Please remember that this is a library book,
and that it belongs only temporarily to each
person who uses it. Be considerate. Do
not write in this, or any, library book.

WITHDRAWN

BASIC PROBLEMS OF ETHNOPSYCHIATRY

BASIC PROBLEMS OF ETHNOPSYCHIATRY

George Devereux

TRANSLATED BY

Basia Miller Gulati
and by
George Devereux

The University of Chicago Press
CHICAGO AND LONDON

THE UNIVERSITY OF CHICAGO PRESS, CHICAGO 60637
THE UNIVERSITY OF CHICAGO PRESS, LTD., LONDON
© 1980 by George Devereux
All rights reserved. Published 1980
Printed in the United States of America
84 83 82 81 80   6 5 4 3 2 1

GEORGE DEVEREUX
professor emeritus at the
Ecole des Hautes Etudes en Sciences Sociales,
is now consultant in ethnopsychiatry at
the Maison des Sciences de l'Homme, Paris.
He is the author of numerous
articles and of ten books, three of which have
appeared in five languages.

Library of Congress Cataloging in Publication Data

Devereux, George, 1908–
Basic problems of ethnopsychiatry.

Translation of Essais d'ethnopsychiatrie générale.
Bibliography: p.
Includes index.
1. Psychiatry, Transcultural—Addresses, essays,
lectures. I. Title.
RC455.4.E8D4713   616.8'914   79–11104
ISBN 0–226–14355–4

To the Memory of my Teacher
MARCEL MAUSS
and to my friends of
the Seminar of Ethnopsychiatry
Ecole des Hautes Etudes
en Sciences Sociales

Contents

Preface to the American Edition

The present volume contains a representative sample of my principal papers on the theory, methodology, and technique of a culturally nonrelativistic psychoanalytic ethnopsychiatry. Though these studies do not cover all aspects of this still relatively new discipline, they discuss enough of the salient features of *one* self-consistent operational theory of ethnopsychiatry to permit its—as yet not wholly foreseeable—further elaboration in one system-adequate manner only.

Though my system of ethnopsychiatry was developed conjointly with a specific epistemology (Devereux 1967a) and a complementaristic general theory and methodology (Devereux 1970 and 1978a) of the sciences of man over a period of several decades, the scheme here presented is wholly self-contained. It suffices to specify that the principle of complementarity presupposes the possibility of at least one (total/partial) psychological and one (total/partial) sociocultural explanation, defines the relationship between the two explanations, and permits the full scientific exploitation of the phenomena under consideration. It also abolishes the temptation to push any type of explanation beyond the point where the law of diminishing returns begins to operate. Above all, it explicitly admits the possibility and the legitimacy of formulating equally satisfactory alternative explanatory schemes.

Precisely because this book analyzes disorder and delusion, it was necessary to follow scrupulously Lagrange's advice, "Seek simplicity, but distrust it!" I have therefore endeavored to bring to light the logic that subtends seemingly chaotic phenomena without trying to juggle out of sight what I still fail to comprehend. Unlike ancient oracles (Devereux 1968b) and fashionable profundity-mongers, I did not attempt to substitute for a meaningful, though as yet incomprehensible, reality a purely verbal rebus inherently devoid of sense.

Nearly all of the studies contained in this volume were originally written, and first published, in English.[1] Most of them appeared as journal articles, but some were contributions to multiauthored volumes. Revised and in some cases further expanded versions of these texts, translated into French, were published as a book, *Essais d'ethnopsychiatrie générale,* by Gallimard in 1970 (reprinted in 1973 and 1977). This French version was translated into Spanish (1973), German (1974), and Italian (1978) and has now been translated from

French back into English, with a few further minor improvements, so that the present version is now the final one.[2]

The publication of this book in French marked a decisive turn of the tide in my professional life. I can only hope that its reception in the English-speaking world will be comparable to its reception elsewhere.

Professor Alain Besançon (Ecole des Hautes Etudes en Sciences Sociales), Mr. Henri Gobard (Université de Paris VIII), and the late Professor Roger Bastide (Sorbonne) (who also wrote a Preface, both generous and insightful, for the original French edition) urged me to assemble these essays into a volume, whose publication was made possible by Professor Pierre Nora (Ecole des Haute Etudes), general editor of the Gallimard series Bibliothèque des Sciences Humaines.

Ralph W. Nicholas and Raymond D. Fogelson (both of the University of Chicago) brought this book to the attention of the University of Chicago Press.

Small grants from the National Institute of Mental Health (M-1669) and the Society for the Study of Human Ecology facilitated the writing of certain of the chapters.

Ms. Basia Miller Gulati translated with great care seven of the chapters (1, 2, 3, 5, 6, 9, and 15) and scrupulously took into account all my suggestions and preferences. I myself retranslated the remaining chapters into English.

In my Acknowledgments I list the copyright-holders of the first versions of the articles contained in this volume, which were reproduced with their permission in a revised form in the French edition and are further revised here.

George Devereux

Acknowledgments

The acknowledgments below appeared in the French edition of this work. All of the essays have been further revised for the present publication.

Most of chapter 1 appeared first in an article entitled "Normal and Abnormal" in J. Casagrande and T. Galwin, eds., *Some Uses of Anthropology, Theoretical and Applied* (Washington, D.C., 1956); it is reproduced with the permission of the Anthropological Society of Washington, D.C. A few passages appeared first in a note entitled "Shamans as Neurotics," *American Anthropologist* 63 (1961): 1088–90; they are reproduced with the permission of the American Anthropological Association.

Some parts of chapter 2 appeared first in an article entitled "Psychiatry and Anthropology: Some Research Objectives," *Bulletin of the Menninger Clinic* 16 (1952): 167–77, and are reproduced here with the permission of the Menninger Foundation, Topeka, Kansas. Other parts appeared first in an article entitled "Cultural Factors in Psychoanalytic Therapy," *Journal of the American Psychoanalytic Association* 1 (1953): 629–55, and are reproduced with the permission of the *Journal of the American Psychoanalytic Association*.

Chapter 3 appeared first under the title "Social Negativism and Criminal Psychopathology," *Journal of Criminal Psychopathology* 1 (1940): 325–38, and is reproduced here with the permission of MD Publications, Inc., New York, New York.

Chapter 4 appeared first under the title "The Voices of Children," *American Journal of Psychotherapy* 19 (1965): 4–19, and is reproduced with the permission of the *American Journal of Psychotherapy*.

Chapter 5 was first published under the titles "The Cannibalistic Impulses of Parents" and "Author's Response" in the *Psychoanalytic Forum* 1 (1966): 114–24, 129–30; it is reproduced here with the permission of the Psychiatric Research Foundation of Beverly Hills, California.

Chapter 6 first appeared as "Retaliatory Homosexual Triumph over the Father," *International Journal of Psycho-Analysis* 41 (1960): 157–61, and is reproduced here with the permission of the *International Journal of Psycho-Analysis*.

Chapter 7 first appeared as "Neurotic Crime vs. Criminal Behavior," *Psychiatric Quarterly* 25 (1951): 73–80, and is reproduced with the permission of the *Psychiatric Quarterly*.

Chapter 8 first appeared (in French translation) under the title "La délinquance sexuelle des jeunes filles dans une société puritaine," *Les Temps modernes* 29 (1964): 621–59; it is reproduced here with the permission of *Les Temps modernes*.

Chapter 9 first appeared under the title "A Sociological Theory of Schizophrenia," *Psychoanalytic Review* 26 (1939): 315–42; it is reproduced here with the permission of that periodical's copyrightholder, the National Psychological Association for Psychoanalysis, Inc., New York, New York.

Chapter 10 first appeared in a different French translation under the title "Les Origines sociales de la schizophrénie," *L'Information psychiatrique* 41 (1965): 783–99, and is reproduced here with the permission of *L'Information psychiatrique*.

Chapter 11 was first published under the title "Réflexions ethnopsychanalytiques sur la fatigue névrotique," *Revue de Médecine psychosomatique* 8 (1966): 235–41; it is reproduced with the permission of the *Revue de Médecine psychosomatique*.

Chapter 12 first appeared as "An Ethnopsychiatric Note on Property Destruction in Cargo Cults," *Man* 64 (1964): 184–85, and is reproduced with the permission of *Man* and of the Royal Anthropological Institute of London.

Chapter 13 first appeared as "Primitive Psychiatric Diagnosis" in I. Galdston, ed., *Man's Image in Medicine and Anthropology* (New York: International Universities Press, 1963); it is reproduced with the permission of the New York Academy of Sciences.

Chapter 14 first appeared under the title "Pathogenic Dreams in Non-Western Societies" in Gustave E. von Grunebaum and Roger Caillois, eds., *The Dream and Human Societies* (Berkeley and Los Angeles: University of California Press, 1966), and under the title "Rêves pathogènes dans les sociétés non occidentales" in von Grunebaum and Caillois, eds., *Le Rêve et les sociétés humaines* (Paris: Gallimard, 1967). It is reproduced with the permission of Professor von Grunebaum and Editions Gallimard.

Parts of chapter 15 appeared first in an article entitled "Cultural Factors in Psychoanalytic Therapy," *Journal of the American Psychoanalytic Association* 1 (1953): 629–55, and are reproduced with the permission of the *Journal of the American Psychoanalytic Association*. Other parts appeared first in "Psychiatry and Anthropology: Some Research Objectives," *Bulletin of the Menninger Clinic* 16 (1952): 167–77, and are reproduced with the permission of the Menninger Foundation, Topeka, Kansas.

Chapter 16 appeared first under the title "Psychoanalysis as Anthropological Field-Work," *Transactions of the New York Academy of Sciences* 2d ser. 19 (1957): 457–72, and is reproduced with the permission of the New York Academy of Sciences.

I express my thanks to all of the persons, journals, societies, foundations, and publishing houses who have authorized me to reproduce my articles. I reserve all rights to the additions, changes, and transpositions of material that have been made in the 1970 French text.

George Devereux

BASIC PROBLEMS OF ETHNOPSYCHIATRY

I

Normal and Abnormal

(1956)

INTRODUCTION

Each science has its key concept, or pair of key concepts, whose precise definition is the principal problem of that science and whose analysis is the best introduction to that field of inquiry. Thus, the key concept of anthropology is "culture," and anyone who understands it may be said to possess the open sesame of this science. If, in addition, he uses it as a counterfoil to the concept "society," he will soon strike an almost inexhaustible vein of productive research problems. The paired concepts "normal" and "abnormal" are the key concepts of psychiatry, and the determination of the exact locus of the boundary between them is the crucial problem of psychiatry, regardless of whether one views psychiatry as a "pure" or as an "applied" science. Yet, whereas anthropologists write a great deal about their key concept, the problem of what is "normal" and what is "abnormal" has received relatively little systematic attention in recent psychiatric literature. This is unfortunate, because the problem is still far from being satisfactorily solved.

Psychiatric anthropology, as a pluridisciplinary science, must concern itself with the key concepts and key problems of both anthropology and psychiatry. It cannot simply borrow psychiatric techniques of investigation and explanation. Indeed, from the methodological point of view, one must differentiate between the *borrowing of techniques* and the complementaristic *conceptual cross-fertilization* of sciences (Devereux 1945 [1978a, chap. 4], 1961b [1978a, chap. 5], 1967c). Truly pluridisciplinary sciences are characterized by this kind of conceptual cross-fertilization—the concepts involved being those that are also the key problems of the several component sciences.

The autonomous science of ethnopsychiatry—that is, of psychiatric anthropology or anthropological psychiatry, the label chosen depending on the *use* to which this pluridisciplinary "pure" science is put—must therefore have as its key problem the coordination of the concept of "culture" with the paired concepts "normal" and "abnormal." It must be brought to bear, first of all, on the problem

3

of determining the exact locus of the boundary between "normal" and "abnormal." This is the principal objective of the present chapter.

ADJUSTMENT AND SUBLIMATION

Since the problem of adjustment—which is not a concept of psychiatry, let it be said—has been thoroughly discussed elsewhere (Devereux 1939a), I shall content myself here with mentioning a few cases that show the logical flaw inherent in this diagnostic approach.

When E. H. Ackerknecht (1943) claims that the shaman, although objectively neurotic ("heteropathological") is nevertheless "autonormal" to the extent that he is perfectly adjusted, he reduces the problem of diagnosis to testing degrees of adjustment. His reasoning leads to vicious circles, such as the following: "In April 1945 the task of a German psychiatrist was completed the day his patient joined the Nazi party. In May 1945 it was finished the day he joined, if he lived in Frankfurt-am-Main, the Christian Democrat party, and, if he lived in Frankfurt-an-der-Oder, the Communist party" (Devereux 1951a [consult the 2d rev. ed., 1969]). This thesis disregards the existence of societies so "sick" that, in order to adjust to them, one has to be very sick indeed (Devereux 1939a). I hasten to add that I am not echoing here anything so controversial as Benedict's psychiatric diagnoses of different cultures (Benedict 1934). What I have in mind is nothing more unusual than the matters discussed in any standard course in social pathology. Broadly speaking, there exist societies so enmeshed in a vicious circle that everything they do to save themselves only causes them to sink deeper into the quicksand. The Tonkawa, as Linton used to say, clung so tenaciously to cannibalism that finally most of their neighbors waged a war of extermination against them. Likewise, in seeking to uproot imaginary "internal enemies" and to avoid encirclement, Germany created (real) enemies for itself on the inside and brought into being a worldwide alliance pledged to destroy Naziism (Devereux 1955a).

The social self-destructiveness of the South, which undermines the mental health of both its "well-adjusted" whites and its Negroes, has been described by Dollard (1937). The case of Sparta, analyzed elsewhere (Devereux 1965a), is similar in many respects. Also, the theory that makes adjustment the criterion of sanity is admittedly indefensible in view of Fromm's (1941) cogent distinction between healthy adjustment and sadomasochistic conformism. The crux of the matter is that there is a fairly simple distinction to be made between external (overt) and internal adjustment (Devereux 1939a). Some degree of overt adjustment is necessary for survival in any society. In a healthy society, the normal person is, in addition, in the fortunate position of being able to introject the norms of his group in the form of a subsidiary ego ideal. In a sick society, he cannot do so without becoming neurotic, if not worse (Devereux 1939a). On the other hand, if a man is rational enough to adjust overtly to a sick society *without also introjecting its norms,* he often experiences so much discomfort and feels so isolated that he eventually escapes from this "double life," either by engaging in an ill-timed and therefore self-destructive rebellion or else by *forcing* himself to accept basically uncongenial norms and becoming a fanatic as a defensive reaction.

From a psychiatric point of view the valid criteria for normality are absolute, that is, they are independent of the norms of any given culture or society but are identical with the criteria for Culture as a universal human phenomenon.[1] Emotional maturity, a sense of reality, rationality, and the ability to sublimate can certainly contribute to the individual's adjustment in a healthy society and insure survival in a pathological one; they are nevertheless logically independent of adjustment itself.[2]

After these introductory remarks, I am ready to embark on a discussion of the problem of normality and abnormality in terms of the key *concept* of anthropology, which is Culture, and the key *problem* of psychiatry, which is the boundary between normality and abnormality.

I shall begin by defining as precisely as possible the aspects of the unconscious that are located within the framework of my own research. I shall examine the problem of trauma, not as a function of the absolute intensity of stress, but as a function of the availability of defenses for use in stress situations (Devereux 1966c [1978a, chap. 2]).

TWO TYPES OF UNCONSCIOUS

The unconscious is composed of two elements: that which never was conscious—i.e., the psychic equivalent of the id—consisting of the psychic representatives or counterparts of instinctual forces,[3] and that which was conscious once upon a time but was subsequently repressed. The *repressed* material is made up partly of memory traces of both outer (objective) experiences and certain internal (subjective) experiences,[4] such as emotions, fantasies, and former bodily states, and includes also the defense mechanisms and a substantial portion of the superego.

I propose to concern myself exclusively with previously conscious but now repressed material, which, from the cultural point of view,

5

can be divided into two groups: (1) the unconscious segment of the ethnic personality and (2) the idiosyncratic unconscious.

1. The *unconscious segment of the ethnic personality* must not be confused with Jung's "racial unconscious." I am speaking here of a *cultural*, not a *racial*, unconscious. The "ethnic unconscious" is that portion of the total unconscious segment of the individual's psyche that he shares with most members of his given cultural community. It is composed of material that each generation teaches the next one to repress, in accordance with the basic demand patterns of the prevailing culture. It changes as culture itself changes. It is transmitted by a kind of "teaching," as culture is transmitted, rather than biologically, as Jung's "racial unconscious" is allegedly transmitted. In brief, it is acquired in exactly the same manner as the ethnic character is acquired—and in this context it does not matter in the least precisely whose theory of ethnic character formation one happens to subscribe to. Each ethnic character structure has both a conscious phase and an unconscious phase, the latter being complementary to the former (Devereux 1945 [1978a, chap. 4], 1961b [1978a, chap. 5], 1967c). Each culture permits certain impulses, fantasies, and the like to become and to remain conscious, while requiring others to be repressed. Hence, all members of a given culture will have certain unconscious conflicts in common.

The material composing the ethnic unconscious is maintained in a state of repression by means of various defense mechanisms, usually *strengthened and often even provided by cultural pressures*. Sometimes, however, the defensive devices that culture places at the disposal of the individual, to enable him to keep such culture-dystonic impulses in a state of repression, are not altogether adequate. In such instances more than just a few persons who have suffered early childhood traumata of an *atypical* sort find it almost impossible to master such impulses and to keep them safely out of sight. When this happens, culture often provides also a kind of *marginal* or halfhearted implementation for such impulses. The *berdache* (transvestite) complex in Plains Indian society (Devereux 1951a) is an example of an official, though marginal, recognition by Plains culture of a form of personality distortion that was in flagrant opposition to the ethnic ideal. Thus, even though the *berdache* grossly deviated from the "heroic self-definition" of the Plains Indian, his (or "her") status was nonetheless at least marginally implemented. However, the fact that it was implemented at all must not prevent one from realizing that the implementation was marginal, amounting to an ex post facto sanctioning of the inevitable. In the last resort, though transvestitism was often formally "sanctioned" by a vision, there is irrefutable evidence that it was nonetheless both ego-dystonic and culture-dystonic. For example, when a vision instructed a certain Plains Indian to become a transvestite, the man committed suicide (Lowie 1924). This individual certainly had the impulse to become a transvestite, for otherwise his vision would not have "given" him this particular directive. His (hidden) impulse was accepted by his culture, but it was so ego-dystonic that the individual chose to kill himself rather than become a transvestite.

The institutionalization—or excessive elaboration—of an abnormal impulse (see chap. 16) emanating from the unconscious portion of the ethnic character must not blind one to its culturally dystonic character.

How culture-dystonic even highly institutionalized homosexuality is may be deduced from the fact that among the Mohave, who did highly institutionalize this deviation, the transvestite is subjected to ridicule and is goaded into scurrilous exhibitions of his deviation (Devereux 1937b). Likewise, the direct participation of a greater part of the group, either individually or collectively, in an activity that is basically abnormal although duly institutionalized cannot be held to imply that the activity is either psychologically normal or syntonic at the cultural level. Thus, Kroeber (1952) stressed that during "epidemics" of sorcery a kind of low-grade paranoia of the laity as a whole is the counterpart of the witches' personal psychopathology.

To anticipate somewhat my later discussion of shamanistic disorders, I add here only that the shaman is exposed early in life to stress situations that are not only numerically *frequent* but culturally *typical*, that is, they originate in the cultural model. Thus his conflicts are permanently localized in his ethnic unconscious.

He also repatterns both his type conflicts (see below) and his subjective conflicts in cultural terms, either by using defenses the culture provides, such as visions, revelations, or initiation rites having palliative "autotherapeutic" qualities, or by undergoing shamanistic treatment intended to cure an organic disease or psychic disorder.

2. *The idiosyncratic unconscious* is composed of elements that the unique and specific stresses the individual has experienced have obliged him to repress. These stresses can be of two types:

a) Stresses resulting from experiences that, without being typical of a given culture—that is, without reflecting the cultural model—occur frequently enough to be recognized and reformulated in cultural terms. Thus, in the *Iliad* (22. 482 ff.), Hector was scarcely dead when Andromache was able to predict in detail the kinds of stress the fatherless Astyanax would experience, the way he would be traumatized, and the deviant behavior he would be forced to adopt. What is relevant here is that what Andromache evokes is not Astyanax's future if Troy falls and he is captured by the enemy (*Iliad* 22. 487 ff.) but rather the fate of any orphan in Trojan society, regardless of rank. "Ethnic neuroses" are produced by this kind of situation.

b) Stresses resulting from experiences that are neither characteristic of a culture nor numerically frequent but that afflict some especially unfortunate individuals. Thersites' traumatizing experiences (*Iliad* 2. 211 ff.) are in marked contrast to those predicted for Astyanax. The unhappy lot of the orphan, widow (*Iliad* 6. 407 ff.), and parents of a man fallen in battle is one of the recurrent themes of the *Iliad* because this type of trauma is a common occurrence in a warrior society. Thersites' woes, by contrast, are clearly quite unusual: he is the ugliest man in the Greek army; he is the only one who is glaringly deformed (bandy-legged, lame, and humpbacked). In a warrior society, which particularly admires strength and male beauty, a deformed boy suffers many completely atypical traumata. The *Iliad* itself (2. 211 ff.) suggests that Thersites' deformities are responsible for his disposition, which is perverse, envious, bitter, and hostile. Moreover, within an army of magnificent heroes, Thersites is doubly conspicuous and deviant. He reacts toward his marginal situation by exhibiting provocative behavior of an obviously neurotic kind, which in turn calls forth equally conspicuous and uncommon reprisals. If one disregards the beating Hera gives to Artemis during the battle of the gods (*Iliad* 21. 489 ff.), Thersites is the only free man in the *Iliad* (2. 265 ff.) who is physically punished by a member of his own group. Thus, idiosyncratic traumata produce conflicts that become permanently localized in the "private" (idiosyncratic) unconscious.

It goes without saying that an individual does not have only an ethnic unconscious and an individual unconscious. He also experiences, in the course of his life, traumata that are in varying proportions both numerically frequent and typical of the culture. What matters here is that the *principal* conflicts of the shaman are localized chiefly in the ethnic unconscious, whereas those of the "private" deviant are localized in the idiosyncratic unconscious.

A further exploration of these differences leads to a radical reappraisal of the concept "trauma."

TRAUMA AND THE UNAVAILABILITY OF CULTURAL DEFENSES

It is indispensable to distinguish systematically between stress—used in this chapter in its conventional sense and not in the strict sense I assign to this term elsewhere (Devereux 1966c [1978a, chap. 2])— and trauma. The term "stress" is applied here only to the harmful *forces* that impinge upon the individual, the term "trauma" to the harmful *results* of the impact of those forces. It is one of the main faults of psychiatric thinking that it considers only the absolute intensity of the stress-producing impact and forgets that the individual may have valuable resources at his disposal for resisting and overcoming the impact he has experienced.[5] In other words, an ordinary rifle bullet can penetrate the thin skin of a tiger and kill him, but it will only bounce off the back of a crocodile.

In human, that is, cultural, situations, stress will be traumatic only if it is atypical or if, though typical in its nature, it is abnormally intense or else premature. Stress is atypical if the culture has no "mass-produced" defense available for relieving or buffering the shock. It is probable, therefore, that the Athenian mother was more traumatized than the Spartan mother by the loss of a son in battle, because the latter was conditioned by her culture to take pride and comfort in sacrificing a son to the city-state (Plutarch *Apophthegms of Laconian Women*). A common stress may nevertheless be the source of trauma if it has a special intensity: it is one thing for a father to lose a son at war, but it is another to lose, as Priam did, nearly all fifty of his sons, including the famous Hector, or to lose, as Peleus did, an only son, when that son was Achilles. Finally, stress is traumatic when it occurs prematurely, that is, when it affects an individual who does *not yet* have access to the appropriate cultural defenses. A major variant of this kind of situation occurs among underprivileged classes, systematically denied access to the defenses the culture reserves exclusively for its privileged members. This matter will not be discussed here, because it has been analyzed in sufficient detail elsewhere (Devereux 1965a).

The matters dealt with in the preceding paragraph sound somewhat complicated when expressed in a formal way, but what is actually implied is a fairly simple and obvious process. For example, a Bushman of the Kalahari Desert seldom if ever falls into deep water; Bushman culture therefore probably does not provide a culturally standardized defense against the culturally atypical strain resulting from falling into deep water: the Bushman child is not taught to swim. Hence, if a Bushman does manage to fall into deep water, he will have to try to get himself out of his predicament by going through a series of idiosyncratic motions, such as calling for help and churning the water as best he can. In brief, falling into deep water is a trauma in Bushman society. It is not a trauma in Polynesian society, where every small child is provided by culture with the "swimming defense."

Even more striking is the contrast between the consequences of a leg wound for Tamerlane, on the one hand, and for a Crow warrior named Takes-the-Pipe, on the other. Since walking was nearly shameful in the steppe culture and no exploit had to be accomplished on foot, Tamerlane's wound, which left him lame for life (Timur-i-leng: Timur-the-Limper), did not prevent him from becoming the sovereign of his people and leader of an immense military empire. But Takes-the-Pipe's limp prevented him from accomplishing one of the exploits required of anyone aspiring to the rank of chieftain: he could not set out on foot and return astride a horse he had stolen from the enemy. He reacted to this form of stress—which in his case, but not in Tamerlane's, had produced trauma *stricto sensu*—by becoming a Crazy-Dog-Wishes-to-Die (Lowie 1925).

A culture or subculture can intentionally reject a defense that is potentially available. In the days when shipwrecks on the high seas were frequent, many sailors deliberately refused to learn to swim. They reasoned that in a shipwreck it would be better for them to sink immediately, without suffering, than to swim about for hours without hope of being rescued and then to drown.

For reasons of expository convenience, I have so far not differentiated between psychological defense mechanisms, such as projection, and cultural materials (or means) for strengthening and implementing such defense mechanisms—projection being implemented, e.g., by means of scapegoating. The defensive *use* of scapegoating can be taught. The defense *mechanism* of projection is not, properly speaking, taught, but it can be culturally developed and fostered—e.g., by teaching scapegoating. It is in this manner that each culture establishes a preferential hierarchy of defenses and patterns them. The chief result of this patterning is ethnic character. However, patterning can influence even broad social processes: identification with the enemy is a defense mechanism, which, on the cultural level, is implemented by "antagonistic acculturation," i.e., by adopting the *means* used by the enemy in order to frustrate his *ends* (Devereux and Loeb 1943 [1978a, chap. 8]).

These distinctions are important for understanding the concept of premature trauma. This term does not denote simply a chronologically early trauma but a trauma that occurs before the infant knows, and/or is capable of using, culturally provided defenses against an injury.[6] For a small child, unable to earn its living, the death of its parents is a premature trauma, since culture provides the child with only *external protection*—e.g., orphanages—but not with internal defenses, such as a sudden, culturally fostered, psychological maturation abolishing infantile dependent needs.[7]

This theory would also account for the fact that traumata causing severe psychoses occur very early in life—mostly at the oral stage, when the infant does not as yet have as its disposal the kind of culturally provided defense against traumata that would enable it to cope with them without sustaining serious permanent damage. Indeed, at this stage of its life—contrary to the assertions made by Kardiner—the infant does not experience the impact of *"cultural materials"* (or *culture* traits) but only the impact of the ethos (or culture pattern) reflected in the emotions and attitudes of its culture mediators: parents, older siblings, and others in its immediate surroundings. It must therefore improvise defenses against traumata. These defenses are necessarily of a strictly intrapsychic, affective-attitudinal type, since that is all the infant is capable of (chap. 5). This view lends additional support to the thesis that psychosis—as distinct from neurosis—always entails a severe impairment of the ethnic personality, and this personality, as stated above, is produced by the impact of the culture pattern rather than by the impact of culture traits (child-rearing techniques) on the immature psyche (Devereux 1951a; Mead 1954). Last, but not least, it explains the singular stability of the ethnic character and its perpetuation, generation after generation, despite cultural change or even the pressures of brutal acculturation (Hallowell 1946; Devereux 1951a).[8]

This hypothesis casts doubt on the paramount importance of child-rearing techniques in the formation of ethnic character, as alleged by Kardiner (1939). Moreover, Linton himself subsequently partly repudiated their importance (1956). In fact, emotionally ill parents traumatize their children even if they follow all cultural rules governing child-rearing techniques, because the atypical affects of the parents mediate to the child a distorted ethos instead of conveying to him the affective equivalent of the real, undistorted ethos. Conversely, this hypothesis explains why children raised in a sick society by mentally healthy parents often become anxious or neurotic (Devereux 1956a).

These considerations account simultaneously for the notorious harmfulness of premature traumata and for the invariable impairment of the ethnic personality of the psychotic, which finds expression in a severe "social negativism" (chap. 3).

Premature traumata can also occur after infancy, e.g., at times when the child or adolescent is either still too young to be able to

11

use certain culturally provided defenses or else—as in Samoa (Mead 1928)—is denied access to certain defenses on the ground that, in using them, he would "presume above his age." A functional equivalent of "premature traumata" occurs also in the case of underprivileged minorities, whose characterological deviations and immaturities (Dollard 1937) I interpret as a consequence of their being denied access to many important cultural defenses, e.g., self-respect, the right to have "honor," etc., that their culture makes available to members of the privileged group (Devereux 1965a). Hence, members of underprivileged minorities tend to be psychologically more vulnerable and are therefore more easily dominated than privileged individuals. The same is true of strangers, who have not yet acquired and/or have not as yet highly cathected the defenses that are most useful in their new environment. In brief, self-realization (the Greek's *aretē*), sublimation, maturity, real independence, and efficiency appear, in the light of this theory, as functions of a free access to all culturally provided defenses.

Some cultural materials, such as myths—which from a certain point of view are defenses—may serve as a kind of impersonal "cold storage" for a number of individual fantasies related to inner conflicts. These fantasies are too intensely laden with affect to be repressed but are also too ego-dystonic to be freely recognized as subjective and as pertaining to oneself. By putting such fantasies into the "cold storage" of culture, one gives them a formal and generalized expression within the impersonal body of culture but more or less keeps them out of idiosyncratic "private circulation" (chap. 16). Partly because the therapist himself knows and uses this "cultural cold storage," these fantasies emerge on the individual level and, in particular, are recognized as pertaining to oneself and to one's own problems—and not merely to some mythical personage (projection supported by culture)—only at the end of an exceptionally successful psychoanalysis. This mechanism is particularly noticeable in the shaman, in whom such "culturalized" fantasies emerge in the form of semisubjective and semipersonalized "experiences," in which myths and subjective fantasies, rituals and idiosyncratic compulsive actions, etc., are inextricably interwoven. This view is perfectly in accordance with what will be said below about the culturally standardized "type conflicts" and "type solutions" of the shaman.

One way in which the individual subjected to a trauma seeks to escape from his difficulty is through the misuse of cultural material that, without such deformation, does not lend itself to symptomatic utilization; or he may select some irrational culture traits that can be used symptomatically without any prior distortion (see below).

This observation leads me to make a distinction between disorders that are prepatterned and those that are not.

ETHNOPSYCHIATRIC TYPOLOGY OF PERSONALITY DISORDERS

The preceding considerations require us to set up an ethnopsychiatric typology of neuroses and psychoses. The claim has been made that, since psychotics are desocialized, psychosis cannot have a sociocultural etiology.[9] This claim is untenable because desocialization is not only a social process but one which is—as will be shown—susceptible of analysis in sociocultural terms.

I want to state once and for all that my ethnopsychiatric typology is perfectly compatible with scientific psychiatric nosologies. Every patient can be assigned a conventional diagnostic label *regardless* of the type of psychiatric disorder he represents within a given culture.

Personality disorders can be divided into four ethnopsychiatric categories:

1. "Type" disorders, relating to the type of social structure (see chap. 10)
2. "Ethnic" disorders, relating to the specific culture pattern of the group
3. "Sacred" disorders, of the shamanistic type
4. "Idiosyncratic" disorders

For the sake of clarity, these four types of "illnesses" will be discussed in a slightly different order.

"Sacred" Disorders, of the Shamanistic Type

The tendency of ethnologists to give far too much atteniton to the supernatural has considerably hampered our understanding of the shaman's psychiatric status. While conceding that the supernatural is culturally often highly elaborated, I feel that the degree of elaboration of a "complex"—whether a cultural one or a psychoanalytically defined one—is not prima facie evidence of its nuclearity and functional importance. Without accepting even for a moment the thesis of wholesale economic determinism (defended today only by certain theoreticians of capitalism and anticapitalism and obsolete from both the scientific and the cultural standpoint, since these theoreticians have not yet discovered the existence of man), I maintain that earning a living, getting married, and other such "pedestrian" activities are far more nuclear in any culture than complex fertility rites or curing rituals, which are but the frosting on the cake. I wish to stress that these remarks imply much more than Kardiner's "genetic" classification of institutions into "primary" and "second-

13

ary" ones (Kardiner and Linton 1939). I am specifically rank-ordering various segments of culture in terms of their absolute importance for *all* members of a given culture.

The view just presented is materially strengthened by the factual observation that, whereas practically everyone gets married, raises children, builds a hut, etc., only a small number of the persons composing a tribe are engaged in shamanistic or other ritual activities on a full-time basis or as a primary means of earning a living. The rest of the tribe are laymen or at best "consumers of the supernatural." Similarly, the Mohave crowds accompanying a transvestite on some scurrilous venture are only audiences. Of course, the members of such crowds are willing to play this role because it enables them to gratify vicariously, without conscious commitment, their own latent homosexual impulses and, at the same time, to gain further strength for fighting these impulses in themselves by witnessing the transvestite's discomfiture (Devereux 1937b).

These considerations are directly applicable also to the shaman. He, too, is a person whose dominant conflicts lie in the realm of the unconscious portion of the ethnic personality. He, too, experiences these impulses as ego-dystonic. Many tribes stress the painfulness of the budding shaman's psychic experiences, and some individuals who receive supernatural "calls" flatly refuse, like the prophet Jonah (Jonah 1:3), to comply with them, as the following examples show. A Plains Indian refused to obey the vision that instructed him to become a transvestite and killed himself instead (Lowie 1924). Among the Sedang Moi, a person who receives the "call" may even drink his own urine in the hope that this act will so depreciate him in the sight of his divine sponsors that they will take back the power they had given him (Devereux 1933–34). The Mohave believe that a potential shaman who refuses to accept the call becomes insane. I personally interviewed such a man who had spent some time in a state hospital with the—to my mind questionable—diagnosis of manic-depressive psychosis. Both he and his tribe felt that his psychotic episode was due to his refusal to become a practicing shaman (Devereux 1961a).

Even those who do accept the "call" occasionally feel that their mode of life is ego-dystonic and therefore commit vicarious suicide. Thus I am inclined to suspect that older healing shamans among the Mohave turn into witches precisely because witches are killed. In fact, society actually expects witches to incite others to kill them (Devereux 1937c, 1961a). There is no real psychological difference between this type of vicarious suicide and the suicide of the Plains Indian who refused to become a *berdache*.

In brief, there is no reason and no excuse for not considering the shaman to be a severe neurotic or even a psychotic in a state of temporary remission.

In addition, shamanism is often also culture-dystonic. This is a point that is amply documented but often systematically overlooked. Thus, the shaman is quite often what I have elsewhere called a "trouble unit" in society (Devereux 1937a). The Mohave say that shamans are both crazy and cowardly. The Siberian shaman is often wretchedly poor and is not highly regarded. The Sedang bitterly resent their shamans, particularly because of their rapaciousness. This very human resentment—reflecting insight into the fact that the shaman is culturally dystonic—even contaminates the attitudes of members of "higher" religions toward their truly saintly members, who are troublemakers from the viewpoint of workaday life. Even so gentle a man as Saint Francis of Assisi met with strong opposition, and the savior of France, Saint Joan of Arc, was burned at the stake as a heretic before being canonized. The opposition of primitive priesthoods to shamans is, moreover, conspicuous and chronic (Linton 1956).

Briefly stated, my position is that the shaman is mentally deranged. This is also the opinion of Kroeber (1952), Linton (1956), and La Barre (1966). By contrast, Ackerknecht (1943), who fails to differentiate between adjustment and sanity, is of the opinion that the shaman is "autonormal" though heteropathological. I certainly do not challenge Ackerknecht's thesis that the shaman is to a certain extent "adjusted." However, as I have already pointed out, he is adjusted to a *relatively marginal segment* of his society and culture, and even though his position is institutionalized, it is ego-dystonic and often quite obviously culture-dystonic as well. The shaman is also much less realistic than ordinary people, and Kroeber (1952) specifically stressed that cultural development is in the direction of greater realism. This thesis—as Kroeber surely knew but did not say explicitly—expresses the classic psychoanalytic viewpoint, which systematically stresses the importance of reality acceptance.

However, Kroeber also held that the shaman is *less insane* than persons whom their own tribes consider psychotic, though he failed to explain what he meant by this specification. If he meant that the shaman's *symptoms* are less dramatic—or melodramatic—than those exhibited by recognized psychotics, his statement is definitely open to challenge, since it is hard to see how anyone's symptoms could be more strikingly florid than those of, e.g., the budding Siberian shaman (Czaplicka 1914). Also, the *obviousness* or *strikingness* of symptoms is not necessarily correlated with the *severity* of the underlying psychopathology. Thus, an acutely schizophrenic individual on a rampage in an acute ward is actually far less "ill," and has a better prognosis, than a "burnt-out" and tractable schizophrenic vegetating in a chronic ward.

Likewise, the diagnostic categories "hysteria, phobia, obsessive-compulsive neurosis, character disorder" are here arranged in an *increasing* order of *severity* and in a *decreasing* order of *obtrusive* symptomatology. In fact, many character neurotics are often practically "symptom free" in the ordinary sense. In other words, the obtrusiveness of symptoms gives no clue to the severity of the underlying psychopathology.

It is possible, of course, that Kroeber meant to contrast the shaman with the recognized neurotic or psychotic, not in terms of the obtrusiveness of symptoms, but in terms of the malignancy of the underlying psychopathology. In that case I can only say that his statement is far too general to be of practical use in the exploration of the shaman's distinctive psychopathology.

Linton (1956), who, like Kroeber, implied that the shaman is "less crazy" than the recognized psychotic, advanced the thesis that he is usually a hysteric. This diagnosis has certain important implications:

a) It contrasts the (neurotic) shaman with the recognized psychotic on the basis of considerations related to the malignancy of the underlying psychopathology rather than to the obtrusiveness of symptoms.

b) The diagnosis "hysteria" suggests a definite etiology and a definite psychodynamic configuration, susceptible of being tested by objective methods.

c) It places the relatively quiet, even depressed, Sedang shaman (Devereux 1933–35) and the violently disturbed Siberian shaman on the same continuum, presumably on the grounds that certain extreme types of hysteria verge on a genuine psychosis and are sometimes almost indistinguishable from certain forms of schizophrenia (chap. 9).

d) It accounts for the florid and exhibitionistic symptomatology of many shamans.

From the strictly clinical point of view, Linton's diagnosis is probably correct and to the point. However, from the point of view of ethnopsychiatry, it fails to account for one crucial fact, namely, that some potential hysterics become shamans while others remain "private" neurotics. Indeed, while it is possible that all shamans may be hysterics, it is quite certain that even in primitive society not all hysterics are shamans.

Theoretical considerations and firsthand observations suggest the same solution: the crucial difference between the shaman and the "private" but recognized hysteric or psychotic lies in the fact that the *shaman's conflicts are characteristically located in the unconscious segment of his ethnic personality rather than in the idiosyncratic portion of his unconscious.* Unlike the "private" neurotic or psychotic, he does not have to evolve most of his symptoms spontaneously. He can express, control, and redirect his impulses and conflicts by using the many—usually ritualized—devices that each culture places at the disposal of those whose conflicts are of the "conventional" type. In brief, the shaman is psychologically ill for conventional reasons and in a conventional way. Quite often— though not always (see below)—his conflicts are simply more intense than those of other members of his group, though fundamentally of the same type and involving the same segment of the personality, the ethnic unconscious. He is quite often like everyone else—"only more so." This explains why the normal members of the tribe echo the shaman's intrapsychic conflicts so readily and why they find his "symptoms" (ritual acts) (Freud 1907) so reassuring. The normal primitive's readiness to respond to the shamans' and witches' conflicts and actions was pointed out by Kroeber (1952). In my opinion, this readiness is due to the fact that the shaman and his performance strike the "normals" as "uncanny"—i.e., as something that their *unconscious* experiences as "disturbingly and unexpectedly familiar" (uncanny = *unheimlich*) in the Freudian sense (Freud 1919). Shamanistic treatment tends, moreover, to reproduce both the morbid process itself and the subjective process of cure (Lévi-Strauss 1958). This fact explains why the shaman's patient experiences the shaman's actions as reassuring.

The shaman provides his patient with a whole set of ethnopsychologically suitable and congenial and culturally recognized defenses (restitutional symptoms) against the idiosyncratic conflicts that torment him. In reality, the shaman does not perform a "psychiatric cure" in the *strict* sense of the term. He simply provides a kind of "corrective emotional experience," as the Chicago School of psychoanalysis calls it, that leads to a repatterning of the defenses without real curative insight. Thus, M. E. Opler (1936) reported that Apache shamans can cure tics (which are notoriously resistant to psychotherapy) by substituting a taboo for the tic. These considerations also explain why, in so many primitive groups, the shaman is someone who has fallen ill and has then been successfully "treated" by a shaman. The most detailed analysis of this kind of "didactic" or "initiatory" illness is to be found in the writings of Kilton Stewart (1954).[10] What seems to happen in such "cures" is simply a changeover from idiosyncratic conflicts and defenses to culturally conventional conflicts and ritualized symptoms, without any real curative insight.

Thus, it is the conventional patterning of the shaman's conflicts and symptoms that differentiates him from the "private" neurotic or psychotic. A careful comparison of the delusions of *a* paranoid Sedang Moi "private" psychotic with the "supernatural experiences" of *any*[11] Sedang Moi shaman shows that the two accounts contain identical elements and differ chiefly in their patterning and orientation, which in the shaman's case are of a conventional type while in the "private" idiosyncratic ambulatory psychotic they are unconventional. Similar correspondences and differences can be observed in our own society between certain socially approved personality types and their "private" (idiosyncratic) counterparts in mental hospitals (Devereux 1955c).

The conventionality or unconventionality of a person's delusions is in itself a matter of considerable diagnostic significance. The patterning and orientation of every Sedang shaman's "supernatural experience"—which is made up of elements identical with those of *a* certain Sedang psychotic's delusions—are the result of what is known as "secondary elaboration," which also takes place—unwittingly—in the remembering and recounting of dreams (Devereux 1951a) and, of course, in culturally significant delusions as well. In the course of this secondary elaboration a conventional pattern is impressed on the (sometimes subverbal) material that emerges from the unconscious. This type of conventionalized secondary elaboration is possible only where "social negativism" is not excessive and unmanageable and where there is still a residual need for remaining integrated, if only marginally, with society (chap. 3).

What matters psychiatrically is not so much the raw content of the unconscious—which is pretty much the same in every human being—but what the ego does with this material.[12] What differentiates the shaman from the "private" psychotic is the conventional, though admittedly still abnormal, patterning of the material that emerges from the unconscious. It is this patterning that is lacking in the "private" psychotic (chap. 2).

As stated a moment ago, the patient who was ill, received shamanistic treatment, "recovered," and became a shaman himself simply underwent a conventionalized repatterning of his conflicts and symptoms without gaining any real insight into his problems and without developing his capacity to sublimate. Ackerknecht (1943) also believed that the shaman is a mental patient "cured without insight"; yet, oddly enough, he attacked me for having said practically the same thing, more rigorously and before he did (Devereux 1942c,

1961a). This, however, is beside the point. What does matter is that Ackerknecht, as a physician, should have known better than to use the term "cured" as loosely as he did. No real psychiatrist would ever call a "remission without insight" a "cure," because the patient in a state of "social remission" remains vulnerable: his old conflicts can erupt anew at any time. No medical man considers a syphilitic really "cured" until it is at least theoretically *possible* for him to contract syphilis a second time and to develop a second set of *primary* lesions. No shaman is "cured" in this sense. He is simply in remission. When subjected to further strain, he does not evolve a *new* neurosis; he simply experiences a new breakthrough of his *old* conflicts and seeks to ward them off by means of the same old symptoms. In other instances his newly acquired defenses become "stale" and lose their efficiency, forcing him to develop additional symptoms —most frequently cultural but occasionally idiosyncratic—exactly the way, after a syphilitic's primary lesions are suppressed by an *incomplete* (suppressive but not curative) treatment, he will eventually develop secondary or tertiary lesions.

The case of Black Elk, a Sioux shaman, illustrates this process in the clearest possible manner. Urged on by a variety of cultural "type" conflicts, Black Elk had a shamanistic vision that received enough social approval and recognition to satisfy him and to relieve his tensions to the point where he could function for a while in a more or less normal manner. However, after a lapse of several years, this "defense," too, became stale and no longer sufficed to hold his conflicts in check. He therefore felt impelled to enact publicly the ritual his vision had instructed him to perform—a task he had so far neglected (Neihardt 1932). In psychiatric terminology one could say that rumination was superseded by acting-out. This development is the typical *vicious circle* of psychopathology. The *primary* defense against a basic conflict creates a series of new difficulties,[13] against which further, *secondary,* defenses have to be developed. A similar process of deterioration can be observed in Mohave healing shamans who eventually become witches. Their initial conflicts are probably related to aggression. Hence, the primary defense consists not in attempts to sublimate but in a "reaction formation" against hostile impulses: the budding shaman denies his sadistic impulses and— turning them around—specializes in healing. Then, when this defense—the therapeutic activity—becomes "stale," a new breakthrough of hostility impels the healer to become a witch. The Mohave Indians understand this mechanism fairly well, since they specify that a shaman can cure *only* diseases that he is also *qualified to cause,* and vice versa, of course (Devereux 1961a). In the end, guilt over the overt manifestation of his hostility eventually impels the Mohave witch to commit vicarious suicide by inducing his victims' bereaved relatives to kill him. Characteristically, he does this in the most aggressive manner possible. He jeers at them, boasts of having killed their relatives by witchcraft, ridicules them for not killing him in revenge, and threatens to bewitch them too (Kroeber 1925; Devereux 1961a).[14] A more obvious example of the manner in which "remission without insight" inevitably leads to a further exacerbation of the fundamental psychopathology, and of the way in which symptom must be piled upon symptom and defense upon defense, would be hard to find. How anyone confronted with such classic manifestations of psychopathological dynamics can continue to speak of "autonormality" or of "*cure* without insight" is hard to understand.

In the face of these observations, some ethnologists, taking refuge from the current disintegration of norms by adopting cultural relativism—whose motto is: "Custom is King, and the King can do no wrong"—persist in denying the shaman's abnormality. Some of their arguments, specious at best and occasionally even false, barely deserve a footnote;[15] others must be systematically refuted.

M. K. Opler, for instance, seems to believe that any field worker is capable not simply of *observing* but of *diagnosing* unusual behavior (see below). This is obviously not the case, for in 1938, when my own psychiatric training was still quite incomplete, I wrote—thinking specifically of my Mohave shaman friend, Hivsū Tupōma—that the Mohave shaman was an exuberant extrovert. However, when, later that year, I did some additional field work, I had occasion to observe him one afternoon, quite drunk, pouring out to me a veritable torrent of frankly delusional material. The following day, when he was sober, he confirmed everything he had told me the day before and begged me to keep his secret because he was not yet prepared to be killed as a witch (Devereux 1961a). Likewise, until a certain night in 1934 I believed my Sedang Moi shaman friend, Hēang, to be a gay, bohemian character. That night, however, he experienced something more serious than a nightmare—he had a genuine psychotic episode *(bouffée délirante)*. His shouts of "Ghost! Ghost!" woke the whole village, and it required several men to hold him down while he fought the ghosts. Now, though it is generally understood that Sedang Moi shamans are on intimate terms with spirits, neither the villagers, unfamiliar with theories of cultural relativism, nor Hēang himself viewed his attack as "normal." All agreed that he had been temporarily insane *(ràjok)*. In short, unless, like occultists, one believes in the objective reality of spirit possession, one must view Hēang's attack as an expression of his latent psychological disturbance.

Opler also fails to understand that the diagnosis of normality is infinitely more difficult to make than the diagnosis of abnormality. A respected citizen may be a true paranoiac but reveal himself as such only when he decompensates and kills his entire family. It is known that a monosymptomatic hysteria or even a common torticollis[16] may mask a latent paranoid schizophrenia. Acute psychotic breaks can occur after cosmetic surgery—surgical correction of the nose, for instance—or after the healing of a neurodermatitis through hypnosis.

Newspapers, too, periodically carry stories about individuals who, considered cured and therefore returned to their families by first-rate psychiatric hospitals, murder someone or commit suicide as soon as they are at home. Nietzsche long ago wondered about the possibility of there being "neuroses of sanity," and N. S. Reider (1950) published a brilliant paper on the neurotic compulsion to seem normal. In short, ethnologists, colonial civil servants, and missionaries, only slightly or incorrectly informed on psychiatric matters, can report only unusual behavior they have had a chance to observe. They do not have the training to make diagnoses; that is a task for trained clinicians. Hence Opler's statement that all the Ute shamans are normal no more deserves to be believed than I deserved belief when I wrote in 1938—that is, at a time when my knowledge of psychiatry was still inadequate—that Mohave shamans are exuberant extroverts.

The preceding remarks pertain only to certain erroneous notions of a purely technical nature. The real source of the fallacious views held by cultural relativists is their refusal to distinguish between *belief* and *experience*. The Ute shaman whom Opler proposes to us as a model of balance and reason *felt* that he harbored within himself a spirit mannikin who swallows evil; he also felt that his shamanistic powers could turn against him and that he was incapable of controlling their inherently destructive tendencies. Finally, he would at times even plead in vain with the mannikin, urging him to refrain from using his malefic powers. Opler sees nothing abnormal in all of this because these beliefs are held by the Utes in general—and, one might add, by numerous other tribes as well. In support of his argument he also cites the misadventures of the son of a Ute shaman who wished to shorten, idiosyncratically, the normal cultural procedure for gaining shamanistic power and promptly had an attack of hysterical blindness. He owed the recovery of his sight to treatment by his father, a leading Ute shaman. Subsequently the young man was able to obtain shamanistic powers by recourse to regular, traditional methods (Opler 1959, p. 110). Since this account demonstrates that the acquisition of shamanistic powers is a "restitutional process," it not only fails to support Opler's theory that the shaman is a normal individual but proves that he is not normal and that shamanism is a restitutional symptom, or, rather, syndrome, provided by the culture. The validity of this view is proved also by the widely held belief that the acquisition of shamanistic powers is always preceded by a psychotic incident.

I have nearly given up hope of convincing the apostles of cultural relativism—as impervious to facts as to logic—that the crux of the matter is simply the *difference between traditional belief and subjective experience*. It is one thing for a physicist to know the formula for the acceleration of a falling body: $s = \frac{1}{2} gt^2$; but it is quite another to experience this acceleration in the form of a hallucination (analogous to what one feels during a parachute jump) each time he utters the formula. Again, it is one thing to read about the Oedipus complex but quite another to *relive* one's own Oedipus complex on the psychoanalyst's couch. Today the Catholic Church itself acknowledges this distinction and consults with a psychiatrist before admitting the authenticity of a vision or other seemingly supernatural experience, even if it is in perfect conformity with dogma, with stereotypes, and with precedents of that "spiritual" experience.

It is almost embarrassing to insist on a point that ought to go without saying, but the obstinacy of cultural relativists forces me to invent two fictitious cases that clearly emphasize the difference between a belief and a subjective experience conforming to that belief.

1. Any mullah knows that the houris in Paradise, as soon as they are deflowered, become virgins again. It is an article of faith for him: he believes it, teaches it, and expects the faithful to believe it. But should a certain Ali ben Mustapha, the village tinsmith, claim that his personal experience has confirmed the mullah's teachings—that he has visited Paradise, deflowered a houri, witnessed the renewal of her virginity, and deflowered her a second time—I do not doubt that the pious mullah would send him straight to a psychiatric hospital or its ritual equivalent.

2. Had Dante revealed in private—and therefore nonrepudiable —conversation what he said publicly in immortal—and therefore repudiable—verses, that is, that Virgil had led him, Dante Alighieri, from Florence through Purgatory and Hell, his friends would have rushed him to a physician and an exorcist for fear that the Church might accuse him of necromancy and heresy.

To return to the Utes, the *belief* that the shaman harbors a spirit mannikin within himself is one thing; for a Ute shaman to *experience the presence* of that homunculus within himself is quite another. To confuse the one with the other amounts to a refusal to differentiate the sociological from the psychological (Devereux 1945 [1978a, chap. 4], 1961b [1978a, chap. 5], 1967b). In short, the shaman is not neurotic because he *shares* the *beliefs* of his tribe; he is neurotic because in *his own* case, and *only* in his case, this belief is transformed, for neurotic reasons, into a subjective *experience,* albeit a culturally patterned one, of a delusional type, which subsequently becomes part of the restitutional syndrome peculiar to shamanism.

It is no doubt even more significant that primitives themselves recognize the psychiatric abnormality of an abnormal condition even when that condition is fully integrated with, and indispensable for, some religious or supernatural rite. I might also add that Plato, who draws a distinction in the *Phaedrus* (244 ff.) between "profane" insanity—insanity pure and simple, which is of concern only to the healer—and the "mystical" seizure having a religious significance, suffered by the Pythia, knew perfectly well that both are cases of insanity. Plato sometimes even seems to wonder whether such episodes of spontaneous, nonritual exaltation are a "divine" or a "clinical" form of insanity. When in the *Cratylus* (396C ff.), for instance, Socrates, obviously in a hypomanic state, pours out a stream of etymological puns and compares his performance, half-respectfully, half-humorously, to a state of mantic exaltation, this seems to indicate that, even for Plato, the boundary between reverential belief and clinical diagnosis is less clear than his *Phaedrus* seems to imply. Furthermore, when he implies that Socrates' exhibition is at least partly abnormal, he is expressing a valid psychiatric opinion. No normal person—even one with the genius of Socrates, not even a Greek, incited by tradition to make etymological puns—could have intentionally released, without even catching his breath, such a barrage of improvised puns,[17] his exaltation increasing with each succeeding one. This kind of situation is psychologically conceivable only when there is a temporary eruption of the "primary process" (Freud) or of the "prelogical mentality" (Lévy-Bruhl).[18] I once analyzed a borderline patient who compulsively broke words up into syllables and played on their etymology "to understand the word," that is, in order to "reconstitute" its meaning (Devereux 1966a, 1967a). I would therefore contend that, in the *Cratylus*, Plato described a clinically abnormal aspect of his illustrious master's personality—and also an aspect of his own abnormality.[19]

What matters most, alas, is that, just like the apostles of cultural relativism, Plato and certain other Greeks formulated the difference between "divine" and "pathological" insanity in cultural rather than psychiatric terms.[20] For the clinician, both kinds of insanity are equally abnormal, and even ethnopsychiatry can say only that "divine" madness is a special form of ethnic psychosis, while "non-divine" madness is an idiosyncratic (individual) psychosis.

Even more interesting in many respects is the fact that in some tribes the shaman may be abnormal in two or even three ways. Thus, the acquisition of shamanistic powers is often preceded by a psychotic episode that, in spite of its supernatural overtones, is nonetheless, in the last analysis, a genuine "clinical" disorder. The shaman may, moreover, be abnormal on both the shamanistic and the idiosyncratic levels. Thus the Mohave believe that all shamans are "crazy," for the simple reason that they are shamans, but that they may, in addition, be victims of an ordinary ("clinical") abnormality. Besides, according to Mohave thought, these two forms of abnormality are mutually independent.[21] Thus, Tcàvàkong was doubly "mad": qua Mohave *shaman* and witch, he had a strictly shamanistic—i.e., destructive and self-destructive—madness, whereas, on the private level, he was *primarily* epileptic and his illness did not differ from the illness of any other epileptic and had, according to Mohave thought, absolutely nothing to do with his specifically shamanistic madness. Likewise, as I have mentioned above, the sudden nocturnal psychotic episode (*bouffée délirante*) of the shaman Hēang was interpreted by the Sedang Moi as an attack of ordinary madness, fitting their "psychiatric" ideas rather than their beliefs about shamans and shamanism. The only difference was that, owing to his fortuitous status as a shaman, i.e., as an intimate of supernatural powers, in his hallucinations he necessarily fought off ghosts rather than, say, tigers.[22]

As for the threadbare argument that considers the shaman's "social usefulness" a proof of his normality, one might as well claim that the poet or the scientist is "useful" because of his neurosis and then claim that his usefulness proves that he is not neurotic. This kind of circular reasoning does not deserve to be refuted, even apart from the fact that the truly creative poet or scientist is creative *in spite of* and not *because of* his neurosis (Devereux 1961c [1975, chap. 1]).[23]

Before appealing to the shaman's usefulness, I must first clarify the way in which he is useful. A stillborn two-headed calf can be more valuable than a normal living calf; as part of a traveling show it can bring in more money than a normal calf—even a prize-winning animal—at the county fair. This does not mean, however, that the two-headed calf is normal.

Wagner von Jauregg was able to arrest tertiary syphilis by inoculating syphilitic patients with malaria, but its usefulness in *this* context does not make malaria a nonillness; it continues to be an illness, of which the patient must then be cured. Similarly, some infectious diseases used to be cured by creating a fixation abscess, which subsequently had to be treated and cured.

The shaman's utility is of precisely the same order. Its nearest clinical equivalent is the utility of the psychotic child who plays the role of "deputy lunatic" for a latently neurotic family. Here it is the family that is ill; the child's fever is not his own but his family's. The child who is a "deputy lunatic" is, furthermore, so "useful" to his family that he may literally be snatched out of the hands of the psychiatrist as soon as his state begins to improve. In fact, if this psychological scapegoat were cured, his family would soon become overtly neurotic (Devereux 1956a).[24] Yet, in spite of the evident "utility" of these children to their families, child psychiatrists persist in thinking that both the "deputy lunatic" child and the family should be treated. The psychic disorder of the shaman is "useful" to the tribe in this sense *only:* like the child, he is mad in the name and on behalf of the "others," whom his "madness" enables to maintain a semblance of psychological stability. Modern society, too, has its "deputy lunatics" (Devereux 1955c), but a discussion of this matter cannot be undertaken in the present study.

L. B. Boyer raises an altogether different problem in a study based on ethnographic work, psychoanalytic sessions, and clinical psychological tests. He convincingly demonstrates that within some rapidly disintegrating Apache tribes the shaman is, on the whole, less neurotic than the majority of the members of the tribe (Boyer 1961, 1962, 1964; Boyer, Klopfer, and Kawai 1964). While I grant the validity of his findings, I think that Boyer is mistaken in considering that they weaken my theory of the shaman's abnormality. I even think that Boyer's findings could have been predicted by and deduced from my own theory, for which they provide the best confirmation available at present.

The crux of the matter is that today the Apache tribes are not simply disorganized but have almost ceased to function as autonomous societies animated by a vital and coherent ethos. Hence the average personality profile of a nonshaman Apache systematically reproduces, point for point and in an almost caricatural manner, my description of the disorganized and impoverished personality of the average reservation Indian (Devereux 1951a [consult 2d ed., 1969]). In such a society the shaman is necessarily *less* disturbed than the nonshaman (even if one does not take into account the fact that he could scarcely be *more* disorganized without being hospitalized). In this type of society the shaman can still derive, from the previously stable but now disappearing aboriginal ethos of his tribe, the "solution" (that is, the restitutional syndrome) for his neurotic conflicts. To put it another way, he still has available at least one type of model—a kind of matrix—that helps him to structure his defenses and restitutional symptoms. By contrast, the nonshaman no longer has access to ancient customs and is, from a psychological point of view, adrift.[25] Hence, "being a shaman," which is a neurosis, has, for the Apache neurotic's total personality, precisely the same organizing functions as those that I long ago ascribed to stabilized neurotics and psychotics (chap. 2).

Nor is that all! Supernaturalism (which I shall show to be antisocial) is notoriously more resistant to even abrupt cultural change than are the practical areas of the culture, which fail when put to the test of daily life.[26]

By contrast the sole competitor of aboriginal supernaturalism is imported supernaturalism, which is just as unverifiable as the aboriginal one. This implies that more or less superficial and syncretistic religious conversions require no radical restructuring of the ethnic personality. The religious movement associated with the Ghost Dance has in no way intensified the Plains Indians' native ferocity, nor have cargo cults cooled that passion for property that characterizes the Melanesians and the Papuans.[27] Finally, and this is the main point, a new ethos endowed with real vitality is seldom able to penetrate an oppressed group in a state of crisis.[28] This no doubt explains the relative impermeability of the ethnic personality to cultural change or decline, a fact emphasized by Hallowell (1945, 1946), Thompson (1948), Wallace (1951, 1961), and myself (1951a).

In short, the Apache shaman lives, even today, cloistered within the confines of his ethnic personality, which provides him with a relatively safe, although anachronistic, shelter. This is not true of the nonshaman Apache, who is forced to incorporate both conflictual and defensive new elements into his personality and even to reorganize, or, rather, first to disorganize, his character structure. In addition, the childhood conditioning he has undergone in a disorganized primitive tribe makes him apriori incapable of functioning well in a modern society that is still efficient. Obliged to improvise all his defensive maneuvers and "solutions" by drawing almost entirely on his idiosyncratic resources, and to do this in a social environment that is affectively incomprehensible to him and to which his childhood conditioning absolutely prevents him from adapting, he will *inevitably* be more disturbed than the shaman, whose behavior is, on the whole, simply anachronistic.[29] The fact that the Apache shaman is psychologically less disturbed than the nonshaman in no way implies that he is not neurotic.[30]

The psychiatric problem of the normality or abnormality of the shaman is not in itself of prime importance. If it arouses so much anxiety, it is only because, behind its commonplace façade, one can glimpse the immense and menacing phantom of our own sociocultural dereism (Devereux 1939a; cf. chaps. 9 and 10 below), our need for charismatic leadership (Devereux 1955c), and our own desperate and mostly fruitless attempts to adapt ourselves to the capriciousness of our times. These endeavors resemble those described with understanding and perspicacity by E. R. Dodds in his *Pagans and Christians in an Age of Anxiety* (1965). It is both saddening and humiliating that few ethnologists, psychiatrists, and sociologists are able to bring to their study of disintegrating cultures, including our own, the kind of realistic compassionateness that good historians of culture, such as Dodds, show spontaneously.

In the following pages I hope to show that the symptoms of "sacred" disorders occupy a key position in the hierarchy of symptoms and reflect the most striking aspects of society's self-disavowal. But before examining the problem of the nature of symptoms, I must analyze the problem of ethnic disorders.

Ethnic Disorders

While ethnic disorders fit modern nosological categories fairly well, they are also structured and arranged by each culture and usually have a name.[31] Moreover, while some of these disorders are supposed to have supernatural causes or aspects and to be curable by esoteric means, they are, unlike shamanism, not directly integrated with tribal supernaturalism. It was no doubt the lack of true integration of epilepsy with Greek supernaturalism that enabled Hippocrates (*On the Sacred Illness*) to say that there was nothing particularly "sacred" in the "sacred illness": epilepsy.

One encounters a wide variety of ethnic disorders in the world. Each culture area, perhaps even each culture, has at least one and often several typical disorders of this kind. In fact, it is my impression, which I will not pause to discuss here, that the number and diversity of ethnic disorders in a given culture reflect its degree of psychological sophistication; that is, they offer an indication of the extent to which the society as a whole takes the individual and his personality into account (cf. note 31). It would thus have been easy to illustrate my theoretical views by choosing one example from central Africa and another from the Eskimos; but documenting a theory by such an assortment of far-flung examples, besides running the risk of disorienting the reader, would not have allowed me to emphasize two critical aspects of the problem, which are the complex patterning of ethnic disorders and their multidimensional character. I shall therefore support my argument with information about a limited number of ethnic disorders, all of which have been relatively well studied and which occur in societies with whose cultures I am particularly familiar.[32] The study in depth of a single ethnic disorder will produce the same results as the comparative—and therefore superficial—study of all disorders of this type (Devereux 1955b [2d rev. ed. 1969]), so that the deliberate restricting of my examples in no way prejudices the validity of my theoretical conclusions.

The ethnic disorders I will most frequently mention are the Malay's *amok* and *latah,* the ancient Scandinavian condition of *berserk,* the *imu* of the Ainus, the *windigo* of the Canadian Algonquians, the Crazy Dog syndrome of the Plains Indians, the heartbreak syndrome of the Mohaves, the transvestitism of these last two groups, and a few others. In most cases the group has explicit theories about the nature and causes of a disorder and clear-cut ideas as to its symptoms, evolution, and prognosis. When a disorder of this type occurs in a particularly dramatic form or threatens to provoke a public crisis, or even when it simply stimulates the group's imagination, it acquires so great a "social mass" (Devereux 1940 [1978a, chap. 1]) that special measures may be taken to control it and possibly exploit it for the benefit of the group. Thus, on the eve of battle, the Vikings counted on some of them to go *berserk* in the heat of the fray and, in that state, to perform great feats of arms, insuring victory. The Crow Indians allotted a place in their battle array not only for the armed Crazy Dog but also for the exceptional one who chose to ride into combat unarmed, although the latter was of no military value to them. The *amok* attack is a recurrent theme in the Malay prose epic *Hikayat Hang Tuah* (Anonymous 1930), whose climax is doubtless the duel between Hang Tuah and his old friend Hang Jebat, who revolted against the king and became an *amok* runner. The cry "*Amok! Amok!*" was a socially recognized signal, to which the Malays reacted (Clifford 1922b) somewhat as we do when we hear an air-raid siren. In fact, the practice of *amok* even affected Malay technology. The *amok* runner who had been speared would press himself forward on the shaft of his enemy's spear until it transpierced his whole body; this enabled him to come close enough to his enemy to kill him with his *kris* (a dagger with a serpentine blade). Hence, the Malays began to make lances whose two blades, forming an acute angle with each other, prevented the frenzied man from closing the distance. This two-bladed spear reminds one of the boar spear of old, equipped at the base of the blade with a transverse bar that prevented the animal from getting dangerously close to the hunter by impaling himself on the spear. It has even been claimed that the United States army exchanged the .38-caliber pistol for the more powerful .45 because a bullet from the latter will knock a man down even if he is only wounded in the hand, whereas the .38-caliber bullet will not make a suitably corseted *amok* runner (*juramentado*) double over, even if he is hit in the stomach or thorax (Hurley 1936). Finally, in many Malay cities, the municipalities used to place forked sticks at street corners to help people overpower the *amok* runner without having to come too close to him. These forked sticks played approximately the same role as call boxes do on our city streets, which permit citizens to alert the nearest police or fire station in an emergency.

Last, but not least, the cultural normalization of such disorders not only allows them to be used as models for individuals who for some reason are psychically disturbed; it also permits the same abnormality to be triggered by a wide variety of different stimuli, as is shown by the extreme diversity of situations that provide a Malay with a reason or incitement to run *amok* (see below).

In brief, ethnopsychiatry teaches—and this is one of its basic contributions—that, particularly in stress situations, *culture itself provides the individual with directives for the misuse of cultural materials*. Linton (1936) called these directives "patterns of misconduct." It is as if the group said to the individual, "Don't do it, but, if you do, go about it in this manner." Before showing that ethnic disorders are indeed patterns of misconduct, I must examine more closely the conduct on which this type of "pattern" is based.

One can criticize Linton on one score only: he applied his brilliant formula to individual deviant behavior only and did not even attempt to specify the nature of the social models by means of which society prepatterns individual misconduct. I was able to fill this gap only in part when, using Linton's views as my starting point, I elaborated the concept of social negativism and suggested, timidly at first, that this negativism could manifest itself not only on the level of individual behavior but also on that of the social process (chap. 3). This suggestion, which I made nearly forty years ago, I now propose to render explicit and to develop into a formal theory.

Every society not only has its "functional" aspects, by means of which it affirms and maintains its integrity, but also has a certain number of beliefs, dogmas, and tendencies that contradict, deny, and undermine not only the essential operations and structure of the group but at times even its very existence. Hinduism, for instance, denies the reality of the sensible world, which is held to be pure illulusion (*maya*). Platonism in many respects shares this way of conceiving reality, and Buddhism so strongly encourages men to shun existence and detach themselves from their fellow men that Alexander (1931) could rightly claim that it constitutes a training for artificial catatonia. The same observations apply equally well to yoga, eremitism, and related attitudes.

On another level, medieval society condemned itself for not realizing the theocratic ideal of the City of God, formulated by Saint Augustine. A number of illustrious popes and theologians maintained that all worldly government is fundamentally evil, and they condemned as sinful certain essential socioeconomic activities, indispensable to the survival of any society, on the pretext that they evidence a sinful attachment to worldly things. Because medieval society would have ceased to exist if these necessary tasks had not been performed, they were accomplished either by circuitous means or by requiring others—Jews, Saracens, and various pariahs—to do them. The Christian could live without sinning as long as the "sinful" pariah sinned in his stead, just as, until very recently, the prostitutes' sexual misconduct permitted girls from good families to remain virgins. In short, while claiming to aspire to the City of God, where these socially useful activities would no longer be necessary, medieval society still found ways to perform—or to have performed on its behalf—these impious activities, thus realizing, *mutatis mutandis,* and in a caricatural manner, Augustine's famous prayer, "Make me chaste, O Lord . . . *but not yet."*

The conflict between the socially negativistic ideal and the functional requirements of a society can also erupt at the individual level. Probably the best-known witness to a conflict of this type is Marcus Aurelius in his *Meditations.* This "Stoic saint" (as J. H. Rose, 1960, calls him), although he fulfilled his imperial obligations not only conscientiously but brilliantly, never ceased to despise them and held them to be obstacles to the attainment of his Stoic ideal. Since it is quite clear that society's contempt of its most useful activities, and of the persons who do perform them,[33] is an expression of its self-destructive tendencies, I hold that Marcus Aurelius's Stoicism suffices almost by itself to explain the decline and fall of the Roman Empire.

Though Linton was clearly not thinking of this type of *antisocial* social ideal when he formulated his concept of patterns of misconduct, it is evident that such attitudes also represent patterns of this type. Indeed, they constitute the pattern of misconduct par excellence, in the sense that they faithfully reflect society's attitude of social negativism and its self-disavowal.[34] Whatever prestige these ideals—or the people who champion them—may have, they represent, nonetheless, types of socially structured misconduct. Like the superstitions and beliefs of those who make up what Americans call "the lunatic fringe"—which exists in every society—they satisfy simultaneously the subjective social negativism of the neurotic and his need to fit into at least one of the many marginal niches or statuses, which range from the ones occupied by the shaman, the Cynic philosopher, the hermit, and other individuals of this type, who are sometimes not considered psychotic by their own group; on through the niches occupied by persons like the *amok* runner or the Crazy Dog, whose condition their group views as an ethnic psychosis; and finally to the niches occupied by the genuinely idiosyncratic psychotics, who have managed to persuade their society that they are insane rather than criminals or sacrilegious persons (chap. 13).

Cultural materials that reflect society's basic disavowal of itself are also precisely the ones that troubled individuals synthesize and give expression to by their behavior—and do this in a manner that can earn them either society's approval or its disapproval. These antisocial social values, which permit the individual to be antisocial in a socially approved and sometimes even prestigious manner, also have another important characteristic. Whereas the majority of cultural traits do not lend themselves to a symptomatic utilization without first undergoing distortion (chap. 2), cultural traits that reflect a society's self-disavowal can, as a rule, be used as symptoms *without* prior distortion.

Materials of this type have three further characteristics.

1. In order to turn them into symptoms, they need only to be hypercathected in a manner that transforms a popular belief into a subjective experience. This is what happens in the case of the shaman (see above).

2. One can transform *rational* cultural materials into symptoms by arbitrarily and illogically associating them with those *irrational* cultural materials that are part of any society's self-disavowal. Thus, when members of a certain fanatical sect fall ill, they refuse medically indispensable blood transfusions on the ground that this is a form of "cannibalism."

3. Since these materials are fundamentally irrational, they can

easily be articulated with modes of thinking and felling rooted in the primary process (Freud) and in prelogical thought (Lévy-Bruhl).

These findings also explain both the frequency of supernatural delusions in psychotics (Dumas 1946) and the fact that supernaturalism contains materials that clearly repudiate culture. It is obvious that every supernatural ritual is essentially opposed to the system of prevailing values of culture as a whole. In fact, the more "sacred" and "restrictive" an action is, the more horror it would inspire were it carried out in a profane context. In some Australian tribes, whose major ritual (*corroboree*) includes a period of sexual license, the ritually preferred sexual partner is often precisely the one who is the most strictly tabooed the rest of the time. At totemic banquets one eats the totemic animal, which is strictly taboo in all other circumstances (Durkheim 1912). After the ox sacrifice (*bouphonia*) the Athenians tried and condemned the knife that had killed the animal (Cook 1940). To insure victory of the Greek fleet over the Persians, Themistocles' soldiers *forced* him to make a human sacrifice (Plutarch *Life of Aristides* 9. 1 f.; *Life of Themistocles* 13. 2 f.). The Arcadian who was *forced* to eat the flesh of a child sacrificed to Zeus Lycaeus (Gk. *lukos* = wolf) automatically became a werewolf for nine years; at the end of that time he became a man again, provided that, during his wolf period, he had abstained from eating human flesh (Cook 1914). In Rome the social hierarchy was completely inverted during the Saturnalia. In Africa there are even rituals of rebellion (Gluckman 1954). These examples, which could be endlessly multiplied, suffice to show that the majority of truly important supernatural rites break the rules and offend the values governing daily life; from a cultural point of view, they often constitute "mirror-image" behavior.

Another expression of social negativism permeated with supernaturalism is a well-known but insufficiently analyzed aspect of shamanism. Shamans are extreme individualists, notoriously hostile toward one another. The Mohave shaman sometimes bewitches one of his fellow shamans simply because the latter's beliefs and practices differ slightly from his own; he therefore refuses to talk about his powers in front of another shaman for fear that this will offend the latter and incite him to magic reprisals (Devereux 1957b). Trials of (magical) strength are very common between shamans. I shall cite, nearly at random, a Greek source (Apollodorus 6. 3–4), Crow data reported by Lowie (1925c), Róheim's (1950) data about Hungarian shamans, and more general data about the type of shaman found in the steppe tribes. In certain tribes the apprentice shaman must consent to the death of one of his kinfolk. Worse still, the Kuanyama Ambo who wants to become a shaman must ask his mother to cohabit with him. If she consents, she dies because she has violated the incest taboo; if she refuses, she also dies, bewitched by her son (E. M. Loeb, personal communication). The relationship between incest and witchcraft is too well known to require further discussion in this context. All of this proves that even if the shaman is socially "useful," as has been claimed (see above), he is also, in many respects, fundamentally "antisocial."

Practically the same thing can be said of hermits, ascetics, and other persons of this type, who must be treated with kid gloves because they are inclined to heap supernatural calamities on anyone who offends them. Although his tormentors were only children, the prophet Elisha cursed them and caused them to be torn apart by two bears (2 Kings 2:24). Similarly, just as shamans engage in trials of (magical) strength with each other, so, according to various important early Christian authors, some Christian ascetics were outrageously arrogant or exhibitionistic persons, competing with each other in "saintliness" and "self-mortification." The data assembled and analyzed by Dodds (1965) lead one to believe that this kind of misconduct was relatively common. During the Greek decadence, certain eminent men were not given to curbing their negativistic tendencies. The Greek Cynics, for example, ostentatiously violated all social conventions, and Lucian reports, in his *Death of Peregrinus,* that Peregrinus, who was first a Cynic and then a Christian before turning to still another creed, masturbated in public. Lucian then describes his suicide in detail: it was a spectacular self-immolation, heralded by flashy advance publicity and carried out during the Olympic festivals, with a stage setting that would outshine that of the greatest modern music halls.

In brief, however great may be their *apparent* integration with the rest of the culture, the supernatural and the irrational always preserve the imprint of their socially negativistic origins; all the sophistry of the apostles of cultural relativism will not convince me that they are a genuinely functional element of any and every genuine culture.

Hence, whatever superficial differences there may be between such generally respected persons as shamans, Stoic saints, and Cynics on the one hand, and the ridiculed Mohave transvestite and the despised prostitute on the other, both types constitute patterns of cultural misconduct within the sociological frame of reference, just as they constitute models of subjective social negativism within a psychological frame of reference. Nor is it at all certain that Stoic saints (and all their ilk) are socially and psychologically less ill than the Mohave transvestite or the prostitute (chap. 7).

Whatever the case, these remarks prove once more that, far from being a marginal component of sociology, psychiatry is instead one of its most reliable grids, because no science can have a better grid than the concepts of another whose explanations stand in a relation of complementarity with its own (Devereux 1945 [1978a, chap. 4], 1961b [1978a, chap. 5], 1967c).

Since all patterns of misconduct belong in many ways to the same type, I can indicate more precisely, already at this juncture, the sense in which ethnic psychiatric disorders fit the patterns of misconduct defined by Linton and "execute" their directives.

Sometimes culture itself provides explicit directives for the misuse of cultural materials, particularly in situations of frequent but atypical stress. The directive that is relevant here is the following: "Don't go crazy, but, if you do, you must behave as follows." Every society has definite ideas about "how to act when crazy." During funeral rites the Nyakyusa simulate insanity in a highly specific manner, since they believe that this prophylactic simulation will protect them from becoming actually insane later on (Wilson 1954). The prophylactic simulation of madness is also attested for other regions (Wallace 1958).

American Indian informants frequently say, "The insane openly mention the names of their dead relatives." Since this is not a common symptom in Occidental psychotics, one must conclude that this is a culturally predetermined form of misconduct and that many psychotic Indians do behave in just this manner. Modern society, too, has definite ideas of "how to behave when insane." People readily believe that the insane make faces, talk at random, get mixed up in their speech, and say "brrr" or "b-b-b-b." Scarcely less naive (and quite as cultural) preconceptions about how the insane "should" behave, feel, and think are embedded in current legal theories. Hence, the psychiatrist appearing in court is often forced to answer questions that are psychiatrically senseless. I once had occasion to testify as an expert at the trial of a man who had shot his wife dead and then, turning the weapon against himself, had shot off a corner of his skull, knocking himself unconscious. The prosecution argued that the accused was sane and simply "grossly selfish" because, when he recovered consciousness, he "selfishly" called to his dead wife to help *him*. My testimony, that this in itself proved that the crime was committed during an epileptic fugue and was completely blanketed by amnesia, was rejected out of hand because it did not dovetail with "legal common-sense" views on how the "insane" *should* behave. Actually, the kind of behavior commonly ascribed to the insane by both the legislator and the layman is seldom seen in mental hospitals. I add that, shortly after being sentenced to prison, the allegedly sane murderer became acutely psychotic.

A fairly good way to study cultural preconceptions about the "proper way of being insane" is to examine the behavior of malingerers, for these persons usually try to conform to the *layman's* notion of how the insane behave and can therefore be shown up as frauds by any experienced psychiatrist.[35]

The earliest diagnosis of malingering was no doubt Palamedes' finding that Odysseus was simulating insanity in order not to have to fight in the Trojan War (Hyginus *Fabulae* 95).

The fact that the impulse to malinger is in itself pathological may explain why one of the Esposito brothers tried to simulate psychosis by ostentatiously eating newspapers. He presumably *chose* this symptom because he was *sufficiently abnormal* to sense unconsciously that oral conflicts play an important role in most psychoses. An even more interesting problem is that of culturally expected and even prescribed transitory eruptions of abnormality. Linton once remarked to me that we will probably never know whether Mohammed was a real epileptic because convulsive seizures were, among the Arabs of his time, not only "the" mental disorder par excellence but were, in addition, so consistently interpreted as tokens of divine backing that Arab chiefs often faked a "fit" just before battle in order to encourage their followers. Odysseus likewise "acted out" the Greek's idea of mental decay when he sought to deceive the suitors (*Odyssey* 17. 336 ff.), just as the fugitive David acted out the Judaic conception of lunacy by allowing his saliva to dribble on his beard (1 Sam. 21:13).

By contrast, the idiosyncratic psychotic tends to develop a symptomatology grossly at variance with cultural expectations and social demands, and, moreover, almost deliberately provocative, simply because his illness is itself an important manifestation of his "social negativism" (chap. 3).[36] Of course this does not mean that an ethnic disorder is to be interpreted as a case of pretense or malingering. *Amok* runners and Crazy Dogs seeks a "glorious" death and generally find it. Among the Plains Indians the coward either sacrifices glory, honored status, and heterosexual satisfactions or may even go so far as to commit suicide to avoid the official "solution" to his problems, that is, transvestitism. In brief, the social stereotypes that determine "how the insane behave" are drawn from "patterns of misconduct," and individuals suffering from ethnic disorders shape

35

their symptoms according to these patterns, which true malingerers in turn deliberately imitate to persuade others that they are really "insane."

In short, among some emotionally disturbed persons the unconscious segment of the ethnic personality is not so disorganized as to incite them to wholesale rebellion against *all* social norms. Although genuinely ill, such persons tend to borrow from culture the *means* permitting them to manifest their subjective derangement in a conventional way, if only to avoid being taken for criminals or witches (chap. 13). This accounts for such "exotic" ethnic neuroses as *amok, latah, imu, windigo, koro,* and many others that are not found in our own cultural repertory. Aberle ingeniously demonstrated (1952) that even though the Siberian equivalent of *latah* in certain respects resembles Gilles de la Tourette's disease, it is nevertheless not identical with that syndrome. Likewise, although the newspapers—and even some psychiatrists—wrote that the paranoid veteran who "shot up the town" in Camden, New Jersey, "was running amok," his psychosis was fundamentally different from that of a real Malay *amok* runner. In fact, his attack was purely idiosyncratic in both its motivations and its manifestations. No culture pattern influenced the course of events in Camden, and, contrary to what occurs in numerous cases of true *amok*, there was no cultural preparation—no premeditation, in the legal sense of the term. Moreover, premeditation plays an equally decisive role in the Crazy-Dog-Wishes-to-Die syndrome (Lowie 1925a and 1935), as well as in a number of other ethnic disorders.

In every ethnic disorder the behavior pattern of the abnormal person not only conforms to what *his* society expects—for instance, from the *amok* runner or the Crazy Dog—but his behavior is also quite often in complete contrast with *our* culturally determined notions of "how the insane behave." In fact the common "lay" ideas on the subject are probably based on the symptomatology of different ethnic disorders obtaining at an earlier stage of our own culture.

If the symptomatology of ethnic psychoses fits cultural expectations, it is chiefly because conventional ideas on "how to act when insane" reflect the specific nature of the conflicts prevailing within a culture—preconceptions determined by the nature of the defenses that that culture provides against culturally penalized conflicts and impulses. Thus, given the nature of Crow culture, the psychically traumatized Crow Indian can, because of his distinctive ethnic makeup, find relief in "being crazy" in accordance with the Crazy Dog pattern, whereas the Malay, because of his ethnic makeup and because of the nature of his culture, will relieve his tensions by becoming an *amok* runner.

This convergence of the states of tension characteristic of a culture and the defenses that it provides against these tensions, on the one hand, and the cultural preconceptions of "how to act when insane," on the other, explains some important facts: the absence, or at least the extreme infrequency, of a certain syndrome in a given society, in which different syndromes proliferate; the variations, determined by the cultural environment, in the incidence and proportion of various syndromes; and, finally, the fact that in a given society the full range of all known psychiatric disorders is rarely observed. Thus, today, the Occidental psychiatrist practicing in an urban environment rarely has occasion to encounter cases of *grande hystérie*, so common in Charcot's time.[37] Similarly, the Mohave Indians were totally *incapable* of understanding my descriptions of obsessive rumination and compulsive rituals. When questioned about obsessions, one of my Mohave informants replied: "I see what you mean; it is like the chief's thinking constantly about the welfare of the tribe." And when I mentioned compulsive rituals, I was told: "So-and-so is always jingling the coins in his pocket."[38] Nevertheless, the Mohave are so prone to "psychological reflection" that it was from Mohave informants and not from psychiatric textbooks that I learned of the existence of *globus hystericus* and pseudo-cyesis (hysterical false pregnancy) at a time (1932–33) when I was unfamiliar with even the rudiments of psychiatry. This comes as no surprise from a culture in which training in sphincter control is remarkably casual and where avarice (anal retention) is one of the capital sins (Devereux 1951d). Moreover, I have so far encountered only a single case of hand-washing of a genuinely compulsive type in a primitive society: the Attawapiskat Cree (Honigmann 1954). Finally, although I cannot diagnose with certainty the native of Dobu who could not stop working, discussed by Fortune (1932b), I am at least perfectly sure that this was not a case of true compulsive behavior.

I shall mention only in passing the absence of true schizophrenia among primitive peoples who have not been subjected to a brutal acculturation process, because I discuss the matter at length elsewhere (chap. 9). In fact, what Occidental psychiatrists sometimes mistakenly diagnose as schizophrenia in a primitive belonging to an *intact* culture is usually a hysterical psychosis or a psychotic episode (*bouffée délirante*). As for Laubscher's (1937) numerous diagnoses of schizophrenia among the Tembu, their accuracy has been challenged even by psychiatrists without ethnological training and especially by those who had not simply read his book but had seen his film—and this in spite of the fact that, at the time Laubscher was working among the Tembu, the tribe was already undergoing a brutal acculturation process. A perspicacious psychiatrist (Domarus 1948), familiar with South African life, has suggested, no doubt correctly, that the Bantu have been able to survive psychologically in spite of very harsh oppression only because of the long period of nursing and relatively satisfactory mothering of infants.

Finally, and this observation is important, it appears that the authentic psychopath—who must be carefully distinguished both from the neurotic or nonneurotic criminal and from the illegalist[39]—is likewise quite rare in intact primitive societies.

The problem of historical change can be reviewed fairly briefly. I have already mentioned the quasi-disappearance of *grande hystérie* in modern urban environments and its persistence in less-developed societies. This is shown by the following incident.

A few years ago an eminent psychiatrist received a manuscript from a psychiatrist, born in the Middle East and practicing there, who had received his training in excellent European medical schools and psychiatric hospitals; the manuscript was so surprising that my colleague asked me to read it and give him my opinion. At first I thought it had been written by an eccentric or by someone trying to be original at all costs; but I gradually came to realize that the author had been treating patients who resembled those Charcot had studied at the Salpêtrière hospital but that, because of his Occidental training, he had tried to fit his clinical data into the straitjacket of contemporary psychiatric thought, whose main axis—or even obsession—is schizophrenia. His approach reminds one of current revisionist attempts to diagnose as latent schizophrenics certain patients whom Freud had diagnosed as hysterics. Such attempts are based not on clinical reality but on certain culturally determined psychiatric thought models (Devereux 1958a [1978a, chap. 10]). One also notes that it has become a commonplace in psychoanalytic circles to say that, whereas the pioneers of psychoanalysis dealt primarily with symptom neuroses and the psychoanalysts of the thirties with character neuroses, the majority of those who consult the psychoanalyst today suffer from an alteration of the sense of their own identity (Lowenfeld 1944).[40]

There is nothing surprising about the fact that the proportions of different psychiatric symptoms vary in terms of the cultural context. Until recently, *many* more men than women have had stomach ulcers. Social-class differences in the distribution of various psychiatric ailments are well documented (Hollingshead and Redlich 1958). In view of these findings, why should one be surprised to learn that the full gamut of psychiatric symptoms is rarely observed in a single society when one readily accepts the absence of malaria among the Eskimos and of snowblindness and frostbite among the Congolese?

Neither differences in the ratios of psychiatric syndromes that one can observe in various societies nor the absence of some known syndromes in every society affects the stability or variability, in a given society, of the proportion of "abnormal" persons to those called "normal." It has been urged—whether rightly or wrongly matters little—that this proportion remains constant in every society and at every moment of history. What does matter is that some scholars (Eaton and Weil 1955) believe that one can conclude from this finding that psychiatric illnesses have a biological origin. This argument is, to say the least, specious. Were it acceptable, one would also have to suppose that physical illnesses do *not* have a biological origin, since the distribution of diseases and the percentage of premature deaths—that is, deaths not due to old age—vary greatly from one society to another. Moreover, the explanation of this fact about psychiatric illness, if indeed it is a fact, would be easy enough to find. If it is true that the percentage of physically incapacitated individuals may not exceed a critical threshold in a given society without causing that society to collapse, it is equally true that too high a ratio of psychiatrically ill persons would have similar consequences (Devereux 1956d).

Lastly, and above all, it is, sociologically speaking, absurd to try to draw rather complex conclusions from the simple ratio between *all* those who are psychiatrically normal and abnormal in a given society. In fact, a society may very well tolerate a relatively high proportion of "abnormal persons" as long as the majority of them are, for instance, hysterics; it cannot survive if the majority are schizophrenic or feebleminded. Likewise, a society whose abnormal members were mostly mentally retarded persons, just below the normal range, would manage to survive, although with some difficulty, if the society were a simple agricultural one or if the majority of its feebleminded members constituted a class of unskilled laborers. This is the equivalent of the finding that if the Elmolo manage to survive in spite of so severe a calcium deficiency that the majority of its members have saber shins, their survival is due to their relatively protected geographical location, on the one hand, and, on the other, to their not being a warrior tribe (Dyson and Fuchs 1937). In a warrior society, such a rate of calcium deficiency would rapidly entail the tribe's extinction. Likewise Sparta, a highly militaristic and rigidly stratified state, was more severely endangered by the low birth-rate of its upper classes (Forrest 1968) than Hungary was by the massacre of the majority of its warrior caste during the disastrous battle of Mohács[41] simply because the Hungarians, unlike the Spartans, rapidly filled the decimated ranks of their warrior nobility with newly ennobled commoners.

To return to clinical problems, one cannot but be astonished when one sees psychiatrists misled by the cultural conformism of some of their neurotic or psychotic patients—even to the point of underestimating the seriousness of their fundamental pathology. The following example will demonstrate this.

An ambitious and educated white woman had married, on the rebound, an Indian farmer, an uneducated but honest and hard-working man. To compensate for her loss of status, she wanted her son to live like a white man and *be a success* in accordance with the standards of white society. In a word, she wanted to make him "mother's hero." However, this halfbreed, a remarkably gifted person, unconsciously identified himself with his father, whom he consciously despised, just as he despised all those of his race. He reacted against the conflicting demands of his mother in a very subtle way: he contrived to fail in everything he undertook in such a way that, by frustrating himself, he at the same time frustrated his mother's ambitions. Moreover, by making *himself* fail, it was first and foremost the despised part of himself, his Indian "half," that he damaged. Thus, in spite of a brilliant freshman year at one of the best universities, when financial difficulties made it impossible for his parents to help him pursue his studies, he chose to leave the university and work in a factory rather than accept help from one of his father's sisters, a "lousy Indian" who had married a wealthy farmer. Also, though he complied with his mother's demand that he should not marry an Indian, he complied by marrying a white girl—but one as uneducated and "primitive" as the most "blanket" Indian. Having by his intelligence attracted the attention of his superiors, he was offered a foreman's job. He refused this promotion and, to justify his refusal, claimed that, if he became foreman, he would have to invite to his home not only his coworkers but also some of the office employees and lower-echelon bosses in the factory—and the latter would consider his apartment (which was in fact quite acceptable) the "dirty wigwam" (sic!)[42] of a "lousy Indian." In short, he failed to achieve any of the typical middle-class values—"education," "success," and "marriage to a white woman"—by setting up, in opposition to them, another white-middle-class value: racial prejudice. His behavior is therefore a typical example of "mock compliance."

Likewise, although he was beset by a severe oedipal complex, he handled it by viewing his father as a "lousy Indian." He denied hating him or being jealous of him because he cohabited with his mother. He said that he was only "indignant" that a "lousy Indian" (his father) could defile "a pure white woman" (his mother) by cohabiting with her (chap. 2). This permitted him to face his oedipal problems (under a cultural mask) without gaining insight into their subjective meaning. Moreover, although he was himself a halfbreed, he did *not* consider his own sexual relations with his (white) wife as a defilement of the white race—doubtless because, owing to her primitive and uncultivated behavior, his wife represented for him an Indian "squaw" and, because of her race, his mother. From some of his allusions—too tenuous for me to cite here but sufficiently convincing to be taken into account—I concluded, further, that it was as if his "white" half made love with the white racial component— with the "whiteness" of his wife—and his Indian half made love with her "primitive," and therefore symbolically Indian, component.

In short, this halfbreed patient took advantage of the fact that race prejudice, like all prejudices, is a symptomatic defense that culture provides to neurotics and used it as a defense against insight into his oedipal conflicts. Now, what betrayed the symptomatic character of his racial prejudice was the fact that he was a halfbreed, for it is particularly absurd for a halfbreed to profess to despise Indians. If he had been a simple southern white, obsessed with the desire to "protect" the honor of white women, his neurosis, though equally pathognomonic, would have been less easy to discern, masked as it was by cultural prejudice.

This clinical observation strikingly demonstrates how a dual cultural allegiance may fit into the series conflict–defense–secondary conflict–secondary defense.[43] This schema provides a particularly fertile frame for the study of religious conversions and of conflicts triggered by acculturation.

Although a definition of ethnic disorders was given at the beginning of this chapter, so many marginal problems have now been raised that, before entering on a systematic study of the cultural patterning and organization of these disorders, it seems appropriate to recapitulate the terms of the definition and to review the principal examples that have been cited.

Ethnic disorders resemble shamanistic derangements in that both use defenses and symptoms provided by culture and developed specifically for that purpose.[44] However, ethnic disorders derive their means of defense from one segment of culture, and shamanistic derangements derive theirs from another. Ethnic disorders differ from shamanistic derangements in the origin of their basic conflicts, which

41

are rooted not in the ethnic unconscious but in idiosyncratic traumata *sufficiently prevalent* in a given culture to force that culture to
take cognizance of them as soon as their frequency or intensity ex-
ceeds a certain threshold. When such is the case, the culture is obliged
to create defenses against these disorders; one of these defenses is
precisely the development of patterned symptoms, which, by permitting the externalization of the disorders in standardized forms,
render them, ipso facto, more easily controllable (see below). Otherwise expressed, only fairly recurrent types of traumata, which culture singles out for special notice and designates as "traumata," elicit
properly ethnic, as opposed to idiosyncratic, disorders, because culture places at the disposal of persons subjected to such strains a
ready-made armamentarium of defenses in the form of prepatterned
symptoms representing one kind of standardized "pattern of misconduct."

The preceding considerations permit a systematic examination of
the origin, evolution, and manifestations of ethnic disorders. In what
follows I shall examine all the significant problems except that of
symptoms—of "signals" (chap. 13)—which are culturally formulated and by means of which the disturbed individual informs his
society that he is "crazy" and, at the same time, specifies that he is
not a *non*crazy deviant—criminal or otherwise.

The main consequence of this cultural patterning of ethnic disorders is to render the behavior of the "patient" not only predictable
but, quite specifically, predictable in terms of the cultural frame of
reference, whereas idiosyncratic disorders are predictable only in
terms of a psychological frame of reference (chap. 2). In the ethnic
psychotic, the predictable segment of behavior will be the behavior
exhibited by *any* ethnic psychotic of the same type. In idiosyncratic
disorders, on the contrary, it will be necessary to try to understand
the psychology of the individual patient, and prediction made on
this basis will apply only to the behavior of *a* (particular) paranoid
individual, of *a* manic-depressive, and so forth. It must be remembered that this distinction between "any" and "a" has a crucial significance, not only, as Russell (1903, 1919) emphasizes, in formal
logic, but also in psychiatry (Devereux 1944b).

The (cultural) predictability of the actions of an individual suffering from ethnic disorders results from a powerful cultural conditioning. Of course the young Malay hopes he will never find himself in
straits so desperate that only one acceptable solution remains open
to him: running *amok*. He knows, however, that, should such a situation arise, he *will have to* become an *amok* runner and *he will
know how to* conduct himself properly. Likewise, it is probable that

every young Viking not only hoped he would be capable of "going berserk" in battle but even *learned* the behavior complex that constituted "going berserk." In Greek and Roman society, suicide, as a solution accessible to the individual in trouble with the law, was thoroughly regulated. The young Greek or Roman certainly hoped that he would never find himself in difficulties of the kind in which society would drive him to commit suicide or would suggest to him that he do so; nevertheless, when matters came to this pass, he did what was expected of him. Thus, although it had unjustly condemned them to death, society did not have to use force to make Theramenes or Socrates drink the hemlock. As for the Roman aristocrat, he was expected to anticipate his own execution—by committing suicide—in order to avoid the confiscation of his property by the state. And when the cowardly Paetus hesitated, his wife shamed him, and, to encourage him to kill himself, stabbed herself before his eyes, saying, "Paetus, it doesn't hurt" (*Paete, non dolet*) (Pliny, *Epistles* 3. 16). I seriously doubt that a modern state could so easily persuade those it has condemned to death that it is their duty to carry out their own sentences so as to spare their countrymen the ritual pollution (*miasma*) of bloodshed.

The argument that ethnic disorders are culturally patterned not only does not contradict but considerably reinforces my fundamental view that, in the last resort, all psychic disorders involve impoverishment, dedifferentiation, and disindividualization. The Malay who runs *amok* ceases to be a highly differentiated individual; he is now nothing but an *amok* runner, his psychic disorder having obliterated and swallowed up everything that was unique in his personality.

The cultural patterning of ethnic disorders also allows two curious facts to be explained:

1. Whether provided by native informants, colonial officials, (Clifford 1898), planters (Fauconnier 1930), or psychiatrists (Van Loon 1926; Yap 1952), descriptions of *latah* attacks are remarkably similar.[45] This tends to prove that Malay informants have not sought to force their accounts into the procrustean bed of the culturally imposed model of this disease. Similarly, the *amok* episodes described in the ancient Malay epic (Anonymous 1922) fit in even the minutest details with modern accounts (Clifford 1922) in regard to both the *amok* runner's behavior and the panic reaction of the civilian population and even of the soldiers sent against him.

2. This explains why nearly every case of *latah* and *amok* appears to be a "classic" case, worthy of inclusion in a psychiatric textbook. The same cannot be said of the idiosyncratic psychotic, who gener-

ally does not have the good grace to facilitate the psychiatrist's task of diagnosis by exhibiting such "textbook" syndromes. In fact, it may be that the relative uniformity of attacks of *grande hystérie,* as observed in Chacot's service, was due not only to the fact that in the 1880s hysteria was the ethnic type neurosis of the Western world but, even more, to the systematic inculcation of "the right way to be a hysteric."

In fact, victims of hysteria lend themselves particularly well to this kind of conditioning because they are notoriously prone to theatrical behavior and are constantly invited to "do their number" for the distinguished professional visitor. Proof that it was not a question of malingering was, moreover, explicitly provided by one of Charcot's "prize patients," who muttered one day, "You really have to be crazy to be able to play the part as expected."

I shall now analyze separately the culturally prepatterned aspects of the various phases that occur in ethnic disorders.

Ethnic character and ethnic disorders. The wide variety of "causes" that in a given society can produce a single type of patterned eruption is sufficient evidence that ethnic disorders are rooted chiefly in ethnic character (and not in the ethnic unconscious). At the risk of repeating myself, I shall state once again that the *amok* attack can result from the widest variety of causes: delirium due to a high fever, rumination of an insult, desire to perish in a glorious conflagration atop a heap of corpses, compliance with the orders of a hierarchical superior, fascination exerted by the *kris,* severe reactive depression, intentional anticipation of *amok* behavior, a kind of autohypnosis that takes the form of a litany on man's being fated to die and the futility of existence, and many others. Despite their statistical frequency, subjective conflicts ("traumata") of the individual *amok* runner trigger only a (temporary) psychosis in him. It is his ethnic character that causes him to become an *amok* runner rather than a catatonic or something else. *Mutatis mutandis,* the same remarks are applicable to other ethnic disorders.

Cultural patterns and clinical labels. An ethnic disorder forms a coherent structure in its evolution, not only from its causes to its resolution, by way of its various manifestations, but also in its specific manifestations. It follows that specific expressions, such as "to run *amok*" or "to go *berserk,*" should be used to designate only the specific disorders of Malays or Vikings, respectively. A Malay does not go *berserk,* nor does a Viking run *amok.* By contrast, in Occidental society only (idiosyncratic) paranoiacs or paranoid schizophrenics can become prey to a blind and uncontrollable homicidal rage. This finding absolutely does not authorize one, however, to conclude that the Malay *amok* runner, too, is paranoid. In fact, what underlies an ethnic disorder is not simply the specific psychodynamic configuration that determines its etiology, but a particular ethnic character as well—one so conditioned as to allow the subject to rid himself of a number of diversified subjective problems by means of one and the same complex of symptoms. This is shown by the fact that a mere attack of malaria may trigger an *amok* attack in a Malay, though it could not do this in a European, even if he had spent a long time among the Malays. I am therefore not convinced that the true *amok* can be observed (Teoh 1972) among Chinese and Tamil citizens of Malaysia.

This finding has an interesting implication: no one is entirely acculturated unless he has reacted to a culturally specific strain with the disorder culturally appropriate to that strain. Thus I have yet to hear of a squaw man (a white man married to an Indian and living as an Indian) who became a Crazy Dog or of a European living among the Malay who became an *amok* runner. In short, a given disorder must conform *in the smallest details* to the prescribed pattern if it is to be considered an ethnic disorder. Thus the term *amok* is inapplicable to the Melanesian's violent outburst, first, because he (usually) uses a lance (Chowning 1961) and not, like nearly all Malay *amok* runners, a *kris* or some other short sword or dagger and, second, because, unlike the Malay's fit, the Melanesian's fit does not always result in homicide. Nor can one compare to an *amok* attack the bloody outbreaks frequently observed among West African soldiers, because they do not use their bayonets but their army rifles and because their attacks do not appear to be culturally patterned (Aubin 1939; Dembowitz 1945). Finally, Sophocles' Ajax and Euripides' Orestes (in *Iphigenia among the Taurians*) are neither "*amok* runners" nor "*berserkers*" when, believing they are killing persons, they savagely slaughter animals—even though the Malay *amok* runner sometimes incidentally kills animals that cross his path. I maintain that both Ajax and Orestes were "werewolves," of the specifically Greek type described by Roscher (1896).

In short, whatever its frequency, a disorder is not an ethnic one as long as it has not undergone cultural patterning. Although in the nineteenth century the sepoys of the Indian army occasionally had seizures of murderous madness—the best-known case being that of Mangal Pande, whose execution was one of the direct causes of the great Sepoy Mutiny of 1857—their fits were nonetheless idiosyncratic, because an ethnic disorder resembling *amok*, but culturally only slightly patterned, existed in only a few limited regions of the Indian subcontinent (Barbosa 1921; Correa 1858; *Encyclopaedia*

Britannica, 1910, vol. 1). Similarly, the British soldier described by Kipling ("In the Matter of a Private"), who went on a bloody rampage, exhibited neither a particularly thorough acculturation nor a desire to imitate Indian culture models. His homicidal psychosis was due to subjective causes and manifested itself in a subjective manner; in other words, he improvised his own symptoms in conformity with his own needs.

The ethnopsychiatrist must therefore reserve specific diagnostic terms for the manifestations corresponding to them: the term *amok*, for example, uniquely for the murderous outburst of the Malay behaving in accordance with the traditional pattern. At the very most, he might also apply it to the behavior of a hypothetical Malay who, having no *kris* or other kind of knife but owning a revolver, runs through the streets shouting "*Amok!*" and shooting blindly into a crowd. My emphasis on the diagnostic importance of the appropriate model is justified by the following case. A particularly sensational psychotic crime—a virtual slaughter—sometimes triggers a "fashion"; that is, the initial incident is soon transmuted into a sort of "tradition" that is patterned, at least in part, by cultural values. A relatively recent example of this is furnished by the slaughter committed by a Texan who shot indiscriminately from a tower into a crowd—a crime that was followed by several similar outbursts of homicidal psychotic insanity. On the other hand, the at least equally sensational murder of eight Chicago nurses found no imitators, doubtless because the killer did not use a firearm. What is involved here is obviously a form of cultural conditioning: the "proper" and "honorable" American way to kill is to kill with a gun. To use a knife for the identical purpose is culturally "despicable," good at best for "dirty niggers," "wops," and other un-American scum (chap. 3).

Pattern and element. Numerous ethnic symptoms are readily mistaken for socially approved kinds of behavior. Thus the recklessness of the *amok* runner or *berserker* is only a paroxysmal manifestation of the courage so prized in the famous Malay or Viking warrior. What makes the *amok* runner's temerity pathological is its social uselessness and the fact that his victims are usually not his enemies but members of his own group. The case of the Crazy Dog is even more revealing. Though he was doubtless as eager as anyone to "count coup" ("score" against the enemy), his ostentatious performance was, nonetheless, an act of pure self-glorification, because sometimes the Crazy Dog went into battle armed only with a quirt and a rattle. This egotistical display of courage had, moreover, a cultural model: it was that of the young daredevil Crow who, avid

46

of glory, often betrayed a carefully laid ambush by riding out of it at breakneck speed so as to be the first to count coup on the enemy. It is to be noted that this practice of self-glorification often had disastrous military consequences.[46]

As for ethnic disorders of our own society, the similarities between the principal symptoms of schizophrenia and the patterns of behavior socially prized by our culture are discussed in chapter 10.[47]

By contrast, the constituent symptoms of idiosyncratic disorders rarely coincide with elements of socially approved behavior. This finding justifies, I think, the utilization of the word "pattern" in Linton's formula "patterns of misconduct," because in every ethnic disorder it is chiefly the pattern, rather than any one of its component elements, that is abnormal, and this abnormality is, in a way, a caricature of the total culture pattern.

Problems in the identification of symptoms. The champions of cultural relativism will predictably assert that the Crazy Dog is normal because his behavior is standardized and culturally controllable. I must therefore demonstrate that there is a parallelism between the definition of conduct qua "symptom" in terms of the absolute criteria of normality and the definition of this same conduct formulated in cultural terms. Among the Plains Indians the coward had at his disposal the solution of becoming a transvestite, whereas, among the Tanala of Madagascar, transvestitism was the refuge of the sexually deficient man, whose impotence, had he married, would have been made public by his unsatisfied wife (Linton 1933). The adoption of the same type of deviant behavior by two different types of individuals under stress proves that transvestitism is a symptom even if it is culturally patterned and fitted into a social niche. Similarly, some notoriously irrational types of behavior that modern psychiatrists recognize as symptoms must necessarily be considered as such even if, in another society, they provide the constitutive elements of an ethnic (or "sacred") psychosis. This is true for glossolalia, which is a clinical symptom for the modern psychiatrist but was a manifestation (a "symptom") of "divine madness" (Dodds 1951) for the Greeks. One can say at the most that the hallucinating Occidental psychotic is *more severely* disturbed than the Plains Indian, whose hallucinations are part of his vision quest (chap. 15).

Trauma, motivation, and social justification. These factors practically coincide in ethnic disorders. Culture itself defines the nature and degree of intensity of the strain or trauma that justifies one's "going crazy." Among the Northern Algonquians only an "extreme deprivation," acknowledged by the society to be of the requisite kind and intensity, justifies—and therefore gives rise to—the *windigo* seizure (Teicher 1960). What Crow culture defines as an "intolerable disappointment" leads to the Crazy Dog syndrome (Lowie 1925a), and nothing it does not define in this manner is capable of motivating or eliciting this ethnic disorder.

If a Crow is to become insane in a *respectable*—that is, *ethnic*—manner, two conditions must be met:

1. The socially recognized stress must be experienced in a conventional manner and must be solved in an equally conventional way: the Crow Indian who fears death has the right to become a transvestite but not the right to declare himself a pacifist or "conscientious objector."

2. To an "intolerable disappointment" of an "appropriate" type, the Crow Indian may react by becoming a Crazy Dog and thus win the respect of the members of his tribe. Such may be his reaction, for instance, if his ambition to become a chief is frustrated (Lowie 1925a). But he is not supposed to react to an "intolerable disappointment" of a type *not acknowledged* as such by "going crazy" in just "any old way"; if caught in this second type of situation, he wins the respect of the others only if he ostentatiously reacts to it phlegmatically and displays exceptional stoicism and indifference toward what even his entourage admittedly recognizes to be an atypical, though terrible, blow.

The following example will illustrate this point. Under certain conditions a Crow could claim the wife of another if he had had an affair with her. A thoroughly disreputable Crow once dared to claim the dearly beloved wife of another man by falsely alleging that he had had an affair with her. In spite of his wife's vehement denials, and even though both he and the rest of the tribe knew for a fact that the claimant was lying, the husband stoically commanded his weeping wife to follow the liar into his tent, thus gaining much prestige for himself (Lowie 1925b). Had he reacted by becoming a Crazy Dog, he would probably have been despised by all, simply because the trauma caused by this situation, though recognized as serious, was not of the "right" kind.

Another telling example is the way in which the Mohave define personal loss and the appropriate response to it. The Mohave weep copiously at funerals and scorn the white man for not having wept at the god Matavilye's funeral (Devereux 1961a [consult 2d rev. ed., 1969]). Though they ridicule the man who allows himself to become upset by the desertion of his wife or mistress, they readily accept that a woman should indulge in a violent display of emotion when abandoned by a husband or lover. In fact, the situation is even more subtly nuanced: the nature of Mohave culture explains why old men deserted by young wives suffer a transitory attack of *hīwa itck* (heartbreak)—a socially recognized but privately ridiculed disturbance—while old women abandoned by young husbands experience nothing of the kind, and why only widows—never widowers—try to commit suicide during the funeral of a spouse.[48]

In short, culturally acknowledged traumata generally provoke ethnic disorders; traumata in which the culture refuses to see a plausible cause of "insanity" elicit idiosyncratic disorders. Because these types of cultural definitions tend to change more slowly than social reality changes, a new ethnic disorder may become quite common before being acknowledged as a product of culture. Thus, because of the progressive disintegration of their social life, Mohave men commit suicide more and more frequently when faced with amorous difficulties, but the tribe as yet refuses to recognize in this emerging pattern the expression of a new ethnic disorder; it correctly perceives the correlation between this type of conduct and the acculturation process (Devereux 1961a [2d rev. ed., 1969]), but it persists in viewing it simply as an idiosyncratic disorder.

The instigation—which must not be confused with motivation—is a formalized signal that triggers both "sacred" and ethnic disorders. Sacred disorders are, moreover, socially functional only if they *can be elicited at will*. A seizure can be triggered either accidentally or intentionally; it can be either self-induced or elicited by an external cause. In a few cases the efficacy of triggering mechanisms can be partially explained in biochemical or neurophysiological terms, but in the majority of cases the sequence "triggering–seizure" appears to be a "conditioned reflex" of a purely cultural order. Furthermore, biochemical or physiological triggers may include cultural components, because, being integrated with a prescribed cultural sequence, they can considerably reinforce and even modify their inherent triggering capacity.

The most common biochemical triggers are alcohol and drugs. Given such well-known phenomena as the "placebo effect" and the clear-cut influence of cultural anticipations and/or antecedent psychological states on the effects of alcohol and drugs, it is evident that this type of trigger needs to be studied also from an ethnopsychiatric viewpoint. As regards alcohol, I have noted elsewhere that the drunken Plains Indian is quarrelsome, whereas the drunken Mohave tends to fall into a sort of stupor (Devereux 1951a [2d rev. ed., 1969]). An alcoholic American woman reacted to different types of alcohol in terms of their cultural definitions: under the influence of champagne she did her best to speak French and behaved like a cute lady's maid of the stage, but under the influence of gin she behaved and talked like an English charwoman, and so forth. Reliance on drugs or alcohol to induce certain particularly sought-after abnormal states is a commonplace phenomenon. Some specialists even think that Viking *berserk* behavior was artificially provoked by the consumption of poisonous mushrooms on the eve of battle (Fabing 1956). Like the modern gangsters who take cocaine or heroin before committing particularly audacious crimes, the dangerous Assassin sect in Persia and Syria consumed hashish.[49] In some modern armies a big shot of rum is regularly distributed to the soldiers before they are ordered to attack. Reliance on alcohol as a preliminary to coitus in puritanical societies is a particularly telling example of the influence of cultural factors on the consequences of intoxication. In fact, since one of alcohol's physiological effects is to decrease erectile potency, it cannot "trigger" sexual behavior except by temporarily abolishing inhibitions; hence the saying "The superego is soluble in alcohol." I strongly suspect that the efficacy of the laurel leaves chewed by the Pythian priestess at Delphi was due less to the drug they contained than to the belief that Apollo's laurel was capable of inducing a "mantic" state. In support of this interpretation I cite the fact that, contrary to the claims of some ancient authors, no trace of toxic telluric gas emanations, or of crevices that would permit such emanations, have been detected at Delphi by modern archeologists. I also interpret frenetic dancing—a frequently used technique for inducing abnormal states—in a similar manner: as a kind of self-intoxication, because physical exhaustion produces a state of self-intoxication (chap. 11). Fasting is another physiological/biochemical trigger.

Neurophysiological triggering. It was long believed that the state of ecstasy induced by the beat of a drum was a mere conditioned reflex. Today it is thought that the drumbeat is *also* a kind of auditory driving, which, like photic driving, modifies the brain waves, inducing an abnormal state explicable in electroneurophysiological terms (Neher 1961, 1962).

Certain kinds of seizure can be triggered either by a cultural stimulus of a conventional kind or by a drug. The Viking could go *berserk* either by ingesting toxic mushrooms or by listening to heroic ballads. An immensely strong but also prudent and good-natured Danish king, wishing to hear such ballads but knowing that they would put him into a state of *berserker* madness, asked his men to bind him hand and foot and watch over him so that, in the *berserk* state, he would not injure anyone (Bérard 1927). One may well wonder what was paramount in the king's mind: the desire to experience the *berserker* frenzy or the desire to hear the ballads. To my mind, his principal motive was doubtless the former. Likewise, the great khan Ogotai took the precaution of charging his men to ignore any death sentence he might pronounce under the influence of alcohol. This permitted him to become as drunk as he pleased without having to bear remorse the next day (Grousset 1941).

Among the Ainu, the *imu* seizure is triggered in a manifestly cultural way, since the standard trigger, "snake," can be either a real snake, a toy snake, or even the simple exclamation "Snake!"—and this in a region that is not infested with poisonous snakes (Winiarz and Wielawski 1936). Since these echolalic and echopraxic states (the Ainu's *imu*, the Malay's *latah*, and the Siberian's *myriachit*) are triggered by a stimulus that produces a startle-reaction, heartless people can amuse themselves at the expense of those afflicted with these disorders by startling them into a seizure. The same type of seizure may also be elicited accidentally and may even become contagious. By shouting at a regiment of Cossacks from Lake Baikal, a furious Russian colonel threw the whole regiment into a state of *myriachit*. Sometimes it is not even a man but an animal that triggers the *latah* attack. The imitative behavior of an old Malay woman who had been thrown into a *latah* seizure by the sudden appearance of a tiger so upset the animal that it fled (Adelman 1955). On the other hand, I know of no truly conclusive case of seizure provoked by a frightening object or by an unexpected noise of purely inanimate origin. This leads me to believe that a hysterical mechanism is at the root of these seizures. The fact that there is often an imitation of the instigator's behavior and that some individuals (a fact attested at least for the Siberians) become coprolalic during such attacks suggests the presence of another important mechanism: that of "identification with the aggressor," so well described by Anna Freud (1946).

In the case of *amok*, a mere object can play the role of trigger. Thus, the *kris* (dagger, short sword) can excessively fascinate an individual about to run *amok* (Fauconnier 1930). Some data even suggest that in ancient Greece the mere fact of seating oneself on a tripod sufficed to induce a mantic attack. Thus, when the Pythia refused to prophesy for Heracles, he took away her tripod in order to seat himself on it and prophesy for himself (Apollodorus 2. 6. 2). Similarly, when the Argonauts, who had lost their way on the sea, met the sea god Triton and gave him a tripod, the god sat down on it, went into a trance at once, and began to prophesy (Herodotus 4. 179).[50]

A particularly interesting triggering technique is the self-induction of the desired seizure by an anticipation of its symptoms or by a preparation for the seizure. When the prime minister of Madjapahit in Java ordered a group of soldiers to run *amok* against the embassy from Malacca, the soldiers started out by killing those of their fellow citizens who fell into their hands—in other words, by acting as if they were already in a state of *amok*. This then permitted them to become genuinely *amok* (Anonymous 1930). Among the Moro of the Philippines, the *juramentado* (*amok* runner) first asks his parents' permission; he then dresses in distinctive clothing, has himself tightly corseted, and performs various other acts, all of which facilitate the triggering of an authentic *amok* attack (Ewing 1955).

This brief survey of the data is far from exhaustive; it suggests, however, that many attacks, both sacred and ethnic, can be elicited by culturally standardized means. In other words, their onset is both positively and negatively controllable.

The manageableness of the patient. Ethnic neuroses are controllable; this is one of their distinctive traits. The instigator of the *imu* or *latah* seizure can, by his own behavior, which the patient will imitate, not only determine the specific manifestations of the seizure but also terminate it, simply by ceasing to goad the victim. The Crazy Dog is easy to control because, being consistently negativistic, he does the opposite of what he is told to do. Thus, when a mounted Crazy Dog gallops toward a group of people eating in front of their *tipi*, one need only shout, "Come, trample on us," to make him turn aside. Moreover, the Crazy Dog is negativistic *only* to the extent to which he is expected to be. Thus, if a warrior wishing to pay homage to this hero, dedicated to glorious death, sends his wife to him for a night, the Crazy Dog proves normally cooperative and cohabits with her without needing the command, "Don't cohabit with this woman!"

The fact that certain Occidental schizophrenics can also be manipulated by means of such "reverse control" (chap. 9) does not permit one to infer that the Crazy Dog is schizophrenic; he is only a Crazy Dog. What is more, his manipulability—his negatively patterned maneuverability—may even become blended with that of the negativistic psychotic. An example of this was provided by a Plains Indian woman belonging to a culture that includes the Crazy Dog pattern. Her psychotic behavior could *also* be controlled by ordering her to do the *opposite* of what one expected of her (chap. 15). What matters, therefore, is that the ethnic psychotic is controllable by essentially cultural means, whereas the idiosyncratic psychotic is controllable only by psychological means.

Termination of the seizure. It is convenient to envisage the process of resolving the seizure in terms of prophylactic measures aimed at preventing symptomatic excesses, especially since data on this subject are relatively meager. Of course, the best way to end the seizure is to cure it. Some seizures are of predetermined length: the Crazy Dog who did not die in combat before the leaves turned yellow was free to give up being a Crazy Dog (Lowie 1935). The classical way of terminating a *latah* attack is to stop goading the subject, who, though sometimes perfectly conscious of what he is doing, cannot halt the seizure by himself and therefore begs the instigator to stop stimulating him. The classical way of terminating an *amok* attack is to kill the *amok* runner. According to Linton (personal communication), this was the situation in Indonesia until it occurred to the Dutch that they could prevent the *amok* runners from finding the glorious death they sought by sentencing to hard labor the ones they managed to capture; this markedly reduced the incidence of *amok* running. Some Northern Algonquians who felt a cannibalistic seizure—a *windigo* attack—to be imminent were so horrified that they begged to be killed (Landes 1938; Teicher 1960). I have noted elsewhere (Devereux 1961a [2d rev. ed., 1969]) that numerous suicides must be considered as attempts to forestall the onset of an acute psychosis.

Among clinical equivalents of social methods of resolving attacks one may mention such well-known techniques as slapping the hysterical patient or dousing him with cold water in order to end his seizure, or else simply leaving him to himself, because hysteria, being a "social disorder" (G. Jaco, personal communication), requires a public. The clinical equivalent of the termination of the crisis by the neurotic subject himself, by recourse to culturally provided means, would be voluntary commitment to a mental hospital or a decision to undertake psychoanalytic treatment.

It goes without saying that my theory of ethnic psychoses in no way excludes the possibility of classifying these disorders also in terms of traditional psychiatric nosology. Thus, the Mohave "heartbreak syndrome" is obviously a classic mourning depression,[51] *imu* and *latah* are almost certainly hysterias, and so on. This is not surprising, for fundamental psychodynamic processes have a universal character even if they express themselves in extremely varied forms. Whether normal or abnormal, whether belonging to one culture or another, the individual relies on defense mechanisms that are basically the same. The normal person differs from the abnormal and the Eskimo from the Bedouin, not in terms of the presence or absence of certain defense mechanisms, but through the patterning of the ensemble of these defenses and in terms of the relative importance his culture assigns to each of them, though the attribution of a coefficient of importance is certainly not a deliberate act but a more or less inevitable byproduct of the prevailing cultural atmosphere.

"Type" Disorders

I designate by the term "type disorder" the psychological illnesses peculiar to the type of society that produces them. From the ethnopsychiatric viewpoint, these are the most difficult to define and the least well known and studied. Some forty years ago (chap. 9) I had already noted their existence (without, however, using the term "type disorders"), but I neglected to follow up this finding, except incidentally. Moreover, the study of these disorders meets with a certain number of difficulties, of which I have singled out two for particular attention.

1. Only the distinction between community (*Gemeinschaft*), whose solidarity is organic, and society (*Gesellschaft*), whose solidarity is mechanical,[52] is workable in the ethnopsychiatric setting. The common distinctions between matrilineal society and patrilineal society or among types of activities (industrial, agricultural, pastoral, or hunting-fishing-gathering) are unusable for various reasons, the main one being that they do not exclude the intersecting and overlapping of categories. Thus the Mohave, who may appear next to the Crow insofar as they are a "warrior" tribe, could equally well be listed alongside the peaceful Hopi, in that they too are "farmers." Given this situation, it is difficult to decide which of the two modes of classification is ethnopsychiatrically the most pertinent. Moreover, I cannot assert that these criteria really concern major types of social *structure* and not simply types of culture *patterns*. This is one of the many problems that arise from the difficulty of distinguishing with precision between what is social and what is cultural.

2. Research in social psychiatry rarely concerns the *total* social structure. Even the best analyses of categories of psychic disorders, considered in terms of "urban zones," on the one hand (Faris 1939), and "social classes," on the other (Hollingshead 1958), fail to specify, and are incapable of specifying, the correlation between a certain type of disorder and a certain type of *total* social structure. To be sure, every urban zone and every social class traumatizes the individual in a different way. The disturbed person may therefore, precisely because of his difficulty, move automatically from one zone or class to another. In our society, for example, a "bourgeois" schizophrenic may finally land in a furnished room, while the alcoholic son of an aristocrat may become a tramp. By contrast, there is no segment of society in which the Sedang psychotic can "end up"; his disorder does not wrench him from the setting of his regular life, nor

does it cause him to "lose status" in any sociologically significant way. At most, he may spontaneously leave his village to wander about in the jungle for a few days, until he dies from a snakebite, is devoured by a tiger, or perishes from simple exposure. Finally, and most important, it must be clearly understood that the "rooming-house zone" has meaning only in opposition to the "residential zone," just as "lower class" (the poor) has meaning only in opposition to "upper class" (the rich)—and *this within one and the same social structure,* characterized precisely by the multiplicity of its "niches," that is, by what Durkheim called "polysegmentation." A simple example will facilitate understanding on this point. A Mohave of 1830, while objectively poor, was lord and master of his narrow *Lebensraum,* or social space. A Mohave of 1930, while objectively richer, was only a poor man, a nothing, in the setting of the immense social space of the United States (Devereux 1961a). In short, psychologically, it is one thing to live in the finest hut in a primitive village and something else again to live in a cabin (doubtless less rough and more comfortable than the hut) which is but a hovel when it is located at the edge of a city boasting luxurious private mansions.

I shall therefore pursue my analysis principally in terms of the typological opposition between *Gemeinschaft* and *Gesellschaft* and shall complete it with a discussion of the dichotomy peaceable/warlike and of different types of warlike conduct.

The ethnopsychiatrist will tackle the *Gemeinschaft/Gesellschaft* dichotomy in terms of the types of social relationships that play a key role in a given society. Parsons (1939) defines three types of social relationships: (1) the functionally specific, (2) the functionally diffuse, and (3) the functionally cumulative. Not being an ethnologist, he does not seem to have realized that none of these three types of relationships is decisive within the primitive *Gemeinschaft,* whose prevailing type of relationship I have called (4) *functionally multiple.* I shall discuss the first three types by following Parson's definitions closely but adding my own psychological commentary. As for the theory of functionally multiple relations, it is my own.

Functionally specific relationships play a preponderant role in all *Gesellschaften,* whose normal functioning they to a large extent insure. These relationships are segmental, often ephemeral, reduced to the essential, efficient, complete from their first moment to their last, and objective to the point of being impersonal—and therefore affectively frustrating. I even think that functionally diffuse relationships have been evolved to compensate people for the frustrations created by functionally specific relationships.

Functionally diffuse relationships often arise from trifles; but, once they are established, they are supposed to be stable, unlimited, and imbued with affective significance at every moment of their existence. A modern father cannot do what his Australian aborigine counterpart does during a famine: play lovingly with his young son all afternoon and then, in the evening, kill him and cook him for dinner (Róheim, personal communication).

Functionally cumulative relationships fall between the two preceding types. One can think, for instance, of an affair between an employer and his secretary. Such "office romances" are in fact common enough for modern society to take them into consideration and even to define how they "ought" to develop. And yet they occur "by accident" and are in principle "optional." If they constitute "patterns of misconduct" (see below), it is chiefly because they juxtapose two types of theoretically incompatible segmental relationships. They can therefore be analyzed sociologically, exactly in the way Davis (1937, 1939) analyzed prostitution and illegitimate births. Like diffuse relationships, they probably result from unconscious efforts to extend and deepen skimpy and therefore frustrating specific relationships.

Since I discuss in chapters 9 and 10 the important role that specific relationships play in the sociogenesis of schizophrenia, I shall add here only that the cleavage element—the *schizo*—of schizophrenia probably represents only a desperate attempt to reconcile mutually incompatible (cumulative) obligations, just as the schizophrenic's attitude of reserve and withdrawal represents an effort to inhibit the tendency, inherent in functionally specific relationships, to spread out of bounds—to become enlarged and transformed into functionally cumulative relationships.

Functionally multiple relationships, which constitute the fourth of the types of relationships under review, play a fundamental role in primitive societies with organic solidarity (*Gemeinschaft*). They differ from cumulative relationships in one essential aspect. Society recognized the "naturalness" of each of the elements that constitute a cumulative relationship, but their *conjunction* may be viewed as a "pattern of misconduct" because it is regarded as likely to hinder the correct functioning of each of the specific relationships that constitute it. Thus, the sexual nexus between an employer and his secretary is assumed to diminish the authority of the one and the efficiency of the other and therefore to impair the smooth functioning of the business. Now exactly the opposite is true of functionally multiple relationships in primitive societies, where it is precisely the pattern of the totality that is socially approved and held to make possible the functioning of each of the constituent relationships. As the Bible describes him, Abraham was simultaneously patriarch, paterfamilias, legislator, judge, executioner, tribal chieftain, generalissimo, high priest, and, in fact, "Lord High Everything Else." Therefore, by sharing the bed of his handmaiden, Hagar, he did not weaken his authority over her but, on the contrary, strengthened it: she did not become less submissive toward him, since his action only increased her desire to serve him. Moreover, if, seen superficially, Abraham can at a given moment act completely (or at least primarily) in but one of his multiple capacities, it is only because, at other times, he is able to act in a different one. He was able to be war chief only because, qua paterfamilias, he could mobilize all his kinsmen and, in his role as tribal chieftain, his whole clan. He could, moreover, raise an army because, as legislator, judge, and executioner, he could get his orders carried out; finally, he inspired confidence in his role as war chief because, in his role as high priest, he could persuade Jehovah to favor his clan.

Functionally multiple relationships also differ from diffuse relationships. The constituent elements of a multiple relationship can, by definition, be enumerated, whereas those of a diffuse relationship cannot. In fact, as soon as one begins to enumerate the constituent elements of a diffuse relationship, one demonstrates by this very act that the relationship is on the point of disintegrating.[53]

Contrary to what happens in the *Gesellschaft,* the *Gemeinschaft* —and particularly the primitive *Gemeinschaft*—is often intolerant of functionally diffuse relationships; this is, in fact, one of its distinctive characteristics. Hence, in such societies passionate love, even between spouses, arouses violent disturbances and occasionally even ends in tragedy (Devereux 1961a). This finding may have some connection with what Mauss said of the relatively weak development of the role and concept of "person" in primitive societies (1950).

Whereas in the *Gesellschaft* the average man is isolated and therefore runs the risk of becoming schizophrenic, in the *Gemeinschaft* he is almost forced into sociability and is in danger of becoming hysteric. These are the "psychiatric type disorders" of these two kinds of societies; one will think of them first whenever one tries to make a psychiatric diagnosis. One must therefore think twice before diagnosing hysteria in an Occidental philosophy professor or schizophrenia in a North American Indian (even in one who is acculturated). Experienced psychiatrists sometimes seem to sense this without managing to formulate the principle clearly. Thus, faced with diagnosing a severely disturbed Indian woman patient who, though raised in a tribal society (*Gemeinschaft*), had later pursued fairly advanced studies and earned a university degree, the medical team was divided: the young psychiatrists were unanimous in diagnosing schizophrenia, whereas all the senior psychiatrists and psychoanalysts agreed on a diagnosis of hysterical psychosis. There is little doubt that this woman, who had suffered severe oral traumata (chap. 15), would indeed have become schizophrenic *had she been raised* in a *Gesellschaft*. Nevertheless, it was fundamentally a case of hysteria overlain by schizophrenoid symptoms. Inversely, at the root of what has been called the "three-day battlefield schizophrenia" of World War II American soldiers, there was a schizophrenic reaction, heavily overlain with hysterical elements. Though from a superficial point of view these two clinical pictures present certain similarities, the pathodynamics underlying them are nonetheless fundamentally different.

More generally, when a member of a *Gemeinschaft*—and particularly a primitive one—happens to suffer a trauma that in a member of a *Gesellschaft* would elicit schizophrenia, he will most often react with a hysteric disorder, but his hysteria will be overlain by symptoms improvised at the idiosyncratic level and resembling those of schizophrenia; the clinical picture will thus be that of a psychotic episode or, at most, a schizo-affective state. Conversely, a member of our society who accidentally suffers a trauma of a nature that would elicit hysteria in a primitive will nevertheless suffer from a form of schizophrenia overlain by improvised hysterical elements.[54] These remarks must not be misconstrued. I do not wish to encourage either the present tendency of making hysteria a catchall and holdall diagnostic label, universally valid the moment one deals with primitives, or the corresponding tendency of attaching the label "schizophrenic" to every modern patient whose diagnosis is uncertain (chap. 9). The psychiatrist's task is to diagnose human beings, not illnesses.

The way in which abnormal reactions are linked with types of societies—and perhaps even with culture patterns—may also be demonstrated by an analysis of the solutions the Crow, the Blackfoot, and the Mohave provided for the conflict between fear of death in battle, on the one hand, and thirst for glory and social ambition, on the other. The Crow had only a single "social ladder": an individual attained the rank of chief only by performing a particular *series* of warlike exploits. Further, it was their custom to work themselves into a state of blind recklessness by loudly claiming to be motivated only by sentiments of extreme altruism, a state that sometimes culminated in a "heroic" and quasi-masochistic self-pity (Devereux 1951a). A Crow chief, about to lead his fierce warriors into battle against a hereditary enemy, made them a lachrymose speech, of almost Hitlerian sentimentality, in which he bewailed the wretched lot of Crow captives and portrayed both himself and his notoriously aggressive nation as a pitiful band of unjustly persecuted innocents, whose misfortunes he would now avenge (Lowie 1935). For the uninformed reader, his speech is touching, even poetic; it is absolutely grotesque for anyone who knows the ferocious aggressiveness of the Crow nation.

The conflict between fear of death and thirst for glory sometimes became so acute that Crow society was obliged to take it into consideration. Thus, those who, for one reason or another, were unable to perform *each* of the warlike feats required of a prospective chief could become Crazy Dogs (Lowie 1925a), whereas those who dreaded death could become transvestites. In addition, the famous warrior who periodically acquired many horses taken from the enemy remained, nonetheless, quite poor because, in order to raise his status, he had to present the horses either to the needy or to those whom he wished to honor. In both cases his generosity à la Robin Hood—made possible by "heroic" banditry—brought him increased prestige.

In contrast to the Crow, the Blackfoot, another typical Plains Indian tribe, managed to reconcile economic preoccupations with martial ambitions. In their tribe, too, social advancement depended essentially on the ceremonial distribution of horses—but of *any horses whatsoever.* An ambitious but poor young man could procure the necessary horses only by raiding enemy territory, whereas a rich young man would be advised by his family to stay comfortably at home and choose from the family's herds all the horses he needed to distribute as prestige-earning gifts (Goldfrank 1945).

Among the Mohave, who are also a warrior tribe but outside the Plains Indian pattern, there were two forms of prestigious status, which, under certain circumstances, could merge: a kind of hereditary "nobility" (*ipā tahāna,* "real person") and an acquired "nobility": that of the great commoner warriors who, on the strength of their feats, gained the status of *ipā tahāna* and could probably found new "noble" lineages.

Now it would seem that certain "noble" Mohave parents urged their sons to become transvestites (Fathauer 1954) in order to avoid the obligation to fight without, at the same time, risking total dishonor, because, except for transvestites, every Mohave man was expected to distinguish himself by some feat of arms. Still, according to all one can learn at present about this matter, a hereditary *ipā tahāna* who showed cowardice without, however, deciding to become a transvestite did not lose his status as a noble; he simply incurred the contempt of the rest of the tribe.[55]

A study of these facts shows that each of these three basically warlike tribes had, in terms of its distinctive social structure, resolved differently the conflict between the fear of death and the desire for prestige and glory. Among the Crow, the coward himself decided to become a transvestite. Among the Mohave, the young *ipā tahāna* was sometimes persuaded by his parents to adopt this solution. The parents of a rich Blackfoot youth advised him to stay quietly at home and increase his prestige by distributing his family's horses. The ambitious Crow who for one reason or another could not become a chieftain had the choice of acquiring an eminent, though marginal (nonnuclear), status by becoming a Crazy Dog. In a similar situation, the young Blackfoot could gain a socially *nuclear* type of prestige only if he was rich enough to distribute horses. It is unnecessary to dwell here on other obvious differences.

The presence or absence of war neuroses constitutes a third difference, which is often psychiatrically significant. It appears that primitive or semiprimitive *warrior* societies (which must not be confused with *militaristic* societies, such as Sparta) are not familiar with this type of neurosis. The relative brevity of primitive and semiprimitive military campaigns does not adequately explain its absence. Though Genghis Khan fought ceaselessly for many years, I have been unable, in spite of a close study of the relevant historical sources, to discover the slightest indication of war neuroses among his warriors. Nor have I been able to find among them even a hint of a simple slackening of enthusiasm for war, whereas at a certain moment the Macedonians of Alexander's army flatly refused to pursue their victorious advance (Plutarch *Life of Alexander* 62), and Napoleon frequently had cause to reproach his generals for preferring the pleasures of their newly acquired wealth to camp life (von François 1929).[56] In fact, to speak of "war neuroses" in primitive societies makes sense only in connection with two diametrically opposed phenomena: the technique that eliminates in advance every anxiety-producing war situation—as in the case of the transvestite —and the outbreak of battle madness of "heroic" character—as in the cases of the *berserker,* the *ghazi* (heroes of Moslem holy wars), the *amok* runner, the *juramentado,* and some others.

These facts show that it is legitimate to speak of "psychiatric type illnesses" determined not by the specific culture pattern of the group but rather by its *type* of social structure. Murdock is therefore right in saying that studies of "culture and personality" should be completed by studies on "social structure and personality" (1949). Now, if one accepts Murdock's suggestion, one is obliged to establish an explicit distinction between "type disorder" and "ethnic disorder." The first is determined by the type of social structure and determines in turn the range of fundamental nosological categories, or pigeonholes, into which real psychiatric disorders will fall. At this point the specific culture pattern intervenes and determines in turn the distinctive formulation ("ethnic disorder") of the type disorder peculiar to a given society. Thus, the short psychotic episode (*bouffée délirante*) is one of the type psychoses of relatively simple societies; when aggressive and self-destructive impulses are superimposed on it, it takes the form of an *amok* attack among the Malay, a Crazy Dog quasi-psychosis among the Crow, and so forth.

A last point now requires consideration. A society (or a culture) may be characterized precisely by the fact that it is highly typical—typical, for example, of societies with organic solidarity (*Gemeinschaft*) as opposed to societies with mechanical solidarity (*Gesellschaft*), or typical of warrior societies as opposed to militaristic societies. The principal characteristic of such a society will therefore be its tendency to incarnate a theoretical "ideal type." Thus, what is really significant about Sparta is the degree of perfection it brought to the realization of the barracks state (considered as a type of social structure) rather than its manner of being militaristic (considered as a sociocultural pattern). What makes Tasmanian culture noteworthy is that it provides a perfect example of primitivism, while American culture is a close approximation of the "ideal type" of industrial society. In extreme cases of this kind it is unlikely that valid *functional* differences can be established between "type disorders" and "ethnic disorders." In any truly primitive society—for example that of the Tasmanians (Roth 1899) or the Phi Tong Luangs (Bernatzik 1958) —hysteria will faithfully reproduce the theoretical conception of this illness as it appears in all the psychiatric textbooks. By contrast, an Occidental philosophy professor will have a form of schizophrenia that corresponds very closely to the "ideal schizophrenia" of textbooks. In both cases the distinctive "ethnic" formulation of the disorder comes close to merging with its basic "type" structure.[57]

Nearly identical considerations permit one to explain why individual and collective neuroses observable in all societies undergoing brutal acculturation—the acculturation neuroses—resemble one another in a fundamental way; even a little probing reveals an undeniable psychological affinity between Melanesian cargo cults (chap. 12) and, e.g., the Ghost Dance religion of the Plains Indians (La

Barre 1970). In both cases, one is dealing with the type disorders of societies in a state of transition. These disorders are "ethnic" only in their specific formulations.

When one is dealing with extreme cases, it is therefore difficult to differentiate on a *practical* level between "type" disorders and "ethnic" disorders, though from a *methodological* viewpoint the distinction remains a valid one. This implies that these double-edged disorders must be analyzed in terms of each of the two frames of reference—and this even when the basic data are practically identical —and it explains why, although the facts and their interpretation involve numerous overlaps, I have thought it necessary to analyze schizophrenia both as a "type" disorder (chap. 9) and as an "ethnic" disorder (chap. 10).

I conclude by stating that the etiology of *any*[58] nonidiosyncratic disorder is essentially determined by the *type of social structure* in which that disorder arises, although its *clinical picture* is chiefly structured by the *ethnic culture pattern*. If the disorders characteristic of modern society—schizophrenia, psychopathic states, and obsessive-compulsive and character neuroses—are so resistant to psychotherapy, this is doubtless due to the fact that the psychotherapist does not realize that the disorders he is dealing with are not *simply* idiosyncratic disorders but are type disorders and ethnic disorders as well.

Our society has its share of ethnic disorders, among which schizophrenia, thoroughly discussed in chapters 9 and 10, has a major place. Psychopathy, which is no doubt another of them, is analyzed in chapters 2 and 7, though not as one of the ethnic disorders specific to our culture.

Idiosyncratic Disorders

The two types of traumata for which culture provides no defense and no symptoms that permit one to bind anxiety or face up to the conflicts that these traumata elicit are (*a*) those that, though statistically frequent, are culturally atypical, so that the culture takes no account of them, and (b) those that (whether culturally typical or atypical) are statistically rare. The individual who undergoes these types of traumata will exhibit an "ordinary," nonethnic, neurosis or psychosis—that is, an idiosyncratic one. Idiosyncratic disorders are characterized by the improvisation of defenses and symptoms—an improvisation that usually operates, to start with, by deforming certain cultural items that originally were not intended to provide a defense against anxiety.

In chapter 2, the four ways of distorting cultural material for symptomatic purposes are treated in detail, so there is no need to discuss them here. But I remind the reader once again that cultural materials that reflect a society's self-disavowal may be used as symptoms without undergoing a preliminary distortion, and they rank high as symptoms in the "patterned" disorders of a given society, that is, in the "patterns" that even idiosyncratic psychotics do not fail to imitate to a slight extent. Still, in the last analysis, the similarities between conventional or patterned disorders and idiosyncratic disorders are not due primarily to imitation or even to that relative uniformity of the ethnic character of all members of the same group. The essential cause of these similarities is the fact that cultural materials of this type lend themselves particularly well to symptomatic utilization. This explains—among other things—why the supernatural is so often (Dumas 1946) and so easily incorporated into delusional systems.

None of this simplifies the task of the ethnopsychiatric diagnostician trying to determine whether a disorder is idiosyncratic or not. The complexity just mentioned may be deplored, but it may not be invoked to justify juggling out of sight the fundamental differences between idiosyncratic disorders and those that are not. It is for us to accommodate ourselves to the requirements of reality and not for reality to conform to our own requirements.

Having analyzed

1. Shamanistic ("sacred") disorders
2. Ethnic disorders
3. Type disorders
4. Idiosyncratic disorders

I shall now briefly mention some of the clinical applications of this theoretical schema.

CLINICAL APPLICATIONS

The psychiatrist turns more and more to the ethnologist for help in diagnosing culturally atypical or marginal patients. Far too often the ethnologist contents himself with saying that "among the Bonga Bonga this type of behavior is normal, this kind of belief is traditional; this sort of personality is well adjusted." Though often true, such statements are almost always insufficient. It is not my intention to minimize the importance of this diagnostic approach, having myself often had occasion to rectify mistaken diagnoses of Indian veterans by stressing, e.g., the difference between delusion and belief (Devereux 1951a). I shall cite in this connection the case of an Indian veteran diagnosed in another hospital as a schizophrenic and subjected to electroshock treatment, which only caused him to become completely unmanageable. When he was finally transferred to Winter Veterans Administration Hospital, where I was working at that time, I was easily able to show that he was not schizophrenic but simply neurotic. Some supportive psychotherapy, given him by a young colleague, permitted him to leave the hospital within six months and return to normal life in the community. All this is routine.

Still, in a diagnostic report, it is not enough to stress the distinction between delusion and belief. The moment one adopts the standards implicit in this limited diagnostic procedure, one becomes unable to provide psychiatric help for an Indian who, after an initial psychotic episode or fugue, goes into remission and defines himself as a shaman (Devereux 1942b). In terms of the "relativist" standards that govern the limited diagnostic technique just outlined, one would have to say that, because this Indian shaman could be considered "culturally normal," he was not in need of psychiatric care; whereas I have demonstrated (see above) that the shaman is either a severe neurotic or a psychotic in a state of remission and is therefore still greatly in need of psychiatric help. Indeed, such a person is in remission *only* with reference to *a* particular social setting: his own tribe. He is more or less well adjusted to that setting and *only* to that setting. *He is not capable of adjusting and, above all, is not capable of readjusting.* By contrast, a normal Indian who is not a shaman may be well adjusted to his culture and yet retain the capacity to adjust to other situations as well (Devereux 1951a). To my mind, the crux of mental health is not adjustment per se but the capacity of the person to make successive readjustments without losing the sense of his own continuity in time (Devereux 1966d). Now, it is precisely this capacity that is so obviously lacking in the chronically hospitalized "model patient": he is perfectly well adjusted to the hospital environment and seems rational and cooperative as long as he is in these surroundings, but he promptly "cracks up" again when discharged from the hospital.[59]

To be effective, the psychotherapy of the shaman does not require that he be stripped of his ethnic character—de-Indianized—or that one persist in completing his acculturation. Nothing justifies such an attempt, not even the fact that, because of his origins—or, rather, because of discrimination—the Indian is clearly at a disadvantage when he tries to live in American society (Devereux 1951a). Moreover, it is not even culturally expedient to rob him of his ethnic character—to de-Indianize him; for every culture, including our own, grows and develops through contact with different cultures, and the

Indian in our midst is an element of constant stimulation—a cultural yeast. The psychotherapy of a shaman must accomplish something entirely different. It must tackle only his shamanistic character—seek to deshamanize him—without attacking his ethnic character structure. It must seek to activate his capacity for *re*adjustment by breaking down his pathologically rigid and relatively marginal and dereistic adjustment to his own tribal milieu *only*.

It may perhaps be objected that Indian tribes *still* need shamans and that, by treating the shaman's illness, one risks depriving the whole tribe of something it needs. I challenge the validity of this argument, for the simple reason that the *role* of an authentic shaman can be played just as well by an adaptable individual who only pretends to be a shaman and therefore does not risk contaminating his "patients" by transmitting his own neurosis to them.

When I was working among the Sedang Moi of Indochina, like most field workers I sometimes practiced first-aid medicine. I soon discovered that, though my native patients were glad to receive Occidental drugs and dutifully swallowed them, they nevertheless went elsewhere for supplementary psychological (magical) support. Thus, after consulting me and receiving a pill and the advice to stay indoors and keep warm, they would proceed to call in a shaman who, on the pretext of a curative ritual, would drag them out into the rainy night —which generally aggravated the cold or indigestion from which they suffered. To put a stop to these harmful interferences, I simply declared that I, too, was a shaman.[60] Henceforth I did not limit myself to handing out drugs; I also performed certain traditional curing rituals, the only difference being that my rituals were performed, not in the rain, but indoors, and they cost nothing!

These practices gave the patients all the ritual (psychological) support they needed, even though I was not psychologically a shaman and therefore did not believe in the supernatural efficacy of these rites but viewed them simply as "first-aid (supportive) psychother-apy"—in short, as a kind of reassuring bedside manner.

Although useful, the diagnostic technique that views the shaman as a neurotic or a psychotic in remission, adjusted *only* to a marginal segment of *his* culture, but considers the ethnic psychotic to be a genuine psychotic, adjusted to a given "pattern of misconduct," is nevertheless related in many ways to the traditional diagnostic technique founded on the criterion of adjustment, which consists of stating that "among the Bonga Bonga, this is normal." In both instances, the major risk is that of mistaking belief for delusion.

For a long time I believed that this limited refinement of diagnostic technique was sufficient for all purposes. Fortunately for two Acoma

Indians, sentenced to die in the electric chair, I discovered just in time that even this more refined approach to the problems of adjustment was not entirely satisfactory. The prison psychiatrist charged with diagnosing the two Indians—who were half-brothers—was sufficiently familiar with ethnopsychiatry not to mistake ethnic character traits for psychotic manifestations. Hence, finding no *culturally neutral* evidence of psychological disorder, he felt obliged to declare them "legally sane." However, this astute diagnostician, who as a psychiatric resident had done a great deal of work with me on cultural problems arising in diagnostic work, continued to be disturbed by an indefinable feeling that he was overlooking something in these men, and he therefore asked me to come and see them at the Medical Center for Federal Prisoners at Springfield, Missouri.

In the presence of the prison psychiatrist, I conversed separately with the two half-brothers, who had not been able to communicate with each other, being confined to individual cells reserved for persons under sentence of death. In less than ten minutes, each, in turn, poured out a veritable flood of data about witchcraft, which perfectly fitted with Acoma belief but nonetheless left me feeling perplexed; for because of my experience in the field, I knew that this kind of material could normally be elicited from an informant only after much hard preliminary work. The point I am seeking to make is quite simple: a traditionally suspicious and distrustful Pueblo Indian—and one, moreover, under sentence of death—who after only ten minutes of conversation speaks freely of his esoteric beliefs and experiences, relating to witchcraft, to a person he is seeing for the first time is acting about as rationally as would a Navy cryptographer who discussed the Navy's secret code with a stranger he had just met in a bar. Following up this clue, I soon discovered that:

1. The two men had ceased to *experience* these cultural beliefs as objective cultural material and had begun to experience them in a delusional manner: "The hand was Esau's, but the voice was Jacob's."

2. Threatened by witchcraft, they had, in terms of Acoma culture, reacted in a wholly abnormal way: instead of ridding themselves of the witch in accordance with Acoma custom, by asking the help of ritual societies in charge of neutralizing witches, they had sought to take the law into their own hands.

It is necessary to make clear the meaning of my statement that these men *experienced* their cultural beliefs in a delusional manner. A brilliant but paranoid electronics engineer may believe that he is being persecuted by radar; he may even design the radar device that "persecutes" him, and his blueprint may include real and considerable improvements on existing radar equipment. In short, his new apparatus may well do *everything* that other radar machines do and do it even better—but, *whatever it does,* it certainly cannot persecute him. In this hypothetical instance, the cultural material is handled quite efficiently but nevertheless in a delusional manner, for in this man's mind electronics has ceased to belong to the realm of physics and has become part of the domain of supernatural persecutory devices.

Once I had determined the *manner* in which these two Indians had distorted cultural reality, it was easy for me to elicit from them personal and idiosyncratic delusional material as well—material that was at variance with the Acoma culture pattern and revelatory of a full-blown paranoid schizophrenia in one of the men and of a psychotically tinged psychopathy in the other.

In short, the idiosyncratic core of these psychoses was covered by a superficial layer of half-shamanistic and half-ethnopsychotic material. This finding, corroborated by a number of other observations of the same kind, suggests certain conclusions concerning ethnic and/or shamanistic psychoses.

1. They may be the first manifestation of an idiosyncratic psychosis.
2. At a later stage, they may mask an underlying idiosyncratic psychosis, in the sense in which a seemingly benign monosymptomatic hysteria may mask a schizophrenia.
3. In some instances, they constitute the terminal restitutional manifestation of an initially idiosyncratic psychosis (see above).

These three possibilities are not mutually exclusive; they represent alternatives that may occur either separately or in combinations of two or three in the development of a large number of obviously idiosyncratic derangements.

A certain number of observations support this hypothesis: a neurosis may be the initial manifestation of an illness that will develop into a psychosis; the psychotic may also present certain neurotic traits, and vice versa; a neurosis may sometimes mask a psychosis, and, in the course of recovery, a psychotic may sometimes become temporarily a neurotic or possibly a psychopath. If this hypothesis is valid, its systematic exploration should be productive.

To return to the diagnostic difficulties mentioned above, it is clear that, in the case of the two Acoma Indians, it was not a question of a belief being mistaken for a delusion but of a delusion that, because of its traditional content, was mistaken for a belief. What made me realize that I was dealing with a delusion was the deviant manner in which the two men handled cultural materials. Obviously, they neither *handled* nor *experienced* these materials according to the usual cultural norms or even in terms of culturally permissible "alternatives" or of the kind of "secondary meaning" that may become attached to a cultural item when it is assigned to a secondary or subordinate matrix (chap. 16). In fact, these Acoma cultural items were not even handled in accordance with some marginal "pattern of misconduct." Traditional beliefs about witchcraft were handled in a purely arbitrary and idiosyncratic manner; the cultural items were "deculturalized"—stripped of their cultural content—in a way that is typically psychotic (chap. 2).

I do not wish to leave this case history suspended in midair. The prison psychiatrist saw the validity of my findings and presented them so skillfully and competently to the court of appeals that the two men escaped capital punishment and were confined in the Medical Center for Federal Prisoners.

CONCLUSION: THE PRACTICALITY OF THEORY

Nearly a dozen years of work in mental hospitals, more than thirty years of teaching psychoanalytic ethnopsychiatry, and years of psychoanalytic practice have convinced me that it is unfair and unreasonable to expect the psychiatrist to become an expert in ethnography (as distinct from ethnology). He cannot be expected to make a detailed study of the culture of each patient he must diagnose and treat. This makes it impossible for him to engage in the practice of what I have called "cross-cultural psychiatry," which requires a thorough knowledge of the patient's culture and which is exemplified in my book *Reality and Dream* (Devereux 1951a [2d rev. ed., 1969]). Recognizing the practical usefulness of this form of knowledge, I used to consider the impossibility of having a command of it as a calamity that might perhaps be palliated but never definitively remedied. I therefore cast about for some means that would allow psychiatrists to diagnose and treat even patients belonging to cultures of which they knew little or nothing.

As long as I looked for an answer to this problem in purely psychiatric or ethnographic terms, I came up against a blank wall. However, when I finally tackled the problem as an ethnologist, that is, not in terms of some particular culture but in terms of the *concept of culture*, the answer became obvious. This proves once more that the mathematician Georg Cantor was right in saying that it is more important to ask a question correctly than it is to answer it—presumably because a correctly asked question provides its own answer. The clue to the solution was the concept of culture as a lived experience, that is, as the *manner* in which the individual experiences and handles his culture both when he is psychically healthy and when he is psychically deranged. What remained to be seen was whether this theoretically correct solution could be effectively used when it became necessary to diagnose persons of whose culture I knew little or nothing. The fact that I had been able to diagnose the two Acoma Indians correctly in spite of my nearly total ignorance of their culture authorizes me to conclude that this technique is valid not only logically but in practice.

In fact, at the time I interviewed the two Acoma prisoners, a diagnosis was so critically needed that I could not consult a treatise on Acoma ethnography. But though I knew little of their culture, I did know general ethnography and clearly understood the function of Culture per se and the nature of the "universal culture pattern" (Wissler 1923). Thus, when these two men told me that they had gone after the witches with their guns, I did not know how the Acoma traditionally dealt with witches, but as an ethnologist I was certain that, *whatever* their specific custom of dealing with witches was, the Acoma, like most societies, had to have definite mechanisms for controlling them. Later on I discovered that the Acoma do, in fact, have ritual associations whose task it is to get rid of witches, just as the Sedang get rid of them by selling them as slaves to the Laotians, while the Mohave do it through witch-killing tribal champions or, more rarely, through lynchings (Devereux 1961a [2d rev. ed., 1969]). I therefore formulated my diagnosis in terms of Culture per se and not specifically in terms of *Acoma* culture, which is but a particular version of a universal culture pattern—a version that was unknown to me at the time.

This experience suggests that a real analysis of the universal culture pattern and a full specification of its nature require that, in every study of culture, one should also take into account the psychiatric perspective. Indeed, regardless of the variety of cultures, the simple fact of having a culture is a genuinely universal experience, and man functions as a "creator, creature, manipulator, and transmitter of culture" (Simmons 1942) everywhere and in the same way. *Pari passu* the Mohave feels about his culture the way the Eskimo feels about his, and the way the American infantryman feels about his Garand rifle is probably identical with the way Rome's Balearic warrior felt about his slingshot.

To return for a moment to the hypothetical paranoid electronics engineer, one may say that his blueprint was *ethnographically* correct but *culturally* (ethnologically) delusional. To take a concrete example, Kempf (1920) described the case of a paranoid patient who, while delusional enough to cut off his penis, nevertheless continued to write articles for the prestigious *Oxford Dictionary;* yet, in stressing the objective quality of this performance, Kempf failed to ask himself what *subjective significance* this work—"scientific" only ethnographically—could have had for the patient himself. I therefore agree with Dodds (1951) that Pythagoras was a shaman,[61] since I believe that his great mathematical discoveries were inspired more by mystical interests than by mathematical ones.

I once called the technique that approaches psychiatric problems in terms of the key concepts of culture "transcultural psychiatry"; today I prefer the adjectives "transethnographic," "meta-ethnographic," or, more briefly, "metacultural" (Devereux 1951a; [cf. 2d rev. ed., 1969]), because those who borrowed the term—without, be it said in passing, ever acknowledging its source—have systematically deformed its meaning by applying it to what I myself have called "cross-cultural" psychiatry (Devereux 1951a); [cf. 2d rev. ed., 1969]).

*Meta*cultural psychiatry, then, does more than palliate the psychiatrist's *technical* inability to become a universal ethnographer. In fact, the approach that views psychiatric problems in terms of Culture rather than *cultures* is also more effective in a practical sense— that is, therapeutically—and is theoretically far superior to any other cultural approach; for it affords a deeper insight into psychodynamics, and this, in turn, leads to deeper ethnological insight into the nature of Culture. Moreover, it undermines once and for all the arrogant claims of the clique of neo-Freudian and pseudo-Freudian "cultural psychoanalysts" who not only boast of their greater sophistication and ethnological flair but also claim that their views are more useful to the ethnologist than those of classical psychoanalysis.

The ethnologist cannot make a real contribution to psychiatric knowledge if he simply assimilates its jargon and, for the rest, is content to trot out his little ethnographic collection of esoteric "curios." He can make a real contribution to psychiatry only if he remains an ethnologist: a specialist of Culture, defined as a patterned way of experiencing both extrasocial and social reality. This, I feel, adequately answers Kroeber's (1948a) claim that ethnopsychiatry is not a part of real ethnology because it does not study Culture. Yet it is only the ethnopsychiatrist who studies both Culture and the manner in which the individual experiences his culture who completes and rounds out—precisely as it should be completed and rounded out—the science of Culture, which "culturologists" (White 1969) sometimes seem to study as though Man did not exist.

As for myself, I feel that by also becoming a psychoanalyst I simply rounded out my training as an ethnologist—that is, a specialist of Culture and of Man. Had I begun as a psychoanalyst, I would certainly have felt the need to study ethnology also, to round out my training as a specialist of the human psyche. In the framework of an effort to understand man in a meaningful way, it is impossible to dissociate the study of Culture from the study of the psyche, precisely because psyche and Culture are two concepts that, while entirely distinct, stand to each other in a relationship of complementarity, in Heisenberg's and Bohr's sense (Devereux 1945 [1978a, chap. 4], 1961b [1978a, chap. 5], 1967c).[62]

2

Ethnopsychiatry as a Frame of Reference in Clinical Research and Practice (1952)

Every research activity implies a certain way of looking at things. The degree to which this manner of looking at things is conscious and explicit is in most instances closely correlated with the value and productiveness of the research work. I propose to outline a way of looking at behavior, and especially at abnormal behavior, that may be of some use in the adaptation of the findings of social scientists to research and practice in psychiatry.

A fruitful way of looking at things for research purposes, and for the achievement of conceptual clarity, may well deviate from the common-sense manner of looking at the same things. Since I cannot enter here into a systematic defense of fruitful though "patently absurd" ways of examining facts, I will offer one illustrative analogy: daily experience "teaches" us that it is manifestly absurd to use a color-blind person as our authority on the appearance of the world. Yet wartime experience has shown that color-blind persons are particularly well qualified to detect camouflaged objects because their perception of form is not interfered with by the additional perception of colors—and the basic principle of camouflage consists in the use of colors to blur the outlines of camouflaged objects. Hence I would willingly stand on my head if, in that position, and *only* in that position, I could make sense of something I was not able to comprehend when I viewed it in my normal position. But—and this is important—I am equally ready, afterward, to resume my normal position in order to integrate what I saw while standing on my head with what I perceive in my normal stance.

Let it be imagined that one can separate human behavior into its component elements—without reference to motivation, goal, or external context. The number of these elements—the range of vocal sounds, the varieties of body movement—is practically unlimited. Moreover, certain mathematical considerations suggest that the

72

number of configurations—the permutations, combinations, variations, and structural arrangements that these elements may form—is even larger than the number of elements themselves. Now, in practice one finds that relatively few of these elements and even fewer of the configurations are actually exhibited over the course of a given person's life. Shakespeare, for example, whose vocabulary was proverbially rich, knew "little Latin and less Greek." And Cardinal Mezzofanti, who spoke some sixty languages, probably never uttered Hottentot clicks and, had he learned Hottentot, would probably have done so only at the expense of some of his English, French, etc.

This selectivity entails no impoverishment, even in a purely numerical sense. Though some behavioral elements and sets of elements of behavior are, in fact, eliminated, this "loss" is more than compensated for in a whole range of ways: for instance, by the subtly nuanced arrangement of the remaining elements and sets within the framework of the selected structures. A comparison will show this: no violin glissando, though it produces in turn all the sounds situated between G and E-flat, has the germinative possibilities of the principal motif of Beethoven's Fifth Symphony, which uses only the G and the E-flat. The structures that remain are enriched also by assigning them to standardized contexts. Thus, though the number 3 is only one of the first ten numbers, in the cultural frame of reference it is also a "magical" number, in religion it is a symbol of the Holy Trinity, and, according to Dumézil (1958), it is the fundamental structural matrix of Indo-European society and beliefs.

The problem becomes even more interesting when viewed from a slightly different point of view. Actually, the constriction of the *range* of behavior appears to be directly responsible for the development in *depth* of the remaining elements. Thus, the cultural meaning of the number 3 quite obviously depends on the elimination of the nine other numbers. Culturally, 3 means more than the series 0, 1, 2, 3, 4, 5, 6, 7, 8, 9, which nevertheless contains it. Its meaning therefore, depends on the fact that it has been isolated (*ausgegliedert*) from the rest of the series.[1] In fact, if the series in question did not exist, 3 would and could have no meaning: it could neither represent "triplicity" nor evoke any of the things that the symbol and concept of "triplicity" evokes.

By combining these two analyses, one is led to a crucial insight: the elements eliminated from actual behavior *inevitably* reappear during the "expansion in depth" of the remaining elements. Two examples, one cultural and one biological, will show this.

1. Totemism is no longer part of the mainstream of Occidental culture. It may, however, reappear spontaneously among small

groups in a state of stress, and it actually did reappear in some units of the American army in 1917–18 (Linton 1924).

2. There are very few types of nonhuman biological functioning and probably no type of nonhuman sexual functioning that do not appear in dreams, neurotic fantasies, or myths. One example will suffice: as a biological human reality, the *vagina dentata* does not exist, and it is barely approximated in the very occasional instances when a vaginal spasm temporarily prevents the withdrawal of the penis (*penis captivus*). Nonetheless, something quite similar to the *penis captivus* is the rule among dogs, who are unable to separate themselves immediately after the male's ejaculation. As for the *vagina dentata* proper, it is a fundamental biological fact among bees. At the end of coitus, the male's penis is torn away and retained within the queen's sexual cavity, where it continues to impregnate her for some time. Everything, including this last detail, reappears as a motif in the myth of the detached penis that remains capable of impregnating a woman. According to Plutarch (*Life of Romulus* 2. 3 ff.), the "father" of Romulus and Remus was a phantom phallus that appeared in a hearth (= vagina).[2] According to Sophocles (*Electra* 417 ff.), Clytemnestra dreamed that the scepter of her dead husband, Agamemnon, thrust into the hearth, sprouted foliage and cast a shadow over all Mycenae. Similar mythobiological parallels will easily come to the mind of anyone who knows some zoology and, especially, entomology.

In accordance with the most immediate and most plausible conclusion to be drawn from these examples, it is precisely the reappearance of elements *eliminated* from the range of observable behavior in the course of the expansion in depth of the *chosen* elements that explains why one can gather the same information either by the study in depth of a single individual or by the cross-sectional study of a number of individuals and (or) cultures (Devereux 1955d [1978a, chap. 3]).

The observed limitations of a given individual's behavior do not seem to be due exclusively to a lack of time or opportunity or to a limited capacity of recall. An inventory of actual behavior does, in fact, reveal a constriction of *potentially possible* behavioral modalities, and it is more convenient to assume that, far from being random, this constriction is, on the contrary, perfectly systematic. The system according to which the range of behavior is constricted has *a structure*. The nature of this limiting and selective structure—of this system of selection—can be defined in several ways, only some of which are of special interest to the psychiatrist. All of these systems have, however, certain traits in common. All reveal that behavior must not be viewed atomistically but in the form of sets of configurations. In fact, the *nonappearance* of certain theoretically possible elements of behavior is always compensated for by a *more frequent and more diversely nuanced recurrence* of certain others; these recurrent elements tend, moreover, to appear in the context of certain clusters rather than others. Thus, I have no difficulty in pronouncing the French sound "u" but find that, when I have not spoken French for some years and then speak French continuously for several hours, certain muscles in my lips and cheeks begin to ache, until I almost begin to feel that French has one vowel only: the "u." Now, the frequent recurrence of the "u" sound is part of the phonetic pattern of the French language.

Such sets or patterns are of special interest: they reveal the implicit axes around which behavioral elements are organized into patterns and structures.

Before I discuss in a systematic manner the various organizing axes of behavior, I would like to describe a hypothetical incident and analyze the motivation involved in terms of four distinct frames of reference.

Let this incident be the following: "On Christmas Eve a man gives the girl he is courting a bouquet of flowers."

Biologically speaking, his action may be viewed as a genitosexual one.

Experientially, he knows that she likes to receive gifts, and that she likes flowers better than candy.

Culturally—being a gentleman of the old school—this man knows that, until one is formally engaged to a girl, one may offer her only candy, books, or flowers. Furthermore, being a member of Occidental—rather than of some primitive—civilization, he feels that freshly cut flowers are more appropriate love tokens than freshly cut human heads. Finally, since both the girl and the man are Americans, he gives her a present at Christmas rather than on New Year's Day, as a Frenchman would.

Neurotically (or unconsciously) the man's choice of flowers is also overdetermined. His gift may reflect his desire to deflower the girl. He may shrink from offering her candy because, for him, feeding is the final token of love and he is not ready, as yet, to commit himself that far. Also, wishing to find in his future wife a giving mother, he expects *her* to feed *him*, which explains why he has so far taken her to the theater and to football games but has been unable to make up his mind to take her to a restaurant. Finally, his unconscious rejects the idea of giving her a book, because he does not wish to encourage her to compete with him intellectually.

There is no need to elaborate this fictitious example further. I have simply emphasized the principle of overdetermination and have showed that the motivating factors can be conveniently divided into four categories corresponding to four axes. My next task is to define these four axes in terms of the basic conceptual frame of reference of psychoanalytic theory.

AXES OF BEHAVIOR
Biological Axes

The art of the ballerina shows that the human being can compete with the dog in being a digitigrade, although nature made him a plantigrade. No structural (skeletal) peculiarities prevent the male rat from exhibiting, during sexual excitement, the kind of lordosis the female rat does; yet he shows no trace of lordosis. However, lordosis *can* appear in the male rat who is castrated early and is then given massive injections of female hormones. A behavioral shift from one area of biological organization to another is displayed by the male monkey: the male who tries to rob a female of her banana can be diverted from the pursuit of this nutritional goal by the sexual presentation of the female.[3] The psychoanalytic theory of psychosexual development also rests on a conceptual framework that presupposes a biological infrastructure of behavior: the individual passes through the oral, anal, phallic-urethral, and genital stages. According to certain common and completely erroneous interpretations of this theory, the tension *emanates* from the mouth, anus, urethra, penis, clitoris, or vagina. This "centrifugal" theory of instinctual behavior is incorrect. What actually happens is something very different. At each stage of psychosexual development, one of these *erotizable* (rather than erogenous) zones becomes the most suitable one for the release of tensions. Thus, the suckling's tensions do not originate in the mouth. It uses the mouth for the release of tensions that come into being elsewhere. The special structural-functional qualities of the mouth then determine certain epiphenomenal forms of behavior—both somatic and psychic—that in their totality may be viewed as "oral eroticism" and that may then become rooted in the personality as an "oral character structure." Thus, the biological axis to a certain extent sets up a bond between the id and the nuclear or body-ego.

Experiential Axes

The organization of behavior through acquired habits, or reaction patterns, has been known since earliest antiquity. Even animals "train" their young in a way. Regardless of whether the impression is made in the sacred halls of a seat of learning or, more vulgarly, upon the seat of one's trousers, *impressive* experiences result in the formation of habits, that is, of more or less uniform, predictable, coherent, and "constricted" behavior. As in the case of the erotizable zones, the conditioned organism begins to develop preferential mechanisms for the release of tensions. These mechanisms then become habits, rooted for the most part in the psyche, by means of countless unconscious fibers, which coordinate them with biological axes and "situate" them with respect to these axes. The inhibited desire to kick someone may find release in frantic foot-wiggling—a movement that is *also* a substitute for the direct expression of masturbatory impulses. The desire to bite may find expression in a kind of grimacing that is correlated *also* with sucking and biting impulses. In brief, experience is a second system of axes for the organization of behavior, existing side by side with the system of biological axes, with which it is unconsciously linked. Although the habit axis is related primarily to the ego, it also includes elements that partake of the superego and the ego-ideal.

Cultural Axes

The third system of behavior-organizing axes comes into being through the subjective experience of culture (chap. 16). This experience is, in its essence, not very different from the one that governs the acquisition of ordinary habits. A significant part of learning— that is, of the child's acquisition of habits—is basically determined by the parents' participation in their culture (Devereux 1951a). Thus, among the Maori of New Zealand, cultural conventions require that well-brought-up girls be *taught* to wiggle their hips (Mauss 1950); in the United States, different cultural conventions motivate parents to suppress this same hip-wiggling, which their daughters tend to develop *spontaneously* as they approach puberty. Yet, genuinely cultural experiences differ from the experiences that teach the child not to touch a hot stove: they have an ideological background that is connected, via the ego, with the ego-ideal and, less closely, with the wholly unconscious superego as well. The latter, needless to say, is connected with the id, which is rooted in biology somewhat the way a corrupt police force is "connected" with gangsters but also, although in an entirely different sense, the way the ridiculous Sheriff of Nottingham was "connected" with a heroic Robin Hood or the way that the Soviet secret police was "connected" with democratically minded "traitors to Stalin" (Devereux 1951a).

To avoid misunderstandings, it is necessary to specify that, even psychoanalytically, culture taken as a whole is not to be confused with either the superego or the ego-ideal, although, qua experience, it is related to both of these psychic instances. Culture is primarily a standardized system of defenses and is therefore linked chiefly with the ego functions (Róheim 1940). Were culture entirely determined by the superego,[4] which is just as absolutistic and dereistic as the id, life in society would become impossible and mankind as a social species would soon become extinct, because a culture centered exclusively on the superego could never, for example, accept marriage as a compromise solution[5] of the conflict between, let us say, oedipal impulses on the one hand and taboos prohibiting *all* sexual relations on the other. In this sense, not even "ethnic character" can be viewed simply as a type of psychic structure wholly dependent on the superego or ego-ideal. Rather it must be viewed as a special form of the structure of the ego, characterized by a distinctive, though variable, arrangement of defense mechanisms (Devereux 1951a). Hence, when one speaks of "cultural axes that organize behavior," one must think first, last, and always in cultural and sociological terms, that is, in terms of *institutions* (Devereux 1961b). One must—if one's scheme is to be both useful for research and conceptually consistent—never think of culture in biological terms, that is, as a group arrangement devised for the satisfaction of the *individual's* biological needs. One must never think of marriage as a "sexual" institution, of economics as an oral-anal ("nutritional") institution, or of law and justice as "safety" institutions. They are all that—but they are neither primarily nor predominantly that. To the social scientist, they are primarily cultural and social institutions only incidentally dependent on biology, just as, viewed biologically, a pianist's hands are primarily a structure of bones and other tissue and are only in the final instance —epiphenomenally and potentially—"artistic" and "cultural" organs.

This kind of conceptual perfectionism is especially necessary for the psychiatrist. The ethnologist who, like Malinowski (1944), explores the biological foundations of society may well broaden his sociological horizon. The psychiatrist who studies mental disorders —which, as I now propose to show, may be viewed as inefficient attempts to reconcile the experiences of the world and the various biological, psychological, and cultural ways of organizing behavior —can reveal the anxiety-eliciting character of this heavily conflict-laden undertaking only if he views the biological *biologically,* the psychological *psychologically,* and the cultural *culturally.* Only thus can he make their contrasting qualities clearly evident.[6] An example will clarify this point. Recent ethnological investigations have shown that traditional conceptions of "feminine psychology" (Mead 1939) or of "child psychology (chap. 5) are, by and large, only cultural fictions. When demanding that women be "feminine" (effeminate) or that children be "puerile," one is usually speaking a cultural, not a biological, language. This is proved by the fact that the American Indian transvestite does not act in a biologically feminine manner, that is, in the culturally neutral sense in which Freud defined feminine psychology. He acts "effeminate" in accordance with the rules of the feminine behavior that prevails among the members of his tribe. Moreover, however "deculturalizing" psychosis may be, even severely regressed Indian psychotics do not act solely in accordance with Freud's culturally neutral standards of child psychology; their behavior is also "puerile" in terms of what their own culture views as "behavior *befitting* a child." In this sense, each culture has a distinctive manner of "masculinizing" its men and of making its women "effeminate" (as distinct from truly womanly) and its children puerile. This "drilling" deeply influences the clinical symptomatology of transvestites and of persons in a state of regression.

Neurotic Axes

The fourth set of axes, which is of special interest to the psychiatrist, is composed of the symptoms of the neurosis and, in more general terms, its structure. Nail-biting may be simply a habit or, among people who do not possess nail scissors, a technique. Among ourselves it is most often a neurotic symptom that serves to express a cluster of diffuse and complexly ramified conflicts, of which nail-biting is only the behavioral nucleus. I do not profess to have anything novel to say about symptoms. As Freud suggested, they may be viewed as inadequate and ineffective compromise formations between certain mutually incompatible demands of the id and the superego. In this sense, Freud's theory obviously implies that symptoms reflect attempts to reconstruct the personality in terms of the logic of the unconscious, which alone can reconcile the irreconcilable. So viewed, all symptoms are restitutional.

Dynamically, the scheme I am presenting does not differ from Freud's. I simply think that by viewing symptoms as attempts to reconcile the mutually contradictory orientations of three incompatible systems—the biological, the psychological, and the cultural —deeper insights can be gained into the meaning of symptoms and of psychological disorders in general. My phenomenological universe is the same as Freud's, and my dynamic interpretation of these phenomena dovetails with his. I am simply using different *conceptual tokens*. I describe, organize, and group new phenomena by using different axes and pigeonholes. I am not seeking to renew the conceptual basis of psychoanalysis; I am simply trying to show that additional insights can be gained by looking at things while, figuratively speaking, standing on one's head or looking through the wrong end of the telescope.[7] In brief, the claim to novelty of my system is not the especially explicit formulation of the principle that symptoms result from efforts made by the individual in a state of conflict to reorganize his behavior, since Freud has formulated this point with complete clarity. My system is new in that it starts from the principle that the symptoms themselves ultimately contribute to a supplementary organization of the totality of behavior. In other words, one can discern the restitutional and reorganizing functions of the illness and its symptoms at the very beginning of a psychological disorder (chap. 1). One need only think of the time, effort, concentration, and ingenuity the obsessed person wastes on obsessive rituals, fads, phobias, and the like. Now, the *need* to develop such a manifestly destructive system of symptoms for organizing behavior arises only when the three other systems are so divergent that there is no possibility whatever of welding them, *by rational means,* into an even moderately coherent whole.

A moment's consideration may now be given to that quality of the axes of organization in abnormal behavior that I have previously called *ausgegliedert* (by contrast with the *eingebettet*[8] quality of axes of organization in normal behavior) (Devereux 1951g, 1952). Now, neurosis and psychosis represent a dedifferentiated and impoverished reorganization of behavior in a form that seeks to effect a compromise between the three other systems of organization—and, what is worse, a compromise that seeks primarily to maintain the emotional status quo. Consequently, the neurotic axes, as reflected, for instance, in symptoms, are usually extremely obtrusive without necessarily being also easily understandable. Their obtrusiveness, moreover, is often of a special kind, for it is a consequence of the abnormality of their context. For example, in some cases of severe regression, the biological axes obtrusively organize even those elements of behavior that are purely cultural in origin. In other instances the neurotic axes of organization are strikingly obtrusive only because they are forcibly *superimposed* on the three other organizational systems of axes, so that they startle one in the way one would be startled to see a bank cashier sorting and arranging banknotes in a purely idiosyncratic order of increasing value, based, for example, on his like or dislike of the persons portrayed on the bills, or to see a librarian shelving books in accordance with the wavelengths of the colors of their bindings.[9]

This peculiarity of the neurotic axes as organizers of behavior gives the abnormal individual's behavior that *spurious* "opacity"—or incomprehensibility—that I have discussed elsewhere (Devereux 1951g).

For the psychiatrist, the greatest problem is to ascertain at the outset to which system of axes an observed pattern of behavior conforms. If a Catholic girl married in a *civil* ceremony—and only in a civil ceremony—to a young Protestant becomes neurotic and fantasies herself to be a prostitute, not much imagination is needed to say that her conflict is in part tied to sexual problems, in the biological sense of the term. When the girl recalls her mother's opinions on "immorality," the habit axis also enters into the situation. Finally, the cultural axis for the organization of behavior is implicated as well, to the extent that the marriage ceremony is primarily a cultural practice. The prostitute fantasies and the possibly provocative behavior of this woman (which are, moreover, balanced by anxiety and depression) can be viewed as a desperate attempt to organize into a whole—a *neurotic* whole—three mutually incompatible universes of discourse.

Now, despite the obvious implications of Freud's theories, too much emphasis continues to be placed on the *disorganizing* effects of a conflict and not enough on its *organizing* effects. Illness is a frantic and inappropriate reorganization, and not primarily a disintegration and disorganization, even though this overall reorganization takes place at the expense of the ego (whose disorganization it actually brings about), which now must learn to run with the hare and hunt with the hounds, that is, to lump together totally incompatible elements. In psychological illness, *the external world is structured at the expense of the ego's structure;* the organism as a whole is kept functioning at the expense of the ego-functions; the world and the organism are made *emotionally* compatible at the expense of realistic, logical compatibility. This, to my mind, is the true definition of psychological illness.

Needless to say, in the course of the therapeutic session itself, one is no more permitted to think in terms of these axes or categories than in terms of any other theoretical concept, including even the concepts id, ego, and superego. In the course of the therapeutic hour one's sole task is to *treat* the patient (Devereux 1953a). Every psychoanalyst who disregards this rule runs the risk of seeing his patient react to his conceptual preoccupations with various resistances. The analyst's nontherapeutic interest in the patient's culture can also elicit great resistances: being aware of it, the American Indian patient may try to turn the hour into an ethnological field session (see chap. 15). On the other hand, the analyst who, after office hours, re-examines the material obtained during the day often obtains insights that are both scientifically valid and therapeutically effective (Devereux 1951a). Similarly, if, during the session, the analyst displays an obsessive interest in theoretical questions and conceptualization, the patient will strive to transform the analytic session into a debate about theory. One of my patients had been treated previously by a psychoanalyst who apparently spent more time thinking about theoretical formulations than in listening to his patients. When I realized that, instead of producing analytic material, the patient was spending the better part of his time discussing psychoanalytic concepts, I said: "Mr. X, now that you are at the head of the class in psychoanalysis, I think, you might, for a change, go back to the analytic couch." This turned out to be an effective interpretation. The patient also seemed to appreciate the fact that someone—at last!—was less interested in analyzing the Oedipus complex per se than the patient's own oedipal problems, which were, be it noted, quite serious and perfectly real.

THE VICISSITUDES OF CULTURE IN MENTAL ILLNESS

What happens to culture and to cultural material in these various neurotic and psychotic forms of organization of behavior is of capital importance not only to the ethnopsychiatrist but also to the psychiatrist who practices in an ordinary clinic. The biological organization of the individual is never known perfectly, and not even the most exhaustive psychoanalysis can fathom the totality of experience qua source of habits and symptoms. One can, by contrast, definitely ascertain whether a given society is monogamous or polygamous and what role charity, honesty, truthfulness, economic success, or religious prejudice play in it. To know this—or to learn it—one need only think realistically. For this reason, the way in which the psychologically ill person uses cultural materials in his illness provides an excellent insight into his true state.

Hence, the formulation of the vicissitudes of cultural materials in psychological illness provides the only valid point of departure for the development of a genuinely *metacultural*[10] and metaethnographic psychiatry—one based on a real understanding of the generalized nature and function of Culture per se, as it is experienced *everywhere* by normal persons and by various types of psychiatric patients. The practice of metacultural psychotherapy requires from the analyst a cultural neutrality similar to the emotional neutrality he is expected to show in the analytic situation in regard to his own residual infantile and neurotic needs.

The human being, whether he is a psychiatric patient or an unusually "normal" analytic candidate, experiences and manipulates cultural materials in five distinctive ways.

1. Normality

Cultural materials can be utilized and experienced in an "up-to-date" way, that is, in a present-synchronic manner that is in conformity with reality. I call this kind of utilization *hygiognomonic,* that is, indicative of psychological health. Culture is recognized and experienced as an originally extrapsychic reality that is later internalized. But my conception of culture as a fundamentally external reality in no way supports the conception that culture is independent of, and wholly external to, man (Kroeber 1952; White 1969). I am referring here to the simple empirical fact that every individual is "enculturated" by other individuals, who incite him to conform to cultural standards. The normal individual's awareness of the fact that culture is something first learned and then internalized is indirectly revealed by the clinical observation that, at the end of a successful analysis, the patient becomes aware of the extrapsychic origins of his superego. This is a common finding in clinical practice. Another characteristic of the normal individual is his capacity to understand and experience culture as a system that structures man's life-space by defining "appropriate" ways of perceiving, evaluating, and experiencing both natural (Devereux 1966c) and social reality (chap. 16). Moreover, culture not only ascribes meanings and values to the *component parts* of the life-space but prescribes the manner of arranging (patterning) these component parts into a meaningful whole. In brief, the normal individual manipulates and experiences cultural items in terms of meanings and values compatible with the *contemporary* social scene, on the one hand, and, on the other, with his true status and chronological age. If he is an American of the twentieth century, he will not believe in the divine right of kings nor will he suspect England of wanting to reconquer the United States. He will be able to see that his boss knows more about certain problems than he does without viewing him, for that reason, as a representative of God or as an imago of his father—or both. Finally, it is hardly necessary to add that a passive and uncritical acceptance of the highly dereistic and unhealthy culture in which one happens to live is not a criterion of psychological health and mature adjustment but a sign of pathological passivity and dependence (chap. 1). The healthy individual simply recognizes the objective reality of the "sick" society in which he must live without introjecting it uncritically (Devereux 1939a). Instead, he will seek to survive in it long enough to modify

83

this cultural reality in the direction of greater reasonableness and an increased efficiency on the human level.

2. Immaturity

Anachronistic adjustment to culture is characteristic of immature or socially and personally regressed individuals, who at least in principle need not exhibit any other type of neuroticism. Such persons recognize and experience culture as such, that is, as something external that has been internalized, but they simultaneously experience and manipulate cultural items in two anachronistic ways.

a) *Social* anachronism occurs when the person assigns to cultural items meanings that they no longer possess in contemporary life. In the perspective of cultural history, this anachronism characteristically manifests itself in "cultural hysteresis": the subject clings to a cultural ideology that was dominant during his childhood or even earlier. For instance, he may believe in the divine right of kings, yearn for, and extol, the good old days, and the like. His social anachronism is generally rooted in personal immaturity and/or regression. Like the Bourbons, he never learns or forgets anything.

b) *Personal* anachronism occurs when the subject assigns to cultural items meanings that are inappropriate in terms of, and incompatible with, his true age and status. Such subjects cannot believe that they are "really" adults, married, and the parents of children or that their real social roles, duties, and rights are more than make-believe, "play," behavior. They view their employer as a father figure and dread him as the child dreads the adult. At the same time, they are convinced that all other adults are truly "grownups" while they themselves are still children, and they react with anxiety, or with surprise and relief, to the discovery that other adults also have areas of infantilism and occasionally doubt their own maturity. In order to preserve the emotional structure and equilibrium of infancy or adolescence, they do violence to objective reality and distort it in order to justify and maintain their infantile emotional equilibrium.

In the therapeutic situation, patients of both types rapidly develop parental transferences, which sometimes manifest themselves first in the guise of sexual demands, whose spuriousness is revealed by their infantile, polymorphous-perverse, ambivalent, and unrealistic nature. When this sexual transference—which is actually a resistance that seeks to destroy and degrade the analysis by turning it into an immature sex play—is interpreted, it is rapidly replaced by pregenital types of demands. This shift may occur even if the analyst remains silent and offers no interpretation whatsoever.

3. Neurosis

In neurosis, culture continues to be recognized for what it is: as something originally external that has been internalized. However, once it is internalized, the cultural material is unconsciously reinterpreted in a manner that gratifies the neurotic's distorted needs. More even than the substance or the purpose of the cultural material, it is the very meaning of the item that is distorted. A cultural item is assigned a new meaning, derived neither from its obsolete traditional social meaning nor even from the meaning that it would have for children whose development is normal;[11] the new meaning usually results from the reinterpretation of a trait belonging to one level in terms of another level: for example, from the reinterpretation of a genital trait in oral terms. A clinical example of precisely this kind of transposition will be cited in chapter 15.

The transference reactions of such patients are not only anachronistic and infantile; they also systematically distort the analyst's behavior already at the level of perception. The pattern of these distortions is determined by the patient's neurotic needs. Thus, a sexual —or rather pseudo-sexual—interest in the analyst may perhaps be complicated from the start by the intrusion of paranoid elements; the patient may, for instance, accuse the analyst of trying to seduce him or test him.[12] Usually the transference is not only based on severe distortions of perception but is often highly inconsistent as well, partly because of massive ambivalences and partly because of the intrusion of mutually contradictory transference elements belonging to different stages of psychosexual development, which enter simultaneously into every transference reaction, as happens, for example, when "sexual" interests are complicated from the start by accusations of seductiveness.

4. Psychosis

The psychotic so deculturalizes culture that it ceases to exist for him, or to be experienced by him, as culture. Culture traits continue to be utilized, but only in a subjective manner and almost without reference to their normal social context. They are, in Merton's sense (1949), empty rituals, which have lost their intimate functional connection with the culture's means-end schemata and value systems. In extreme psychotic regression, in which the principal behavior-organizing axis happens to be precisely the axis of the illness, culture traits cease altogether to be used as cultural materials, which automatically imply a feeling of common or shared experience. From then on, they are no longer utilized qua culture but in a purely autistic manner, without reference to the cultural context that gives them their cultural meaning. They are degraded and deculturalized to the point that they become simply means or channels of expression for psychotic needs. For the psychotic, a chair may become a throne—both literally and in the sense of the language of the nursery (i.e., a toilet). Similarly, the table will become an altar, the bed a rack, the door a booby trap, and so forth (chap. 4).

The manner in which a severely regressed schizophrenic utilizes discourse illustrates this process particularly well. The schizophrenic's discourse—the "word salad"—only seems complex and diversified. It has ceased to be discourse in the strict sense because it is intended no longer as interpersonal communication but merely as a means of "self"-expression. Furthermore, what the schizophrenic seeks to "express," most of the time, is not what can actually be verbalized, because the drives he expresses are organized in terms of noncultural and therefore nonverbal axes. Words are used merely as emotional vocalizations: as means of expressing subverbal instinctual needs.[13] "Reasoning" is used only to express the irrational demands of the superego. In brief, cultural material continues to be utilized, but *for noncultural ends*. It suffers a loss of function and a degradation, as when a scalpel is used for murder (chap. 16).

For the psychotic, people are not whole persons endowed with independent reality and existence. They are now only partial objects: actors in a shadow play. They exist only as bearers of meanings external to their real personalities—as symbols of something that exists inside the patient himself. Hence, the patient can preserve his sick and rigid emotional equilibrium only if he abolishes the cultural reality of human beings as a cultural element and transmutes it into something noncultural. If the patient's pathological emotional equilibrium demands, for example, that sex should not exist, then he (she) must cease to view men as men and women as women. If subjective paranoid needs demand that everyone should persecute the patient, then the most benign or commonplace approach will be viewed as a threat. In fact, the more commonplace it is, the more dangerous it will seem, because its very banality threatens to upset the only equilibrium the patient still has: his sick and rigid emotional organization. It was, I think, for this reason that a woman patient refused to believe Dr. Fromm-Reichmann's (1946) assertion that she accepted the patient "as she was." The patient kept on asserting—not without reason—that the real objective of Dr. Fromm-Reichmann's therapeutic efforts was to *change* her.

In such cases, a true transference usually cannot be established by the patient's own efforts. The keystone of the entire psychotic edifice is its *private* character, which is an extreme manifestation of what I have previously denoted by the term "social negativism" (chap. 3). In the early stages of analysis the therapist must therefore seek to deprive these structures of their private character (Devereux 1953a; Kubie 1952); to this end, he must intrude into, find a place within, and participate in the creation of the psychotic edifice. Figuratively speaking, the patient must first learn to experience his psychosis as a kind of *folie à deux* before the analyst can partly neutralize the psychotic edifice by depriving it, surreptitiously, of its wholly "private" character. Since the psychotic is not a proselytizer, this is difficult but not impossible. Only when this partial neutralization of the psychotic system, now no longer completely "private" ("socially negativistic"), has been accomplished can the psychoanalytic therapist resume his distance and "externality" and, instead of sharing an artificial *folie à deux,* become its *object*—"become the patient's psychosis," one might almost say—by the establishment of a transference relationship based on, and rooted in, a constant reality-testing, which gradually leads to a reenculturation of the patient. The axiom that the psychosis cannot be abolished before its private character is destroyed simply means that the reestablishment of some kind of object relationship—of whatever nature—must always precede the cure. The patient must be partially *resocialized,* or at least *"regregarized,"* before he can be *reenculturated.* This view is fully compatible with what is known of the child's need to have a firm relationship with his parents before he can accept them and can let them function with regard to him as "mediators of culture" (Devereux 1956a). In two recent papers Nathan (1978a, 1978b) has brilliantly expanded and refined my theory of the role and vicissitudes of cultural materials in psychosis and has devised a technique for its therapeutic application.

5. Psychopathy

Psychopathy is characterized by *one* very special and complex vicissitude of culture. Whereas the psychotic's social negativism causes him simply to repudiate culture per se, the psychopath is, in a sense, actually waging a systematic and provocative war against culture (Cleckley 1950). However, I feel that, contrary to accepted views, the psychopath fights culture, not by giving free rein to his instincts, but by means of reaction formations both against his instincts and against sublimations suggested by his culture. I have therefore proposed the term "defense-ridden psychopath" as a substitute for the term "instinct-ridden psychopath" (chap. 7). I also suggest that, unlike the immature person and the regressed schizophrenic, the psychopath does not behave in a truly infantile manner and does not seek to fight his way back to the instinctual "Garden of Eden" (Róheim 1940) of early childhood. The psychopath seeks to "act out" a conception of adult behavior resembling that held by frustrated children who, as a result of particularly severe traumata during weaning or toilet training, delegate their own omnipotence to the frustrating adults (Devereux 1955c). At that stage in the development of his sense of reality, the child thinks of adulthood as a new avatar of the infantile instinctual paradise and defines adults as impulsive, autistic, unpredictable, and instinct-ridden autocrats, whom it can hope only to conciliate and manipulate to its own advantage. It is this childish conception of adult behavior that the psychopath seeks to "act out" in his own conduct (Devereux 1955c). The psychopath is fully aware of the external origin and reality of culture but fails to internalize it sufficiently. He understands intellectually the values and meanings with which cultural items are endowed but fails to respond emotionally to these culturally determined values and meanings. In fact, the psychopath often specializes in exploiting other persons' loyalties to cultural values. His predatory "skill" is simply a consequence of his callously and cold-bloodedly manipulative approach to that which other persons most cherish. The true psychopath does not simply seduce lonely women "for the fun of it," nor does he burgle their homes. Instead, he exploits their yearning for matrimony—which is a cultural value—in order to swindle them out of their money (which is *also* a cultural value). The psychopath is a plausible and successful confidence man precisely because he appeals to the basic cultural loyalties of his victims. An imaginary example may help to clarify this point. A feebleminded *thief* may steal a woman's wedding band and be quite unaware of the fact that this woman values her ring far more than its monetary value warrants. He may therefore melt it down and sell it as bullion. The psychopath, on the other hand, is fully aware of the high "sentimental excess value" this object has for his victim. Hence, instead of melting it down, he may try to induce the woman to ransom her ring, the amount demanded being computed partly on the basis of the gold's cash value but *especially* on the basis of the sentimental value the ring has for "the sucker." In other words, the psychopath thinks of himself as a "realist" in a world of "suckers." It is in this sense only that we may define psychopathy as "semantic insanity" (Cleckley 1950). Usually the psychopath's "semantic insanity" is simply an emotional scotoma. He is unable to internalize certain cultural meanings and values (though he "knows" them as well as the next person) and therefore cannot truly empathize with the cultural loyalties of normal persons. On the other hand, he is fully capable of taking a *predatory* advantage of other persons' allegiances to cultural values. The above considerations clearly indicate why—except under quite unusual circumstances—the psychopath is incapable of developing a genuine transference. I therefore suggest that in the opening phases of therapy one might attempt to outdo the psychopath at his own game, thus forcing him to cease "acting out" the frustrated child's conception of the omnipotent and ruthless adult and to accept, instead, the complementary role of the frustrated child at the mercy of the "psychopathic" therapist.

In the original (1953) version of this article I suggested this technique simply as a theoretical possibility, because I had not at that time had occasion to analyze psychopaths. I admitted at the outset that this method, too, might fail, like so many other methods proposed for the treatment of psychopaths; theoretically plausible, they proved ineffective in practice. I can now report that I have used this method in the treatment of two patients who in certain respects were psychopaths and that I obtained fairly satisfactory results.

The above remarks have definite diagnostic implications. The manner in which the patient manipulates cultural materials necessarily indicates whether he is immature, neurotic, psychotic, or psychopathic. This finding, in turn, affects both the prognosis and the therapeutic policy to be adopted. In addition, even though I have described, above, only the *initial state* of the transference and the patient's *initial pattern* of manipulating cultural materials, the same diagnostic criteria can also be used at other stages of the psychoanalytic therapy. Precisely because, in the course of analytic therapy, the patient alternates between improvement and relapse, a continuous reappraisal of his current diagnostic status, by means of an analysis of the manner in which he currently handles and experiences cultural materials, is particularly desirable.

It is this area that the ethnopsychiatrist must explore with the greatest thoroughness. The ethnopsychiatrist is not a luxury, indicating by his presence that a hospital or medical school is rich enough to afford him or enlightened enough to feel a need for his services. His services are indispensable in diagnostic work because his specific training qualifies him to assess the cultural normality or abnormality of the manipulations and reinterpretations to which the patient subjects cultural materials and of the ways he uses them. This, as I have indicated, is an especially sensitive and precise diagnostic procedure (chaps. 1 and 13).

In therapy, the ethnopsychiatrist's role is equally important. I spoke previously of the need for cultural neutrality when appraising the *true* meaning of a given trait in contemporary society and, more narrowly, its meaning in the patient's own subgroup. This neutrality can sometimes be achieved unassisted, but that is an arduous and uneconomical way of doing things. It is easier to have someone handy to whom tuxedos are no more "natural" than the primitive's warpaint nor wedding rings more obviously indicative of married bliss than a close haircut is.

On a purely practical level it is obvious that the average psychiatrist has no time to study in detail the cultural peculiarities of all who come to him for treatment—every Ozark mountaineer, reservation Indian, or Cajun. That is what the ethnopsychiatrist is there for. But the ethnopsychiatrist has an additional task of which we are, barely, becoming aware: the development of a *culturally neutral psychotherapy,* comparable to the nonevaluative emotional neutrality of psychoanalytic psychotherapy. Only the development of such a system of psychotherapy will enable the New York psychiatrist to treat with equal efficiency a refined southern lady, an Eskimo sealhunter, and a Filipino scout.

In short, what is particularly needed is a system of psychotherapy based *not* on the *content* of any particular culture—as the psychotherapy described in my book *Reality and Dream* (1951a) was based on the specific content of what I have called "Wolf" culture[14]—but on an understanding of the nature of Culture per se: on an insight into the meaning of *cultural categories,* which, as the French sociological-ethnological school of Durkheim and Mauss stressed long ago, are identical with the great fundamental categories of human thought. This culturally neutral—or *metacultural*—psychotherapy is still in the making, and I, for one, have devoted many years almost exclusively to the pursuit of this one goal, which, though seemingly still far away, has, despite many false starts and mistakes, lost nothing of its appeal in the course of time.

3

Social Negativism and Criminal Psychopathology (1940)

I propose to formulate a theory of social negativism based essentially on the sociological analysis of delinquent or criminal behavior in the neurotic or psychotic. The feebleminded delinquent and the psychotic whose illness has an organic basis are excluded. Individuals exhibiting "psychopathic personalities" or "character neuroses" are included in the neurotic and psychotic group, since the concept "psychopathic personality" is devoid of sociological meaning (Devereux 1939a). To the social scientist, delinquent and criminal personality types fall into two distinct groups.

The first and probably most important group is composed of individuals who in some respects are more realistic than their social environment, whose misevaluations and inconsistencies they reject, either consciously or unconsciously. Individuals of this type are able to adjust to a more congenial environment, as did certain beachcombers and "squaw men"—men who uprooted themselves and fled nineteenth-century civilization to settle in tropical countries or Indian tribes and take native wives.

The second group includes potentially neurotic or psychotic individuals in whom transplantation to a less congenial environment may trigger a latent psychological illness. The high incidence of neuroses and psychoses among migrants, and generally among persons having great social mobility, is significant in this context (Faris 1939). Hence, I have included this second subtype in my study, calling it simply "neurotic or psychotic delinquent."

For the sake of brevity I shall designate the neurotic or psychotic who exhibits delinquent or criminal behavior a "delinquent defective," laying stress on the order of these two words.

The central problem of criminal psychopathology is to determine the position the delinquent defective should occupy in the series ranging from the so-called normal individual to the violent individual in quest of a sometimes psychotic justificatory ideology.

91

The concept of criminal psychopathology rests on two assumptions:

1. Criminal behavior is symptomatic of a conflict and, like every symptom, involves "neurotic gain" insofar as it allays the anxiety aroused by the conflict. Pragmatically and socially, such neurotic gains are subject to the law of diminishing returns (chap. 1).

2. There is a functional relationship between the type of crime committed and the nature of the conflict. In many cases the anxiety produced by a given conflict can be allayed only by the performance of a particular type of criminal act. Criminal acts of another kind not only fail to allay that form of anxiety but may even exacerbate it to an intolerable extent. One need only think of the scorn some criminals have for others who commit "despicable" crimes; thus, during World War II, a group of American gangsters brutally attacked criminals whose activities undermined the nation's war effort.

The second assumption explains why certain delinquent defectives, as well as certain allegedly nondefective criminals, limit their criminal behavior to one or a few types of crime, executed in a manner that is both systematic and characteristic. The type behavior of a given criminal is thus, in a way, his seal or "trademark." It bears the imprint of his personality makeup as much as would a poem he might write. This analogy is far from superficial. The extreme conditions of criminal "work" are, in fact, scarcely more constraining than is the nature of marble for the sculptor or the grammatical structure of the language for the writer (Devereux 1961a). In support of this analogy, I recall not only the creation of new words by Lewis Carroll and James Joyce but also the fact that Thomas De Quincey viewed murder as one of the fine arts.

On the practical level, criminologists recognize and implicitly exploit these regularities in the behavior of known criminals. When a certain type of crime is committed, the list of suspects excludes, a priori, criminals who are definitely known *not* to engage in that particular type of criminal activity. In brief, crime, like other social activities, exhibits a certain number of directly observable regularities that permit one to make experimentally verifiable predictions. The successful utilization of these insights into the criminal's modus operandi is, moreover, a validation of my assumptions. In logical terms, my second assumption is thus, technically speaking, a conceptual scheme facilitating the comprehension and manipulation of the phenomena to which it refers.

The next problem confronting the social psychiatrist is the difficulty of detecting and of correctly diagnosing defectiveness in the delinquent, and this immediately raises the particularly difficult problem of normality and abnormality (chap. 1), since, for reasons to be specified later, neither the criminal act itself nor the technique used to accomplish it is a reliable diagnostic signpost.

Neurotic and psychotic *behavior,* which must not be confused with psychological *illness* as such, is partially definable in terms of cultural norms, from which, by definition, it deviates.[1] A given type of behavior that in our culture is prima facie evidence of psychosis (meaning, in this context only, simply a *deviation*) may, in another culture, be simply a form of socially standardized behavior susceptible of being *elicited* from any "well-adjusted" individual in certain socially determined circumstances and may even be an essential prerequisite for social recognition (Benedict 1934). Unfortunately, the cultural definition of normality and abnormality (Wegrocki 1939) —even at the level of behavior alone—makes it extremely difficult to diagnose the element of deviance that is present in the criminal act of the delinquent defective. Though there is no book of criminal etiquette for the use of the "proper" criminal, the deviant character of a crime is nevertheless always obscurely felt. In fact, when English newspapers used to stigmatize a crime as being a "particularly shocking and un-English one" or when American police immediately attribute a certain type of crime to a person of a particular nationality, this only means that something about the crime under consideration strikes the observer as so "foreign," "improper," or perhaps even "crazy" that he finds it impossible to understand it through *empathy.* It should be remembered that in this context the term "empathy" refers above all to an essentially sociocultural factor. Thus an American, with his frontier tradition, is less scandalized by the Indian custom of scalping the enemy than he is by the Galla custom of using the genitals rather than the scalp as a trophy, although the Indian practice is basically no less horrible than the Galla one. The reason for his reaction is that nothing in his culture prepares the American to feel empathy for the Galla custom.

In brief, despite obscure hunches, sometimes validated by later findings, the diagnosis of defectiveness in the delinquent must be made without reference to the *nature* of the crime or even to the fact that a crime has been committed. In fact, although the delinquent defective's crime is functionally linked to the nature of his neurosis or psychosis, it may happen, in the case of a subject with a "psychopathic personality," that what is deviant is the whole behavior pattern rather than its "molecular constituents." In such a case, a diagnosis of latent psychosis is extremely difficult to make if, despite protestations of faith in a dynamic viewpoint, one surreptitiously clings to the categorizing spirit of psychodiagnostics of a neo-Kraepelinian type—whose sole advantage is that it enables one to make elegant statistical studies of isolated diagnostic *labels*.

My main task is thus the analysis of the term "deviant behavior." As a rule, neurosis and psychosis become observable when the individual's behavior begins to deviate both from his own previous behavior ("onset of present illness") and from social standards. The nature of the problem becomes blurred only when, in clinical practice, one begins to suspect that the neurosis or psychosis existed in a latent state long before it began to influence observable behavior. This difficulty is to be expected, since, except in limiting cases, the observation of differences (discrimination) is easier than that of similarities (induction).

Now, psychopathology all too often disregards one of the fundamental aspects of the nature of a causal proof. When *A* is our standard, it does not suffice to be able to explain why *B* is different from *A;* it is also necessary to explain why *C* is similar to *A*. In psychiatry, it does not suffice to explain why John Doe has become psychotic if one cannot explain at the same time why Richard Roe, beset with similar problems and conflicts, has become neither antisocial nor psychotic. One cannot juggle this problem out of sight with magic words like "constitution," "environment," and the like. A series like surgeon–anatomist–butcher–assassin–homicidal maniac is a continuum and should be analyzed as such. It is at this point that problems arise. Modern society correctly sees the anatomist as a highly sublimated type of personality. On the other hand, in the Middle Ages he was viewed as a vampire, and a mad one at that.

Now since, all things considered, surgery, anatomy, and homicidal mania are so many different ways for the individual to cope with his aggression, the question of sublimation cannot be reduced to establishing whether a specific manifestation of aggressivity is or is not socially acceptable. It is simply not enough to call socially acceptable behavior "sublimation" and socially unacceptable behavior "symptom." Yet many "experts" routinely reason in these terms. Even some psychoanalysts believe that they have helped the patient to sublimate his conflict when all they have done is to replace a socially unacceptable symptom or misevaluation with a socially acceptable one without bringing the patient one inch closer to that culturally undistorted *reality acceptance* that is the touchstone of sanity.

Of course, the acceptance of the sociocultural environment as an order sui generis of reality is an important and integral part of the process of reality acceptance. Too often, however, social reality is accepted *at the expense of* certain more basic realities that a culture has seen fit to reject, for reasons of its own. All too often the only difference between the well-adjusted "sublimated" individual and the "unsublimated" "deviant" is that the former accepts—often far too completely—the reality of his society, while the latter does not, although he may have achieved a higher order of reality acceptance with regard to *non*social areas of reality. There is, above all, a fundamental difference between "introjecting" society uncritically and *accepting* it as a reality to which one has to adjust realistically and, when necessary, with a critical realism.

Matters of mere adjustment and conformity have very little to do with reality acceptance. This is shown by the fact that no clearly *significant* differences have been observed between the conflicts experienced by "sublimated" normals and those experienced by nondelinquent neurotics and delinquent defectives. One may conclude from this that in terms of present-day sociocultural knowledge—which is to be distinguished from pure speculation—many of the sociological and psychological explanations for the delinquency of John Doe are merely a posteriori rationalizations, which prove, at most, that it was *possible* for him to drift into neurosis and/or crime but do not allow one to give any necessary and sufficient reason for the fact that he *actually did* deviate from standardized conduct. With a few exceptions, such as Merton's theory (1949), most of our so-called sociologistic "explanations" prove nothing beyond the possibility and the opportunity for deviancy to occur. They do not and cannot explain why the possible and the opportune actually materialized in one case and not in another.

The occasional presence of some degree of sublimation and adjustment even where an anxiety-generating conflict exists proves that anxiety can be allayed by standardized and/or normal means as well as by deviant, or both criminal and deviant, means. This leads up to the main question: Why do only some individuals subjected to psychological discomfort select (generally unconsciously) a deviant and/or criminal symptom as the most suitable means of allaying their anxiety and of ventilating their conflicts?

My principal thesis is that deviant criminal behavior has the same origins as deviant noncriminal behavior; it differs from it in a single, but crucial, respect, that of *social negativism*.

It is not my intention to discuss here the theory according to which the criminal's mistakes, which lead to his identification, capture, and punishment, are motivated by an unconscious desire for self-punishment (Reik 1925, 1932). Nor shall I discuss the finding of both Krafft-Ebing (1875) and the Mohave Indian tribe (Devereux 1961a) that some crimes are committed chiefly to elicit punishment and therefore represent an indirect form of suicide—"vicarious suicide."

Plausible as these theories and beliefs are, they do not imply that the existence of moral masochism and the desire for punishment permit one to infer from them the existence of a (*biological*) *death* instinct. An early socialization, however unsuccessful it may have been in some respects, suffices to explain why even the most antisocial criminal cannot totally escape his social training.[2] Only socialization can instill in man the desire for punishment or even the understanding of what "punishment" means. My most trustworthy Mohave informant assured me that there is no word for punishment in the Mohave language, probably because, under aboriginal conditions (Devereux 1950b), Mohave children were treated with the utmost gentleness and patience.

In short, the problem of defining deviant behavior, qua symptom, is still unsolved: crime is what a culture recognizes as crime. In Western society parricides and matricides are usually severe neurotics or psychotics, and this in spite of the fact that their victims generally deserve their fate. Quite the opposite is true in civilizations in which the killing of the old parent is a gesture of filial piety, thoroughly regulated by the cultural norm and therefore, in spite of its senselessness, incapable of allaying surges of *neurotic* anxiety. Habitual thieving may be resorted to in our civilization as a means of allaying anxiety and solving a personal conflict, although a neurotic belonging to one of the so-called "criminal tribes" of India could not resolve his conflict by kleptomania, which in his tribe is the norm, not the exception.

Data like these force one to reject a simplistic phylogenetic-regression theory of symptoms. It is hard to see why, in one culture, a given type of symptomatic behavior should be normal, and its opposite a biological "regression," while the contrary is "true" in another tribe. If, among ourselves, kleptomania is held to be a regression to, let us say, roughly the stage of monkeys or jackdaws, then presumably, among the criminal tribes of India, strict honesty would be a regression to Adam and Eve before their expulsion from the Garden of Eden. This just does not make sense. Paradoxically, however, a partially phylogenetic theory of symptoms is possible and even necessary, although it presupposes a way of approaching the problem that differs in almost every respect from the currently accepted one. Unfortunately, I must postpone until a later date the presentation of this theory, because some of its details have yet to be worked out.[3]

The ontogenetic-regression theory of symptoms, while probably true in the main, raises two problems of radically different natures, even if one does not take into account the fact that ontogeny more or less duplicates phylogeny.

The first difficulty is due to the fact that most studies in child development have hitherto been carried out in Occidental cultures. The situation has been somewhat modified by the proliferation of similar studies in non-Occidental cultures, although these researches are almost always pursued within a frame of reference derived from the earlier studies of Euro-American infants and children. Hence one sometimes wonders whether the distinctions drawn by child psychologists between "infantile" and "adult" behavior are biological findings or cultural preconceptions. What a priori possible modes of behavior a culture discards in the process of socialization (chap. 2) by calling them "infantile," and what other modes of behavior it encourages and finds worthy of incorporation into a—culturally conceived—adult behavior pattern, depends largely on cultural norms and on methods of socialization. Freud's formulations of the stages of psychosexual development are relatively neutral from a cultural point of view. Yet, even they cannot be automatically transposed to the study of primitive childhood, as is done all too often.[4] The latency period, in particular, seems to be essentially a cultural product (Devereux 1951d), and yet it is precisely this stage that Freud tried to explain in paleobiological terms.

The second question is of an entirely different kind. Because child-development specialists are at the same time *adult* members of a culture, less concerned with defining what a child *is* in himself and how he *behaves* than with what he *should* be and how he *should* behave, many apparently scientific ideas concerning authentic childhood behavior are, in the last analysis, nothing more than the self-serving projections of adults (Devereux 1968a). One cannot provide a valid formulation of the ontogenetic theory of symptoms until a culturally neutral and truly disinterested model of childhood behavior has at last been formulated.

THE INDIVIDUAL PSEUDO-SOLUTION OF
META-INDIVIDUAL PROBLEMS

The crux of the conflicts and problems encountered by the patient is well stated by Jung (1928): "We always find in the patient a conflict which at a certain point is connected with the great problems of society. . . . Neurosis is thus, strictly speaking, nothing less than an individual attempt, however unsuccessful, at the solution of a universal problem."[5]

Freud partially anticipated this viewpoint when he said that others' behavior, if it differs even slightly from our own, is construed by us as a criticism of our own standards and ways[6] and hurts our narcissism. He called this reaction the "narcissism of small differences" (Freud 1921).

These two statements contain most of the necessary elements for an understanding of the factor I call *social negativism*.

Human conflicts, which culminate either in "sublimation" or in neurotic or psychotic, criminal or noncriminal, behavior, are the outcome of certain situations that can occur *only* in *human* societies. I have attempted elsewhere to demonstrate this with reference to the problem of schizophrenia (chaps. 9 and 10), and I have further suggested that, the higher the civilization, the more complex become the problems of adjustment with which it confronts the individual. Hence one might expect certain types of conflicts to be functionally interrelated with the complexities of a civilization. I am indebted to Róheim for the information that *consistently* antisocial individuals are practically unknown among the very primitive tribes of Central Australia; he also reports that such individuals tend to become almost mythical figures. I myself found few or none among the Mohave and only a few among the Sedang. Three factors may account for the absence of *professional* delinquents (criminals), whether "normal" or defective, in primitive society:

1. In primitive society, adaptation to the total social situation is easier than among ourselves because society is simpler and its members constitute a "community" (*Gemeinschaft*) rather than a "society" (*Gesellschaft*) (Tönnies 1926).

2. Elton Mayo plausibly suggests that, in primitive society, socialization is more consistently encouraged than it is among ourselves.

3. Complex societies set up goals that many of their members cannot attain by socially standardized *means*, or else they overemphasize the *means* by which normal human goals can be reached (chap. 1). This leads to structural inconsistencies on the social level. Merton's (1949) brilliant analysis of this situation leads to the conclusion that "the consequences of such structural inconsistencies are psychopathological personalities and/or antisocial conduct and/or revolutionary activities."

Such findings lead me to conclude that deviant conduct—whether merely neurotic or overtly criminal—is able to allay personal anxiety and express part of the subjective conflict *because* these modes of behavior deviate from social norms. Moreover, if the human being experiences the different behavior of others as *a criticism of his own behavior*, then it is possible that the socially negativistic deviant wishes (at least unconsciously) to behave differently *in order to* strike at the narcissism both of his fellows and of society as a whole.

It is obvious that, in the last analysis, what traumatizes the individual is the total social situation (the "law") and not the persons representing society (the policemen). Malinowski (1926, 1927a, 1927b, 1932) rightly suggested that the Trobriand father cannot be the *virulent* oedipal traumatizing agency for his child that the Occidental father is, simply because his society does not delegate to him either the function of socializing his child or the necessary authority to do so. This implies that the father—or any other "mediator" of culture—is merely the channel through whom the *irrational* components of a society are introjected in the form of a superego. If an individual is intelligent enough to perceive, or is at least sensitive enough to feel, that the traumatizing agent is not an individual but the dereistic and structurally inconsistent society or culture to which he belongs, then one must expect his aggression to be directed toward the *agency* that assigns to selected individuals the role of traumatizing others, and not toward the individual who happens to be merely an agent of the traumatizing society. The recognition of the fact that it is the inconsistencies of the sociocultural structure that are the real traumatic agent necessarily presupposes a certain amount of intelligence; but then, many studies indicate that the intellectual level of most groups of psychotics is not much different from that of the average adult population.

The experiments of Maier (1939) and of many others who have placed rats in very baffling situations, in which action is *forced* upon them though no solution to the problem confronting them exists, is significant for evolving a situational theory of deviance.

In this specific sense, deviant behavior—whether criminal or not —is aggressively "critical" of the *total* situation that permits the frustration of one individual through the agency of certain other individuals selected for this purpose and empowered to effect it. This view tallies perfectly with Freud's first formulation of the problem of aggression and with the frustration-aggression hypothesis derived from Freud's formulation by Dollard and his associates (1939).

One can distinguish so-called "normal" from criminal and non-criminal deviant behavior as follows:

1. Pseudo-sublimation, that is, symptoms that conform to social standards, represent on the social level the tendency toward "homonomy," which Angyal (1938) postulated as a general principle. The individual accepts society as a reality and conforms primarily to the means, and secondarily to the goals, proposed by society.

2. Deviance, that is, the cluster of symptoms that deviates from the social standards, can, on the social level, represent a tendency toward an "autonomy" or toward a bionegativity, in Angyal's sense. Deviance implies a rejection not of the *reality* of society, as in schizo-

phrenia (chaps. 9 and 10), but a nonacceptance of its values and of the social functions it assigns to the individual.

There are two main types of social negativism:

1. Noncriminal deviant behavior is unconsciously chosen or constructed to exclude both socially acceptable behavior and socially penalized (and therefore criminal) behavior (chap. 13). The noncriminal neurotic or psychotic rejects his social ties partially or completely and almost ceases to be a "social animal." This extrasocial position may sometimes even be socially recognized. Medieval society provided certain persons with the pseudo-extrasocial positions of "outlaw" and "excommunicate," which, technically speaking, were in many respects genuine "social" statuses. Among the Sedang, the individual who refuses to conform to some major rule must renounce his human status and "become a boar" (Devereux 1937a). In simpler societies such a renunciation may be a violent assertion of one's functional individuality and of one's uniqueness. This is a meaningful form of behavior in the framework of social history, since Mauss (1950) has shown that the *concept* of "person," and the social actualization of the individual's uniqueness, are late developments. For my part, I think that the limited actualization and structuration of the individual's uniqueness are due largely to the early diffusion of affective bonds in primitive society (Devereux 1942a). Finally, in "aggression by isolation" the individual can (unconsciously) "select" any mode of behavior that deviates from socially accepted behavior. He will therefore choose those that (*a*) best correspond to his neurotic needs and (*b*) usually form a culturally partly preestablished structure (chap. 1).

2. Criminal behavior must, in certain respects, be the *exact opposite* of social norms. Hence the criminal's field of choice is as limited as that of the "bohemian" determined to *épater le bourgeois* (shock the staid middle classes). Now, whereas the aggression element is very pronounced in social negativism, the apparent rejection of all social ties is in the last resort a mere rationalization, since criminal behavior is directed against society itself.

Neither in neurosis nor in delinquency is the existence of society questioned, and behavior continues to be determined by the social norms—but henceforth negatively so, in that it must exclude all conformity with them. Thus, though these symptoms yield a neurotic gain precisely because they harm society (by hurting the narcissism of those who conform, by constituting an aggression against the norms, and so forth), they nonetheless call for recognition by society, for they attract attention to the deviant and elicit a social response. This is true even of the schizophrenic (Bleuler 1912). Every clinician knows that when a psychiatric hospital is visited by a party of, say, psychology students, the patients readily put on their most showy "act" for them.

Society, in turn, accords an explicit recognition to every deviant—even to the most extreme ones—and sometimes in very surprising ways. Both Róheim (1932) and I (1937b) observed, in two different primitive societies, that the incestuous male is "condemned with admiration." The robber baron of the nineteenth century—an antisocial being if ever there was one—is to this day viewed as an ideal by a few right-wing extremists. The "glamour" of the deviant presupposes, within limits, the imperfect acceptance of norms, even by very well-adjusted individuals, who can therefore identify with the "hero"—the "great criminal" or the "eccentric" who dares defy the norm.

Now, though people admire the great surgeon and the great criminal, they have nothing but contempt for the "on-the-fence" position of the neither-fish-nor-flesh hangman, who—like the cowardly slacker he is—gives free rein to his aggressivity by accepting social goals of a *marginal* type and socially standardized means of attaining them. This may explain why aggressive individuals prefer to become surgeons or criminals rather than hangmen.

The clinching argument is that in other societies the deviant behavior of "neurotics" and "bad people" sometimes closely parallels what our society views as the acme of good behavior. In certain societies, cooperativeness, generosity, and sincerity are sometimes—though *not always*—as symptomatic of neurosis as are, in our culture, openly antisocial activity, egoism, and insincerity. Both Fortune (1932) and I (1933–35) were able to study fairly well sublimated but nonetheless deviant individuals who belonged to two particularly "tough" primitive civilizations. These cases are paradoxical in that they show that genuine sublimation can *also* become a source of neurotic gain if it satisfies the residual social negativism of the adult individual living in a fundamentally "sick" society (Devereux 1939a).

Whether social negativism manifests itself in mere deviance or involves antisocial activities as well depends mostly on whether the individual's negativistic trends are passive or active.

Active social negativism can manifest itself in three ways, which differ from each other quantitatively rather than qualitatively—that is, in terms of the relative size of the segment of society at which the antisocial behavior is directed. All things considered, the *less* generalized and *more* personalized the deviant's social negativism is, the smaller will be the area of the social body which his behavior affects. This area often varies with the intelligence of the defective delinquent.

1. On the most personalized and restricted level, aggression is directed against the person whom society has placed in a strategic position—one that permits him to frustrate the subject. The victims of such crimes are usually members of the defective delinquent's family and his immediate associates.

2. On an intermediate level, aggression is directed at no one in particular. Who the victim is depends largely on opportunity and other secondary motives. Social negativism expresses itself on a fairly low level of abstraction and at the expense of almost any member of society. The crimes committed by habitual delinquents generally fall into this category. Part of the neurotic *gain* that this type of crime yields consists of the unhappiness it causes to the criminal's own family and close associates (chap. 8). It is this that links crimes of this group with the more highly personalized and very direct crimes of the previous group.

3. On a higher level of abstraction, aggression is generally directed toward society as a whole, although the concrete form of the act by which the rebel's social negativism expresses itself can vary a great deal. Thus aggression against society may range from gratuitous assassination of a statesman by an eccentric (alias "anarchist," "bolshevik," "fascist," or other unspecified "subversive element") through treatises on revolutionary tactics, *bad* novels of social criticism, and so forth, to terrorism and revolution. Hence, civilized states rightly distinguish between freedom of speech and explicitly antisocial tendencies, expressed in writings that plead—allegedly in the abstract—for an overthrow of organized democratic society. I recall in this context that even animal herds reject and expel those of their members whose aggressive behavior constantly disturbs the herd.

I strongly stress that, being no advocate of either cultural relativism or other theories based on the *Vox populi, vox Dei* principle, I consider neither the generosity of a certain old Sedang man nor Spartacus' slave revolt to be *in any sense* pathological. I do hold, however, that—marginally and epiphenomenally—both *also* gratify social negativism as such, even if the old Sedang's kindness, like the revolt (but not the terrorism) of Spartacus, was essentially a sublimatory mode of behavior.

In fact, the more brutal and dereistic is the society whose norms one rejects and against which one rebels, the more social negativism the sensitive human being will exhibit, simply because life in a society of that kind cannot really encourage confidence in society as such. This may explain why it is so difficult to restore order and to reestablish normal social life after a revolt—even a legitimate and successful one—against a brutal and obtuse system. People seem to be traumatized and to need time to regain their faith in the mere possibility of a decently organized society (Devereux 1978a, chap. 11). This simple finding explains the prolongation of disorders and the replacement of one dictatorship by another. These phenomena of social pathology need not, however, be viewed as reasonable or even necessary. The most effective "revolutions" are those that are the least chaotic and most peaceful.

The fact that every society is in a sense contrary to the basic psychobiological *Anlage* of man represents an entirely separate problem, which was discussed in chapter 2. It does not come within the scope of this analysis of social negativism, which is concerned with this tendency as it manifests itself essentially within the framework of a society characterized by at least a minimum of decency and realism. On a practical level, my analysis of social negativism is therefore applicable to Athens rather than to Sparta and to France, England, and the United States rather than to the regimes of Hitler, Stalin, or Mao Tse-tung. The theory itself is, however, applicable to even the most perfect society imaginable, because a totally nonfrustrating society is—alas!—a contradiction in terms.

One direct consequence of the theory of social negativism is that, *within a strictly sociological frame of reference,* the *temporal* order of the *valid* psychoanalytic equation proposed by Osborn (1937), Father = Society, must be reversed to read Society = Father (or member of the group, or policeman, or organized government). What enables one to link the sociological viewpoint with the psychoanalytic one is the fact that the parents' capacity to harm the child depends on the status and function society assigns to him.

The analysis of social negativism is made considerably more complicated by the existence of partially or totally pathological societies, whose structural inconsistencies place a superfluous burden on the individual. On the other hand, the very existence of the state of adjustment, which is often *as neurotic and as remote from reality acceptance as antisocial behavior,* shows that a socially nonnegativistic, well-sublimated individual is often able to allay his anxiety by means that are *not in the least* antisocial. I therefore hold that *systematic* social negativism, *whatever its level of abstraction,* is as dereistic as any other form of neurosis or psychosis and perhaps more so. This is why the psychotherapy of the delinquent defective, whether he is a parricide or a demagogue, proves particularly difficult. His neurosis is clearly also the expression of a *pathological* social negativism, which is simply a dereistic method of facing the problems that every person living in society faces.

The psychiatrist can resolve such problems efficiently only if he follows Burrow's (1937) advice to rid himself first of his own social neurosis and then recognize the fact that the criminal often views his crimes as good and just actions according to his *own* lights.

The preceding formulation, evolved in an empirical manner, constitutes a large part of the conceptual scheme in terms of which I propose to analyze the fundamental problems of ethnopsychiatry.

EPILOGUE

Some fifteen years after writing these pages, I psychoanalyzed a young neurotic delinquent who hated society and its laws rather than human beings. Such, at least, was his attitude until he came to understand that in early childhood he had mostly hated persons whom society had authorized to behave toward him in a particularly frustrating, unfeeling, and harsh manner. One day, even though he had often tangled with the law, he began to speak warmly and affectionately of a certain policeman who had *misused* his influence on a movie-theater employee to get the patient into the theater without a ticket. An analysis of this incident showed that the *only* manifestation of affection and loyalty which the analysand viewed as authentic was the willingness on the part of an adult—"the hereditary enemy of youth"—to commit an illegal act in favor of an adolescent or a child. Lawful acts of generosity quite simply did not count for him. In addition, this patient viewed the performance of an illegal action as a proof of rationality, because he held all rules, of whatever nature, to be useless and dereistic. It took me nearly a year to bring this patient to the point where he understood that even lawful acts of affection and kindliness can be authentic. At about the same time, I managed to make him realize that some rules are like the bones of the body: they make a variety of voluntary movements possible but do so only "at the cost of" a decreased *general* flexibility. A total flexibility would, of course, exclude the possibility of any movement whatsoever.[7] As soon as he had grasped this, he not only refrained from all delinquent acts but sought to forestall, by kindness and persuasion, the gratuitous rebellious actions of other young delinquents. Finally, since he had neither the means nor perhaps the talent to become a doctor, he decided to become a policeman in the Youth Division of the police force and to dedicate his life, through acts of kindness, to helping young people avoid clashes with the law.

4

The Voices of Children
Psychocultural Obstacles to
Therapeutic Communication
(1965)

According to the great mathematician Georg Cantor, it is more important to ask a question correctly than it is to answer it. This is a profound statement, since the askers of questions—the gadflies of the intellect—are those who force us to take cognizance of things we do not care to see. Perhaps the greatest gadfly in the history of psychoanalysis was Sándor Ferenczi, whose real greatness as an answerer of questions is overshadowed by the even greater services he rendered by asking questions and by focusing one's attention on certain disturbing aspects of reality that do not readily fit any pigeonhole of one's habitual frame of reference.

In one of his last papers, "Confusion of Tongues between Adults and Children" (1955), Ferenczi brought into focus, in his inimitable and intellectually restless manner, a problem no one really wanted to notice. He answered it, moreover, in a manner that does not wholly satisfy everyone, myself included. Nonetheless, without the stimulus of that paper I might never have become aware of this problem and therefore could not now venture to offer my own analysis of the almost insuperable difficulties of communication between the child and the adult. In fact, I even suspect that Ferenczi's disturbing paper would have affected me as little as it seems to affect most people had I not had comparable experiences of my own when trying, as an anthropologist, to communicate with primitives. Indeed, anthropological field reports are replete with examples of complete misunderstandings between primitive and modern man (La Barre 1947). An example of such a misunderstanding may help to clarify the nature of the problem.

Case 1.—A Lengua Indian of the Gran Chaco, South America, traveled nearly 150 miles to accuse the missionary and anthropologist W. B. Grubb of having stolen a pumpkin from his garden. Greatly taken aback, Grubb insisted that he could not possibly have done so, since he had not been anywhere near this man's garden for many months. The Lengua Indian readily admitted this fact and also conceded that Grubb had not actually stolen the pumpkin. Nonetheless, he asked to be compensated for the (unstolen) pumpkin because he had seen Grubb steal it *in a dream* (Grubb 1911).

This example—which could be duplicated, one way or another, by comparable data from many primitive tribes—shows that, in order to grasp what a primitive is really saying, one sometimes has to derail one's normal train of thought and operate intellectually in a manner closely resembling what Freud calls "the primary process" and what the now unjustly unfashionable Lévy-Bruhl (1910–31) designated by the term "prelogical mentality." I hasten to add that comparable misunderstandings can occur when one communicates with members of other civilized groups or of social strata somewhat removed from one's own. Last but not least, one has to remove a great deal of defensive wax from what Reik (1948) so picturesquely calls "the third ear" in order to grasp the real meaning of the statements of neurotics and psychotics or, for that matter, the real meaning of the dreams of normals. These difficulties are immeasurably increased when the neurotic or psychotic patient also happens to be a primitive (Devereux 1951a, 1951f, and chap. 15). If, in addition, he is a child, communication is often reduced to a minimum. This is readily apparent to anyone who cares to glance through my verbatim accounts of interviews with three neurotic Mohave children (1961a).

For simplicity's sake, I will limit myself to one striking aspect of these interviews. Among the Mohave, all children, no matter how young they may be, are entitled to realistic sexual knowledge, and a great many of them have complete sexual relations before reaching the age of ten (Devereux 1951d) without incurring parental or tribal disapproval. I therefore felt free to ask those Mohave boys direct questions about their sexual experiences. Moreover, I arranged to be accompanied by a skillful adult interpreter, because I felt that his presence—as a character reference, so to speak—would guarantee that I would not betray them to the school authorities. The interpreter's presence had a decisive influence on these interviews. When asked about their sexual activities *in English*—the language of their puritanical teachers—the youngsters denied certain activities, but when my interpreter repeated the same questions *in Mohave,* they almost invariably admitted the very practice they had just denied in English. The children apparently felt that they could admit in Mohave what they felt they had to deny in English, because both sexual acts and verbal ribaldry, prohibited in an English-speaking context, are accepted by the Mohave.

Before one chuckles about the naiveté of such unconscious hair-splitting, one might do well to take a critical look at oneself. As recently as thirty years ago no educated American woman was simply pregnant—she was *enceinte*. Even today some American women own no underwear—only "lingerie." And none of them ever wears a bosom-support, only a "bra"—from *brassière*, which is not even the proper French word for the unmentionable item that the French call a *soutien-gorge*.

The purpose of the present essay is to elucidate the real function of the utterances of children and the devices adults resort to in order to conceal or distort the essence of what children seek to express by means of language.

Though the title of my paper is at once too broad and too narrow, I chose the term "voice" advisedly, since, in my opinion, a great deal of what children seek to express is expressed by means of what one might call "sound effects" rather than by words. Hence, insofar as there *is* a communication, it represents primarily "metacommunication" rather than a cut-and-dried conceptual communication. Everyone is of course familiar with the fact that the way one manages one's voice is an important qualifying and supplementing device in one's linguistic behavior. The relevant literature on this topic, which actually pertains to what is common knowledge (witness, for example, the French quip "C'est le ton qui fait la musique") is well summed up by Hymes (1961). As Owen Wister's proverbial Virginian knew, it is the manner, the tone of voice, in which a statement is made that reveals its true meaning: when a stranger presumed to call him an s.o.b., the Virginian pulled his gun and snapped, "When you call me that . . . smile!" Many child patients and even some adult ones are almost obsessed by the nonconceptual, vocal-expressive, concomitants of speech and react more to the voice and facial expression of their interlocutor than to his actual utterances.

Case 2.—A very depressive and neurasthenic young man in analysis was almost obsessively preoccupied with the presence or absence of smiles on the faces of his interlocutors. If they failed to smile, the most neutral and even the kindest utterance was suspected of being hostile. Conversely, the roughest remark, when accompanied by a smile, was uncritically defined as a friendly utterance.

Other patients respond primarily to the inflection of the interlocutor's voice rather than to the conceptual content of his speech. The inflections of the voice—its acoustic qualities—seem to possess the

107

capacity to produce almost physical sensations. Expressions such as to "lash out at" or "to speak in a caressing voice" show a dim awareness of the fact that the quality of the voice is perceived more or less as a physical contact. This is true even of animals.

Case 3.—As a great dog-lover, who has spent many years of his life in close relationship with them, I have made certain relevant observations, two of which I will now summarize.

a) One of my dogs, perfectly trained to understand the sternly voiced command "Go away," would, when the command was uttered in a *caressing* voice, react to the voice rather than the phonetic pattern and, instead of going away, would approach me.

b) When playing the piano or eating, which kept my hands busy, I could *talk* to my dog in a certain tone of voice to which he reacted as though I were physically petting him: his motion responses to my voice were identical with his motions when I actually petted him. One of my dogs, who particularly enjoyed having the base of his spine scratched and would, when so petted, rapidly turn his stern toward me, often responded to a caressingly uttered endearment by doing just that and actually wriggling as though he were being scratched.

On the postpubertal human level, certain types of voices notoriously have an almost irresistible erotic quality for certain individuals. Thus it is not entirely a matter of juvenile mass hysteria when bobby-soxers respond with manifest sexual excitement to the voices of certain popular singers.

These data—which could be further substantiated by means of the experimental findings summarized by Hymes (1961)—indicate that the voice in which a statement is uttered is an important second level of communication. It is a metacommunication, operating primarily on the level of the emotions; the type of information it conveys is not a conceptual one. It is, rather, a very archaic (and therefore extremely powerful) form of the communication of affective states: a type of communication best designated as "contagion" and closely related to types of communication found in animal aggregates. Indeed, when the sentinel animal of a herd of wild creatures utters a so-called warning cry, which causes the herd to stampede, anyone not guilty of anthropomorphic thinking readily realizes that what the sentinel communicates to the herd is not the objective finding "There is a lion in the bush" but the subjective experience "I am afraid," which then induces a similar subjective experience of fear in the rest of the herd. Similarly, a so-called stirring piece of music, like the French *Marseillaise* or the Hungarian *Rákóczy March,* can induce martial exaltation even in an Austrian or a Swede who, though accustomed to respond to Western musical idioms, may be unaware that these are battle marches, and, moreover, the battle marches of alien nations.

In extreme instances, metacommunication by means of a specialized form of voice production can completely obliterate the conceptual content of articulated speech.

Case 4.—I have published elsewhere (1956a), in some detail, an interview with a severely neurotic boy in his early teens who did not speak but simply squawked like Donald Duck and therefore could not engage in a verbal therapeutic interaction. When brought to my office, the boy moved around, behaved with normal curiosity, and did not do anything peculiar except for squawking like Donald Duck whenever articulate speech was called for. Suddenly it occurred to me that the true meaning of his communication was precisely the fact that he concealed his *thoughts* and communicated only his *feelings*. Since the word "squawking" denotes the explosive expression of angry grievances, I simply told the boy that I was aware of his pent-up anger, directed at everyone and everything, and encouraged him to express his anger in words, promising not to punish him, no matter how insulting he became.

The results were startling, to say the least. For the first time in many months the boy began to speak normally, pouring out a torrent of grievances, rage, and threats in perfectly articulated but angry-sounding speech. He poured over me a veritable stream of almost magic curses: He hoped that my books would crumble and disintegrate into dust because I refused to lend him a technical psychiatric book that he wanted to borrow. He put on me the curse of lung cancer because I would not give him a cigarette, and so on.

The expression of strong emotions may render the clear articulation of the conceptual content of speech impossible even in adults, both primitive (Devereux 1961a) and modern.

Case 5.—A patient had a secret baby-word, which represented for her the essence of everything obscene and exciting. After two years she told me of the *existence* of this word but refused to utter it because it seemed far too exciting and obscene. When with endless patience, I succeeded in making her utter this word, she voiced it in a literally window-shattering, inarticulate bellow, so that I could not even guess what she had said. Many additional sessions were required before she consented to—and could—pronounce the word halfway intelligibly, and further weeks elapsed before she could utter it with normal clarity and in a normal voice. In fact, she could do so only when, as a result of her analysis, the word had lost its magical quality and immense emotional charge.

This patient also had another vocal device for obstructing communication. It consisted in mumbling so constantly and so badly that nearly everything that was emotionally important remained utterly unintelligible. In fact, her mumbling prevented both myself and an experienced training analyst, who had treated her abroad for a while, from putting her on the analytic couch, since in that position even her ordinary speech was just barely intelligible.

One day she reported that her overly modest father would, when urinating, always open the faucet wide so that his urination would be inaudible to his children, and during the same session she mentioned other ways of obliterating sounds by means of monotonous and persistent noises. The parallelism between her mumbling and her father's recourse to a "sound screen" was immediately pointed out to her, with quite dramatic results: it became possible during that very session to put her on the couch and to continue to do so for the rest of her analysis, which was entirely successful (Devereux 1966b).

A third technique of using the voice to obliterate communication was resorted to by an American Indian patient. The case is quite complex and can only be briefly summarized.

Case 6.—During World War II the patient's combat team advanced on foot toward the battle line. It was overtaken en route by a semimotorized unit, to which the patient's admired, hated, and loved older brother belonged. Half an hour later the patient passed a wrecked jeep, which had received a direct hit and contained his brother's charred corpse. In narrating this dramatic episode, the patient always spoke at first with mounting excitement. However, when he came to describe the actual sight of his brother's corpse, his voice became coldly objective and his face showed no trace of affect. Every effort to mobilize the affect related to this sight in the course of his therapy (which, for administrative reasons, had to be short) failed. An attempt was therefore made to remobilize this repressed affect by recourse to sodium pentothal.

Under the influence of the drug, the patient once more narrated the entire episode, his voice reflecting much anguish and deep emotion. However, when he came to the crucial scene, he suddenly lapsed from English into the language of his tribe. This was a startlingly unforeseeable subterfuge, since, according to the patient and also to his fanatically Christian parents—who considered everything Indian, including their tribe's language, as "heathen" and therefore not to be learned—the patient knew only a very few words of the language of his forebears. Apparently, it was desperately important for the patient to isolate the factual, conceptual side of his experience from its emotional side, especially in the therapeutic situation, which calls for the "deprivatization" and communication of the *total* experience. Unable, because of the sodium pentothal, to inhibit the *affect* that this tragic spectacle had elicited, he whisked its *factual content* out of sight by suppressing conceptual communication through recourse to his tribe's language, which he supposedly barely knew and which I, of course, could not understand at all.

Although some of the above data pertain to neurotic adults rather than to children, they nonetheless shed a great deal of light on several functions of speech in the child, which will now be scrutinized one by one.

EXPRESSION VS. COMMUNICATION

Adult cultural preconceptions lead one to assume that all vocal behavior represents—and is actually intended as—communication. Yet in reality much verbal output is *not* intended as communication. I do not mean this simply in the sense of Talleyrand's famous saying, "Speech was given to man to enable him to conceal his thoughts."[1] The point is rather that the human baby's vocal output at first resembles animal outcries in that it is primarily, and even exclusively, *expressive behavior*. It more or less automatically reflects the child's emotional state only; it does *not* imply *intentional communication*. A baby may scream when he is hungry or when his diapers are wet. Yet he does not scream because he expects, by doing so, to gain relief from discomfort. He does not *experience* or *view* or *intend* his vocalizations as communication or as a means of getting help. He does, of course, slowly learn that his screams bring milk or dry diapers. In brief, because he learns that his purely expressive vocalizations have certain consequences and thus, almost in the form of a conditioned reflex, learns to connect his screaming with the bringing of milk, he will henceforth use screaming as a genuine communication, directional and intended. Nonetheless, one must remember throughout this discussion that the child's *first* vocalization is purely expressive behavior and that it *expresses* affects rather than *communicates* thoughts, wishes, or facts.

It is equally clear that the hungry baby animal's vocal output does not represent a conceptual communication *for* the mother animal. It represents primarily a symmetric affective contamination of the mother, just as the sentinel animal's cry of alarm, expressing only its own fright, elicits a general stampede, *in which the sentinel animal itself also participates*.

One important distinction between animal and human behavior must, however, be made. The sentinel animal's (inducing) fright and stampeding is exactly duplicated by the (induced) fright and stampede of the rest of the herd. The two behaviors are parallel. By contrast, the mother animal's nursing response to her baby's whimpering, while also representing affective contamination or contagion, elicits not parallel but complementary (or symmetric) behavior. *Later on,* perhaps, the young animal will cry to ask for milk. But, *in the beginning,* it cries only because it is hungry and may even make sucking movements with its lips. Its mother thereupon begins to yield milk and nurses it. Similar complementary behavior, induced by emotional contagion implemented through the production of sound, is represented by the mating behavior of tiger and tigress. Each expresses its own sexual excitement by certains "mating calls," and the two (seemingly) "call" back and forth until they meet and engage in sexually complementary behavior (Corbett 1946).

On what is culturally an infinitely higher level, expressive behavior that almost coincidentally represents *also* a kind of communication is best exemplified by so-called absolute music, whose basic and overridingly important objective is pure expression. Of course, the composer does hope for listeners and may therefore work hard at making his expressive behavior perfect, using the most recondite devices of harmony, counterpoint, musical architecture, and instrumentation. Yet, despite everything, he unconsciously aims only at an affective contamination of the listener. He does not seek to teach the listener counterpoint, nor, even in an alleged piece of program music, like Debussy's *La Mer,* does he seek to initiate the listener into the mysteries of oceanography.

At this point I would like to stop for what I consider an important aside. The child's conception of the possibility of communicating at all—of contaminating and of actually informing—is the result of its mother's standard responses to its expressive behavior resulting from its discomfort—a behavior that at first does not seek to inform anyone of anything. It is my feeling that the formerly fashionable technique of scheduled feeding, which ignores the child's expressive voice production, had disastrous results, not only for the development of the child's emotional potential in adulthood but also for the growth of its verbal articulateness, especially in a situation of exchange, i.e., in a conversational context. Thus, as Michael Arlen remarked somewhere, an Englishman who can utter three consecutive sentences without interrupting himself with "haw," "hmm," or some other noise is held to talk too much. Yet, precisely because the Englishman is not emotionally frozen, England has produced—perhaps as a substitute for articulateness in personal relationships—some of the world's most deeply felt and expressively worded poetry and scholarly as well as scientific works whose style is thoroughly literate. Where nonresponse to the child's early vocalizations is more marked and there is an impairment of the capacity to feel, one observes that these frozen persons sometimes become great technicians of impeccably articulate and smooth style—as cold as the nose of a puppy or a short story in the *New Yorker*. In the intellectual realm it leads to an artificially impersonal and therefore completely segmental and unrealistic behavioral science—intellectually slick, devoid of empathy, as clever as the handiwork of a sophisticated cuckoo-clock maker and just about as meaningful in human terms (Devereux 1961c).

This, then, is the first roadblock in the path of communication between child and adult: what is exclusively expressive behavior on the part of the child the adult insists on construing as communicative behavior. What seeks, at most, to produce an affective contamination is compulsively perceived as a factual statement.

The area in which this complete misunderstanding manifests itself most conspicuously is perhaps the realm of so-called children's lies. The adult focuses his attention on the (seemingly) conceptual and factual content of what the child says—and accuses the child of lying. However, all along, the child is resorting to seemingly declarative statements only to induce in the adult a certain affective state that will either parallel his own or be complementary to it. In a folktale, the shepherd boy's "deceitful" shouts of "Wolf, wolf!" were perceived by people as a cold-blooded misrepresentation of facts. Yet, from the viewpoint of the shepherd boy it was simply expressive behavior, reflecting fright and loneliness and aimed, perhaps only preconsciously, at eliciting a response from the villagers, safely ensconced in their huts.

Nonoverlap of Conceptual and Affective Response

A second major obstacle to communication between child and adult is twofold.

First of all, concepts and facts do not have the same meaning for the adult and the child.

Case 7.—The following incident was narrated to me by a highly cultured old Hungarian lady in the presence of her psychologically sophisticated daughter and the daughter's brilliant graduate-student son, both of whom confirmed the incident in every detail. During the terrible aerial bombardments of Budapest in 1944, when the boy was still very small, his grandmother took him one evening to stay with some friends whose apartment seemed less vulnerable than their own. Unfortunately, precisely that night a bomb fell so near to the friends' apartment that the plaster began to fall from the ceiling. The boy reacted with panic and—crying and shouting—accused his grandmother of having brought him to that place in order to murder him.

One specific aspect of this situation deserves special notice. The boy was at the time too young to understand what had happened to him in terms of "causes" located outside his immediate family circle and narrow field of vision. He could not conceive that bombers, miles up, sent by perfect strangers, should seek to kill *him,* quite impersonally. The same problem also confronts adults with limited horizons (chap. 9).

Case 8.—In 1933–34 I tried in vain to make the Sedang Moi understand that the depreciation in the value of their produce was due to the economic crisis then affecting the Western world. They could not understand how events in distant countries could affect their dealings with itinerant Vietnamese or Laotian peddlers. For them, the Western countries were farther away than the land of the gods and the spirits.

Case 9.—In Steinbeck's *Grapes of Wrath,* the expropriated Okie farmer first tries to shoot the men who are tearing down his fences but is told that they were sent by the local banker. He then wants to shoot the banker but is told that he takes his orders from the big New York banks. Finally, in despair, farmer Joad exclaims: "Then whom am I going to shoot?"

Scapegoating—a phenomenon as common among ourselves as in primitive societies—shows how difficult, or even impossible, it is to admit that distant, complex, and almost anonymous forces can affect the very core of our existence. As far back as 1939 (chap. 9, below) I indicated that the subjection of the individual, living in a complex society, to anonymous and impersonal forces, which wholly escape his control and nonetheless affect him in his very being, is a decisive sociogenetic determinant of schizophrenia.

One specific aspect of this nonoverlap of the semantic significance of facts and concepts for children and for adults is that, for the child (and for the primitive and the neurotic as well), the symbolic implications of an object often outweigh its practical, objective implications. To a mature adult the toilet may be a throne or a devouring monster's maw only in a dream—or, rather, in a nightmare. To the child, it may be primarily a throne and a threatening maw and only secondarily and incidentally a hygienic device. In the same way, for an Australian, the bull-roarer[2] is the sacred voice of a god, such as Daramulun. For a modern child it is simply an amusing toy. It is said that Bernfeld once warned analytic candidates—somewhat tongue-in-cheek—never to forget that, even though a plane is primarily a phallic symbol, it can, incidentally, also take one from Vienna to Paris. Hence, even when one is listening to a perfectly normal child, it is advisable to ascertain whether, when he speaks of airplanes, he is talking primarily about a phallic symbol or whether he is realistically thinking of the joys of riding a plane to visit a doting grandmother.

Second, a seemingly very different, yet basically somewhat similar, obstacle to communication is the fact that the affects of children do not fully parallel the nearest comparable affects of adults. The result is that the adult's ideational and conceptual reaction to his affective state X_a does not overlap with the child's ideational and conceptual reaction to his own, similar but not identical, affective state X_b. Thus a child in the pregenital stage may express its oral longings in clearly oral terms—behaviorally, verbally, conceptually, by fantasies, and in every other way possible. By contrast, a grown woman beset by unconscious oral longings, but having at her disposal a fully developed genital apparatus and opportunities for sexual gratification, may experience—in connection with basically oral wishes—a strong genital-sexual arousal and seek coitus, quite unaware that she assigns an oral meaning to coitus, equating milk and semen. This point is of some importance and will be illustrated by the following two examples.

Case 10.—Among the Mohave Indians it is a standard cultural belief that after the sixth lunar month of pregnancy the fetus in the uterus ingests *orally* and feeds on the semen deposited in the pregnant woman's vagina by her sex partner (Devereux 1948a).

Case 11.—The coital fantasy of a neurotic woman consisted in the idea that a small baby boy within her uterus (or abdomen) ingested her husband's semen (Devereux 1966b).

The behavioral and ideational correlates of the affective state of anger may also largely depend on the stage of psychosexual development the subject has reached. In a baby, anger may elicit biting fantasies. In a three-year-old, anger may elicit ideas of soiling with feces or else of frustrating the object of his anger by defiance or by withholding the feces or their equivalent. In a boy in the phallic stage, anger may arouse ideas of piercing and cutting into pieces.

The point I seek to make is that the three-year-old who informs (perhaps by a tantrum) his four-year-old brother that he is angry (tacitly) implies that he wishes to soil his foe. The four-year-old—given his phallic definition of aggression—will, however, "understand" that his younger brother means to attack him with a phallic dagger. Even grosser misunderstandings of the realistic or fantasied

115

consequences of an emotional state can arise between child and adult. A small child who realizes that his parent is angry may imagine that the parent will devour him, because, for the small child himself, aggression means biting and devouring. Conversely, the parent, witnessing the small child's anger, may visualize the child as attacking him with his fists—as *he* might attack another adult—and have the surprise of his life, and a sense of being tricked, when the child bites him instead.[3]

Conversely, a given expressive action, "normally" reflecting an affective state *A* in the child, may be misinterpreted by the adult as reflecting another affective state, *B*, because, in *his own* case, such behavior *would* reflect affective state *B*. Two examples of misunderstandings between Westerners and primitives may help us clarify this point.

Case 12.—If a member of a certain African tribe, whom I have just met, spits into my extended hand instead of grasping it and shaking it, I will (wrongly) feel that he is insulting me. Actually the African simply means to tell me by this action that his trust in me is so great that he is willing to put a portion of himself in my hand, certain that I will not use it for the purpose of bewitching him.

Case 13.—When the Portuguese explorer Albuquerque reached the city of Malacca, he tried to honor its Malay king by placing a gold chain around his neck. He nearly got killed for his pains, because he "grossly insulted" the king by attempting to touch him and by raising his hands—holding the gold chain—above the level of the king's head.

SUPPRESSED UNDERSTANDING AS A
FURTHER OBSTACLE TO COMMUNICATION

Communication between adults and children would be quite bad enough if they really did not understand each other. What greatly aggravates the situation is that the infantile core of the adult understands only too well what the child is expressing and what its actions mean—and desperately seeks to suppress this understanding because it represents a threatening temptation to regress to childhood attitudes, to revive childhood fantasies, and to engage in primary-process thinking.

Ferenczi (1955) suggests that one source of the confusion of tongues between adult and child is that, while the one is using the language of tenderness, the other may be using the language of (erotic) passion. This point is of crucial importance, and even Ferenczi did not fully explore all of its important implications. He feels, for example, that the adult may become sexually aroused by the child's tenderness or that the child may become sexually aroused by the adult's tenderness. This is true enough on the conscious level. What really complicates the situation, however, is that the adult may be sexually aroused by the child's tenderness *because of the underlying (infantile) type of sexuality present in the child*. Conversely, the child may be sexually aroused by the adult's tenderness *because of the adult sexual feelings lurking behind the adult's tenderness*.

The amount of scotomization that can take place in this particular area of communication is truly frightening. Diderot suggested long ago that the child is a potential murderer and incestuous rapist who simply lacks the force to act out his impulses. Moll and Freud created a scandal by openly discussing infantile sexuality, which was culturally scotomized despite various manifestations of infantile sexuality, such as the erections of sucklings. Slowly, society came to terms with the fact of infantile sexuality. In his early work Freud also indicated that many children are actually seduced by adults. Subsequently, however, he shied away from this conclusion, asserting that the child simply fantasies such seductions. However, as I have had occasion to point out elsewhere (Devereux 1953b), counteroedipal impulses have been systematically minimized by psychoanalysts, though even the myth of Oedipus and Chrysippus itself reveals them; and I have specifically demonstrated (Devereux 1965c [1978a, chap. 7]) that oedipal impulses are elicited by the (alleged) counteroedipal impulses of parents. The present attitude seems to be that it is all right for the child to have oedipal impulses but that one had better not discuss too much either the (so-called) counteroedipal impulses or the (so-called) countercannibalistic impulses (chap. 5). Personally, I am even inclined to question the "counter" part of these terms. One should speak of Laius and Jocasta complexes and describe the Oedipus complex as, respectively, a *counter*-Laius complex or a *counter*-Jocasta complex, representing infantile murderous and sexual urges elicited by the antecedent murderous and sexual impulses of the parents. In brief, one must remember that for every parricide or matricide there are probably millions of cases of abortion and infanticide (chap. 5); that for every incestuously raped mother there are thousands of children seduced by adults. In citing these I am simply complying with Bernfeld's advice not to forget that planes *also* have realistic functions and are not purely phallic symbols. More than anyone else, the analyst should avoid scotomizing facts, for, when he puts his mind to scotomizing reality, he certainly does a good job of it!

One favorite adult device for dealing with the more disturbing

aspects of communication between child and adult is to blame everything on the child. Hence, the Oedipus complex was discovered long
before the Laius and the Jocasta complexes, which are simply not
very fashionable. I think I am the only classical Freudian analyst
who in recent years has been seriously interested in this matter
(Devereux 1953b; 1955d; 1978a, chap. 7; and chap. 6, below). In-
credible as it may seem, the law, usually about as blind to psycho-
logic realities as a bat, is more realistic in this respect, at least on the
sexual level: it makes the adult responsible for sexual acts involving
children. However, it makes up for this realism by utter unrealism
in punishing the rare cases of parricide or matricide with much
greater ferocity than it punishes the innumerable cases of abortion
or infanticide. Indeed, abortion is lawful in many civilized countries, sometimes even for economic reasons. But the killing of aged
dependent parents is not permitted in any civilized land, although
it is customary in some primitive and archaic societies, such as Herodotus' Padaeans (Herodotus 3. 99).

The logical sleight-of-hand by which the adult shifts responsibility to the child consists essentially in insisting on understanding the
child's *primary*-process utterances in terms of the *secondary* process.
The whole maneuver reminds one of the incredibly funny and grotesque scene in Multatuli's *Max Havelaar* (1868), where the dry-as-
dust merchant Droogstoppel analyzes and dissects a fine poem in
terms of strict, common-sense logic.

In communicating with children in this devious way the adult engages in an important defensive maneuver. He professes to seek to
inhibit the child's sexuality and aggressions while actually seeking
to control his own and to blame his own relevant impulses on the
child. This defensive maneuver serves, on the one hand, to block
overt and conscious understanding; on the other hand, and simultaneously, it permits adults to express complementary (and seemingly adult) infantile-regressive affects in the guise of considered and
rational (so-called "disciplinary" or "didactic") actions (Devereux
1956a).

TENDENTIOUS MISDEFINITION OF THE CHILD

It is a truism enshrined in an old adage that he who wishes to shoot
his dog need only say that it has rabies. John Dollard, in *Caste and
Class in a Southern Town* (1937), pointed out that the white man
justifies his oppressive acts by developing a stereotype of the Black
and then inducing Blacks, by every means at their disposal, to behave in conformity with the stereotype. Exactly the same policy existed in Sparta with regard to the Helots (Devereux 1965a). Forcing

those who are discriminated against to behave in the desired (degrading) manner is quite easy; all one needs to do is to deny them access to, and the use of, the defense mechanisms that are available to the socially favored group (chap. 1).

Such a stereotype exists also with regard to children, who are more or less discriminated against nearly everywhere; they are weighed and measured by adult standards and are found wanting. On this basis, the adults develop a defect-centered stereotype of the child, which is couched in primarily negative terms: a child is what a self-respecting adult is not. This makes about as much sense as saying "A dog is what a fish is not" and then seeing to it that the dog does behave in a maximally *un*fishlike manner—for example, by not allowing him to swim. I would therefore like to differentiate between two technical terms by saying that "childlike" denotes the spontaneous, authentic, and positive behavior of the young organism as a whole, while "puerile" denotes the behavior that one inculcates in children to make them fit a culturally determined and negatively worded stereotype of the child (chap. 8).

I propose, furthermore, the following fundamental distinctions:

1. The childlike child is, within the framework of psychobiological standards, the *complete* specimen of a young organism; in the framework of sociocultural norms, it is an *incomplete* specimen of the adult.
2. The puerile child is, within the framework of psychobiological norms, an incomplete and distorted specimen of a young organism; within the framework of sociocultural norms, it is a *complete* specimen of the child (Devereux 1968a).

I cannot, for lack of space, elaborate on this point and will therefore cite only one obvious example: the fact that the child thinks in terms of the primary process. What one does not recognize is the extent to which one's longing to disinhibit one's own unconscious and primary process causes one to encourage children to read fairytales and incites one to reward, by approving chuckles and narcissistic rewards, their "cute" but irrational sayings. In brief, one rewards children in every possible way for modes of thought and expression that one discourages in the adult. This exactly duplicates the discriminatory process described by Dollard (1937), by which general irresponsibility, sexual randomness, lack of economic foresight, vaudeville cuteness, and ritualized humility are encouraged in Blacks in order to make their oppression and depreciation seem justifiable.

In brief, as I stated forty years ago (chap. 9), one teaches children so well to be puerile that they have a very hard time of it, indeed, in learning how to turn into adults. The procedure presupposes a particular type of "discontinuity in cultural conditioning" (Benedict 1938), because adjustment to child status is so contrived as to render a subsequent adult adjustment especially difficult. Moreover, children are even taught, in every possible way, the most effective technique of getting on adults' nerves. Thus, as I have indicated elsewhere (chap. 8), one literally incites rebellious adolescent girls to misbehave sexually by conveying to them in countless ways the information that this is the easiest and most effective means of exasperating adults.

On the practical level, many studies are vitiated from the start by the fact that even competent observers fail to realize that what they are studying is not authentic and spontaneous childlike behavior but the puerile behavior that society, through psychologists and educators, teaches children in order to make them fit this stereotype. The stereotype in question is then studied as though it were a genuine product of the "nature" of children. This is clearly a vicious circle.

These defects are not limited to psychological and biological research on child development, for the same misconceptions can also be found in many psychoanalytic studies of children. I have already referred to the fact that in their conceptualization of child psychology many psychoanalysts remain uninterested in counteroedipal and countercannibalistic phenomena. One hears a great deal about parental seductiveness in case histories, but when it comes to generalizations and conceptualizations one is prone to return to the safe treadmill of the spontaneous Oedipus complex and—if pressed for an explanation—to prefer to appeal to the Ice Age myth, evolved by Freud in one of his (rare) lesser moments, instead of to the obvious counteroedipally induced sources of the Oedipus complex and behavior. I believe in the universality of the Oedipus complex. However, I believe in it not because it is biologically determined *in the child* but because the Jocasta complex is biologically determined *in the adult* (Devereux 1956a [1978a, chap. 7]), who therefore induces it in every single child that is born and will be born, now and forevermore.

The willful misunderstanding of children's real nature usually oscillates between the stereotype of the vicious little instinct-ridden brute and the sexless and aggressionless little cherub. Sometimes the two images exist side by side, on two different levels of awareness. I have mentioned elsewhere (1956a) that the word "cherub"—so often applied to children to stress their sexless sweetness and touching immaturity—derives from Cherub; the latter in turn derives from

120

kirubu, which in Mesopotamia denoted the hypervirile man-headed bulls of religious statuary. A nice blend of the two is present in the figure of Cherubino in Mozart's *Marriage of Figaro,* derived from Beaumarchais's play. In the instructions preceding the play, Beaumarchais insists that the role can be played only by a young and pretty woman, although it is the role of a romantic teen-age boy in love with a grown woman whom, in Beaumarchais's later play, *La Mère Coupable,* he seduces and makes pregnant!

My last appeal, therefore, is to those who, for two thousand years, have dinned into all-too-willing ears Solomon's advice, "Spare the rod, spoil the child," and have—to the adult's joy and ill-fortune—consistently soft-pedaled Jesus' admonition: "Suffer the little children to come unto me, and forbid them not." My own plea is much more modest: If we but forbid them not our *ear,* we might, in due time, develop a real science of child psychology, free of stereotypes, and therefore raise children who could build a better world than the one they have inherited from us.

[*Addendum 1977.*—My often criticized remarks concerning the anteriority of the Laius and the Jocasta complexes have been fully confirmed in the meantime by the current pornography wave—which includes sadomasochistic practices—involving children (see *Der Spiegel* 22 [1977]: 174–83). My mistake—as so often—was that I published my findings and conclusions twenty or even thirty years before they could be accepted.]

5

The Cannibalistic Impulses of Parents (1966)

If one has humbled oneself all one's life long in order to avoid painful conflict with facts, one tends to keep one's back bowed in one's old age before any new fact which may appear.

S. Freud (1916–17)

The present study has two purposes.

1. It seeks to present a body of data attesting the existence of parental cannibalistic impulses and to demonstrate that these impulses underlie a psychic structure which—qua structure—comes into being in adulthood and is therefore neither a simple elaboration of infantile "cannibalistic" impulses nor a reaction to such impulses: in short, one is not dealing with *counter*cannibalism. An even moderately objective scrutiny of related data—psychological, historical, ethnological, and zoological—shows that exactly the contrary is true: the parents, through their own cannibalistic impulses, elicit in the child specifically cannibalistic impulses, which must not be confused with mere oral-aggressive impulses. Hence it is the specifically cannibalistic impulses of children that are to be interpreted as reactive, *counter*cannibalistic, manifestations. I am deliberately using the term "children," as distinct from "infants," since the infant is incapable both of thinking in conceptual terms and of engaging in fantasizing that has specifically cannibalistic connotations, just as an animal is incapable of committing *incest,* in the human sense of the term (chap. 16).

2. Second, I shall examine the singular lack of psychoanalytic interest[1] in the problem of the cannibalistic impulses of adults and a fortiori of those of the adult qua parent. I shall do so in order to show that the systematic refusal to take this important problem into account is not an accident and that it must be viewed as the result of both psychologically and culturally determined scotomizations.

PARENTAL VS. FILIAL CANNIBALISTIC IMPULSES AND ACTS

In an earlier paper (1953b), I showed that the so-called counter-oedipal attitudes of parents are actually prior to the oedipal attitudes of children and serve, in fact, as triggering mechanisms for the latter.

Here I seek to demonstrate that the allegedly countercannibalistic impulses of parents are prior to the reactive and therefore genuinely countercannibalistic impulses of the child. In essence, my argument is based on an analysis of the unconscious reciprocal relationship between the proverbial, characteristic, and *real* oral cravings of pregnant women and those *imputed* to the infant, and especially to the unborn and to the aborted or murdered neonate. The word "imputed" is of crucial importance, since, in the case of unborn or dead children, one can be dealing only with gratuitously *imputed* cravings.

The analysis of such impulses, gratuitously and arbitrarily imputed to the fetus or to dead babies, which cannot possibly have a realistic basis, brings out well the unconscious attitudes of the adult both toward the living child's *real* oral cravings and aggressivity and toward the adult's own oral needs, which he projects upon the infant. He will even go so far as to *exploit* the real and intense oral cravings felt by the infant by suitably distorting and reinterpreting them for the purpose of masking his own neurotic reactions to such infantile cravings. This maneuver strikingly resembles that of certain neurotics who, during their analysis, systematically appeal to (*their* conception of) reality in order to justify and to rationalize their neurotic attitudes. Thus, an American Indian woman analysand responded to my efforts to make her gain some insight into her provocatively hostile behavior by blaming all her setbacks on racial discrimination, which, according to her, was the sole cause of all her misfortunes (chap. 15).

The quite real oral (alimentary) cravings of pregnant women are part and parcel of the folklore of pregnancy. Two examples, chosen at random, will show this.

If an unmarried Swahili girl suddenly develops unusual cravings for certain foods (malacia), her parents promptly subject her to a physical examination to ascertain whether or not she is pregnant. The fact that such girls also tend to take an intense dislike to some young man or woman living in the same house underscores the aggressive components underlying the pregnant woman's food cravings during pregnancy (Velten 1903).

Hawaiians believe that after the first few months of pregnancy women experience a strong craving—*hookaukau*—for some special food, such as certain kinds of seafood or fruit. Thus, Kekuipoiwa, while pregnant with the future King Kamehameha the Great, craved to eat the eyes of the man-eating *nihui* shark, which were obtained for her at great risk. Thereupon, the *kahuna* (medicine man, diviner) predicted that she would give birth to a chief whose eyes would flash with a tiger shark's anger and who would have the power of the *nihui* shark. This prophecy frightened the chiefs so much that they conspired to kill this dangerous child.[2] In commenting on this incident, our ethnological authority specifies that it is not the food eaten by the mother that affects the character of the unborn child; rather, it is the inborn nature of the fetus that induces special food cravings in the mother (Handy 1934). In other words, the *responsibility* for the mother's violent oral cravings is *attributed* to the unborn child. Moreover, these Hawaiian data resemble the Swahili data in stressing the hostile, even "man-eating," character of the oral cravings of at least one mother, who is linked with the man-eating shark *nihui*.

ORAL CRAVINGS IMPUTED TO DEAD INFANTS

Two examples, chosen among many, suffice to illustrate this fantasy.

A Hawaiian woman—apparently in a state of advanced pregnancy—walked to a distant village to visit relatives. While en route, she miscarried a fetus sufficiently developed for her to determine that it was a male. She wrapped the fetus in her undergarment and placed it under some convolvulus vines, intending to pick it up after the visit and take it home to her husband. She then calmly went on and visited her relatives, as planned. While walking back to her own village, accompanied by her brother, she looked in vain for the bundle where she had left it. It had disappeared. A few weeks later, while she was fishing, her nipple was seized by a small shark, who began to nurse at her breast. The fact that the markings of this shark resembled those of the undergarment in which she had wrapped the fetus made her realize that the sea gods had taken the fetus and transformed it into this shark, which many Hawaiians subsequently saw at a certain spot near the shore. Similar stories are told by other Hawaiians (Pukui 1934).

This narrative stands in need of comment. The fact that a woman in an advanced state of pregnancy—as one may judge from the state of development of the fetus—took such a long walk for a very trivial reason and reacted so casually—not to say callously—to her miscarriage, suggests that one is dealing here with a pseudo-miscarriage. In other words, this woman's long walk suggests a—perhaps only preconscious—intention to induce an abortion by means of overexertion. It is true, of course, that the Hawaiian data surveyed in connection with my study of abortion among primitives (1955b [rev.

ed., 1976c]) did not include overexertion as a means of inducing abortion. This, however, is almost certainly a fortuitous omission, for abortion was quite common in Hawaii, and it is unlikely that the very widespread technique of overexertion was not practiced there.[3] Data on abortion for most primitive tribes are, moreover, extremely sketchy and fragmentary. In brief, in this case the tenuous motivation of a strenuous walk in a state of advanced pregnancy, taken in conjunction with the mother's casual attitude, would seem to suggest either an intentional abortion or one induced "accidentally on purpose." What is certain is that this miscarriage, whether actively intended or passively endured, was the organizing focus of an abortion fantasy.

If an Aleut girl kills her illegitimate baby, its ghost will haunt the village every night in the shape of a *k'dah* bird, which can be heard crying. Since this haunting can produce major disasters, it is necessary to put an end to it. The murderess therefore exposes her breasts, so as to lure the bird to them. The bird is then captured and ripped apart. This ends the haunting (Veniaminov 1840).

The data just presented indicate that intense oral cravings are commonly imputed even to dead infants and that the reincarnation of the infant as a nonhuman creature endowed with evil powers is viewed as the actualization of these cravings; this is true both of the man-eating shark of the Hawaiians and of the disaster-causing *k'dah* bird of the Aleuts.

Discussion

The beliefs just described have no bearing on the actual oral cravings of real infants. They simply reflect the nightmarish and revengeful quality that adults *impute* to the *genuine* oral cravings of children, and they demonstrate once more—if that is necessary—how neurotically unrealistic many of the ideas adults have about children really are (Devereux 1956a). These beliefs, which are no more than the projection of adult needs on the child, show only what adults (apparently) *need* to believe about children. According to Freud (1912b, 1915), the instincts become monstrous only as a result of repression; from this one may conclude that, though it is permissible to visualize the infant as a hungry wolf cub, it is not permissible to visualize him as a psychotic werewolf. The infant who bites the nipple does not know it is *human* flesh, and his bites do not suffice to prove that he dreams in the cradle of feasting on corpses at Dracula's wedding with a vampire. The refusal to call the baby a crazy werewolf does not imply that he is therefore a cherub. I have shown elsewhere (1968a) that both conceptions of the infant are self-serving adult fantasies. A baby is neither angel nor devil; he is simply a baby. It has been claimed at times that the analysis of certain depressives and alcoholics proves that cannibalistic fantasies go back to the oral period. I will criticize this theory for failing to differentiate between facts, on the one hand, and the (inherently unprovable) reconstructions of *certain* analysts and the retroactive fantasies of *certain* patients, on the other hand. For my part, I refuse to participate in this kind of intellectual acrobatics, because our understanding of the early childhood psyche is, in general, no more than a series of more or less plausible hypotheses.

I shall now scrutinize some aspects of the oral cravings of pregnant and parturient females, both animal and human. It is a well-known fact that cravings for certain specific foods may be mobilized by what Cannon called "the wisdom of the body" (1939). Thus, when rats who have been experimentally deprived of some important nutritional element are presented with a variety of foods, only one of which contains the needed substance, they will select that particular food. Similarly, zoologists hold that the female animal that has just given birth to her young devours the placenta and the cord because they contain certain active substances that help her body achieve the hormonal shift from the pregnant to the lactating state. Sometimes the craving to devour the placenta and the cord can even lead to the devouring of the young. Lorenz (1954) describes the sucking jaw-and-lip movements the bitch makes when she is cleaning up her newborn puppies' navels. Sometimes this sucking becomes so intense that it culminates in her devouring the puppy, the first bite being taken from the puppy's navel. The eating of the afterbirth as a therapeutic measure is also reported from some of the most backward tribes of eastern Siberia (Devereux 1955b; Ploss, Bartels, and Bartels, 1927).

The impulse to eat the afterbirth—and possibly even the baby— is also quite strong in the human species, though this impulse is culturally implemented only in the form of a projection and/or reaction formation. Thus, in many primitive groups elaborate precautions are taken to hide and otherwise safeguard the afterbirth and the cord from scavenger animals.

A more explicit and culturally implemented defense against maternal cannibalistic impulses is the taboo that requires the Mohave mother not to eat any meat whatsoever during the postpartum period (Devereux 1949b). Elsewhere, maternal or parental cannibalistic impulses are only vicariously implemented. In New Guinea, every woman of a certain tribe must take her firstborn baby to the ravine where the farrowing sows are kept and must then throw it to the sows, who promptly devour it. The woman then takes one of the farrows belonging to the sow who first attacked her baby and nurses it at her own breast (Dupeyrat 1954). A less obvious example is the sacrifice of children to Moloch: the infants were thrust into the *maw* of this bronze deity.

Still more relevant is the actual eating of one's children or the marketing of their flesh during medieval famines and even during the great postrevolutionary famine in Russia. This formerly occurred also in Java, where the compulsory cultivation of cash crops repeatedly caused disastrous famines (Multatuli 1868). In at least two Australian tribes—the Ngali and the Yumu (Róheim 1932)—the women even abort—or are made to abort—in times of famine in order to feed the rest of the family. In another Australian tribe (Howitt 1904) the smallest baby was killed by knocking its head against the shoulder of an older sibling; its flesh was used to feed the older siblings and also the rest of the starving family. In brief, in times of famine, child cannibalism was quite common among primitive Australians; it was deemed preferable to kill a useless baby than a useful dingo hunting dog. The peculiar technique of killing the baby by knocking its head against its sibling's shoulder was probably intended to exonerate its parents. It would, however, be quite erroneous to suppose that Australian aborigines do not love their children. So great an expert on Australia as the late Géza Róheim once cited a case to me—whether from a published source or from personal observation I can no longer recall—in which a small child with whom his parents had been affectionately playing during the day was killed and cooked for dinner. The familiar parental endearment, "I love you so much I could eat you," is almost an echo of this incident. I shall return to this matter shortly.

Thus, the eating of children in times of food shortage is far from rare. By contrast—and this is what is most significant—hungry children do not seem to kill their parents in order to eat them. In fact, I have never heard of such a case in either primitive or modern society.

So far I have dealt chiefly with child cannibalism motivated by famine. As regards ritual cannibalism, the situation is somewhat different, for here, although the ritual cannibalization of children by their parents and by the ritual associates of the parents is quite common—for example in connection with the *poro,* or with the leopard-men rites of West Africa (Beatty 1915), or in the cult of Zeus Lycaeus (Cook 1914)—in certain instances it is also deemed an act of piety for children to eat parents who die of natural causes (Herodotus 3. 38).

127

Among many Algonquian tribes of Canada, a partly economically and partly neutrotically motivated form of cannibalism is practiced by those experiencing an attack of the *windigo* illness. Teicher's monograph (1960), which summarizes everything known on the subject, reports and analyzes seventy *know*n cases. The patient who becomes a *windigo* experiences intense cannibalistic cravings, often directed at his own children. Sometimes, probably to make this urge more ego-syntonic, he hallucinates them as beavers, which are considered a delicacy.[4] When the cannibalistic urge becomes uncontrollable without ceasing to be highly ego-dystonic, the *windigo* either begs to be killed or else flees into the forest, where he will have no opportunity to eat a human being, and especially not one of his own children or kinsmen.

The point I am seeking to make is an extremely simple one, although legislators and psychoanalysts have chosen to ignore it: law and public opinion penalize parricide infinitely more severely than infanticide, as though the impulse to commit parricide were especially strong and therefore needed to be curbed by especially violent means. Statistics, however, tell a very different story: throughout the course of history, infinitely more children have been killed either before or after their birth by their parents than parents have been killed by their children. Child sacrifices, too, are much more common than parent sacrifices. Books on history, ethnology, criminology, comparative religions—and even the daily press—all tell the same story. These are hard facts, which simply cannot be reconciled with the perfectly arbitrary thesis that the cannibalistic impulses of children are not only more intense than those of adults but are also dynamically and genetically prior to the cannibalistic impulses of adults and that, moreover, the children's fantasies of their parents as potential cannibals are groundless. These hard facts cannot be disposed of by the often repeated and untenable thesis that "reality cannot be analyzed," especially when this reality consists of human beliefs and practices. Nor can one circumvent the inescapable conclusions to which these statements lead by insisting that, since everything originates in childhood, adult cannibalistic impulses must also originate in childhood. This is equivalent to reasoning as follows: crawling is instinctual and matures into walking and running and (sometimes) into winning an Olympic race; this "proves" that the infant, in crawling, is *already* dreaming of Olympic victories. Because I disagree with this kind of strictly "culturalist" nonsense, I have been called a heretical "culturalist" psychoanalyst (Coodley 1966; Ekstein 1966). The fallaciousness and speciousness of the argument concerning the childhood origin of adult cannibalistic impulses when used in this context—and it has actually been so used —is easy to discern. Indeed, even though childhood does condition all of man's later development, it is not the *genetic* or *biological* substratum that is responsible for cannibalistic impulses but the subject's personal experience in childhood—in this case, the impact of the adults' cannibalistic impulses on the infant's psyche. Postulating innate "cannibalistic impulses" is a methodologically undesirable multiplication of entities, already objected to by Newton, and is, moreover, incompatible with ordinary biological knowledge. This type of reasoning ("Which came first, the chicken or the egg?") disturbingly resembles the kind of *pseudobiologia phantastica* of which too many examples still survive in certain dark corners of psychoanalytic theory. I shall return to this point later. For the moment it suffices to state a very simple fact: it is never the child but always the parent who says, "I love you so much I could eat you." In Duau, it is the father who takes his little son's penis in his mouth and "tenderly" pretends that he will swallow it (Róheim 1932). This, too, is a fact hard to dispose of by appeals to traditional "theory." Lagrange's famous statement, "Nature is not concerned over the analytical[5] difficulties with which it confronts the scientist," might profitably be taken to heart by psychoanalysts. Freud teaches the same lesson when he insists—although in a most unfortunate context[6]— that he has always bent his back before facts.

The real problem confronting one, therefore, is not so much to acquire an objective understanding of the child's genuine (though reactive) cannibalistic impulses (impulses whose existence no one would deny) as to explore the reason why adults have the need—at once conscious and unconscious—to derive their own child-directed cannibalistic impulses from the allegedly innate cannibalistic urges of the child, which the adults impute to him, both gratuitously and uncontrollably. On this point, the experts are no more lucid than laymen.

I would question, first of all, the *nightmarish quality* customarily attributed to the child's oral cravings, since one obviously can postulate the existence of cannibalistic impulses in the child without necessarily being obliged to view the child's entire psyche—as Melanie Klein and some of her followers do—as a self-perpetuating chamber of horrors. The extremeness of these imputed characteristics makes them a priori suspect; here, if anywhere, Shakespeare's dictum about protesting too much is applicable. Moreover, such a conception of the infantile psyche is altogether incompatible with the Hartmann-Kris-Loewenstein theory (1947) of the infantile ego. The least one can say of a conception of the child's psyche that justifies much parental sadism is that it is "self-serving," just as an eighteenth-century theory that made animals into mere machines, "only behaving as though they felt pain but actually feeling none," was "self-serving" in that it authorized and justified a great deal of callousness toward animals.

The failure to recognize specifically adult forms of cannibalism is a second obstacle to insight into the real (derivative) nature of infantile cannibalistic—as distinct from spontaneous oral—impulses (such as the desire to bite). If one compulsively starts from the theory that "everything begins in childhood, since man was a child before he became an adult," one is forced to disregard such specifically adult forms of "cannibalism" as that of the bitch or sow who eats her young, to say nothing of the fact that such complex and highly structured behavior *could* not be manifested in a fully developed form in the very young, for small puppies or piglets do not have young which they could eat; moreover, they do not, in fact, eat their mother, nor do they apparently try to do so.

Given the many studies devoted to infantile cannibalistic impulses, the widespread tendency to avoid any discussion of parental cannibalism clearly suggests that what is involved here is a scotoma. In spite of the great rarity of actual cases, much is written about the child's wish to castrate his father, but very little has been written about the parent's wish to castrate his son. There are, at most, passing references to threats to castrate masturbating children. Yet the actual castration of the child by the father, or at the instigation of the father, is a fairly common occurrence. In both China and the Near East, certain parents sold their children to be made into eunuchs. In Byzantium, eminent families often had their sons castrated, in some cases to insure that they would become high court officials and in others to save their lives, since many emperors—always afraid of being dethroned—sought to rid themselves of the scions of aristocratic families. It can be noted, further, that castrating boys to preserve their soprano voices became forbidden less than two hundred years ago.

This list could, moreover, be considerably extended if one included in its scope the castration of children by parent substitutes. States, leaders, and kings alike have assumed the right to castrate children. In Kansas, the actual castration (not simply the sterilization) of feebleminded children was routinely performed in some state institutions as late as 1949. The principle of castrating the feebleminded was even vehemently defended by Hawke (1950) in the official organ of the Kansas Medical Society. By contrast, the only instance known to me in which a father was castrated by his son was reported by Herodotus (8. 105–6): Hermotimus was captured as a boy and sold to Panionius, a merchant of eunuchs, who castrated him. Having become Xerxes' favorite eunuch, Hermotimus pretended to be grateful to Panionius and invited him to visit him with his family. When all the family was in his power, he forced Panionius to castrate his own sons and the sons to castrate their father.

There is a striking parallel to be drawn between the psychoanalysts' lack of interest in parental castrative impulses—no systematic discussion of this point having ever been undertaken—and their similar lack of interest in parental cannibalistic impulses.

THE CHILD AS PARASITE

The conception of the child as one who devours his parents can be readily documented. The Papuans of Geelvink Bay perform many abortions, claiming that children destroy their parents (Rosenberg 1875). Similarly, the Mohave Indians hold that after a certain degree of intrauterine development is reached, the fetus feeds on the semen that the mother's sex partner injects into her vagina (Devereux 1948a). The concept of the fetus as a malignant tumor in its mother's womb exists even among certain doctors. Thus a physician, commenting, in the course of a serious discussion, on a vulgar ditty in which the fetus is referred to as a "tumor," assured me that "medically speaking" the similarity between an embryo and a tumor is rather close. Perhaps the most sublimated fantasy of infantile cannibalism is the tenacious myth of the pelican father, who supposedly feeds his brood by tearing open his own breast, though in reality he feeds his young with partly ingested food stored in a sac under its beak. It is, I think, no coincidence that the favorite poem of a young psychiatrist who had recently become a father was the famous French poem about this bit of "unnatural history." In fact, though he spoke French rather poorly, this young colleague took the trouble to learn this poem by heart and recited it in and out of season.

In reality, among most animals and birds who carry food to their young in their beaks or mouths, there occurs a *temporary inhibition of the swallowing reflex.*[7] This inhibition may conceivably represent a greater strain for the adult animal or bird than does the inhibition of the hand-to-mouth reflex in man or the inhibition of the claw-to-beak reflex in predatory birds, who carry the prey to their young in their claws.

Certain parents do sometimes deprive themselves orally for the sake of their children. Among the poor this deprivation is largely quantitative, except that, in times of real scarcity, it is the breadwinner who has the right to the lion's share, in order to be able to keep on working. Among the richer classes the deprivation is usually qualitative. Tidbits (from "teat") are usually reserved for the children.

Case 1.—An analysand reported that his well-to-do parents always reserved the tidbits for the children. One day, however, when the analysand protested against some parental exaction and contrasted the freedom of his friend X with his mother's oppressive control, the mother replied: "In this house you get the tidbits. The same is not true in your friend's home. I know for a fact that one day your friend X was eating a raisin pudding and set the raisins aside, saving them all for the last mouthful. His mother let him do it, but when he was ready, at last, to eat his hoard of raisins, she simply reached over and took them for herself. We do not behave that way toward you. Therefore we are entitled to absolute obedience." This remark casts a flood of light on at least one of the reasons why parents find it advantageous to exaggerate the oral needs of their children—even of those in the latency period. It is hardly necessary to add that this man's analysis disclosed that the obedience demanded by his parents practically required *flexibilitas cerea* and amounted to a total "devouring" of the child's distinctive identity.

In brief, the oral self-denial of the parents to gratify the oral needs of the child is a mechanism whose animal prototype is the inhibition of the swallowing reflex.[8] It is as though the parents reinterpret what is simply a reflex mechanism for them as a kind of infantile oral aggression and as clear evidence of cannibalistic impulses, which they therefore feel to be characteristic of children's mentality; the pelican myth could be explained in this manner.

Speaking tentatively, one might suggest that the adult's *tendency* to correlate the feeding of children by their parents with the (alleged) cannibalistic impulses of children may be linked with a fairly complicated mechanism observable in the parturient bitch. After the bitch has eaten the placenta and a certain (sufficient but not excessive) length of the cord and has licked the puppy clean, an inhibition of her swallowing reflex occurs. Without the inhibition of this reflex, she would eat the puppy itself. However, the reflex is not inhibited until the placenta and the cord have been swallowed. Indeed, when Lorenz (1954) gave a bitch who had just finished cleaning up her litter another newborn puppy, whose navel cord had already been removed, he noted that the bitch sought to bite off and eat the (nonexistent) cord and that, in doing so, she bit the puppy's navel area and would actually have devoured the puppy itself had Lorenz not stopped her. One may wonder, then, whether the inhibition of the swallowing reflex in the animal who is bringing food to its young may possibly be an extension of the inhibition of that reflex that occurs when the cleansing of the newborn puppy has been completed.[9]

Degrees of "Cannibalism" in Babies

A curious cultural variation on the theme of cannibal babies is the belief that some babies are more cannibalistically inclined than others. According to a very ancient Hungarian folk belief, which demonstrably goes back to the time when the Hungarians still lived in Asia, shamans are born with teeth and bite their mothers' nipples (Róheim 1950). Exactly the same belief is found among the Mohave Indians (Devereux 1947), who also believe that, if a pregnant woman's husband kills a snake, the child's head will resemble that of a snake and its bite will be poisonous.[10] The mothers therefore do not nurse such babies but—sometimes successfully—try to keep them alive by feeding them mush (Devereux 1961a). In certain other tribes the baby's cannibalistic impulses are believed to be directed chiefly at other babies (sibling rivalry).

Case 2.—An American Indian woman patient, possessing the equivalent of a college degree, made the following statement in the course of her analysis: "When I was a child, my favorite story was an old Indian tale about a cannibal baby. This baby would sneak away from its cradleboard at night and devour other babies, returning to its cradle at dawn with its mouth smeared with blood and with bits of baby flesh caught between its teeth. I used to feel so sorry for this cannibal baby; it must have felt very uncomfortable with bits of flesh caught between its teeth! . . . I wished I could make it more comfortable by picking its teeth [clean]."[11] The tribe to which this woman belonged was characterized by an especially high degree of both sibling rivalry and aggressive adult competitiveness.

The identification of this adult woman with the mythical cannibal baby was even more far-reaching than the above data indicate. Angry because she had been weaned quite early,[12] not only by her own tribe's standards but even by modern Western standards, she developed early in life a marked aversion to milk and boasted of having drunk coffee from the time she was six months old. She would also wax almost lyrical about the "wonderful smooth, bland taste of Delaware Punch" (a not very popular—but blood-red—soft drink). Finally, she ferociously envied men because, as she saw it, they could gain access to a woman's breast under the pretense of cohabiting with her (see also chap. 16).

This case provides some interesting clues into the nature of childhood cannibalistic impulses. They indicate them to be:

1. Elicited by severe oral frustration at an early age
2. Reinforced by elements of sibling rivalry, especially if the formerly frustrated child is obliged to watch the nursing of younger siblings
3. Structured into fantasies by means of stories, such as the tale of the cannibal baby. The structuring of this type of fantasy can, of course, be furthered also by the type of cannibalistically worded tenderness ("I could eat you") found in Europe and America or by the Duau-type paternal "caress" mentioned above, or, simply, by behaving toward the child in a manner having oral-cannibalistic connotations.

Sometimes the parents themselves suggest cannibalistic behavior to their children—for instance, when they say that certain cookies look like human beings or animals and that it will *therefore* be *fun* to eat them. Boehm (1935) is mistaken in thinking that this proves infantile cannibalistic impulses; the facts he cites prove precisely the opposite.

Certain overt or implicit castration threats are also often "cannibalistically worded": "The cat will take your penis,"[13] "A bird will peck at your penis," and so forth. Equally significant is the fact that among many Siberian tribes both reindeer and dogs are castrated by biting off their testicles (Bogoras 1904–9). In certain parts of Hungary young rams are castrated in the same way (Rohan-Csermák 1949).

COUNTERCANNIBALISTIC IMPULSES

The rare allusions in psychoanalytic literature[14] to the cannibalistic impulses of adults never, or hardly ever, state in so many words that parental cannibalistic impulses are "reactive" and therefore "countercannibalistic." Yet that is precisely what they seem to imply. Be that as it may, no one has so far made the essential point that parental cannibalistic impulses toward children are *primary*, whereas the corresponding impulses and fantasies of children are reactive and should therefore be viewed as countercannibalistic. This conclusion seems inevitable in the light of the aforementioned data, selected from masses of evidence,[15] which supporters of the theory of infantile cannibalism refuse to take into cognizance. It is hard to escape these simple facts. Though some have tried to do just that, their theory, which presupposes that, since all psychic phenomena start in childhood, cannibalistic impulses must *also* start there, is based on a *pseudobiologia phantastica* and leaves unsolved the following two crucial problems.

1. Reactive fantasies, too, can start in childhood. Therefore, the presence of infantile cannibalistic fantasies does not suffice to prove that they are innate, for they can just as well be—and, in fact, are—reactive and "learned."

2. The cannibalistic-behavior pattern is too complex and requires too high a degree of conceptualization to come into being in early childhood, that is, before the child knows the difference between animate and inanimate, let alone the difference between human beings and animals.[16]

Indeed, in order to be a cannibal, one must first be able to differentiate between human and animal flesh, just as, in order to be a vegetarian, one must be able to differentiate between meat and vegetables. This point, of capital importance, can be illustrated by an example drawn from mythology. Thyestes, tricked by Atreus into eating the flesh of his children, was engaging in cannibalism only in the crudest and narrowest descriptive sense of the word. Seen psychoanalytically, he simply *ate meat* for dinner. And if it be speciously argued that Thyestes *knew unconsciously* that it was his own children's flesh, this also means that his unconscious awareness presupposed a conscious awareness, not only of the difference between meat and human flesh, but also the difference between the flesh of his own children and that of other human beings. In the sense here defined, Thyestes did not practice cannibalism and, even less, familial endocannibalism.

A few words should now be said about the place of biological facts in psychoanalytic reasoning. It would be foolish to deny the psychological importance of man's biological substratum. It is equally senseless, however, to forget that psychoanalysis is quite specifically a strictly human psychology. In fact, it is the only psychology that applies to man as a human being. This implies that, in psychoanalytic discourse, physiological and zoological data can be used only for the purpose of characterizing or defining the terrain on which, and the raw material by means of which, certain dynamic processes characteristic *only* of the human psyche unfold themselves.

This, too, was clearly stated by Freud, in the memorable passage of *Totem and Taboo* (1912–13) in which he correlates the genesis of the Oedipus complex with the coming-into-being, or at least with the differentiation, of man as a culture-creating being, distinct from the animals. The fact that Freud then proceeded to provide, as an afterthought, a gratuitous "biological" and "paleopsychological" explanation for all this—although the facts, illuminated by his flash of genius, spoke so clearly that no further explanation was needed—is best forgotten and is certainly not to be imitated by proposing

135

paleopsychological speculations, which all truly scientific psycho-analysis must repudiate.

SUMMARY

1. There exists a reciprocal relationship between the cannibalistic impulses of parents and those of children.

2. The available facts lend no support to the (implicit) assumption of official science that the cannibalistic impulses of children are primary while those of parents are secondary or reactive.

3. On the contrary, massive data prove that the child's specifically cannibalistic impulses are induced by, and therefore epiphenomenal to, parental cannibalistic impulses. Once established, the cannibalistic impulses of the child can, however, enter into a relationship with the preexisting cannibalistic impulses of the parents, thus creating a relationship of mutual induction.

4. The bypassing of parental cannibalistic impulses in psychoanalytic literature suggests the presence of massive resistances against this insight—even more massive, perhaps, than those that account for the fact that the child's Oedipus complex was discovered long before the so-called *counteroedipal* complex of the parents, and this *despite* the fact that one of Freud's first discoveries was the role of (real or imaginary) parental seduction. Hence, any attempt to clarify the real sources of cannibalistic fantasies and impulses must include an analysis of the resistances and scotomata which impede the perceiving and understanding of these phenomena.

5. There is a striking discrepancy between the large amount that is known of the neurotic attitudes of children toward adults and the little that is known of the neurotic attitudes of adults toward children (Devereux 1968a), which can assume the form of self-exonerating fantasies (Freud 1925; Devereux 1951a) about the nature of children, disguised as scientific discourse. As a result, the bilaterality and reciprocity of adult-child relationships and the attitudes that engender them have been quite systematically underestimated and even dodged. Notable exceptions are Ferenczi's memorable paper on the confusion of tongues between children and adults (1955) and also certain of Spitz's papers on "hospitalism" and other subjects (1935, 1945, 1946a, 1946b, 1949). These papers blazed a new trail because, unlike many others, their authors did not assume a priori that in the interaction between child and adult it is the child only who speaks the "jabberwocky" of the primary process and the unconscious (chap. 4).

6. My refusal to view the infant as a rabid werewolf does not mean that I therefore view him as a cherub. I have shown elsewhere

(1956a) that both these conceptions of the infant are self-serving adult fantasies. A baby is neither angel nor devil—it is simply a baby. It is incumbent upon us, as adults, to understand the baby and accept it for what it is.

In conclusion, I propose to cite a case that highlights both the strength of the adult's pedophagic (child-eating) impulse and the stubbornness with which even the enlightened scientist denies its existence. I shall cite an absurd *lapsus* I myself committed shortly after writing not only this study but a book that was entirely concerned with the way the countertransference and the preconceptions of the scientist influence scientific work (Devereux 1967c).

The text of Aeschylus's *Agamemnon*, verses 1215 and following, is perfectly clear: Cassandra is speaking of children devoured by their father—by Thyestes. *Nonetheless,* I claimed—mistakenly— that Cassandra was referring to Agamemnon's children, who were indeed seriously endangered but quite alive (Devereux 1967d). I realized my error only when Professor E. R. Dodds brought it to my attention.

If this inexcusable *lapsus,* committed just when I was warning my fellow psychoanalysts against exactly this kind of error, does not suffice to prove both the reality of the pedophagic impulse and the scientist's refusal to acknowledge it, nothing will. The essence of all research that has man as its subject is the scientist's dogged struggle against his own blindness.

6

Retaliatory Homosexual Triumph over the Father: A Clinical Note on the Counteroedipal Sources of the Oedipus Complex (1960)

Certain neglected aspects of the Oedipus myth prompted me some years ago (Devereux 1953b) to suggest that the oedipal fantasy involves not only the slaying of the father and cohabitation with the mother but also—quite specifically—a homosexual triumph over the feminized father. I propose here to document this latter aspect of the oedipal fantasy by means of a rather thinly disguised dream of the David and Goliath type, in which, despite an inversion of affect in the critical scene, the homosexual triumph is clearly present.

The clinical material about to be presented was obtained from a talented young artist, born and raised in a French-speaking tropical country, after several months of twice-a-week face-to-face therapy. He had sought treatment for sexual difficulties, and specifically for a potency disturbance, which had appeared when he first fell in love with his second cousin, who was also the first woman he had ever loved. His trouble disappeared rapidly after he realized that it was due to oedipal anxieties and to his fear of becoming emotionally unfaithful to his mother.

THE DREAM

I am in a bathtub with a male cousin of my own age; we are engaged in some kind of physical contest with some older and stronger men, one of whom is my older cousin. Somehow I have the feeling that the cousin in the bathtub and I are not our present age but much younger; we are boys struggling against adults and must defend the bathtub against them. I reach down, grasp my older cousin, who is one of the assailants, by the ankles,[1] and lift him up with a violent jerk, which causes him to fall on his back outside the bathtub. He is lying on his back, completely immobile. I emerge from the bath-tub and bend over him. I am worried, thinking I may have killed him.

Associations

Before discussing the patient's associations, I must mention that, despite the excellent education this young artist had enjoyed, his dreams were of a rather transparent type, of the kind one finds among primitives and children and often among certain hysterics (Devereux 1951a). While the physical setting of his dreams was drawn from his own civilized background—steamships, physicians, bathtubs, and automobiles—and the dream situations were such as one commonly finds in the real lives of the educated classes of this young man's own country (which was still, on the whole, quite back-ward), as well as in Europe and America, the structure and the plot of his dreams were "primitive," in that wishes and fears were pre-sented in them in an almost undisguised form. Moreover, like some of my American Indian patients (Devereux 1949a, 1951a, 1951f, and chap. 15), this young man had little trouble in producing significant associations to his dreams quite rapidly and in understanding their latent content with a minimum of help from me. I would cite in this connection Róheim's view (1933) that the primitive's superego (dream censor) is patchy and full of gaps and also the ethnological truism that the primitive differentiates less categorically between reality and dream than members of Western civilization do. Also, though Kroeber (1952) is correct in stating that the evolution of civilizations is, generally speaking, in the direction of greater real-ism, I think it helpful to specify that so-called advanced cultures, which differentiate sharply between reality and fantasy on the *logi-cal* level, continue *in practice* to take collective fantasies for reality and sometimes to take reality for fantasy (chap. 10).

a) The *attacked and seemingly killed cousin* had been the object of some clearly sadistic-castrative roughhousing with the patient at a time when the patient was still very young—in the late latency period—and the cousin was a young adolescent. One day, after the boys had been swimming in the nude in their private swimming pool and were standing near the water, the patient suddenly grabbed his cousin's penis—which, for some reason, had become erect—and began to run around the pool, dragging his older victim behind him. Since the patient had a firm hold on his cousin's penis, it was impos-sible for the latter to defend himself effectively without hurting him-self; he had to trot behind his smaller assailant for quite some time before the latter agreed to release him.

b) The *bathtub* led to two associations. The patient compared it to the pool near which the sadistic scene just described had taken place. He then remembered that, when he was swimming in, or playing near, that pool in childhood, he sometimes peeped through a crevice into the dressing cabin to look at the enormous nude buttocks of one of his family's native woman servants. Throughout his childhood this woman's huge buttocks had fascinated and excited him so much that he sometimes refused to be *bathed* until bribed by being shown the large buttocks of this female servant. When I asked him whether the shape of the bathtub made him think of anything, he immediately replied that it made him think of the female genitalia. At that juncture I pointed out to him the role played by the day's residue in the formation of the bathtub image: his physician had, in fact, just instructed him to take hot sitz baths as treatment for a nonspecific urethritis and mild chronic prostatitis—sitz baths that he was unable to take, since he had only a shower in his small apartment. It should be added that, some weeks earlier, this shower had been the scene of a violent and (unusually) completely successful lovemaking between the patient and his second cousin, whom he planned to marry as soon as possible and subsequently did marry.

c) The *big attacking the small*. When this aspect of the situation was pointed out to him, the patient spontaneously replied that the elder cousin obviously represented his father—a gross, huge, and fat man—attacking him while he was with—inside—his mother. This association is explained by the highly seductive behavior of the mother, who had made her son an ally against his father and an accomplice in her more or less open liaison with another man. She demanded, moreover, to be made the confidante of her son's quite promiscuous adolescent sexual adventures. In fact, in various subtle ways, the mother maneuvered her son into the position of a young gigolo, partly supported by money that she diverted to that purpose without the father's knowledge. As for the theme of paternal aggression, which came up in connection with the theme of the *big attacking the small* in the bathtub, it had already inspired earlier and more explicit dreams (and a subsequent dream as well; see Devereux 1965c [1978a, chap. 7]) and during his childhood had provided the patient with material for fantasmatic panics in a waking state.

When the patient wondered why, in this dream, he had transformed his father into the cousin, I reminded him that, somewhat earlier in the hour, he himself had stressed that he had always refused to call his uncles and aunts "uncle" and "aunt" but had instead insisted, to the great scandal of his conservative and authoritarian family, on calling them by their given names, as though they were cousins rather than uncles and aunts: merging the generations instead of keeping them apart. For technical reasons I made no reference to the fact that, in treating him like a lover, his mother, too, had minimized the gap between the generations and that his second-cousin-and-fiancée, when only ten or eleven years old, had been intimately caressed and almost seduced by one of her uncles, who, in so doing, also ignored the gap between the generations. I should mention that this incident had worried the patient a great deal when he found out about it, since he rightly felt that this traumatic experience had been responsible for his fiancée's initial inability to obtain an orgasm.

d) *Throwing a large opponent by grasping his ankles* was readily seen by the patient as a further means of emphasizing the difference in size between the assailant and the attacked, and he spontaneously associated it with his grasping his cousin's penis.

e) The *concern over the possibility that he might have killed the cousin* was presented in a spirit of self-justification by the patient: as proof that he had not *meant* to kill his assailant. When I pointed out to him that he had no "rational" reason for assuming that a mere fall would kill his assailant and that the *fear* that he might have killed him therefore meant that he had actually *wished* to kill him and felt conscience-stricken about it only afterward, the patient spoke angrily of earlier aggressions this cousin had committed. In fact, he suddenly held up one of his hands and pointed to a scar on his palm—evidence that, before the penis-pulling episode, he had been wounded by this older cousin with a nail in the course of another bit of roughhousing. This wounding of his palm with a metal nail led to associations to a Cocteau film in which someone tries to drive the flat head, rather than the point, of a nail into wood—a scene that the patient quite spontaneously related to homosexual impulses. (The patient's further associations to this topic are not germane to the present discussion.) In brief, the patient showed himself to be as incapable as a primitive of differentiating between reality and dream, since he cited an act of aggression committed in *real* life as justification for the *dream* slaying of his cousin.

f) The *position of the victim*. Since the patient was an artist, highly sensitive to movement and positions,[2] I asked him to describe carefully the position of the figure on the ground that he was examining so solicitously. With a marked expression of surprise on his face, he stated that the seemingly dead cousin was lying on his back, his thighs somewhat spread, *like a woman preparing to be penetrated by a man, and he did not seem to have a penis*. At this point, I reminded the patient of the nail wielded by his cousin, which had inflicted the wound on his palm; of his own spontaneous association to the "homosexual" significance of a nail being driven in head (glans?) first; and of his justification of the dream murder in terms of the real wound. This partial interpretation was readily accepted by the patient.

Interpretation of the Dream

"While you were near (or inside [= bathtub]) your mother, your father attacked you homosexually. You retaliated by killing and feminizing him: he has no penis and lies on his back in the position of a woman about to have sexual intercourse."

The validity of this interpretation was confirmed in the following dream, which the patient reported in the course of the next session.

DREAM

There are very large stools in the toilet. They are alive. I cannot quite explain how I knew that they were alive, but the fact that they were alive was quite clear to me in the dream. Then, again in some manner that I cannot explain, these large stools transferred themselves from the toilet to the washbowl. Also, there were little bits of stool on the floor and—perhaps while transferring themselves from the toilet to the washbowl—the large stools devoured the small stools.

Associations

This dream puzzled the patient so much that his first associations consisted entirely of attempts to clarify its manifest content. Thus he grappled in vain with the problem of how he "knew" that the large stools were alive, with the manner in which they transferred themselves to the washbowl, and so forth. Next he explained that the large stools' devouring the small stools seemed to be a particularly aggressive act. When I suggested that the devouring of small stools by big ones was rather like cannibalism and, specifically, like child cannibalism (chap. 5)[3], the very startled patient promptly declared that this interpretation fitted his own feelings perfectly. He added that the large stools were obviously those of a corpulent adult person; in fact, they were probably the stools of his father, who had a markedly large abdomen.[4] Next, a brief exchange of remarks led him to conclude that the small stools were his own. Asked whether, as a child, he had received enemas, the patient, once more startled, said that he had in fact received many enemas, which he both disliked and dreaded, and he spontaneously added that the small bits of excrement, which the large stools devoured, resembled the small fragments of feces that he used to extrude after being given enemas.

I then suggested a correlation between the enemas and the prostatic massages he had recently received for diagnostic purposes, in order to determine the cause of his recent urethral discharge. At that point the patient suddenly remembered that, when he had had gonorrhea during puberty, his prostate had been massaged several times by his own father, who was a physician.

Paradoxically, many months later, in the course of an attempt to elucidate the causes of his recent and unwarranted bouts of jealousy (Devereux 1965c), the patient suddenly mentioned the positive aspects of his father's personality for the first time. This led him to reconsider his earlier interpretation of the symbolism of the nail that in the Cocteau film was being driven headfirst into wood: "I told you, when I first spoke of this matter, that this way of driving in a nail—which, as I realized, symbolized the penis—seemed to me a kind of 'inversion'—like something 'inverted' and therefore 'homosexual.' Yet the head [glans] of the penis is the real penetrating tip of that organ, so that, at least insofar as the nail represents the penis, it is not an inversion to drive it in 'head' first." It is significant that this remark was made at a time when his jealousy had abated and certain feelings were beginning to come to the surface—positive feelings (untainted by neurotic elements) that he had felt in his childhood toward the father whom, until this point in his therapy, he had so consistently criticized.

Discussion

In relatively early Greek legends, Laius's doom was explicitly correlated with the rape of the child Chrysippus (who is a substitute for Oedipus). Laius then repeated this homosexual aggression on his own son—but at a symbolic level: he pierced Oedipus's ankles [with a nail?]. In retaliation for these two crimes of counteroedipal (Laius complex) homosexual aggression, his son Oedipus slew him, symbolically emasculated him, and triumphed homosexually over him (Devereux 1953b).

In the first dream reported here, the patient—who represents himself in dream as a mere boy—successfully wards off the attempts of his larger and older cousin (= uncle = father) to invade the bathtub (vagina = mother's womb = sitz bath = shower = scene of a highly successful and violent lovemaking with his second cousin, whom he formerly unconsciously equated with his mother). He upsets the assailant by grabbing his ankles (as he had once grabbed his penis): the patient is a little David, triumphantly warding off Goliath's attack. Thereupon the defeated invader seemingly dies and lies on his back, without a penis and in the position of a woman about to be penetrated. The murder, castration (penis-pulling episode), and homosexual triumph are explicitly justified by the patient by skipping—in a characteristically "primitive" manner—from dream to reality and showing the scar of the wound his cousin had once inflicted on him by means of a nail. The homosexual nature of this earlier attack is revealed by the association that "driving a nail in headfirst" has a homosexual meaning.

CONCLUSION

I conclude from the Oedipus myth that a homosexual triumph over the feminized father—an attack justified by the father's earlier homosexual aggressions against the son—is an integral part of the oedipal fantasy. This hypothesis is fully supported by this singularly transparent dream. I conclude, moreover, that the successful resolution of the oedipal ties and conflicts calls for a fantasized homosexual triumph over the father. Both conclusions are fully substantiated by the fact that this dream occurred at a point in therapy where the patient had recovered his sexual potency, even in his relationship with his second cousin and fiancée, though this relationship had originally been impaired by his unconscious tendency to equate his girl cousin with his mother. Finally, for the first time in his life, he proved capable of loving a girl in a mature way, which (culturally) required completion by a sincerely desired marriage.

The immediate reason for the appearance of this dream at this particular time was the disturbing recurrence of the symptoms of a nonspecific urethritis and mild chronic prostatitis—aftermaths of several earlier bouts of gonorrhea. The symbolization of the oedipal situation by means of cousins (= uncles) is overdetermined: it can be associated with the girl cousin's own oedipal experience with an uncle, with the fact that the girl cousin had formerly been equated with the tabooed but seductive mother, and, last but not least, with the fact that the girl cousin's family and the patient's family had an old family feud of considerable bitterness, further complicated by snobbish prejudices related to subtle shades of skin color. The patient's courtship had consequently been bitterly rejected by the girl's family, which ignored him to the point of refusing to return his greetings on the street. At the time this dream was dreamed, the rejection displayed by the cousin's family had become especially offensive, for it was increasingly apparent that the girl would marry the patient no matter how strongly her family opposed the match.

A very interesting aspect of our data remains to be examined: the older cousin's wounding of the patient's hand was avenged both in real life, when the patient grabbed his cousin's penis, and in the dream, when he grabbed his cousin's ankles. Realistically, a small and weak individual may indeed attack a stronger enemy, or beat him off, if he can attack a vulnerable spot of the strong opponent's body (the penis) or take advantage of his short stature to grab his ankles, thus throwing him off balance. In the present case, the attacks on the cousin were viewed as acts of retaliation for the cousin's having pierced (wounded) the patient's hand. They therefore constitute an analogy to the Oedipus myth.

It would take a whole book to discuss adequately each variant of the Greek myth of the traumatizing of Oedipus's ankles[5] and to examine each of the many hypotheses, ancient as well as modern, that have been proposed to explain it. I shall therefore comment here on only a few points.

1. According to Lévi-Strauss (1958), the name of Oedipus's grandfather, Labdacus, can mean "the Lame One," and his father's name, Laius, can mean "the Left-Handed One"; the name Oedipus itself means "the One with Swollen Feet." The first two of these etymological derivations are offered tentatively, because the meaning of many proper names in Greek mythology is still open to debate. Lévi-Strauss calls attention also to some similarities between Oedipus and various individuals mentioned in Pueblo Indian myths who are lame or afflicted with an unsteady gait.

2. Herodotus (5. 92) mentions a girl named Labda ("the Lame One"), a member of the Bacchiadae clan, who were the oligarchs of Corinth. Because of her handicap, she was unable to marry within her own clan and therefore married a man from Petra. Without her handicap, the girl would have married a relative—an uncle, perhaps —as did so many girls of the Greek aristocracy. Things being as they were, an unusual marriage, both hypogamous and exogamous, had to be arranged for her. When the oracle predicted that she would give birth to a son who would wrest power from the Bacchiadae and become tyrant of the city, ten young Bacchiadae were sent to kill the child; but when the child smiled at them, none had the heart to kill him. As predicted, this child, called Cypselus, became tyrant of Corinth.

3. The myth of Jason, while less striking, is also relevant. Jason's father, Aeson, was dethroned by his half-brother, Pelias, who tried to rid himself of his nephew as well, but Jason was saved by his friends. An oracle advised Pelias to distrust a man wearing one sandal only. When Jason returned to his homeland, wearing but one sandal, Pelias sent him off in search of the Golden Fleece, to be rid of him. Eventually Pelias died, not by Jason's hand, but victim of the machinations of Jason's wife, Medea. It is difficult to elucidate

the detail of the single sandal. A man wearing only one sandal is necessarily "lame"; but it is also known that some Greeks, when going into battle, wore but one sandal in order to get a better footing.

4. The technique of attacking a person by grabbing or wounding his ankles or feet is repeatedly mentioned in Greek tradition. The "grabbed foot" can, obviously, be only the ankle.

a) According to one version of the myth, when Hephaestus was defending his mother, Hera, Zeus grabbed him by the foot and cast him out of Olympus (*Iliad* 1. 591 ff.). In another version, Hera herself, perceiving that she had given birth to a crippled child, threw him out of Olympus (*Iliad* 18. 395 ff.).

b) In Sophocles' *Trachiniae* (vs. 777), Heracles, crazed with pain through contact with a tunic smeared with Nessus' blood, grabs Lichas—the messenger who has innocently brought it to him—by the foot and hurls him violently against a rock.

5. There is even an example of reciprocal aggression involving the ankles. In the *Iliad*, Achilles drags Hector's *dead body* behind his chariot, obviously attached by the ankles. But Murray (1960) has reconstructed an older and more barbaric tradition, according to which Hector was dragged *alive* behind his vanquisher's chariot. In support of his thesis, Murray cites Sophocles (*Ajax* 1031), Euripides (*Andromache* 339), and, particularly, Virgil's *Aeneid* 2. 273, where the ankles of the dragged Hector are said to swell up (*tumentia*)—which means that he was still alive while being dragged about. Inversely, Achilles, whose own ankle (regularly mistranslated as "heel") was proverbially vulnerable, was killed by an arrow (= nail) shot through this vulnerable part by Hector's brother, Paris. An ankle for an ankle: the symmetry is remarkable. But the series is not yet ended: Paris was killed by the poisoned arrow of Philoctetes, who for years had had a gangrenous foot, caused either by a serpent's bite or by a poisoned arrow.[6] One can also cite the comic comparison Pseudo-Lucian seems to make, in his *Ocipus* ("swift-footed"), between an athlete (grown gouty) resembling Achilles (but this epithet is never applied to Achilles in the *Iliad*) and Oedipus Swellfoot. These few facts, to which could be added many others of similar import, show that, for elusive reasons, ankles (feet) have a significant though little understood symbolic value in Greek mythological thought.

These examples, thought-provoking in themselves, would be strengthened by a more detailed clinical investigation conducted in conjunction with an exhaustive philological exploration of the problem of the wounded or grabbed ankle in Greek tradition. In the present state of our knowledge, the data merely permit one to consider the symbolic equation ankle = penis to be as "natural" as the symbolic equation snake = penis, which no one would contest.

Methodologically, the present data suggest that the psychoanalytic scrutiny of myths and other ethnological data can alert the clinical psychoanalyst to the existence of intrapsychic patterns and processes that, sooner or later, he will also meet in a therapeutic context. This demonstrates the ultimate clinical value of so-called applied psychoanalysis.

7
Neurotic Crime vs. Criminal Behavior
(1951)

Psychoanalysts are, as a rule, less successful in interpreting and treating criminal behavior than neurotic behavior. This is a striking fact, especially if one is inclined to accept the by now commonplace proposition that neurosis, perversion, and criminality are three possible means by which the organism, in a kind of misguided attempt at self-healing, seeks to alleviate internal tensions and anxieties.

That our understanding of the dynamics of criminal behavior is limited is not due entirely to the fact that few criminals have been psychoanalyzed, although the lack of clinical material on which to base sound theoretical conclusions assuredly impedes a fuller understanding of criminal behavior. It is one of my basic theses that our failure to understand the dynamics of criminal behavior is rooted essentially in an appalling confusion between isolated criminal acts and consistently criminal behavior, which constitute two entirely distinct categories of phenomena. On the clinical-investigative level, psychoanalysts and psychiatrists have collected a considerable amount of material about the dynamics of the isolated illegal acts of otherwise law-abiding citizens; they have then transposed these insights to the habitual criminal in an attempt to interpret "criminality in general." In short, they have engaged in illegitimate extrapolations, applying conclusions drawn from one set of phenomena to the other without ever seeking to prove that the nexus between the two sets is necessary and genuine rather than imputed and spurious.

This confusion is probably rooted in part in the investigators' unconscious scotomata, which are especially restrictive and deceptive because they are disguised as insight and empathy. In seeking to understand the motivational structure of habitual criminality, the investigator responds to the material produced by his subject by an echo emanating from his own unconscious, which, as it happens, is in this case a distorting and fallacious pseudo-echo. Indeed, the region of the investigator's unconscious that "responds" to the behavior of the habitual criminal is a segment of the investigator's id, which the investigator mistakenly assumes to be the counterpart of the motivational structure underlying habitual criminal behavior.

It is the central thesis of this essay that drawing conclusions from the similarities between the occasional or unique illegal act of the "average" normal-neurotic law-abiding citizen and the habitual criminality of the professional criminal leads to a logical impasse because the similarities between these phenomena are in fact superficial, not real. Any attempt to link the two disregards the fact that the *Homo unius criminis* is, in every significant respect, radically different from the habitual criminal.

I hardly need stress that I am not attempting to revive here the appallingly naive and fallacious myth of the "born criminal," which I wholly repudiate.

To be specific:

1. Only a kind of genetic speculation approximating what I have called *"pseudobiologia phantastica"* can cling to the myth of the "born criminal" when there exist in India religious groups (the Thugs) and even whole tribes rightly called "criminal tribes."

2. Only genetic speculations of a Lamarckian type of *pseudobiologia phantastica* can postulate the existence of "innate criminals" when it is known that what in early Anglo-Norman times was a felony (e.g., killing the king's deer), punishable by a brutal mutilation, is today no more than a misdemeanor. Conversely, certain acts that a few centuries ago, or even a few decades ago, were perfectly legal are today severely punished.

At this point it can be objected that I myself affirm that it is of the essence of every neurotic symptom, every perversion, and every criminal act that, *if* it is to alleviate anxiety, it *must be* a culturally deviant or even antisocial form of behavior (chap. 3). I continue to believe in the correctness of this thesis, which assigns a testable clinical significance to the subsidiary statement—which has gradually degenerated into a shibboleth—that neurosis, perversion, and criminality are, within limits, mutually exclusive phenomena. In this strictly limited phenomenological sense, it is indeed legitimate to postulate a nexus between the single criminal act and habitual criminal behavior.

It must be stressed, however, that this genuine phenomenological similarity, and the similarity between the underlying anxiety-controlling functions of these acts, cast no real light on the structural aspects of illegal behavior patterns and do not, a priori, justify depth-psychological attempts to postulate a fundamental similarity between the dynamics of an occasional crime and the dynamics of habitual criminality.

One cannot but be surprised that the confusion between isolated criminal acts and habitual criminality should have persisted with such tenacity in the teeth of crushing empirical evidence to the contrary. It is a matter of common knowledge among penologists that the authors of crimes of violence, and especially the authors of the most "revolting" murders (parricides, infanticides, etc.), are model prisoners and the best of all possible rehabilitation prospects, whereas the habitual pickpocket is almost beyond redemption. Even the law knows this, and certain courts act on this knowledge when, regardless of the nature of his crime (which is often a relatively "minor" one), they sentence the habitual recidivist to life-imprisonment. Thus, psychiatrists are apparently almost alone in stubbornly clinging to the myth of a fundamental similarity between isolated crimes and habitual criminality.

THE UNIQUE CRIMINAL ACT

I propose to consider under the heading "unique criminal act" two types of illegal modes of behavior:

1. Truly unique criminal acts, premeditated or otherwise, as exemplified by the appalling tragedies of ordinary people who impulsively kill an enemy, rape a "date," etc.
2. The occasional and, realistically, often almost meaningless illegal acts of neurotics, as exemplified by kleptomania, etc.— acts so ego-dystonic that they are frequently blanketed by selective amnesia

Individuals who perform either or both of these types of illegal acts are usually neurotics, characterized by a considerable amount of free-floating anxiety, which their armamentarium of neurotic symptoms does not succeed in binding either securely or permanently. These illegal acts may hence be viewed as supplementary emergency symptoms and probably as representing a breakthrough of instinctual forces, which, as Freud convincingly demonstrated, become distorted into monstrous shapes as a result of being repressed (Freud 1912b, 1915).

Thus, what these acts primarily represent are temporary failures of repression. They should therefore be classified as neurotic symptoms rather than criminal acts. This means that their interpretation does not require a minute consideration of character structure. Rather, it calls for interpretations in terms of the subject's intrapsychic economy and the constellation of dynamic checks and balances between his id, ego, and superego.

HABITUAL CRIMINALITY

Habitual criminality—including the "genteel" criminality of those of whom Blackstone said that he who does everything not prohibited by the law is a blackguard—does not represent, primarily, a temporary breakthrough of repressed instinctual forces and is therefore not indicative of an inability to repress or even, perhaps, of an inability to sublimate. Habitual criminality should therefore probably be interpreted as a manifestation of a character structure whose armor (Reich 1945) is predominantly composed of certain defenses that work very well indeed—in fact, that work overtime—in repressing *healthy* instinctual drives. This theory presupposes that *these* defenses happen to be criminal ones.

The occasional neurotic "criminal's" leading presenting symptom is closely related to his basic neurotic problem. Hence, his occasional "criminal acts" are to be viewed as temporary failures of his noncriminal repressive defense mechanisms. These failures are triggered by the momentary inability of the neurotic's *habitual* neurotic symptoms to control the load of tension and anxiety generated by his basic conflict, which may be an oedipal, an aggressive, or any other kind of conflict.

In contradistinction to the neurotic "illegalist," the habitual criminal has (subjectively) "solved" his basic conflict once and for all. His repressions and other defenses, which hold his repudiated instincts and conflicts in a viselike grip, seldom if ever fail him. The entire system of his defenses has been deposited, layer by layer, in his character structure, until both his basic conflicts and his basic impulses are inaccessible to, and concealed from, not only the criminal himself but anyone who does not undertake a well-nigh endless exploratory analysis of him. The criminal behavior of such an individual is not open to the almost "direct interpretation" of hysterical symptoms, which reveal the basic conflict by the very manner in which they disguise it. There is probably an even less obvious relationship between his behavior and the basic conflict underlying it than there is, e.g., between the specific hidden conflict of an obsessive-compulsive and his overt symptoms. One of the greatest of all obstacles to the discovery and interpretation of the criminal's basic conflicts is the blatant obtrusiveness of his symptomatology, which completely obscures, instead of merely failing to reveal, its direct relationship with his basic conflicts.

These considerations are, admittedly, theoretical. But if my hypothesis—that habitual criminals are basically different from occasional neurotic criminals—is used to investigate the problem of "crime," it will be seen to provide the only logical answers.

There is at least one (rather consistently disregarded) bit of psychiatric evidence that reveals with the utmost clarity the real structure of criminal behavior. In an elaborate obsessive-compulsive neurosis each symptom can be "irrelevant" with regard to the basic conflict, though an examination of the overall pattern of the symptoms reveals, from a bird's-eye view, if not the basic conflict itself, then at least the skeletal outline of the psychic process by which a given conflict led to the formation of a large set of symptoms—symptoms that, viewed separately and superficially, seem unrelated to the real nature of the basic conflict.

I refer here to the striking fact that many habitual criminals, seeking to achieve an only "moderately" objectionable aim, will utilize means that lead to the commission of a far more serious crime (e.g., murder during a holdup) or, seeking to avoid detection and escape punishment for a "mere" burglary or misdemeanor, will murder e.g., the policeman who tries to capture them. Sometimes this extreme pattern is repeated even in prison, as witness murders committed by men seeking to escape from a prison to which they have been sentenced for only a few years. This pattern has—mistakenly I think—been interpreted primarily as a self-punitive mechanism, i.e., as a marginal manifestation of the wish for expiation or as a manifestation of outright moral masochism.

In contradistinction to this thesis, I believe that this type of criminal behavior reveals a pattern that duplicates almost minutely—point by point—the process by which the criminal managed, in childhood, to overcome his basic conflict by means of symptoms (criminality) that were ethically infinitely more vicious, and realistically far more dangerous to himself, than any unbridled "acting-out" of all the fantasies connected with that conflict would have been. For example, many a criminal prefers to kill rather than masturbate, or, like Hitler, to plunge the world into a war rather than be a passive, dependent homosexual.

If these considerations are valid, then the term "instinct-ridden psychopath" is a misleading one; the correct designation would have to be "defense-ridden psychopath." Such a person's career is the exact reverse—or is it?—of De Quincey's ironical remark that, once a man starts out with murder, there is no saying what he might stoop to: he might even end up as a petty thief, a drunk, or even a blasphemer.[1] His overreaction to every crisis or tension, his use of a cannon where a penknife would suffice, as regards both the means used to perform the criminal act and the attempts to escape the penalties of his crime, reveal, in drastically sharp contours, the distinctive characterological impairment of the habitual criminal and "criminal psychopath," whose major problem is no longer his initial conflict but rather the constantly new set of secondary conflicts brought into being by his excessive defenses against his relatively innocuous initial conflict.

Viewed in this light, the habitual criminal is no longer an enviable "negative ego-ideal": a superman, acting out in unfettered freedom every one of his impulses. Rather, he appears as a caricature of the puritan and the fanatic—as a "saint manqué" or "saint à rebours," whose aggressive defenses, like those of the criminal, are so excessive, luxuriant, and incongruous as to conceal the tiny acorn of conflict from which grew the mighty oak of his "saintliness."

Hence, just as the figure of the saint seems to many a tangible proof of the "divinely superhuman" in man, so the figure of the criminal has led to the conception of the "diabolically superhuman" in man. In fact, in some not wholly unprejudiced quarters, both the saint and the sinner have been viewed as direct proof of the inadequacy of psychoanalytic theory, which is concerned with the "merely"(?) human.

CONCLUSIONS

In the first approximation—and with special reference to illegal behavior—the difference between neurosis, perversion, and habitual criminality is as follows.

1. In neurosis, the core of the conflict is the struggle between the instincts and the defense mechanisms—especially the forces of repression. Whether they are isolated or recurrent, neurotic criminal acts reflect only a temporary failure of the defenses. The breakthrough of repressed forces is usually triggered by moral masochism, as witness the fact that it almost automatically elicits punishment and expiation, which placate the superego. This proves that one is dealing with the return of the repressed. The defenses may or may not be characterologically anchored, depending on whether one is dealing with a symptom neurosis or a character neurosis. What matters most here is that character neuroses differ from habitual criminality in that, in the former, it is the *impulse*—and *not* the *defense* against it—that is "criminal."

2. In perversions, the conflict is chiefly between pregenital and genital instinctual needs, the former being used—sometimes quite masochistically—as defenses against the latter. The pervert's "criminality" is thus either simply a matter of social convention (i.e., as in homosexual relations between adults) or else, as in the case of neurotics, the result of a breakthrough of aggressive pregenital impulses (lust murders); or, finally, it may be the highly ineffectual means by which the pervert seeks to avoid the consequences of an illegal sex

act, e.g., when he tries to avoid punishment for rape or pedophilia by murdering the sex object. Only the last type of perverted behavior bears any real—though still only partial—resemblance to habitual criminality.

3. In habitual criminality the socially relevant conflict is a product of the need to maintain and to protect characterologically anchored, excessive, and criminal defenses against various—and often "normal"—instinctual needs. The habitual criminal's defenses against instinctual needs are criminal in nature and, on the level of reality, create, for both society and himself, problems far more severe than those that would result from the uninhibited acting-out of his instinctual urges. Only in this respect does the criminal resemble the pervert who kills in order to cover up, temporarily, a far less objectionable sexual act. However, the pervert differs from the habitual criminal in that the latter's superego is structurally modified to permit the maintenance of criminal defenses against instinctual pressures. Predatory criminal behavior can even be made both ego-syntonic and superego-syntonic by the pretense that it is a subculturally sanctioned means of earning a living, i.e., that it serves the need for self-preservation. True and intense (morally) masochistic and self-punitive mechanisms are fairly rare in the habitual criminal.

In this paper I have sought to differentiate between the neurotic "illegalist," whose symptomatic defenses sometimes fail him, and the criminal, whose (criminal) defenses work overtime and whose analysis and therapy must be focused, first and last, upon his characterologically generalized and armored *excessive* defenses. I have also explained the failure of "psychoanalytic" treatment, especially of habitual criminals, conducted on noncharacterological lines by mere "detectives of the unconscious." In short, I have tried to bring criminality within the scope of the universally human subject matter of psychoanalysis. Last, but not least, I have attempted to provide theoretical support for Freud's empirical dictum that neurosis, perversion, and criminality are inherently distinct phenomena.

8

Female Juvenile Sex Delinquency in a Puritanical Society (1964)

INTRODUCTORY NOTE (1979)

Appearances to the contrary notwithstanding, the situation described in this study, which was written nearly twenty years ago, has not been modified in any essential respect by the current "sexual liberation"—or, rather, "compulsory promiscuousness" (Devereux 1955b [1976c]) of adolescents. Impersonal fornication, in which not the partner but only the scenario matters (Nathan 1977), has become practically mandatory, while "la nouvelle pudeur" has tabooed the word "love" quite as much as the affect it denotes. In short, the traditional duty to "fall in love," coupled with the taboo on intercourse, has simply been turned upside down, preserving intact the old dread of complete involvement. As a result, both impotence and the inability to achieve a vaginal orgasm appear to be on the increase, while clitoridism has been granted the status of an ideology.

The community's increasingly casual acceptance of biologically normal adolescent sex behavior has deprived such acts of their previous functions; they have ceased to be efficient means of expressing self-destructive rebelliousness. This has led to increasingly radical misuses of sexuality. Since early defloration no longer shocks most adults, its role as a means of creating a scandal appears to have been taken over not only by very early pregnancies but even by an indifference to, or even a conscious quest for, venereal disease—a quest encountered formerly only in severely self-destructive patients (Laforgue 1944). Normal coitus is, moreover, increasingly combined with, or even replaced by, perversions, precisely because the real, if unconscious, goal of the perversions is the diminution of the orgasm's intensity (Devereux 1967b). In the most extreme cases, rebelliousness practically ceases to have a manifest sexual component. Its unconscious—and largely pregenital—libidinal component is manifested more and more through drug addiction, gratuitous crim-

155

inality and vandalism, "political" terrorism, and, last but not least, by conversion to pretentiously cryptic ideologies, some of which even profess to be "psychoanalytical" or "Freudo-Marxistic."

I am using the term "ideology" here in a sense close to the one it has in the writings of Alain Besançon (1977). In the light of Besançon's findings, I view ideologies as psychoses masked by the empty trappings of scientism. The validity of this conception is confirmed by clinical data. Nathan (1977) found that patients championing the currently fashionable ideology of chaotic ("communal") sexuality *spontaneously* give up that ideology as soon as the analysis has resolved their subjective problems.

Of course, the parents of adolescents continue, as before, to provide them with clues to the way of using sexuality in a maximally self-destructive and socially negativistic manner. The fear that one's adolescent daughter may lose her virginity is sometimes replaced nowadays by concern over her "protracted" virginity; in one such case the daughter had just turned sixteen. The voyeuristically tinged strict supervision of adolescents, meant to prevent them from engaging in coitus, is today fairly often replaced by an almost obsessive curiosity over the sex life of one's adolescent children. In fact, one now often encounters what can only be called a "primal-scene curiosity in reverse" (chap. 6). More than one "modern" mother serves breakfast in bed to her adolescent daughter and her lover; another examines her son's bedsheets to determine how often he has cohabited with his girlfriend during the night—"fearing that he may have strained himself by over-doing it."

In short, as in Mao's China, there still are traffic lights—though (if the stories one hears are true) in China the red light now means "go" and the green one "stop."

Only the law remains caught in its traditional cultural lag. It will probably get around to making virginity a misdemeanor by the time a "new puritanism"—whose first signs are already discernible—becomes fashionable once more.

INTRODUCTION

I propose to discuss female juvenile sex delinquency from the viewpoint of psychoanalytically oriented social science. The anxiety-arousing nature of this problem has so deeply affected current theoretical and therapeutic views that my first task will have to be a careful scrutiny of the "scientific" definition and treatment of such girls from the viewpoint of the *Wissenssoziologie* of psychiatry, i.e., from the viewpoint of that half-historical and half-sociological science that seeks to explain and understand the theories and practices of psychiatric science in terms of its roots in, and its articulation with, the culture that produces it (Devereux 1958a [1978a, chap. 10]).

To avoid seemingly *ad hominem* polemics, I shall not cite by name the authors with whose views I disagree, but it should be clearly stated that most of the writings that I implicitly criticize were written by some of the ablest and most conscientious authorities on juvenile delinquency. Specifically, two of the case histories referred to below—those of "Hilda" and "J."—were presented by well-qualified and experienced psychiatric research workers at a colloquium devoted to the problem of the female juvenile sex delinquent. I feel that the analysis of what our culture, as represented by the science it produces, thinks and does about such girls will promote a real understanding of the roots and functions of this type of delinquency.

Methodological Considerations

A genuinely fruitful discussion of the sociocultural aspects of what is called female juvenile sex delinquency requires a preliminary clarification of the precise relationship between the sociocultural and the psychological-psychoanalytic explanation of a given behavior.

It is often alleged that the psychologist and the social scientist systematically compete with each other for the right to explain certain phenomena, though actually they offer entirely different explanations, which stand in a Heisenbergian complementarity relationship to each other (Devereux 1945 [1978a, chap. 4]; 1961b [1978a, chap. 5]; and chap. 16, below) and either of which can completely and satisfactorily explain why what happened did, in fact, happen. Indeed, a given human act can be made to seem inevitable in terms of either sociocultural or psychological-psychoanalytic explanations of it (Devereux 1961a).

The next point to be clarified concerns the commonly held illusion that the neurotic, the psychotic, and the delinquent are hard to understand. Actually, such individuals are much simpler, much more dedifferentiated, and considerably more derivative than normal persons are; they are much less colorful, imaginative, original, and individualized. The illusion that they are complicated, almost to the point of being incomprehensible, is a consequence of a refusal to examine them in terms of a suitable frame of reference (Devereux 1951g and chap. 2, above). A homely example may help us understand the degree of confusion that inevitably results from attempts to study a phenomenon in terms of an unsuitable frame of reference. Let us suppose that someone gives me a dog but persuades me that the animal is actually a cat. It is obvious that, as long as I persist in believing that what I have is a cat, its behavior will be completely incomprehensible to me. However, the moment I realize that the supposed cat is actually a dog, its behavior becomes completely understandable, predictable, and controllable. It is one of the key methodological theses of this essay that a great deal of what we think and feel about deviants is as frustratingly self-defeating as the belief that a dog is a cat.

This proposition is, unfortunately, especially applicable to our most cherished "scientific" ideas about children in general and about "problem children" in particular. The child's and the adolescent's closeness to the unconscious, his greater affectivity, spontaneity, and imaginativeness, and the fact that he has not yet gone to seed, both intellectually and emotionally, greatly disturb the adult. The adult scientist has therefore developed what he complacently believes to be a genuine "child psychology" but what is all too often nothing more than a codification of the things that he, as an adult, *wants* to believe about children and adolescents. This is quite in accordance with Julius Caesar's maxim that people believe what they want to believe. Specifically, many of the behavioral scientist's objective findings supposedly pertaining to *children*—i.e., to biologically immature human organisms—are actually scientific findings about certain *puerile traits* that our culture has *taught to,* and *imposed upon,* children. In other words, adults teach *children* to be *puerile* in a *particular,* culturally determined, manner and then call the *study* of the *products* of this inculcated puerility "child psychology" (Devereux 1956a).

The last methodological point to be made—which is intimately related to the preceding one—is that Western adults grossly underestimate young people in general, and their capacity to evolve sublimations in particular, as the following incident proves.

Case 1.—Years ago, I gave the star athlete of a certain university a failing midterm grade; this elicited frantic telephone calls from the dean, the athletic coach, and others. In response to these messages, I called the young man into my office and said to him: "You probably know that the university authorities are burning up the wires about your midterm grade; and you, I am sure, feel that these people are your friends and that I am your enemy. I think, however, that *they* are your real enemies. They—not I—are the ones who do not respect you. They think that, simply because you are an athlete, you are necessarily an imbecile—someone who can earn passing grades only with his muscles. I, however, believe that you are just as intelligent as the others and can earn passing grades with your head. I will therefore disregard the grades you have made so far this

term, because they are not really *your* grades but those of your pro-
tectors and advisers. Now go home, study hard, and give yourself
the breaks to which you are entitled." This athlete's final grade for
that term was a well-earned B-plus.

MISPLACED OR SELECTIVE EMPHASIS

Human beings can be destructive in a great many ways, only a few
of which are labeled "delinquent," "antisocial," or "abnormal."
Many other *objectively* destructive and/or self-destructive types of
behavior are actually highly valued and socially rewarded and bring
prestige rather than opprobrium to those who perform them. Thus
it is certain that all murderers, from Cain onward, have slain fewer
people than are killed by admired heroes in a fair-to-middling war.
There have been fewer actual suicides since Judas hung himself than
people who, with full social approval, have led lives of senseless
asceticism and self-denial—lives (so-called) that were socially more
costly than out-and-out suicides. Such lives are typified by that of
the Malay *amok* runner, who, seeking a glorious death, slays a dozen
innocent people before he himself is slain (Anonymous 1930). These
are facts—though, unfortunately, men often refuse to see objective,
statistically verifiable facts unless they fit their prejudices. Thus, to
take a particularly striking example, one hears a great deal about
the body-destruction fantasies of children—or, perhaps, of Melanie
Klein—directed especially at their pregnant mothers or unborn siblings; about their infantile cannibalistic impulses directed against
the maternal breast; about their murderous hatred of the father; and
so on. Yet, cultural history teaches us that countless women have
been aggressively aborted in a hostile way, not by children, but by
adults (Devereux 1955b [2d rev. ed. 1976b]) ever since, according
to Herodotus (3. 32), Cambyses kicked his pregnant sister-wife in
the belly; that children have been systematically cannibalized by
their parents, not only in aboriginal Australia (Róheim 1932) but in
times of famine in most so-called civilized countries; and that countless fathers have sacrificed their children to Moloch or have simply
killed them the way tomcats sometimes kill a litter of kittens. Also,
men apparently do not choose to remember that, long before Oedipus killed Laius, the latter had tried to slay his infant son (Devereux
1953b). Compared to this mass of actually perpetrated adult acts of
aggression against children, the number of pregnant women aborted
by their children, of parents cannibalized by their offspring, or of
fathers slain by their sons is negligible.

These comments do not imply that I deny the psychic reality and
functional importance of children's fantasies of body destruction

and their cannibalistic and oedipal urges, all of which are certainly universal and quite as important as they are thought to be by Freud and those who, like myself, adhere to the classical analytic tradition. I am simply suggesting that one should discard the untenable pseudo-analytic shibboleth "Reality is not analyzable" and then, precisely *because* of a legitimate preoccupation with infantile *fantasies,* pay attention to types of actual *adult* behavior that reveal the *basic nature* of unconscious parental destructiveness and seductiveness.[1]

I am also struck by the large number of articles dealing with transference and the scarcity of papers on countertransference. Yet the latter mechanism is, both scientifically and therapeutically, more important than the former, since nearly every insight obtainable through the analysis of the transference can *also* be obtained through the analysis of *other* data, while the analysis of the countertransference yields needed insights *not* obtainable by other means (Devereux 1967c).

A comparable misplaced selective emphasis in the approach to sexually delinquent girls manifests itself in the fact that the way in which their problems are studied differs from the way in which the problems of neurotic, psychotic, or aggressive girls are studied.

This difference is highlighted by the fact that two excellent case histories presented in a certain colloquium provided surprisingly few *relevant* data about "Hilda's" and "J.'s" parents, though it is routine procedure to provide complete and *relevant* data about the parents of aggressive, neurotic, or psychotic girls.

The data about the mother in "Hilda's" case history are deceptively rich, but closer scrutiny reveals that they pertain almost entirely to events preceding "Hilda's" birth and provide no information about the mother's attitude toward sex during the crucial years of *"Hilda's" life.* Moreover, as regards "J.'s" father, we are, in effect, given no information whatsoever and are simply left to wonder what kind of father would break his daughter's nose.[2]

It seems legitimate to assume that these puzzling omissions are significant byproducts of certain biases that distort the perceptiveness of even the most conscientious therapist and research worker (Devereux 1967c).

Superficially, one might argue that these serious omissions simply reflect the adult's automatic assumption that parents—at least when acting in a parental capacity—are, as a class, more often right than wrong. Since this peculiar bias is especially frequently observed in cases where only the child, not the parent, is in treatment, it might be tempting to explain it by saying that it is more convenient for the therapist or research worker to blame everything on the person who is in treatment than on some other person who is not available for a scrutiny and interpretation of his or her conduct.

Actually, however, this bias has much deeper roots and affects psychotherapeutic work with adults as well as children. Even a cursory review of the psychoanalytic literature shows that we are prone to analyze the adult patient's *oedipal* conflicts much more carefully than his *counteroedipal* problems, though in the end it is the analysis of his counteroedipal problems that will enable the adult to be a good parent.

It is unnecessary to recapitulate here my historical and functional analysis of the psychoanalyst's extraordinary lack of interest in counteroedipal problems, which has enabled him to scotomatize the numerous and even blatantly pedophilic counteroedipal incidents in those portions of the Oedipus myth that pertain to events preceding the birth of that ill-fated hero (Devereux 1953b).

For present purposes, it is entirely sufficient to stress the contrast between our readiness to highlight the role of parental errors in the genesis of neurosis and psychosis and our striking proneness to minimize the role of parental counteroedipal impulses in the genesis of *sex* delinquency. In fact, as one reads case history after case history of sex-delinquent girls, one begins to wonder whether the pre-Freudian fantasy of the nonoedipal, nonsexual, cherubic infant is currently being replaced by the opposite fantasy image, that of the nonsexual, noncounteroedipal parent, in order to avoid the necessity of establishing unpleasant correlations between the sexual acting-out of the child and the counteroedipal impulses of the parents.

Case 2.—A sexually rather conventional but otherwise highly aggressive juvenile delinquent complained in his analysis that *he* was made quite uncomfortable by his widowed mother's seductive insistence that he play the role of an escort whenever they had dinner together in a restaurant. At the same time, this young man's clinical file recorded at length *his mother's* complaints that her son embarrassed her by flirting with her in public. The data obtained in the course of the analysis conclusively proved that it was the mother, not the son, who was seductive and that the mother's accusations represented simply a projection of her own counteroedipal wishes upon her son.

To sum up: this section demonstrates that our perception of the sex-delinquent girl is misleading and distorted because it systematically assigns far more importance to sexual acting-out than to nonsexual symptoms, and it highlights oedipal problems without tracing them back to those parental counteroedipal urges that elicit the child's or adolescent's oedipality in the first place.

PROBLEMS OF DEFINITION

Many of the technical terms that modern psychiatric nosology employs are also condensed definitions. The technical label "Female juvenile sex delinquent" is no exception to this rule.

Now, it is a well-established fact that any label that is also a condensed definition becomes a major obstacle to the further development of science the moment the definition itself ceases to be adequate. The classical example of the captious semantic misuse of the label-as-definition is the celebrated "refutation" of Freud's conception of hysteria by the Viennese physician who argued that men cannot possibly have hysteria because they have no uterus (*hystera*).

The time has come to reconsider the *definitional* validity of the nosological label "Female juvenile sex delinquent." Of these four words, only one—"delinquent"—has either sociocultural or psychological-psychoanalytic validity. The other three are so inappropriate that they distort, rather than clarify, the nature of the syndrome under consideration.

For reasons of expository convenience I propose to scrutinize first the term *"sex,"* which, though disguised as a neutral label, is actually the key word in this definition. I shall show that, when seen in the context of the other three words that make up this label, the word "sex" has certain wholly incorrect and even tendentious implications.

A. "Sex"

1. It is *not* true that "sexually delinquent" girls revolt *in order* to enjoy forbidden sexual pleasures. In the actual, operational means-end schema of such girls, coitus is not a *goal* but a *means* to an end. It is, moreover, chiefly a means to a nonsexual, and sometimes outright masochistic and/or aggressive, end. Hence, the very use to which such girls put their sexual organs and functions represents a disastrous degradation and/or tragic negation of sexuality, just as the use of a violin as a club represents a degradation of both the violin and the person who uses it as a weapon.

2. The delinquent girl who uses her sexual "equipment" masochistically or aggressively not only uses sex as a means to *non*sexual ends but, incidentally, also shows that—like the misguided puritan she is—she is in revolt against genuine, mature sexuality. Indeed, she is not so much delinquent *by means of* sex as delinquent *with respect to real sexuality,* which she compulsively degrades, because

she dreads it quite as much as the neurotically puritanical girl dreads it, and perhaps even more. (See further, below.)

B. "Female"

Once these facts are understood, one must also automatically challenge the way the term "female" is used in the diagnostic label under consideration. When it is conjoined with the term "sex"—which, as I have already shown, is inappropriately used—the term "female" seems to imply that these persons are genuine *women,* in the complete, sociopsychophysiological sense of that word. In reality, however, they are female only in *gender,* i.e., only in the anatomical sense in which a "masculine" lesbian is "female." Specifically:

1. She is not "female" *socially,* since her behavior deviates even from the few sensible norms still surviving in our sexually confused society.

2. She is not "female" *psychologically,* since she is unable to love in a healthily feminine way and is unable to experience the psychological components of normal sexuality and orgasm.

3. She is not "female" *physiologically,* since she usually experiences no physiological climaxes and does not wish to bear children —or else, if she does, she views pregnancy as a gesture of revolt.

Case 3.—In a certain therapeutic school, students in psychotherapy were brought in groups to the psychiatric-clinic building. One day a group of girls, who had just arrived, refused to go to the offices of their respective psychiatrists. Instead, they came in a group to my office to complain about the "unreasonable restraints" imposed by the school authorities on their petting and other quasi-sexual activities. I listened to them carefully, expressed my complete approval of real and mature lovemaking, and asked them if they were prepared to commit themselves emotionally to their petting partners and to contemplate the possibility of eventually marrying them and bearing their children. This question elicited a loud chorus of nos, together with protests that they were still too young to go to such "extremes." I responded by saying that one cannot ride with one foot in a Cadillac and the other foot in a baby carriage, that I would champion their rights as women the moment they ceased to be *infants,* but that, until then, I could not ask the school authorities to treat as *women* persons who still wished to be *children.* To my surprise, the room suddenly became very quiet. Several girls nodded thoughtfully, and the group thanked me and quietly left my office. This incident should be remembered when I discuss, below, the proper way of handling the delinquent behavior of such girls, since all I did was to oppose the creative *goal* of *mature* sexuality to the destructively used *means* of *immature* sexuality and to stress that they were children rather than women, though, chronologically, they were old enough to be women if they *chose* to assume the great rights and *noblesse oblige* duties of that estate.

C. "Juvenile"

The preceding considerations immediately lead to the problem of the grossly incorrect, the almost factitious, use of the term "juvenile" in the diagnostic label under scrutiny. Standard nosology uses the word "juvenile" in a wholly arbitrary, Humpty Dumpty manner, making it mean whatever we want it to mean.

In theory, the term "juvenile" is a *legal* concept, taken over by psychiatry and allegedly justified by sociological considerations. It is a spurious concept, both in psychiatry and in therapeutic education.

1. The "biology" underlying the legal concept "juvenile" is a *pseudobiologia phantastica,* pure and simple. The fact that these individuals are, sexually, not really juveniles is indirectly admitted even by the law itself, which permits sixteen-year-old girls to marry with parental consent even though marriage calls for *more* wisdom and maturity than does the casual fornication of "juvenile" delinquents. One is also inevitably led to inquire whether young American southerners are biologically different from young northerners, since many southern states (in 1950) permit marriage at much earlier ages than northern states do.

2. The transfer of the concept "juvenile" from jurisprudence to the social and behavioral sciences is illegitimate unless one can demonstrate that even the properly educated teenager is *inevitably* and *necessarily* inferior to the most uneducated adult—or even to the average adult—in *socioculturally significant ways* and that society does *not* call on the "juvenile" to perform *socioculturally significant services.* As regards the first specification, society unquestioningly accepts the enormously important mathematical discoveries of such teenagers as Pascal and Galois, the poetry of the teenager Rimbaud, and the compositions of the child Mozart, but it coldly ignores a great French poet's warning that "valor does not wait for the fullness of years." Hence, society treated Galois—a duelist and patron of prostitutes—and Rimbaud—a nineteenth-century "hippie"—as juvenile delinquents and granted no vote to Pascal and Mendelssohn, who even as minors were consistently sensible and mature. As regards the second specification—socioculturally significant services —society permitted, and in fact demanded, that Louis II de Bourbon, Prince de Condé ("Le Grand Condé") defeat, with grossly outnumbered second-rate troops, Spain's best troops at Rocroy, but,

because of his "tender" age (twenty-two), kept him under his father's thumb and away from the woman he loved. Society deems average eighteen-year-olds sufficiently mature to be drafted, to know that *dulce et decorum est pro patria mori,* and to earn the Congressional Medal of Honor but regards them as too immature either to vote for a city dogcatcher or to be a candidate for that exalted office. In fact, even the United States Army, which the adolescent serves as an elite soldier, feels that he is not old enough to make sexual decisions —to marry—without the approval of his chaplain and commanding officer.

[*Addendum, 1979:* Until fairly recently it was more or less possible to challenge these conclusions by an appeal to a hypothetical period of "adolescent sterility" (Montagu 1939). Should such a period exist, which I venture to doubt, one could argue that nature provided it for the purpose of enabling adolescent girls to learn to love as women before having to learn to love also as mothers. But the existence of such a period is quite improbable. According to Peter Fuchs (1978), Omar Arab girls of the Wadai, who marry before reaching puberty, often become pregnant during their first ovulation.

In our own society girls reach puberty much earlier than their mothers did, and the pregnancy of barely nubile girls has become far from rare. Though a better diet is probably partly responsible for these phenomena, one must also envisage the possibility that both early puberty and early pregnancy may be partly due to a culturally encouraged early sexual arousal and rivalry. Where girls were formerly proud of being the first of their age-mates to reach puberty, and, more recently, the first to be deflowered, there are faint indications that some girls now wish to become pregnant sooner than their age-mates.

Now, it is a fact that psychological factors, such as rivalry, can facilitate impregnation. Some women believed to be sterile become pregnant as soon as they decide to adopt a child or soon after having adopted one (Orr 1941). When King Anaxandridas' wife failed to bear him a child, the Spartan government forced him to take a second wife. Hardly had the second wife borne him a son, Cleomenes, than the first wife bore him three sons in rapid succession: Dorieus, Leonidas, and Cleombrotus (Herodotus 5. 41, etc.). The Bible also mentions such occurrences. Hagar's pregnancy appears to have elicited the first pregnancy of the long-sterile Sarah (Gen. 21:1 ff.). The pregnancies of both Leah and Rachel appear to have been elicited by rivalries, not only between the two sisters (and cowives) but also between the two sisters and their respective handmaidens, Zilpah and Bilhah, whom, during their own initial period of sterility, the two sisters caused to bear children on their behalf to their husband Jacob (Gen. 30). Now, whereas these biblical cases may well be mythical, the Spartan case cited by Herodotus is certainly historical and had momentous historical consequences.

In short, as noted in the introduction to this chapter, it is possible that early defloration is now, in some cases, replaced as a token of rebellion by precocious pregnancies.]

The alleged incapacity of the adolescent girl to be a psychologically and socioculturally functioning woman can be brought into focus by asking whether Shakespeare's fourteen-year-old Juliet is a juvenile delinquent. The possible objection, that Shakespeare's Juliet is a figment of the poet's imagination, is untenable. Shakespeare's realistic Elizabethan audience would have laughed *Romeo and Juliet* out of court had it not, on the basis of valid experience, taken it for granted that fourteen-year-old girls can be, and often are, emotionally mature women, capable of being good wives in a society that permitted and even encouraged them to grow up emotionally. Indeed, even Shakespeare's eloquence could not have "put across" Juliet's capacity to love deeply and meaningfully had the Elizabethan age, and the Renaissance in general, not known of many young girls capable of being authentic women. Had this not been so, Shakespeare would have been compelled to make his Juliet not fourteen but twenty years old, simply because theatrical audiences will accept the impossible—such as the existence of ghosts—but not the preposterous—such as emotionally mature ten-year-old wives.

It is therefore crucially important to know why Shakespeare's Juliet is *not* a juvenile delinquent while the Juliet of Leonard Bernstein's *West Side Story* is. Any cogent answer to this question implies a scathing condemnation of our handling of adolescence.

A word should also be said about adolescent aggressiveness in general. In a lecture given in the 1950s before the Tulsa County Mental Hygiene Society, I stated that adolescents are idealists who, if given nothing worthwhile to fight for, will fight simply for the sake of fighting. I postulate that young hoodlums of either sex are destructive only because we give them nothing more creative to fight for than college football, split-level houses, insurance policies, and the flabby pseudo-ideology of the status-seeking "organization man" [and now—in 1979—of the anti-status-seeking and anti-organization man]. The Western adult's lack of idealism—of true dedication and commitment—has made our world almost uninhabitable for the adolescent, who, unlike the adult, has not yet gone to seed and has as yet developed neither an intellectual potbelly nor a fatty degeneration of the heart. Hence he reacts with greater violence to this moral, ethical, emotional, and intellectual deprivation than does the adult, because he seems to have a greater need than most adults have for the better things in life—for the things that make man human in a more than taxonomic sense. In fact, delinquency may in some cases be simply a manifestation of inhibited and frustrated creative potentialities. An edict of Emperor Han Wu Ti (140 B.C.) instructed his officials to appoint brilliant but untractable men to high positions because "exceptional work demands exceptional men," and, when properly handled, "a bolting or kicking horse may become a most valuable animal." The Hungarian adage, "The more tempestuously the grape juice ferments, the better will be the wine," has the same implication (Anonymous, n.d.; Devereux 1944a).

Our juveniles are not juvenile because *biology* so ordains it. They are juvenile because *we have deliberately made them puerile* and have discouraged their strivings toward a true maturity—one that would put our own compalcent pseudo-maturity to shame. They are delinquent because the goals we offer them are shamefully "flat, stale, and unprofitable." They kill as hoodlums, for two dollars and a bottle of hooch, because we give them no opportunity to fight as heroes for true freedom—for that of Periclean Athens—instead of for "mom's apple pie," which (according to the newspapers that reported this World War II utterance with cloying sentimentality, professing to find in it an authentic philosophy of democracy) is what at least one American soldier felt he was fighting for.

Speaking as a former United States Naval Reserve officer who volunteered for service—and even speaking simply as a man—I feel that it was infamous not to have told the soldiers of a democracy *what* they were fighting for. It is more appalling still to have brought up a generation of Americans in such a manner that they did not know, *without being told,* what they were fighting for. One may be certain that Aeschylus fighting at Marathon and Salamis, and Socrates, the Athenian hoplite (armored combat infantryman), who was the last to retire from the stricken field of Delium, making threatening faces at the victorious Boeotians, did *not* fight for mom's apple pie and did *not* need to be told that they were fighting for Athenian democracy or that their democracy was worth dying for (Devereux 1956a).

In brief, our female juvenile sex delinquents

1. Are, through our own fault, *not* female, except anatomically.

2. Are *not* juvenile—except that we so define them and therefore prevent them from attaining a true emotional maturity, which is entirely compatible with biological adolescence.
3. Do *not* indulge in real sex but use sexuality as a means to an aggressive or masochistic end and in a manner that actually sins against true, mature sexuality.
4. Are delinquent—both pseudo-sexually and sadomasochistically—because we did not allow them to mature sufficiently to be able to engage creatively in mature sex, which implies love, and did not give either sex a chance to fight for anything more meaningful than sports laurels and platitudinous economic goals or to seek glory and achievement instead of popularity and a raise in pay.

In a word, *we have the so-called female juvenile sex delinquents whom we have made and therefore deserve.* A society that discourages maturity, degrades love, cheapens valor, sneers at ideals, and pursues shoddy objectives can expect nothing better than sons who are either hoodlums or else timid conformists and daughters who are either sluts or else champion church-social pie-bakers. The sickness is *ours*—*they* only have *our* symptoms. *We* carry the germs—though *they* have the fever. It is *we* who are disoriented and anxiety-ridden; *they* are but our "deputy lunatics"—the scapegoats of our sins of omission and commission (Devereux 1956a). [*Addendum 1979:* The anticipation, by several years, of the somewhat similar ideas of the so-called anti-psychiatrists is to be noted.]

SYMPTOM CHOICE

My 1956 conclusion (Devereux 1956a) that the child or adolescent acts out the illness of its parents—that it has the symptoms appropriate to the latent immaturity and psychic illness of its parents—leads directly to the problem of symptom "choice." I place the term "choice" in quotation marks to indicate that the deviant child's freedom to choose its own symptoms is largely spurious. My purpose in this section is to explain how the deviant girl's symptoms are imposed on her by her environment and why she usually manifests her deviancy by means of maximally tabooed *sexual* behavior rather than by some other means.

This subject is, needless to say, a quite general one, and I have discussed it in some detail in two other publications (Devereux 1956a and chap. 3, above). For this reason, I will concern myself here exclusively with the disturbed girl's "choice" of sexuality as her preferred means of symptom formation. However, before tackling this matter, an important point, likely to seduce one into overstating the matter, must be taken into consideration. As stated elsewhere (Devereux 1956a), one sees so many sexual problems in hospitalized or imprisoned children and adolescents because, in our society, the adults find adolescent sexuality more disturbing than adolescent aggressiveness, especially if the adolescent happens to be female. A sexually inhibited girl can be a borderline schizophrenic or be grossly aggressive and yet escape hospitalization or arrest, while a sexually active but psychiatrically less ill girl will almost inevitably be either hospitalized or sent to a girls' reform school, because adults find her behavior *more* disturbing than the behavior of the aggressive or schizoid girl.

Yet, even if one takes into account this arbitrary preselection of one's patients, problem students, and reform-school inmates, the fact remains that girls are especially prone to engage in sexual acting-out. It is this overdetermined phenomenon that will concern me most in this section.

1. In the methodological section, I referred to the neurotic's relative unimaginativeness, which also manifests itself in his symptom formation. It takes infinitely less originality and inventiveness to form the most bizarre symptom than to create a wise maxim, a two-line poetical epigram, or a simple folk song. Specifically, though even a minute detail in a neurotic's dream can be a complexly overdetermined, and surprisingly multivalent, condensation (Freud 1900), it is quite apparent from the works of Sachs (1942), Kris (1952), Kubie (1958), and myself (1961c [1975, chap. 1]) that genuine artistic products are even more complexly overdetermined, condensed, and multiple-structured. This fact alone would suffice to explain why the neurotic eagerly borrows the ready-made symptoms that the culture so obligingly makes available. Needless to say, it is, in itself, a sign of the deviant girl's sickness that she is willing to "oblige" us by accepting the symptoms we so eagerly place at her disposal. Exactly as a drunk's willingness to use a violin for a club is proof of his unmusicality, so the delinquent girl's readiness to use sex destructively proves that she is not feminine enough to resist the temptation to misuse her sexuality.

2. I have, since 1940, systematically stressed that symptom choice is negatively determined by the social mores (chap. 3). The element of revolt present in every distortion of the personality (Jenkins and Glickman, 1947) requires for its manifestation—and also for the alleviation of the underlying anxiety—a socially tabooed symptom (chap. 3). In fact, the extent to which the individual deviant's symptom is tabooed—i.e., whether, at one extreme, it is simply a socially

marginal ("lunatic-fringe") act or else a mere superstition (Devereux 1954c) or, at the other extreme, expresses outright revolt and "social negativism"—is a fair measure of the role that revolt plays in the total disease picture (chap. 1). Now, since in our society sex is the maximally tabooed type of female misconduct—a fact of which all girls are well aware—it is literally inevitable that sexual misconduct should be the rebellious girl's most conspicuous symptom, possessing all the qualities of the "signal symptom" by which the disturbed individual alerts society to his abnormal state (Devereux 1961a). In brief, by vociferously tabooing female adolescent sexuality, we practically suggest to the young girl the most effective way for her to exasperate adults. Through the very act of telling the girl *not* to be sexually active, the adult reveals to her *his* most vulnerable point, thereby practically inviting her to direct her attack at that particular spot[3]—and, if she does, he condemns her. In brief, it is quite evident that "sex as a symptom" is suggested to the girl by society itself, albeit by negative suggestion, and is accepted by her because it fits her social negativism.

3. The delinquent girl's choice of sexual misconduct as her leading symptom is also positively suggested to her by society in two additional ways:

a) By means of "patterns of misconduct," which, according to Linton (1936), seem to tell the individual deviant: "Do not do such and such a deed, but, if you do, you must proceed as follows!" Thus, in Goethe's *Faust* (act 1, scene 19) Valentin tells his sister Gretchen, "Since you are already a whore, you might as well be a whore all the way"—though it is quite obvious that Gretchen was not a whore but an innocent girl tenderly in love with the tormented and irresponsible Faust. Students of the problem of sex delinquency in girls time and again hear of similar contemptuous and unjust "implicit directives" addressed by parents to young girls who are anything but tramps. By defining a single sexual act, performed by a naive girl in the throes of puppy love, as a major crime or mortal sin and the girl herself as wayward and promiscuous, such parents literally direct and force their daughter to be what they deem her to be. This interpretation is strongly supported by Sperling's (1950) very cogent analysis of the trauma as a command—and, needless to say, of the command as a trauma. An example will clarify this point.

Case 4.—The analysis of a seriously delinquent youth, in his late teens, revealed that he felt *obliged* to be a delinquent simply because his mother—who was, by definition, infallible—insisted that he was worthless; this literally made it mandatory for him to prove her right. Hence, in his analysis he readily and insightfully accepted all interpretations of his shortcomings but reacted for quite a while to any confrontation with his very genuine assets and increasingly numerous sensible actions by not appearing for his next analytic session (Devereux 1956a).

b) Society also suggests suitable means of revolt to the disturbed girl when it seeks to impose injudicious and unrealistic patterns of behavior on her, for she can caricature these by reducing them *ad absurdum*. Much of the remaining portions of this essay will be devoted to the demonstration that the sex-delinquent girl is, in essence, a *caricature of the pathological puritan* she is expected to be and feels obliged to be.

THE SEX-DELINQUENT GIRL:
CARICATURE OF THE PURITAN

As a preliminary to discussing the way in which the *reductio ad absurdum* mechanism operates in sex delinquency, it is necessary to recall the considered opinion of many thoughtful and responsible persons that the sexual mores of our society leave much to be desired, not only ethically but in terms of realism and common sense.[4] What is less commonly recognized is the fact that, despite the actual wording of our relevant laws, society at large actually interferes more consistently with heterosexuality than with perversions. To take only one—but an extremely convincing—example, better hotels and apartment houses in the United States usually refuse accommodations to obviously unmarried heterosexual couples but not to manifestly homosexual ones. As for children, they are more severely punished for heterosexual play than for masturbation.

Two striking case histories will demonstrate the social pressure against normal heterosexuality, involving mature object relations.

Case 5.—A warmhearted and somewhat promiscuous girl of twenty, living in a medium-sized and extremely conservative town, said that the local mores literally forced her to be promiscuous. "If I dated a man regularly, people would assume that I was having an affair with him; but if I date a different man every night, no such suspicions will arise. Since my body and soul need a man, I am forced to be promiscuous, though I want to love just one man." The fact that this was no self-deception became evident when, after her marriage, she remained perfectly faithful to her husband—a sometimes quite difficult, though affectionate and sensual, man.

Case 6.—A small-town schoolteacher reported almost the same thing. She felt that she had to put on "holier than thou" airs—to be a model churchgoer and to participate in all civic activities. Safely ensconced behind this puritanical façade, she could afford to pick up transient soldiers and enjoy sexual intercourse with them, since anyone who saw her with a soldier simply assumed that she was engaged in some volunteer U.S.O. (social work) activity. By contrast, had she "gone steady" with one man, the town would have suspected "immorality"—and her contract with the school board was drawn up in such a way that the least breath of scandal would have led to her instant dismissal.

It is the central thesis of this paper that the so-called female juvenile sex delinquent acts out sexual delinquency in a manner that on closer scrutiny appears almost slavishly conformist and conventional.

This point is fully corroborated by two admirably chosen—because typical—case histories presented at a certain colloquium. Neither of the two girls discussed was actually interested in coitus per se or in that complete communion the Mohave Indians describe in the maxim "When two people make love, their bodies make love with each other and their souls make love with each other," and whose psychological aftermath they characterize by saying, "One always knows who made love the night before, because the ones who have carry themselves proudly, and their eyes sparkle" (Devereux 1950a). This Mohave philosophy or psychology of the sex act is the diametrical opposite of ours, which proclaims that, after coitus, all beasts are sad (*Post coitum omne animal triste*).[5]

It is a well-established fact that many so-called sex-delinquent girls are not interested in coitus and even disapprove of it. They are mainly interested in being accepted by men—and, therefore, at least noticed by women—even if they have to pay for this acceptance with an abject sexual compliance. This, needless to say, is precisely what so-called "nice" girls also do—though they do it somewhat more judiciously and far less compulsively and indiscriminately.

The validity of this thesis is strongly supported by the fact that these two case histories, which form the background of this paper, failed to reveal whether "Hilda" or "J." could have orgasms. Since it is unlikely that this omission was due to an oversight, it must have been determined by the fact that the experienced and insightful social workers who compiled these case histories automatically—and rightly—took it for granted that these two girls, like many others of their kind, *could not* experience even a physiological spasm, let alone a true and complete psychophysiological orgasm. By contrast, "nice" girls who are in love do, as a rule, have both physiological (vaginal) and psychological orgasms. Given the well-known dynamics of female orgastic frigidity (Deutsch 1944–45; Hitschmann and Bergler 1936), this finding forces the conclusion that girls like "Hilda" and

"J." are actually *more* puritanical than "nice" girls and would think it "wicked" to have orgasms—except, perhaps, when "raped" and therefore ostentatiously "innocent."

It is extremely important for my entire argument to demonstrate conclusively the validity of my thesis that, in certain women, guilt over *coitus as such* has been effectively replaced by guilt over *orgasms,* in accordance with the well-known quip: "An English gentleman can do anything he pleases as long as he *does not enjoy it.*" This thesis explains the puzzling fact that many women submit to joyless and almost impersonal sex acts quite readily but do so nearly always in a spirit that is close to penitence and self-degradation.

Case 7.—A brilliantly intelligent and rather promiscuous young woman, who had never experienced orgasm during coitus, went from man to man, supposedly looking for someone who could give her a climax. However, when a fine man, very much in love with her, finally did give her an orgasm, she immediately terminated the affair.

Case 8.—A middle-aged, intelligent woman analysand, raised by a mother who positively loathed and despised sex, had had no intercourse with anyone except her husband, by whom she had several children. In the course of her analysis, the patient declared that, the moment her mother died, she would have to discontinue marital relations entirely, "because my mother would then discover that I have intercourse with my husband and also that I hate her." When it was pointed out to her that, since she was the mother of several children, her mother could not help knowing that she had had sexual relations with her husband, the analysand immediately realized that what she was trying to conceal from her mother was not simply that she hated her and that she had engaged in marital relations (sex = revolt) but the far more "scandalous" fact that she actually *enjoyed* sexual intercourse and had orgasms easily and rather consistently.

Case 9.—An intelligent woman analysand of about forty, active in charity work, was married for a number of years to a sickly and almost completely impotent husband, to whom she remained faithful until his death. Soon after being widowed, a friend of the family made love to her and gave her an orgasm of such intensity that she sobbed uncontrollably for several minutes. When, at the end of the first tryst, the man, who seems to have been genuinely attracted to her, asked her when they would meet next, the woman replied: "Never! I would soon become completely enslaved to a man who could give me such exquisite pleasure, and this would cause me to neglect my *higher* duties toward my children and also toward the charitable organizations for which I do volunteer work."

Case 10.—A young married woman developed an incapacitating agoraphobia and severe anxiety states when a major automobile accident caused a prolonged occupational and sexual incapacitation of her colorless and never very potent or economically successful husband. When the husband recovered sufficiently to engage, from time to time, in intercourse, the wife discovered that she had become incapable of having orgasms. Simultaneously, she developed an acute fear that she might become irreversibly "uncontrollable" and might go to pieces emotionally, especially in the analyst's waiting room. After some nine months of analysis this young woman had a dream: She fell flat on her back in the street in such a manner that her skirts flew up and displayed her pretty underwear. Her associations revealed her conviction that, if she allowed herself to have orgasms with her still only slightly potent husband, she would soon become sexually uncontrollable and promiscuous. Her analyst—who at the time was only a candidate—suggested that this was much more likely to happen if she did *not* allow herself to have orgasms with her husband than if she allowed her sexual tensions to be relieved by her at least occasionally successful marital relations. The next day the patient entered the analytic chamber looking positively radiant. Her first words were: "I have been had last night! My God, how I have been had!" This episode was followed *almost immediately* by a total and permanent disappearance of her orgastic frigidity and agoraphobia, by a startling diminution of her anxieties, and by a recovery so swift that the supervising analyst urged the candidate to terminate the analysis many weeks before the latter was willing even to contemplate doing so. It should be added that, in this instance, the supervising analyst was quite right; for when an unforeseeable chain of events made it possible, a year later, to test the resolution of the transference, in a situation involving considerable strain, it was found to be complete.

In brief, the negative attitude of many women toward sexual pleasure and, more specifically, the orgastic impotence of many female juvenile sex delinquents indicate that they view coitus not as a creative pleasure but as a masochistic gratification. In fact, their attitude is quite comparable to the views of certain heretics who held that man must humble himself before the deity by engaging in degradingly immoral activities. Hence, many sex delinquents cohabit not to *obtain pleasure* but to *prove their depravity*. In short, as stated before, their sexual acts are "signal symptoms," informing society of their emotional illness, degradation, and self-contempt.

The underlying masochism of such an attitude cannot be exaggerated, and it is highlighted, rather than concealed, by the concurrent presence of markedly sadistic elements. Indeed, the masochist invariably manages to be masochistic and self-depreciatory *in a manner that also affects others in an adverse manner.* Figuratively speaking, the self-despising masochist is someone who likes to dive into a cesspool—*but only after making sure that innocent bystanders will also be spattered* in the process. This observation explains why the self-contempt of the promiscuous girl so readily turns into a resistance to therapy.

Case 11.—A fourteen-year-old adopted girl had been completely promiscuous since the age of twelve. In therapy she declared that she would not cooperate because her promiscuousness was the worst thing on earth and made her undeserving of any help. This was of course an overdetermined resistance. If she had been able to maneuver me into saying that promiscuousness is *not* the worst sin, she could, on the one hand, have construed my utterance as a further "command" to be a quasi-prostitute, and, on the other hand, she could have brought about a termination of her treatment simply by telling her puritanical adoptive parents that I "encouraged" her in her evil ways. Interestingly enough, her previously always prosperous parents found it "financially necessary" to terminate her treatment *the very moment* she ceased to be promiscuous—with the result that, after going home, she became pregnant in a matter of weeks. These facts suggest that her parents simply could not tolerate her recovery (Devereux 1956a).

Another devious type of conformism is the seemingly nonconformist promiscuousness of many delinquent girls. It is well known that promiscuousness is in part an indirect search for an oedipal relationship, since the promiscuous girl's heart belongs to her father, in accordance with the well-known symbolic equation Big Man (daddy) = all men (Devereux 1955a). Her many lovers simply represent various aspects of the father. At the same time, the fact that such a girl gives her body to many men and her heart to none represents an abject compliance with tacit counteroedipal parental demands. Indeed, it is well known that many parents who are extravagantly proud of their young daughter's "popularity"—as proved by the fact that she "dates" many men—strenuously object to her becoming emotionally involved with any *one* man, nominally because she might have sexual relations with such a man but actually because they view the girl's love for an "outsider" as a real betrayal. This parental attitude—which is quite common—has finally led to the almost grotesquely paradoxical situation that today [in the

175

1960s] "nice" adolescents revolt against parental counteroedipal claims by "falling in love" and "going steady" at a strikingly early age.

The inherent degradingness of coitus with despicable partners and with mere pickups is also a roundabout manifestation and masochistic phrasing of puritanism. Indeed, the mechanism described, *for men only,* in Freud's article "On the Universal Tendency to Debasement in the Sphere of Love" (Freud 1912) is present also in the promiscuous girl, though it is probable that the rapid emancipation and masculinization of women is largely responsible for the increasing obviousness of this mechanism in modern American girls. Indeed, where previously it was the privilege of the princess to elope with a gypsy violinist or to order handsome serfs to her bedchamber, today even the middle-class girl has the opportunity to associate with young hoodlums and middle-aged beatniks. In brief, partly because of their increasing masculinization, many modern girls are increasingly unable to take their sex cleanly, pleasurably, without anxiety, and in a spirit of self-respect, pride, and dignity. Quite often such girls are able to engage in sexual relations only if an "appropriate" punishment or self-degradation is already built into the act itself. They therefore select contemptible partners or unsuitable physical settings, have sexual relations under conditions which make the risk of discovery and disgrace extremely great, refuse to take adequate contraceptive precautions, select partners likely to infect them with venereal disease, or even openly demand that their partner despise them.

Case 12.—A young man, approaching the end of his analysis and already capable of genuine object relations, reported with considerable distress that his girl friend had repeatedly warned him that she would leave him if he fell in love with her; she also specified that she wanted only to be "screwed," not "made love to."

A further reason why promiscuous girls feel compelled to combine sex with degradation is that they have accepted in the most literal sense the maxim "The wages of sin is death." Hence, they feel compelled to turn this maxim into a Mertonian (Merton 1949) "self-fulfilling prophecy" by combining pleasure with punishment. For example, one of Laforgue's patients did not rest until she had acquired what she called her "trinity": gonorrhea, syphilis, and chancre (Laforgue 1944). Other girls achieve the same objective by carelessness with contraception, so that they have to undergo abortion after abortion (Devereux 1965b). Needless to say, the phenomenon of the neurotic "self-fulfilling prophecy" can also be understood in terms of Sperling's (1950) interpretation of the trauma as command, though it is necessary to add that such pathological distortions of admonitions occur only when the demand itself is largely nonfunctional and irrational and relies solely on "hallowed authority" for its prestige. Rational demands, susceptible of becoming part of the ego ideal—as distinct from the superego (Devereux 1956a)—seldom, if ever, elicit such a disastrously warped pseudo-compliance.

SEDUCTIVE APPEARANCE VS. ACCESSIBILITY

Sometimes a relatively minor culture trait or segment of behavior sheds a great deal of light on some major orientation, value, or conflict. It therefore seems worthwhile to discuss, at least in passing, the relatively minor matter of the delinquent girl's characteristically "seductive" dress, which is, demonstrably, nothing more than a symptom of her misguided and concealed puritanism.

The entire matter is neatly epitomized in "Hilda's" case: her skirts were so skintight that she had to be sewed into them; in practice this meant that these "beautifying" garments, supposed to suggest accessibility, actually made "Hilda's" body quite inaccessible. The same thing is true of the leotard and skintight torero pants worn by many delinquent girls. What matters in this context is that this *negative correlation* between the *appearance* of accessibility and *actual* accessibility is highly characteristic of female dress in general. Almost every cosmetic and costume device used by women to attract men actually decreases their practical accessibility. Elaborate coiffures and makeup must be protected, while elastic girdles encase the female body in a veritable armor. Moreover, many nondelinquent girls are quite aware of these facts and systematically use the "need" to protect their perfect makeup and clothes as an excuse for fending off male advances.

On a more subtle level, the delinquent girl's tastelessly showy and "sexy" dress actually protects her against emotional involvements. Since attire of this kind repels emotionally mature males, who are capable of love and demand genuine love in return, the delinquent girl's "uniform" functions as a kind of "psychosocial sieve," which repels the emotionally mature man, whom she might come to love, and attracts the emotionally immature man, who is incapable of loving and cannot tolerate being loved.

Last but not least, it can be conclusively demonstrated (Devereux 1960a) that, in both the female and the male, the excessive or outlandish decoration of the body is directly motivated by a sense of personal worthlessness:

The female's use of heavy makeup and showy clothing represents a defense against anxieties related to her castration complex, one of whose major symptoms is an unconscious belief in the defectiveness and repulsiveness of her sex organ and, by extension, her entire body (Devereux 1960a).

The male's sartorial excesses are more complexly motivated and are sociocultural rather than idiosyncratic in nature. For a variety of reasons society chooses to ascribe to certain men an altogether unrealistic amount of charismatic power or inherent excellence. Since, as Lowie so insightfully expressed it, man is not a total abstainer from reason, though he indulges in rationality with "fanatical moderation" (Lowie 1929), men whom society chooses to deify—as it deified certain Roman emperors—or addresses as "the Shadow of Allah on Earth," etc., welcome the splendid regalia of their status, which help them to forget that they, too, are mere mortals.[6]

In this sense, then, exaggerated female costumes represent, by and large, a compensation for the lack of a penis, while an overly splendid male costume is a kind of mask that facilitates the impersonation, by a very human and altogether imperfect being, of a preternaturally perfect Róheimian "group ideal" (Róheim 1932).

What male and female sartorial excesses have in common is that they promise more than mere human beings can deliver. In fact, one of the objectives of wearing such impossibly promising attire is precisely to inhibit demands that the promise be kept: just as it is forbidden to challenge the Shadow of Allah on Earth, Ruler of the Universe and King of Kings, to *prove* his omnipotence, so elaborate makeup, tight girdles, and skirts one is sewed into often justify the refusal to translate the promise of accessibility into actual accessibility, which would reveal both the bodily blemishes and functional inadequacies of the spurious Aphrodite Pandemos whom the delinquent and insecure girl seeks to impersonate.

As a final comment, I must point out that provocative clothing, intended to suggest a (spurious) accessibility, is today no longer uniquely characteristic of the delinquent female. There was a time when one could distinguish at a glance between the respectable wife or maiden, on the one hand, and the streetwalker on the other. In fact, around 1900, it was even possible to tell at once whether a respectable young female was a wife or a maiden, because the latter wore simple pastel-colored frocks and no jewelry or makeup (Clermont-Tonnerre 1928). This is no longer the case, since today's so-called virtuous women and maidens have learned not only the art of wearing attractive clothes but even bodily cleanliness from women of easy virtue.[7] This process is actually only one aspect of a type of interclass acculturation characteristic of demoralized societies, in which, as Sorokin (1937–41) has pointed out, the upper classes borrow certain cultural traits and behavior patterns from the lower classes.

These considerations have a direct bearing on the problem of the delinquent girl's preference for extremely "sexy" clothing. Since the fashions of the professionally "sexy" segments of the female population are today almost immediately adopted by "respectable" women, the deliberately nonrespectable woman must search for more and more extreme means of advertising her unique availability, even if, in the pursuit of this objective, she is finally obliged to select a distinctive attire that, while suggesting functional accessibility, actually makes her physically almost inaccessible.

A curious variant of this maneuver is the studied unglamorousness, lack of makeup, and "conservative" long hair of the modern female "beatnik," who is actually more drab than the most modestly dressed *jeune fille* of yesteryear ever was. This observation highlights the fact that there is no predetermined, basic, and *direct* correlation between genuine accessibility, on the one hand, and glamorous attire and nonconfining clothes on the other. Culturally determined fashions—which change constantly—alone decide precisely what type of costume is at any given moment *readily understood* to *signify* that its wearer defines herself as sexually accessible and is seeking to convey this self-definition to the male half of the population by means of clothing and cosmetic devices that represent metacommunication in the strictest sense of that term.

Of course, despite the (theoretically uninviting) drabness or the tight "sexy" attire that differentiates the delinquent girl from the "nice" girl—the *fille* (prostitute) from the *jeune fille*—both seek to attract men by suggesting that they are, in one way or the other—for money or "thrills," or for true love and marriage—available. The difference lies in the fact that, in the last analysis, the delinquent girl lacks the self-confidence of her nondelinquent sister. She therefore first overprotests and overadvertises her availability and then, when the chips are down, consents to gratify the man but, as we saw, *not herself,* since, being a puritan in disguise, she is orgastically frigid and emotionally incapable of love.

THERAPEUTIC AND EDUCATIONAL IMPLICATIONS

Social stresses and strains that *produce* psychopathological distortions of the personality demonstrably determine also the nature of the particular psychiatric nosologies, theories, and therapeutic practices that the society in question induces its scientists to evolve (chap. 1 and Devereux 1958a [1978a, chap. 10], 1961a). This process can be highlighted by several striking and very relevant examples.

179

Broadly speaking, the best and most sophisticated psychoanalytic theory of neuroses and psychoses explicitly recognizes that

a) The chief antagonist of the analyst is not the patient's id but his superego, and
b) The main instinctual component of psychiatric illness is not (mature) sexuality but pregenital sexuality fused with aggressive impulses.

These facts have been misunderstood by most laymen and also by some insufficiently sophisticated psychoanalysts. In accordance with the culturally determined biases of the society to which they belong, such persons tend to view the instincts as a kind of monstrous booby trap (Devereux 1951a [2d rev. ed., 1969] and systematically ignore Freud's explicit statement (1915) that the instincts we observe in the course of our analytic work are the wretchedly distorted products of repression and not the natural instincts in their unrepressed, pristine condition.[8]

Laymen, in particular, persist in thinking that psychoanalysis deals exclusively with problems created by sexuality rather than with those, related to man's aggressivity, that distort, or at least inhibit, the evolving of mature genital sexuality.

A closely related distortion of authentic psychoanalytic theory concerns Freud's valid finding that learning (related to the reality principle) is sometimes used as a defense against instinctual surges —that the cathecting of the external world sometimes diverts attention from inner drives.

Under the influence of our—partly culturally determined—dread of the instincts, Freud's sound observation was interpreted by some to mean that learning actually requires instinctual frustration. That this is a distortion of Freud's theory is easily proved by sound experimental demonstrations that (latent) learning can and does take place, even in mere rats, in the absence of instinctual frustration and reward (Tolman 1951). It is sufficient to introduce into psychoanalytic theory the commonsense Tolmanian distinctions between learning and behavior and between latent and manifest learning to dispose, once and for all, of this distortion of Freud's real thought.

These distortions of genuine psychoanalytic theory, which most thoughtful psychoanalysts explicitly repudiate, possess, nonetheless, a cultural impetus sufficiently strong to have led to the weird nosological concept of the "instinct-ridden psychopath," though it is quite easy to prove that such persons are actually superego-ridden psychopaths (chap. 7). Moreover, these individuals, who supposedly seek to perpetuate an infantile instinctual paradise, actually seek to enact in adult life the *child's conception* of adult behavior (Devereux 1955c). In brief, the contrast between the psychoanalyst's conception of neuroses and psychoses as distortions due to the superego, and his conception of most types of delinquency and psychopathy as distortions due to the instincts, is largely due to a methodological error. This error consists in treating the *quantitatively* greater role played by (manifest) aggressivity in delinquency than in the neuroses and psychoses as though it were a *qualitative* difference. Once this point is made clear, the contrast between neurosis and psychosis, on the one hand, and delinquency, on the other, is readily seen to be *quantitative* rather than *qualitative*. This interpretation of the contrast does not conflict with Freud's implicit view that delinquency is in some ways the obverse of neurosis, since the superego —which is the etiological factor in both forms of personality distortion—produces one type of conflict and symptomatology in neuroses and psychoses and an entirely different set of conflicts and symptoms in delinquency.

The *pseudo*-psychoanalytic theories discussed in the preceding paragraphs, which have been evolved under the pressure of certain cultural biases, are largely responsible for the inadequacies and inefficiencies of the therapeutic and educational procedures derived from them. This is not at all surprising, since, as stated above, identical social strains lead to culture-specific personality distortions, to culturally determined scientific (psychiatric) theories, and to culturally determined therapeutic and educational-rehabilitational procedures. In the case of sex-delinquent girls, this cultural bias has led to the illusion that they are hedonists rather than (unconscious) puritans, that they are "sexy" rather than pregenital, and that they are actuated by the pleasure principle instead of by sadomasochism.

It is one of the basic theses of this study that the delinquent girl's sexual acts are what I have elsewhere called "red-herring symptoms" (screen symptoms) (Devereux 1953a), which, precisely because they upset the adult, divert his attention from the *real* anxieties that beset these girls. The cultural "scandalousness" of these symptoms impinges so strongly on the observer that he sometimes forgets that he is a psychoanalyst and begins to think like a naive Watsonian or Guthrian behaviorist. The same phenomenon can be observed in connection with the perversions. Some years ago, at a meeting of the American Psychoanalytic Association, I pointed out that, in terms of classical psychoanalytic theory, a perversion is not simply a *motorically* deviant type of sexual activity, tabooed by society; it is, above all, a *psychologically* immature and deviant attitude, toward both the genital act and the sexual partner, *that can be present even*

181

during the motorically most conventional type of sexual relations within marriage—for example, in the form of neurotic fantasies or the unvoiced pretense that one's sex partner is some other, more desirable, person.

Hypnotized by the delinquent girl's ostentatious "red-herring" sexual misconduct, psychotherapists as well as educators have come to see the delinquent girl exactly *as she wishes to be seen:* as a rutting "id machine," running wild, instead of as a puritan whose superego has gone berserk. They therefore concentrate all their efforts on controlling the (screen) symptoms instead of coping with the real problems besetting these girls. This explains why we continue to use monastic segregation, cold showers, tranquilizers, and the like to cope with problems that demand psychoanalytic insight and why we cooperate with the delinquent girl's contempt for, and dread of, mature sexuality by a further depreciation of sex.

Governor Alfred E. Smith once declared that the cure for the ills of democracy is not *less* democracy but *more* democracy. The same principle should also be applied—*mutatis mutandis*—to the rehabilitation of the sex-delinquent girl. Since we do not view a neurotic mysophagist as a gluttonous gourmet, we seek to persuade this compulsive eater of carrion that man's proper food is not garbage but tasty and hygienic food. We do not encourage him to develop anorexia nervosa! Yet the latter is precisely what we tend to do in our work with the sex-delinquent girl. Our proper therapeutic and educational objective is to restore the self-despising delinquent girl's self-esteem to the point where she can deem herself worthy of genuine and mature love experiences. In order to achieve this aim, we must attempt to replace her neurotic dread of psychosexual genitality with a striving for mature genitality. In brief, we must raise her level of aspiration so as to make her more exacting in the realm of sexuality and must persuade her that she deserves to—and can—attain true genitality. It is not enough to interfere with her immature, masochistic, and frigid promiscuousness. It is even more necessary to persuade her that such acts are almost insurmountable obstacles to the attainment of an unambivalent, anxiety-free, and mature genital character structure and of the capacity to love. We must inhibit her psychologically pregenital acting out, not because it "shocks" *us* or because it is "sinful," but because it prevents *her* from enjoying the legitimate delights and rewards of mature genitality and love to which all human beings are entitled.

I believe in the *vis medicatrix naturae* and in man's inherent desire for happiness and maturity. I therefore believe that psychological illness can be cured only if we pit man's striving for health against his illness. I know from experience that patients react first with surprise and then with hope and a new determination to recover from their illness to the suggestion that the joys of maturity are greater than those of continued immaturity.

Case 13.—The patient also mentioned in Case 10—who regained her orgastic capacity when it was pointed out to her that the best way to control her promiscuous impulses was to enjoy her legitimate marital relationship—reacted with great surprise when it was pointed out to her that the joys of maturity *exceed* those of immaturity. This idea struck her as entirely new, perhaps because, like so many other systematically infantilized patients, her parents had selfishly persuaded her that adulthood means nothing but dreary toil and renunciation (Devereux 1956a). The particular session in which this thesis was first advanced was an important turning point in her treatment.

Case 14.—A seemingly highly successful and prosperous analysand, who had a marked tendency to "please himself" but systematically avoided major emotional and intellectual involvements, invariably responded with genuine emotion and new and meaningful insights to the psychoanalyst's comment that he was passing up the best things in life. Otherwise stated, every confrontation with the *availability* of mature satisfactions triggered a new forward step in this patient's progress toward recovery.

It is important to stress, quite explicitly, that the delinquent girl, confronted with the ideal of mature, guilt-free genitality, does *not* respond by asking for an immediate "laboratory demonstration" or by an unmanageable intensification of the transference relationship, though one suspects that the *dread* of such a possibility plays a major role in the therapist's and educator's reluctance to pit the ideal of mature genitality against the delinquent girl's red-herring symptom of self-defeating pseudo-sexual acting-out. In reality, both delinquent and nondelinquent analysands almost invariably react to attempts to raise their sexual level of aspiration by a *diminution* of their *neurotic* transference demands and by an appreciable increase in their cathecting of *reality*. This finding is not at all surprising, since it is basic psychoanalytic theory that a maximally genital character structure necessarily implies the capacity for maximal genital enjoyment and for truly gratifying object (love) relationships.

Needless to say, attempts to raise the level of aspiration of such girls are successful only if their analysts and educators are completely sincere. Indeed, though such girls are severely disturbed, they are not necessarily fools as well. They therefore sense whether the analyst is a hypocrite, who dangles an unattainable carrot before them, or whether he actually believes them capable—and worthy—of attaining true maturity. Above all, they invariably sense whether the analyst's attitude is genuinely objective and helpful or whether his extolling the satisfactions of true genitality is actuated by an unconscious seductiveness, representing an acting-out of the countertransference.

SUMMARY

1. The phenomenon of so-called female juvenile sex delinquency is a product of certain characteristic stresses of our society.

2. These same social stresses are also responsible for our distorted conception of the nature of this type of deviation and, specifically, for our failure to grasp that such girls are pathological and masochistic puritans rather than uninhibited "id machines," operating solely in terms of the pleasure principle.

3. The therapeutic and educational methods and procedures derived from this incorrect conception of the deviation under consideration are inevitably doomed to failure, because they deal with behavioral appearances instead of psychoanalytic realities.

4. The true challenge is not the delinquent girl but her analyst or educator, since his culturally determined anxieties and *wissenssoziologisch* analyzable biases induce him to treat a *maladie imaginaire* rather than the real problems of the delinquent girl, who acts out her nonsexual problems by pseudo-sexual means.

9

A Sociological Theory
of Schizophrenia
(1939)

> I never realized there were so many things in our culture.
> *Mbrieng, my* best *Indochinese informant*

According to the great mathematician and physicist, Henri Poincaré (1901), if a phenomenon admits of one explanation, it will also admit of a number of other explanations, all equally satisfactory. I propose here to examine schizophrenia exclusively from the sociological viewpoint and to offer *a* sociological theory of this psychosis. I say *a* sociological theory and not *the* sociological theory because it may be possible to find other sociological theories of this psychosis.

In examining a problem from a restricted viewpoint, one may lose sight of certain important details. On the other hand, one is almost certain to bring to light a number of hitherto unsuspected details and correlations that would be missed altogether—or whose significance would be missed—by someone investigating the same problem from the "normal" viewpoint. Furthermore, by restricting the field of vision, one automatically decreases the number of (necessarily) undefined basic concepts, the multiplication of which often leads to a set of postulates that is (in the mathematical sense) not wholly coherent and compendious. Finally, one must bear in mind that Emile Meyerson (1921) justified partial explanations by stating that any complete explanation of a phenomenon implies denying that phenomenon by reducing it entirely to other phenomena.

In this chapter I shall consider schizophrenia as an exclusively functional disorder—a disorder of the type that can be produced in animals only under carefully contrived laboratory conditions, whereas it occurs "spontaneously" in man, who lives in society and possesses a culture. This observation leads me to an investigation of the connection between functional disorders and sociocultural factors.

In the original version of this study (1939) considerable space had to be devoted to the refutation of certain erroneous hypotheses that were fashionable at the time. These polemics can now be substan-

185

tially abridged; I mention them only briefly to show how many absurd opinions can be advanced on the subject.

1. Despite elaborate theorizing and a certain number of experiments, attempts to prove that all psychological disorders are due to organic and/or congenital factors constantly lead one to give the Scottish verdict, "Not proven." Yet, attempts to revive this theory continue to be made. The relatively constant statistical incidence of psychological disorders in all societies has been offered as proof of the organic or congenital etiology of—or organic predisposition to —psychological illness (Eaton and Weil 1955). Now, it is obvious that this theory implicitly presupposes the genetic and constitutional identity of all nations and all races—which is manifestly false. The simple fact that there is variation from one race to another in the percentage of persons belonging, for example, to the O blood group suffices to show this. I have proposed (1956d) a much simpler explanation: A society loses its capacity to survive if the proportion of individuals suffering from psychological illnesses, related to the flaws of that society or culture, attains the point of saturation (chap. 10).

2. The theory that the wear and tear of modern civilization is responsible for functional psychological disorders is now fortunately outmoded. Pseudo-Hippocrates described this type of disorder long before ethnologists and psychologists went into the field to gather empirical evidence of the existence of functional disorders among primitives.

3. Equally outmoded is the thesis according to which functional disorders observable in primitive society are due to the "inferiority" of these races. This view has been invalidated by all the empirical findings of comparative psychology.

4. Some twenty years ago, in a private discussion, someone suggested to me that the seemingly identical incidence of functional psychiatric disorders in primitive[1] and advanced societies may be due to an important though unrecognized difference, namely, that in the primitive population a smaller percentage may *become* psychologically perturbed but that, once perturbed, the primitive *remains* psychiatrically ill for a longer period of time than does the Occidental patient, who has access to modern psychiatric facilities. In short, the "turnover" in the psychiatrically ill subsection of a primitive population may simply be lower. Now, so far as I know, existing data do not suffice to substantiate this hypothesis, which should perhaps be tested through field studies. There is, however, at least one well-established fact that is incompatible with this hypothesis: in many primitive groups the life-expectancy of the psychologically perturbed person is quite short, for he is often poorly supervised

and cared for and at times is even badly mistreated. Two examples will substantiate this. In Basutoland, it has been found (G. I. Jones 1951) that an unduly large proportion of the victims in human sacrifices were psychologically impaired individuals. Among the Sedang Moi, the psychotic often escapes from his village and disappears into the jungle, where he perishes from exposure, hunger, snake bite, and the like (Devereux 1933–35).

In short, functional disorders are as prevalent in primitive as in modern society. Only one highly significant distinction between the two exists: schizophrenia is practically absent in truly primitive societies. To my knowledge, this was first pointed out by Seligman (1932). It is true that Laubscher, in 1937, diagnosed many cases of schizophrenia among the Tembu, but a careful examination of his book and film led me to question, as early as 1939, the accuracy of some of his diagnoses. Moreover, and this is of capital importance, at the time Laubscher studied the Tembu they were already in the throes of a brutal and oppressive acculturation process. Information that has come to light since the publication of his work—which is excellent and rates as a precursor in the field—corroborates my initial thesis, that true ("nuclear") schizophrenia is never encountered among populations that have not been subjected to a brutal acculturation. Furthermore, the appearance of authentic cases of schizophrenia in so-called underdeveloped regions—a fact reported in recent field studies—was perfectly foreseeable on the basis of my theory, because today there is scarcely any tribe sufficiently primitive or sufficiently isolated to escape the violent and massive pressures of acculturation (Devereux 1961a). In terms of my initial theory I can now (1970) predict that schizophrenia will be one of the most common functional disorders for some time to come among societies that were, until recently, primitive and are now undergoing rapid social and cultural transformations. [*Addendum 1979*: It is becoming increasingly evident that when a laborer from an underdeveloped country has a *"bouffée délirante"*—which, in his own social setting, disappears in a matter of days—is hospitalized in the industrialized country in which he works, his illness can become chronic and turn into a schizophrenia (Devereux 1978b).]

The word "primitive" must, of course, be taken in its strictest sense. Though an Arab, Hindu, or Malay peasant or laborer may be as illiterate as a Papuan and may live nearly as "primitively," he is nonetheless a member of a high civilization. The degree of evolution of a civilization is not determined by the degree of cultural development of its lowest representatives—regardless of the size of that group within the total population. In America, the best college faculties, not the hillbillies of Kentucky, and, in Polynesia, the learned priests, not the ignorant fishermen, are indicative of the cultural development of their civilizations. This point is crucial because, as will soon become apparent, one of the causes of schizophrenia is precisely the gap between the complexity of a culture and the inherent limitations of the "field of competence" of even the best minds that participate in it.

What, then, in a culture, and in its degree of cultural development, is functionally connected with the presence or absence of schizophrenia? Neither the "temperament" of a culture (Linton 1936) nor the ethnic character of its representatives is among the determining factors. Even fifty years ago schizophrenia was as rare among the strongly extroverted Khirghiz of Astrakhan as among their neighbors, the sullen, introverted Kalmyks (Skliar and Starikowa 1929). The presence or absence of schizophrenia thus seems to be functionally related *only* to the development of the culture, although its frequency can be correlated with other cultural factors (chap. 10).

My first duty is therefore to specify what I mean by the "development" of a culture. As a first approximation, I shall define culture as the sum of all shared techniques that are not biologically transmitted. *These techniques are not juxtaposed at random; they form a closely interwoven whole;* they are organized along certain general conceptual lines (chaps. 2, 16), which constitute the skeleton or "pattern" (Benedict 1934) of the culture. One need not imagine this skeleton to be made up of anything tangible, such as crafts. One could think of it as a kind of conceptual blueprint to which the contractor, as well as the bricklayer, conforms at every step in building a house. Speaking anthropomorphically, this skeleton is the personality of a culture; speaking theoretically, it is the structure of its invariants.

Now, precisely because these techniques constitute a consistent pattern, the existence of technique A generally excludes the presence of technique "non-A" and implies, and even requires, the presence of other techniques—B, C, and so forth—which are functionally interrelated with it.[2] While one might think of this as "organization," I prefer to call it "simultaneous causality"; this concept, evolved by the philosopher Joseph Petzold, implies the coherence of "spatial" structures.

I shall first analyze the significance, for the study of schizophrenia, of a culture's theoretically quantifiable *richness* in cultural *traits* and then the significance of the *complexity* of its organization of these traits.

1. *The richness of the cultural inventory.* Every culture can be

broken down into culture traits or culture elements. The fact that certain of these traits can be further broken down into simpler traits is relatively unimportant. What matters is that they can be broken down only into more elementary culture traits and *not into something else*. Every culture is composed of a certain number of such traits organized into patterns, which assign a contextual meaning to them.

The first of two fundamental differences between "higher" and "lower" cultures is to be found in the number of traits composing them. Consider cultures A, B, and C. A is composed of x traits, B is composed of y traits, and C of z traits. If $x > y > z$, then one can arrange cultures A, B, and C in one, and only one, order of increasing complexity of inventories, namely, C, B, A. Though it is assuredly impossible to make a complete inventory of any culture, this difficulty is only technical. It is self-evident that modern American culture contains more traits than Malay culture, and the latter more traits than Tasmanian culture.

It is in terms of this definition of cultural richness that I first propose to interpret the problem of schizophrenia.

Culture-and-society is essentially an environment—of a special nature, no doubt, but an environment nevertheless. The individual has to orient himself as much within this environment as in the physical one. That is to say, he must be able to find his way about in the cultural environment by understanding its signs, symbols, and signals, by knowing its rules, etc. Efficient and useful orientation in both the physical and the cultural environment involves a certain number of inborn aptitudes as well as a certain amount of learning. It is impossible, however, to learn to orient oneself in a given environment unless that environment has a certain degree of logical consistency—has, as a characteristic trait, the presence of certain regularities. Thus, one could not learn to swim if water were one day lighter than air and the next day as viscous as axle grease. The survival of even the simplest virus depends on certain regularities in its environment. In short, the organism extrapolates from past experience—either biologically (although in a non-Lamarckian way) or else by "learning"—to possible future experience; it "makes" predictions and then acts in conformity with them. Living matter extrapolates from real experience to future experience, which it comes to view as a kind of "generalized image" (or program) evolved, as an abstraction, from the mass of previous experiences.

The number of physical laws of which man has to be aware in order to orient himself in the world of daily life is surprisingly small. Even the youngest child soon learns that lifting a stone involves a certain expenditure of effort and that he cannot see in a dark room. He then infers that lifting a table or seeing in a dark forest at midnight involves similar difficulties. In other words, the child relies on the constancy of physical laws. So does a plant.

Orientation in the sociocultural sphere is much more complex, in spite of the fact that culture has a specific pattern—a structure—which implies the presence, in culture and cultural processes, of certain regularities that are not only empirically accessible but often explicitly formulated.[3] Thus, when I greet a friend, he does not, as a rule, pull a gun on me. Man counts on such regularities for his cultural orientation.

Unfortunately, the number of sociocultural traits and regularities is very large. If one assembled all the laws, bylaws, statutes, and rules and regulations to which a citizen of Chicago, Illinois, or Bordeaux, France, is subject and added to it a list of his religious duties, as well as a copy of Emily Post's *Opera Omnia,* one would assemble a library that would far exceed in size a treatise on all aspects of the physical universe. This suggests that orientation in any cultural environment is much more difficult than orientation in the physical environment and also that orientation in a culture rich in traits, such as American culture, is more difficult than orientation in a simple cultural environment, poor in traits, like that of the Semang of the Malay Peninsula. In terms of my basic assumption, it is precisely this *difficulty in orientation* that causes functional disorders in man, who has a culture, and prevents their spontaneous occurrence in animals, who have none. Now, since there is practically no schizophrenia in primitive societies unless they are subjected to a brutal process of acculturation, which necessarily implies a multiplication of traits that are not *immediately* coordinated with the preexisting patterns, one can conclude that the high rate of schizophrenia in advanced cultures is functionally related to problems of orientation. This is, of course, a partial explanation, which will be investigated, first of all, in terms of the individual's participation in his culture.

Man's capacities are not unlimited. The most brilliant of physicists may be completely "at sea" in the realms of philology or law. This leads me to a readily demonstrable second fact: there is no appreciable difference in the mental endowment of the various races. Still, in response to those who (even in the 1970s) continue to advocate the opposite view, I am prepared to propose a more sophisticated formulation of my viewpoint, although I myself am in complete disagreement with these opinions. Let it be assumed, for the sake of argument only, that the white race is more intelligent than the Bushmen. This hypothesis does not permit one to postulate a simple and direct relationship between the degree of development of a culture and the "inborn" intelligence of the *carriers* of that culture, for the simple reason that an Australian or Bushman can learn to live in modern society. One is therefore forced to concede that the difference between "white" and Bushman intelligence cannot be as great as the difference between modern culture and Bushman culture. In other words, the most brilliant biologist shares in a smaller part of modern culture than a clever Bushman shares in Bushman culture. This is obvious to ethnological field workers. Few, if any, native informants of average intelligence will fail to provide fairly adequate information about all major, and perhaps even minor, aspects of their own tribal culture. On the other hand, a student of modern culture will time and again come up against a blank wall and be advised by his informant to consult someone with specialized knowledge. Moreover, though there are also specialists in native cultures (shamans, smiths, and so forth), the totality of their knowledge is not *utterly* beyond the average native's reach. Anyone who is familiar with the history of science knows that certain men, such as Aristotle, had a command of the whole knowledge of their times. Today the humanistic ideal, which was also the ideal of the French encyclopedists and, later, of the *Universalgenie*, has disappeared, simply because it has become unattainable. The rapid increase of the culture traits composing modern civilization has outpaced the increase in the mental capacities of the white "race" during the same period of time.

One of the fundamental differences between primitive and civilized man is that the former shares in almost all aspects of his tribal culture, while the latter shares in only a small segment of his. This is even expressed socially (as my discussion of initiation ceremonies will show further on).

I have applied Mach's theory of scientific experimentation in thus formulating the problem. According to Mach, an experiment consists in holding n factors constant and varying one other factor (and sometimes more than one). It is my belief that, in doing so, I have not unduly simplified our problem.

I will here examine, first, the development and socialization of the primitive child, then that of the modern child. Every primitive child has a biological father and mother. Whether a primitive culture officially admits or denies (Róheim 1937) this biological relationship is irrelevant. It suffices to say that there is always a man and a woman toward whom the child has certain duties and from whom, in turn, he may expect certain favors. The totality of this set of mutual obligations can be grasped by means of the functional analysis of kinship systems. The importance of such reciprocal duties has been repeatedly stressed by Malinowski (1934) and others. Nevertheless, in addition to his biological parents, the primitive child sometimes has another set of relatives to whom he has obligations and from whom he may expect favors analogous to those that characterize the parent-child relationship. Thus Linton (personal communication) attached great importance to the fact that in many primitive communities a child may, when hungry, toddle up to a considerable number of women with a fair expectation of being nursed. Among the Mohave Indians (Devereux 1947) an orphan's maternal grandmother, even past her menopause, will be able to nurse it if she submits to galactopeic treatment. Also, in many primitive communities, the staff of authority is wielded chiefly by the mother's brother. All of this leads to an early dispersal of both the libidinal attachments and the antagonisms (Devereux 1942a) that in our own society characterize, almost exclusively, the relations between parents and children. If one assumes that a child's libido and aggressivity are not unlimited, it is easy to see why, in many primitive societies, one does not find the emotionally charged tangle of undercurrents characteristic of modern families, composed, as they are, of a very small number of closely related individuals.[4] When affective ties are widely dispersed, strong conflicts do not arise. Hence, it is unnecessary to ascribe hidden virtues to primitive children in order to explain why they are, as a rule, well-behaved and friendly toward strangers. Functionally speaking, the child frequently has, not one mother (or father), but $mother_1$, $mother_2$, and so forth (or $father_1$, $father_2$, and so forth). This statement gives a new meaning to so-called "classificatory" kinship systems, which lump together the mother, the mother's sister, and even the mother's female maternal cousins under the common appellation "mother." One would ascribe an undue amount of naiveté to the native if one assumed that he is *unable* to distinguish between $mother_1$ (his biological mother), $mother_2$ (his mother's sister), $mother_3$ (his mother's maternal female cousin), and others. This terminology simply implies similarity of the relationships existing between the child and any individual member of the class of individuals lumped together under the common (*relational*) term "mother." What was just said about "mothers" may also be said of "fathers," "brothers," and so forth. *No problem in extrapolation is involved here.* The child does not generalize from $mother_1$ to $mother_2$. He perceives the relationship between himself and the class of individuals he refers to as "mother" on a very low level of abstraction. Hence, just as in modern society, it is only in pathological cases that the child extends to all other mothers the antagonism he feels toward mother$_x$.

Socialization consists in a gradual severing of the tense, affectively overcharged bonds that exist between the child and the members of the restricted (or biological) family. Now, in primitive societies— where, as I have just shown, relationships of this type do not, as a rule, obtain—the child at a comparatively early age forms mild attachments and antagonisms toward a large proportion of the individuals composing his social group and is therefore well prepared —emotionally, at least—to become a full member of the tribe when he is still very young. In other words, he knows both emotionally and intellectually a large number of individuals because his social universe—unlike that of our own children—has never been restricted to a narrow circle of relatives and close friends. This may also explain the primitive's quasi-automatic obedience to custom, which ethnologists find so hard to understand.

In the field of concrete knowledge, the primitive child learns at a very early age the rudiments of most tribal techniques and lores. Little girls of five and six are not seldom accomplished housewives, and boys of twelve have perhaps one or two raids to their credit. Hence, the primitive adolescent is more or less completely and satisfactorily oriented in all segments of his sociocultural environment. He is both emotionally and intellectually ready to be initiated into full tribal membership. (This may also explain why legal maturity occurs at so early an age in simpler civilizations.) True, he may, later on, acquire additional knowledge (as one may discover new details by continuously traveling a well-beaten path). He may also form new "affective" attachments. But—and this is of crucial importance —his subsequently acquired knowledge is already implicitly contained in what Tolman (1951) would call the "cognitive map" of his sociocultural territory—a map he acquired at an early date. Either this is so or the whole theory of culture patterns and the theory of the structural coherence of all cultures must be thrown overboard.

Now, figuratively speaking, no man can know more than, let us say, a thousand individual coconut palms. If these thousand palm trees are scattered over, and form the sole vegetation of, the remote island that his tribe inhabits, then, little as he may know of *each* of these trees, he knows all there is to know about his sparsely wooded region. If one replaces coconut palms with *culture elements* and geographical territory with *sociocultural territory,* one assigns a concrete meaning to the statement that the adolescent primitive is fully oriented in everything that now composes, or is ever likely to compose, his world. In *this* world he can never be disoriented. He may know some specific nook or cranny of it better than another; but, if he must suddenly abandon his profession as a smith and become a potter, or if he must suddenly leave his own village and move to a neighboring one, he can, on a very low level of abstraction and extrapolation, adapt himself almost immediately to the new situation, which is *sufficiently* similar to his first environment not to elicit in him the kind of dysphoria that is produced by disorientation.

It might, of course, be supposed that the initiation ceremony—which often includes severe physical ordeals—would cause psychological "upsets" in the individual undergoing it. The facts, however, do not seem to support such a view, because, even if such upsets occur, they apparently do not lead to the initiate's *cultural* disorientation.[5] In primitive societies, status is, in general, very clearly defined, and the duties and obligations of each status are more or less known to *all* members of the tribe. Hence, the assuming of a new status—or accession to a new age grade—does not involve disorientation (Benedict 1938). It may be objected that initiation rituals often consist in imparting "secrets" to the new initiates. Unfortunately for this argument, these "secrets" are, as often as not, of a *negative* nature. A typical example of this kind of secret is found among certain Northwest Coast Indians. The initiate is informed that the great secret is the fact that *there is no secret!* This may come as a shock to the initiate, but it does not disorient him.

There is no need to deny that the transition from adulthood to old age is not always smooth, even in primitive society. Linton (in Kardiner 1945) describes this situation among the Comanche Indians as follows. The unsuccessful warrior finds solace in becoming a mild, wise old man, as prescribed by Comanche culture. The extremely successful warrior, upon entering the class of old men, is still sufficiently surrounded by a halo of fame to accommodate himself without resentment to his new status. Only the mediocre warrior will show resentment, and he vents his envy by becoming a wizard and bewitching the young warriors who are beginning to acquire fame on the battlefield. In brief, in Comanche society, as in many other primitive societies, the rights and duties of the various age grades are so varied and so well known that almost any temperament will find at least one phase of adulthood congenial. For him who does not, there remains the recourse of becoming a shaman, which I shall discuss below (see also chap. 1).

One of the most important characteristics of primitive life is the absence of what may be termed "the refusal to grow up and to assume responsibilities," so common in our society and so admirably described by the novelist Peter Mendelssohn (1931). Among primitives the advantages of being an adult are forcibly impressed on the child at the earliest opportunity. This is well exemplified by the social implications of Arunta food taboos. A number of such taboos are imposed on the young (Strehlow 1907–21), and, if they do not comply with them, the somatic signs of physical maturity—which would free them from these irksome restrictions—will fail to appear: the girl's breasts will not become pendulous, the boy's facial and body hair will not grow, and so they will remain forever subject to these taboos. And even though Mead (1928) reports that the Samoan child is loath to "presume above its age," she nowhere mentions an instance of a "refusal to grow up." With the exception of a few special statuses—that of the homosexual for sexually feeble men among the Tanala (Linton 1933), for example, or that of the shaman in various cultures (Devereux 1961a)—primitive society offers few niches into which people desiring to remain infantile may withdraw.

And yet the age at which the child is initiated is usually a critical one. Not only does the initiate enter upon a new and fuller social life, but his pubescent body now makes new demands—sexual and other—so that he (or she) must adjust not only to a new status but also to a new physiological pattern (Devereux 1967b). Yet, because of the absence of stork or other mythologies *ad usum Delphini,* the arrival of sexual maturity is unaccompanied by *disorientation* (which is not to be confused with a socially prescribed or purely neurotic *fear*). This would explain, at least in part, the absence of the latency period among so many primitive tribes, where the passage from the infantile-erotic to the adult-erotic stage is, as a rule, free of psychological blocks (Devereux 1951d).

These observations bring me to the subject of virginity and continence. According to Róheim (1933), the Australian feels that a virgin is *alknarintja*—a savage being, demonic, untamed, and almost sacred ("sacred" in Durkheim's sense; that is, dangerous); she has to be deflowered (and, in some groups, violently deflowered) before becoming a full member of the tribe. Similarly, the Mohave Indians believe (Devereux 1941) that not until they marry do twins cease to be visitors from heaven and become true members of the rank and file. In this sense, continence—ritual or otherwise—could be interpreted as a fixation at a stage of unsocialized infantilism. I have shown elsewhere (1939c) that incest is prohibited because it diminishes social cohesion. This viewpoint is fairly close to that of Freud and of Zuckerman (1932), who consider sex to be the basis of social life. In fact, setting a high value on virginity seems incompatible with the occurrence of puberty rites. Deflowering seems to sanction on the motor level what puberty sanctions on the endocrine level: initiation into the full sexual life of the adult.

Thus, at no stage of his life is the primitive likely to become disoriented—as long as the fabric of his culture and the destiny of his tribe are not subjected to very strong interference from without. Among many primitives the child is, intellectually at least, a "little man" in every sense of the word, who, because of the relatively simple structure of his cultural milieu, may safely extrapolate from the familiar to the less familiar. Actually, even his juvenile behavior is often viewed primarily as *incomplete* adult behavior (Devereux 1968a).

The situation just described is so different from the one obtaining among ourselves that a brief and partial enumeration of differences will suffice for present purposes. In our society, libidinal bonds as well as antagonisms are not diffused but are canalized within a narrow circle of relatives and close friends. Emotional dispersal occurs late, and socialization is accompanied by many upsets. The French proverb, "One cannot please the whole world and one's own father at the same time," expresses this situation. The modern child is trained to adapt himself to narrow, specific, and often idiosyncratic demands and privileges. His many "aunts" do not act as a *class* of aunts but as a random group of individuals, although language suggests an *inexistent* identity of relationships. The child is so well trained to *be* a child that it has difficulties in *ceasing to be* one. Puerility is artificially prolonged by doting or tyrannical parents, who hate to see their "baby" grow up. One cannot help being struck by the fact that "dutiful, pure daughters" and "mama's little boys" furnish an unduly large proportion of schizophrenics. The incidence of both male and female virginity in schizophrenics is also disproportionately high.

Last of all, to encourage the prolonging of puerility past its normal duration, adult life is depicted as one of incessant toil, while childhood is always represented as a golden age (Devereux 1956a). "The black bull of life will gore you all too soon" has been whispered into the ears of more than one schizophrenic and adolescent suicide. Hence, the refusal to grow up is characteristic of our modern society, to a degree that few who have not *lived* with primitives would suspect.

Intimately connected with the inherent complexities of civilized life is the artificial delaying of legal maturity past the age of sexual and intellectual maturity, although this delay sometimes manifests itself precisely in those areas of a complex society that are the most backward—for instance, in rural Ireland (Arensberg 1950; Arensberg and Kimball 1940). The age at which one becomes a full member of the community is apparently a function of the complexities of that culture. Until the advent of legal maturity, the child and the adolescent are trained not in life but in a profession. This explains the comparative sanity of modern nations in their professions and their comparative infantilism in all matters connected with life and with larger issues involving social problems.

2. *The problem of structural complexity* is linked only empirically with the comparative "richness" of cultures. Theoretically, it is possible to imagine a culture with a complex structure but having few culture traits, and a culture with a simple structure but rich in traits —in spite of the fact that one source of the richness of a culture is precisely the multiple context of each trait (chap. 16), which confers on it a variety of meanings that are also culture traits.[6]

I shall now analyze the nature and the complexity of modern civilization. The primitive *can be* and *is in fact* aware of the "total" pattern of his social and cultural milieu. He can be aware of it at an early age because his milieu is so structured that it can be comprehended as a whole on a comparatively low level of abstraction by extrapolating from the familiar to the less familiar. (I say "less familiar" instead of "unknown.")

Modern man is confronted with a more difficult situation. It is very difficult to detect the total American pattern in a complex sociocultural milieu containing such diversified structures as great universities and illiterate Louisiana Cajuns, Long Island estates, Chicago tenements, and Wyoming ranches. To the casual observer these subpatterns of American life contain few similarities indeed. Seen mathematically they are invariant in a few respects only. It is impossible to extrapolate effectively from one's knowledge of any of these subpatterns to other subpatterns, at least not on the low level of abstraction of which the average man is capable. Thus the total pattern —which is highly abstract—cannot be expressed in literary plots. This explains why the "Great American Novel" has not yet been written and may never be written.[7] The level of abstraction on which the *general* American pattern would emerge from the jumble of disparate anecdotes is simply not the proper subject matter of even the highest form of literature. The pattern does not appear on a pictorial, objectified level (the equivalent of mechanical models in classical physical theory); it can be observed only on a level of abstract inferential units and conceptual schemes (the equivalents of what Bridgman [1932] called mathematical models). In this sense, in earlier quantum theory the electron *was* a ball of electricity, but at present [1939] it *is* a differential equation (Dirac).

I might suggest in this regard that the greatness of Greek tragedy is directly related to the limited dimensions of the Greek city-state and the relative simplicity of its organization; a plot involving only a handful of characters could reflect this society's structure in its totality. Suggestive as this hypothesis seems, it cannot be elaborated in the present context.

Many persons still try to orient themselves in the dense jungle of the American sociocultural pattern with the help of a map depicting the sociocultural pattern of the back yard in which they grew up, although they would not attempt to drive from New York City to Los Angeles by relying on a map showing only the streets of Muncie, Indiana. The street map of Muncie is on such a low level of abstraction that, if one sought to find one's way around the United States by extrapolating exclusively from it, one would most certainly go astray. The map of the United States is on a higher level of abstraction; it contains only the most salient features of the street map of Muncie. Unfortunately, the average man has had it hammered into him all his life that his home town is the navel of the universe. Little wonder, then, that he pretends to understand the universe in terms of its hypothetical "navel" instead of trying to discover, at a higher level of abstraction, the total pattern of the universe of which this "navel" is but a subpattern or functional part. I can make this quite clear by giving a legal example. The Constitution of the United States is the general pattern of all American state constitutions, city ordinances, and so forth. Any federal or state law, and any city ordinance, becomes void if it is declared unconstitutional by the United States Supreme Court. The decision that a law is unconstitutional is equivalent to saying that it is *not* invariant with regard to the Constitution in some fundamental respects. Although this is so, I defy the most astute expert in extrapolation, the most versatile lawyer, to reconstruct, from a city ordinance concerning the removal of garbage, the whole text of the United States Constitution *by extrapolation only*. The two are simply not on the same level of abstraction. I further defy the same lawyer to reconstruct, by extrapolating solely from the California statutes concerning arson, the Virginia statutes concerning vagrancy, although both are on the same level of abstraction. On the other hand, any first-rate ethnologist can, from the detailed account of a single important ceremony, give a fairly good picture of the rest of the culture without using either comparative material from other tribes or his knowledge of the given culture area.[8] Extrapolation will suffice, as a rule, because primitive cultures are synthesized (integrated, patterned) on a rather low level of abstraction.

In brief, the primitive knows all the trees of his *sparsely* wooded island, while the modern man knows, at most, all the trees of a small section of his *densely* wooded continent. The primitive can wander about his whole island without becoming disoriented. Modern man can barely leave his own back yard without becoming lost.

Moreover, modern man is not safe even in his own back yard. "Progress" will seek him out on his North Dakota farm, on his Long Island estate, in his laboratory. The back yard in which he grew up is not the same as the one in which he "still" lives. Radio, labor issues, international complications, will make secret inroads into his walled garden, and no "No Trespassing" sign can protect him. Modern man lives on an escalator. In order to keep his position constant *with respect to the walls,* he must run swiftly backward, thereby modifying his position *with respect to the steps* of the escalator. The primitive's escalator simply moves more slowly. Whether one refers to this motion as "change," "progress," or even "radicalism," there exists a dynamic process with which no single individual, no single nation—not even the united forces of the world—can successfully interfere. Protesting against this change is as sensible and as effective as Voltaire's protest (in the name of Reason!) against the great Lisbon earthquake (Voltaire, *Epître sur le désastre de Lisbonne*).

One can refuse to take cognizance of the change in one's back yard and can continue to extrapolate from the 1918 back yard to the 1970 back yard.[9] Even if one has left one's native back yard to live in another, one can continue to extrapolate from the old back yard to the new one. In a simple culture, having a low rate of change, one could "get away with it"; in a modern culture, one can elect to become schizophrenic. A refusal to date and in other ways identify one's sociocultural environment, coupled with the tendency to orient oneself to it by extrapolating, on a low level of abstraction, from one's first back yard implies an improper evaluation of reality—which can have disastrous consequences. In our complex and changing modern civilization, *the wages of improper evaluation is schizophrenia.*

The whole problem of schizophrenia as a "social psychosis" is contained *in nuce* in the following anecdote: a certain research institution, which decided to send an expedition to the North Pole, dispatched a scouting party to inform itself of the natural resources of the country through which the expedition proper was to travel. The scouting party traveled 500 miles northward and returned with a learned statistical report, which concluded that, *by extrapolating from its experiences en route,* it could guarantee that the expedition would find a hot-dog stand every quarter of a mile, right up to the North Pole.

Every single case history of schizophrenia with which I am conversant contains—implicitly or explicitly—strong indications of disorientation in a changing environment. Thus I was able to help a feeble-minded catatonic reorient himself in society by teaching him *first of all* to orient himself within the limited social universe of the hospital ward to which he was confined; this permitted him, after years of hospitalization, to leave the hospital and take up an independent life again (Devereux 1944b). In the light of these considerations, the Chicago studies comparing the distribution of schizophrenia in stable and disorganized urban areas acquire a new significance (Faris 1934; Dunham 1937; Faris and Dunham 1939). Also, if one agrees with Linton (1924) that the First World War created a subculture ("trench culture"), one sees in a new light Nolan Lewis's statement (personal communication) that many schizophrenic soldiers recovered almost miraculously when the Armistice was signed, for, with the war's end, the sociocultural area in which they were disoriented had disappeared. Similarly, Dhunjibhoy (1930) pointed out long ago that only Hindus who had been overseas or had lived in strongly westernized Indian communities developed true schizophrenia. In this sense, war neuroses, prison neuroses, immigration neuroses, and other disorders of this type can all be considered products of improper orientation.

Thus, ineffectual efforts to adapt to a changing environment *may* result in schizophrenia, although the environment as such does not *cause* schizophrenia. It causes only a special type of adaptation to take place. What the nature of this adaptation will be in a particular case is not, as a rule, predictable if one lacks knowledge of the subject's capacity to abstract. It may be objected that schizoid personalities are—according to Kretschmer's school—characterized by great meticulousness and by being highly addicted to theorizing. The question is: to theorizing *on what level?* Extrapolating is a theoretical process. It is not, however, the proper one to use in a complex and rapidly changing cultural environment. I suggest that the propensity to theorize to which the Kretschmerian school—always rather loose in its terminology—refers is precisely the tendency of schizophrenics to extrapolate—*and only to extrapolate*. It may be objected, further, that schizophrenics are often quite intelligent. Were they not, they would not try to theorize (extrapolate) or seek to use cognitive maps in orienting themselves. What matters is that their maps are either obsolete or refer to another territory. Some so-called stupid people escape schizophrenia by ramming their fists into their eyes and so

200

avoiding the fact that there has been a change in the world around them; others do so by asking every passerby for directions at every step. It is enough to think in this connection of the notorious "distractibility" of manic-depressives, who react to *every* stimulus emanating from the environment. To put it bluntly, the average "intelligent person," not trained to evaluate correctly and to abstract on a high level, is in the position of a skilled barber who is asked to shave a marble statue with an ordinary razor blade. It can't be done, although the whole social fabric tries to make one believe the contrary. [*Addendum 1978:* This fictitious example anticipated the theory of the "double bind." In the original 1939 text it stood in place of two actual cases that I was not then at liberty to publish: (1) a coed was told by her parents to be popular at college, to get admitted to a fashionable sorority, etc., but was forbidden to use lipstick, to date boys, etc.; and (2) a coed lived in her parents' home with her husband, whom she had married with their full approval; yet they considered it shameless for her to have sexual relations with her spouse under their roof. The maxim "The end justifies the means" would not have come into being were such double-bind situations exceptional in complex—i.e., schizophrenogenic—societies.]

There is something radically wrong with the system of reality evaluation in which Western man is trained when the front-page headline screams "SECRETARIAT WINS!" and a small item on the second page reports that a famine has caused 20,000 deaths in India. I therefore assert that *modern civilization does not suffer from dictatorships or revolution but from socio-politico-economic schizophrenia*[10] due to an absence of realism and to hasty extrapolation.

The preceding pages may have given the impression that the primitive is completely oriented with regard to all matters related to practical life. This is not strictly true, and the primitive's disorientation with respect to a certain part of his total life even provides the main clue to the nature of schizophrenia. There occur, even in primitive life, certain situations not readily or completely understandable in terms of extrapolation or analogy alone. The "motion" of the stars and the sun, the changes of the moon, and, in general, all events classified by the primitive under the heading "supernatural" transcend the realm in which he can be completely oriented with the help of extrapolation alone. It is in this sense that Xenophanes (frag. 15 Diels [1922 ed.]) could assert that man has fashioned God in his own image. The "natural" order of tribal social organization is extended, as Durkheim (1912) has shown, to include animal and vegetable and even inorganic "beings" and objects, as well as the whole pantheon of supernaturals. This type of extrapolation is at the root of totemism, the doctrine of mystic participation, and various other products of primitive-archaic thinking.

Yet even the primitive often realizes that his extrapolation process sometimes fails and that he is not completely oriented with respect to the supernatural world. I have mentioned elsewhere (1938) that the Sedang Moi of Indochina, though fully aware that their oracles are fallible, continue to practice divination "because it makes us feel good." In an attempt to adapt himself to the supernatural world, the primitive has evolved a set of (socially acceptable but nevertheless dereistic) rituals, beliefs, and modes of reasoning that induce him to believe that he is oriented in that world. And it so happens that *all the modes of thinking and reasoning that Storch (1924) calls archaic-primitive and discovers also in schizophrenia belong to this class of* (socially established) *pseudo-orientation in a supernatural world.* This I believe to be the main basis of my thesis and the crux of my whole argument. As Kroeber (1934) has pointed out, the primitive is not *always* prelogical; he acts in a perfectly matter-of-fact manner whenever ordinary issues, with which he can cope perfectly, are involved. *Only* in situations involving some stress (or disorientation) does he begin to act and reason prelogically, that is, by means of Freud's "primary process." Conversely, Lévy-Bruhl has repeatedly pointed out that modern man, too, sometimes acts and reasons prelogically, and—to judge from the examples he cites—Lévy-Bruhl must have been at least implicitly aware of the fact that modern man, too, thinks prelogically only in situations of some magnitude, involving disorientation phenomena and affective stress.

The same holds for Freud's analysis (1912–13) of similarities between primitive and neurotic behavior. The primitive instances he mentions belong chiefly to the sphere of culturally organized attempts to deal effectively with the supernatural—that is, with a sphere in which the primitive is disoriented. If schizophrenic behavior and the content of dreams are regressions to the "archaic," then the segment of primitive, culturally determined behavior to which schizophrenics regress is already a regression, precipitated by disorientation, from the archaic to the infantile primary process. There is nothing neurotic or schizoid about the matter-of-fact manner in which the Micronesian constructs his geographical maps with sticks and the California Indian collects acorns, because geography and the gathering of acorns do not involve serious problems of orientation.

In the present frame of reference, schizoid mechanisms, and, in general, the whole symptomatology of schizophrenia, can be understood as so many (individual or collective) attempts to become

202

adapted to a milieu in which one is disoriented and to neutralize the dysphoria resulting from disorientation.

There is, first of all, an attempt to deny that one is disoriented, an attempt to repress the feeling that one is lost in the wide open spaces of the world beyond the safety of the walled garden. Like a cage-bred bird, the patient is disoriented outdoors and tries to fight his way back into the cage in which he lived in 1918—the cage that is no longer there in 1970. This entails a regression to 1918 patterns: a genuinely schizophrenic regression to infantile patterns.

To accomplish this regression, the schizophrenic must first of all exclude from his Conscious every stimulus that reminds him that the date is 1970, not 1918. Thus, there is a gradual attrition of his responses to stimuli—and especially to stimuli that *indicate the actual date:* namely, 1970. Moreover the stimuli that continue to elicit a reaction are not evaluated by him in adult terms and therefore do not elicit adult reactions. They elicit only infantile reactions, because they are interpreted and evaluated in infantile terms (chap. 2). Naturally, with the passage of time, fewer and fewer stimuli are "acceptable" to the schizophrenic in their adult meaning. This explains why, after its onset, schizophrenia is characterized by a decrease in the rate at which new stimuli and new knowledge are absorbed. Soon all that is left to the schizophrenic to operate with are memories and stimuli that can be interpreted in an infantile manner or can even be deculturated (chap. 2). Though many schizophrenics have no systematized delusions, their pattern of behavior is nevertheless perfectly consistent, in that it is *systematically* dereistic and infantile. They are also consistent in insisting on extrapolation as the sole means of understanding the world. This implies that a *method* rather than a *system* is important to the schizophrenic—which explains in part the meticulousness of many schizoid personalities.

The obstinate use of only one (highly inadequate) method for investigating and systematizing knowledge leads to a highly disorganized view of the world (delusional system). This rigidity can be usefully contrasted with the versatility of the paranoiac, to whom all methods are acceptable as long as they provide grist for his mill, that is, support the main thesis of his coherent delusional system. Comparison of these two modes of having delusions brings out, in a useful way, the contrast between the two attitudes.

The adoption of one—and only one—(infantile) method of investigating and apprehending the world is doubtless connected with the well-known fact that it is often comparatively bright youngsters who become schizophrenic. An intelligent child senses at a very early

203

age the variety of the environment, but he obtains this insight before he has acquired an efficient method for exploring, systematizing, and evaluating reality. He tries to cope with this disturbing situation, which causes a sort of intellectual vertigo, with the only method he has at his disposal: the (infantile) method of extrapolation. A duller or more extroverted child would perhaps react to it with a manic-depressive psychosis, which is not a real "private" method but a series of bursts of alternating subjective affective states; by means of this pseudo-method he will attribute a (pseudo) structure to the external world in order to make it (pseudo) intelligible.

Of almost equal importance is the fact that in modern "civilized" society youth is trained for a profession rather than for life per se. This specialization—this narrowing of the field of interest and of training, for which extrapolation is a quite adequate method of inquiry—teaches him that *under given conditions* one may cope with (a segment of) reality by relying solely on the method of extrapolation. This encourages him to extend this method to the world as a whole.

Unfortunately, it is one thing to view the world from a specific point of vantage and then, starting from that viewpoint, to elaborate, at a high level of abstraction, a conceptual scheme that fits it, but it is quite another to make a regular practice of extrapolating, on a low level of abstraction, from the sole segment of reality with which one is familiar to the rest of the world.

In the sphere of actual behavior this type of extrapolation leads to *stereotypy*. Disparate elements are assimilated to each other by means of identification, and the whole is "understood" on an infantile level and elicits only gross, "all-or-none" reactions—and only a few of them at best. This process can best be understood by analogy with the distinction between epicritic (differentiated) and protopathic (undifferentiated) sensibility—and, by extension, behavior—the protopathic type being observable chiefly in neurotics and psychotics (Rivers 1920). It can be illustrated by a case history cited by Bleuler (1912). When told to play the piano, a certain patient obediently brought his hands to the keys, only to bend his fingers up and back at the last moment: "protopathic" compliance, "epicritic" dissent. The problem of ambivalence, intimately connected with this kind of behavior, will be discussed below.

The clinical picture is one of autistic thinking and behavior and often gives the misleading impression of an impoverishment of the intellectual life and a decrease in the affect mass. In appearance the patient has managed to restrict his world to the segment of reality in which he still manages to orient himself. By retreating from the world, he *seems* to abandon, one by one, his advance posts, which prove indefensible. Figuratively speaking, he seems to inflict on himself the torture of the green cowhide: he seems to be sewed up in it, and, when it shrinks in the sun, he is reduced to an inert lump of pathologically vegetative life. He seems to have restricted the world in which he lives to a single extensionless and contentless point in the multidimensional space-time world of reality.

I believe this traditional interpretation to be a fallacy. The chronic schizophrenic reacts to the external world by restricting his *behavior* to a few rudimentary reactions, such as digestion, peristalsis, and breathing. The functioning of his sensorium is equally infantile and undifferentiated. He continues to perceive reality, but only as an infant would: without values and shadings. Hence my formulation concerning the decreasing rate at which stimuli penetrate the organism-as-a-whole simply means that the number of *differentiated* stimuli has decreased, although the range of reality from which the stimuli *spring* has *not* shrunk. Figuratively speaking, the patient still sees; but where he formerly saw horses, men, tables, and so forth, he now sees only "objects." Even less does he see $horse_1$, $horse_2$, . . . $horse_n$. At best he sees *a* horse, and this horse is for him the equivalent of all other horses. Likewise, *all* shadows are malignant, *all* vegetable matter is edible, and so forth.

Although prior to the onset of his disease the schizophrenic had absorbed as much concrete knowledge and had as many sense impressions as any normal man, these memories are now lumped together into a few gross categories, in the exact sense in which, in thermodynamics, one speaks of "all oxygen molecules" in a gas model. This lumping-together does not mean that his memories now stick together in a solid mass; it implies only that, according to the schizophrenic's "theory"—and his "experience"—"all horses are the same."

For the schizophrenic, new sense impressions are similarly lumped together because they are not properly evaluated. Hence no new sense impression is sufficiently differentiated to be capable of imposing on his reactions an organization in conformity with a consistent behavioral policy, nor can it impose a structure on his personality. All sense impressions have the same strength and value, all memories are equally significant, and so on. His world remains composed of the same number of "absolute" elements, but they are lumped together into fewer and fewer classes.

In the end, when the number of classes is reduced to as few as two, the patient lives in a world of rudimentary "all-or-none" gross reactions. The elements composing these two classes are of equal strength; they are, moreover, so thoroughly mixed that the world becomes as homogeneous as the mind observing it.

This can immediately be interpreted in physical terms. Let, for the time being, the elements of the world be equated with molecules and the affect mass with the kinetic energy of the molecules. Consider, now, a bowl of water into which red ink has been dropped—or hot water, for that matter. The two will mix: the color (or temperature) of the bowl's contents will become homogeneous: they reach a state of entropy. The total molecular and energy content of the system remains constant. The *system* (not simply the *energy*) has, however, become so degraded and disorganized that it can produce no further work.[11] It can be reorganized (sorted out, made nonhomogeneous) only by adding energy to it. Then, when it is once again nonhomogeneous, it can produce further work.

The comparison between these two processes is not a mere play on words. The gradual involution of the intellect, the gradual "identifying" of all things, was linked by Meyerson (1921) long ago with the second law of thermodynamics (law of entropy).

These observations cast a new light on what some insist on calling the "success" of insulin and electroshock therapy. To my mind, any shock, regardless of its nature, simply breaks up (disturbs) the homogeneity of the external-internal world of the schizophrenic. An analogy will serve to make my views clearer. When the motor of a toy boat stops, the boat also stops. If a shock is then imparted to the bowl of water in which it floats, the boat will move about until the ripples produced by the shock die—and this even though the molecules within that body of water never stop moving about at random (Brownian movement). They simply can't "get together" on a common direction. Last, but not least, the shock does not *rewind* the boat's motor and fails to create any permanent structure—which is, by definition, nonhomogeneous. The shock only adds to the system a quantity of energy that is promptly dissipated.

To return to the subject of insulin and electric shock: whatever their effects may be, it is certain that they are not genuinely *structure-producing*. At best they disturb the homogeneity of the system long enough to allow some former, segmentary, and more or less obsolete structures to reconstitute themselves momentarily and to begin to function again as structures. If shock therapy—physical, chemical, or psychological—is useful at all, it is because some patients, unapproachable by any other means, become amenable to genuine therapy as long as the disturbance caused by the shock lasts. In other words, the only effect a shock (of whatever kind) can have is to make the patient (temporarily) *accessible* to therapy—*therapeutizable;* the shock *in itself* is not a therapeutic procedure in the strict sense of the term.

In another sense, schizophrenia is an adaptation to loneliness. Certain chronic schizophrenics can almost be described as "closed systems," in the physical sense of the word. However, loneliness *in itself* does not produce schizophrenia. Certain modes of *adaptation to loneliness* do produce this psychosis. To begin with, a schizophrenic's loneliness is artificial. It is, moreover, already an adaptation to the patient's terror of a more abundant and therefore more complex and demanding life—a life that ends naturally by becoming part of the physical environment, by dying. The schizophrenic simply anticipates death. He runs away from death so fast that, before he knows it, he has almost returned to the quasi-inorganic state preceding conception.[12] In order not to be killed by life—and Claude Bernard said that "life is death"—he pretends that he was never born (Menninger 1938). All this is metaphorical, but, were one philosophically inclined, in the eighteenth-century sense of the word, one could write pithy aphorisms on the fact that our body is surrounded by— embedded in—a layer of dead cells, because direct, *unorganized*, contact with the environment is death.

This type of adaptation is not unknown in politico-socio-economic matters, where infantilism is rampant. In the era of bombers [1939!] the British still blessed Providence for the British Channel, which was no longer a natural moat protecting Britain's ivory tower from invasion. The French aristocracy, intellectually alert and hospitable before the Revolution, became clannish in the extreme between 1814 and 1830. American isolationism was never more consistently stressed than in the years immediately preceding World War II, that is, just when the world became a functional whole.

This type of adaptation is not merely infantile but even phylogenetically archaic; it closely resembles the encystment of microorganisms when the environment becomes unfavorable. In a milder form it is represented in the hibernation of the bear family, the "playing-dead" defense of certain animals (Rivers 1920), and the decreased exchange between organism and environment that occurs during normal sleep. This type of adaptation can be carried so far as to defeat its own purpose. The gradual extinction of the lungfish was made the subject of a brilliant biological novel (Smith 1932).

The results of this type of adaptation clearly resemble schizophrenia. Anoxemia (decreased absorption of oxygen) causes symptoms resembling schizophrenia (McFarland 1932). It is also well known that if dreams—which, as noted by Hippocrates (*On Dreams*) and Aristotle (*On Divination in Sleep*), are the product of the mind when it temporarily withdraws from interaction with reality—were enacted, the resulting behavior would astonishingly resemble the clinical picture of schizophrenic behavior. As regards the social level, two examples should suffice. Man tends to conform to the requirements of stronger individuals as well as to those of the community. Now, according to Kempf (1917), the weaker male baboon protects himself from the stronger one by (pseudo-homosexual) sexual presentation, fear prostitution, *catatonia,* and *flexibilitas cerea.* As for "supernaturalist" ideologies, having already discussed their obvious similarities with schizophrenic delusions, I need mention them only in passing.

The forms of adaptation of the types just described, whose goal is the preservation of life, oblige the organism to change in a *number of ways* in order to keep a *few* (life) functions constant. I obviously refer here to Cannon's (1939) principle of homeostasis, which, as Wardlaw (1932) has shown, is a direct consequence of the third law of thermodynamics. I am, however, far from certain that this formulation of the principle of homeostasis is directly applicable to the "organism-as-a-whole" in its *normal* state. To my mind, normal homeostasis does not try to keep *anything* constant in the strict sense of the term. Rather, it tries to keep the *variations of state* within certain limits, or poles, while initiating and favoring change *within these limits;* for the *process,* like the *experience* of life itself, consists of such controlled changes.[13]

A very interesting mode of protection against disorientation is provided by the modern family. In the United States, in the 1930s, 75 percent of male schizophrenics and 45 percent of female schizophrenics were unmarried. This discrepancy can be explained by the fact that women usually marry at an earlier age and live in a less diversified world. The modern family is simply an *égoisme à deux,* a highly infantile, sheltered, lax existence, which can be made to change as slowly as one wishes. All too often it is a haven of stagnant infantilism in an adult, changing world. That this is not the case in primitive society has been well proved by Malinowski (1934). The primitive family includes all relatives and was, until recently, a complex organization—and also one that, given the primitive condition of these societies, was perfectly effective.

I shall now turn to the subject of ambivalence, which may also be interpreted as a problem of orientation—or, rather, as symptomatic of disorientation. I have already noted that undifferentiated (protopathic) obedience and differentiated (epicritic) disobedience occur simultaneously in schizophrenia. Bleuler (1912) has shown that the impulse opposite to the one that one implements or wishes to implement at a given moment is often hallucinated as an external command. The patient does not know what to do, nor does he care. More often than not he complains that he is forbidden to do what he wants to do. It is not false—although it is certainly not sufficient —to say that this resembles man's tendency, where morality and faith are concerned, to externalize a particular "order of things" as being "divine," "natural," or "legal." Bleuler's observations do not merely fit my theorem regarding the equivalence of all stimuli that get lumped together in a very few categories; they could also have been predicted on the basis of my theory. The schizophrenic simply sees all sides of the situation simultaneously. If he simultaneously wants and does not want to do something, the whole world becomes divided into arguments pro and con. My views are further supported by Bleuler's comment on the apparent "flirting" of the patient with his interlocutor. He pretends to withdraw but does so in order to subtly stimulate the interlocutor. This parallels in many ways the behavior of "nice" girls. They make love to a man by permitting him to make love to them. Lundborg's suggestion (1902) that the patient wishes to move but cannot—in other words that his situation resembles a kind of *myotonia*—also implies the principle of the equivalence of all stimuli and memories, which the patient simply cannot unite into consistent patterns permitting a definite action.

Further proof is afforded by the problem of random behavior on the symbolic level ("word salads")[14] and on the motor level (apraxia). Both resemble the Brownian motion of molecules in an apparently immobile body of water. William A. White's sagacious remarks on the problem of fluctuating attention are also very much to the point. Speaking facetiously, the schizophrenic no longer knows *"à quel saint se vouer"*—all saints being equivalent: Saint Jude is no longer specifically the patron of lost causes, nor Saint Anthony the finder of lost things. This is a dynamic conception of the schizophrenic's pseudo-psychasthenia, and it compels one to distinguish clearly between alternative symptoms occurring *at a given stage* of the disease and chains of symptoms, which develop *in the course of the disease.*

It is of special interest to note that some particularly characteristic traits of schizophrenic behavior reproduce certain fundamental cultural practices. [Cf., now, Nathan 1978.] Examples of this are plentiful. Since I cannot cite all of them, I shall take as a paradigm of these similarities one characteristic of schizophrenic speech. For "ugly," the schizophrenic says "not beautiful" or even "not not-ugly." A large number of languages differ from the Indo-European group in their way of responding to a negative question. For instance, the Sedang *married* man replies to the question, "Have you no wife?" by saying, "No" (that is, "it is untrue that I have no wife"). An English-speaking person could reply, "Yes" ("I do have one"). Classical literary Greek shows a marked preference for the negative mode: "And the hero was not unmindful of Apollo's exhortations" —and this even where the meter in no way requires this kind of formulation. Classical Malay has its own way of handling the active and the passive; it prefers to the active form, "I see a horse," the passive form, "A horse is seen by me." The British have a pronounced tendency to express themselves in negatively formulated meioses:. "not bad" for "good." The double negative frequently occurs in American slang: "I ain't done nothing" (and I seriously doubt that the use of this incorrect mode of expression is due solely to an ignorance of grammar).

Another central characteristic of schizophrenia is *active* negativism, because it allows the observer to evaluate the schizophrenic's real awareness of reality and his orientation to it. Lowie (1935) has brilliantly described the culturally prescribed active negativism of certain Crow Indian warriors known as "Crazy Dog Wishes to Die" (as the result of a disappointment). These warriors *systematically* do the opposite of what they are told to do. Thus it is possible to make them dance by saying "Do not dance." It is possible for a group to avoid being ridden down by one of them by saying, "Come and trample on us."

However, Crazy Dogs do *not* do the opposite when it is *not* expected of them: when pretty women—eager to have intercourse with these heroes who are about to die—sneak into their tents at night. It would be worth testing the "absolute" orientation of actively negativistic schizophrenics by, let us say, forbidding the use of the toilet to those who have consistently refused to use it. This would indicate whether they are truly disoriented or whether "being contrary" is part of their "ritual" (figuratively speaking) of being insane. This experiment would test Anton's interesting suggestion (1904) that negativism is what I consider bizarre reactions to be: a defense against suggestibility (Devereux 1959a).

Less than a year after I had written this article (1939), I had occasion to observe a nondeteriorated chronic adult schizophrenic—who had certainly not read my article—*spontaneously* use this technique of negative suggestion to control the systematically negativistic behavior of another young schizophrenic, who was more or less his protégé. He *commanded* this young man to do what he should *not* do but habitually did do; and he *forbade* him to do what he should in fact do. The result was that the young man became completely controllable, at least in this area (Devereux 1944b). I myself used this method some twelve years later with a temporarily psychotic and extremely negativistic Indian woman who came from one of the tribes in which the Crazy-Dog behavior pattern of "contrariness" occurs. She too became perfectly controllable as soon as she was commanded to do the opposite of what was actually expected of her (chap. 15).

Dog-owners and parents are also familiar with the fact that, when one calls a dog or a child to take a bath, the dog or child will not merely refuse to come but will retreat: will show active negativism. The mechanism of suggestibility—and the subject's own resistance to his suggestibility—could further be tested with Ainu patients afflicted with *imu* (Winiarz and Wielawski 1936) and with Malays afflicted with *latah* (Van Loon 1926), diseases characterized by both positive (or negative) echolalia and echopraxia. It would be interesting to see how these patients would react to suggestions or patterns that were highly repulsive to them. There is an element of rebelliousness in active negativism that has never been given sufficient attention (chap. 3). Negative suggestibility, as exemplified by impotency on the wedding night, does not seem to occur frequently in primitive tive cultures.

The schizophrenic's tendency to destroy a piece of work he has just finished is interesting both biologically and culturally. Gratuitous destructiveness is —phylogenetically—a very primitive trait in man, monkeys, and other species. Furthermore, it is reminiscent of certain primitive behavior, as when the potter chips the new pot or the Navajo woman deliberately makes a small error when finishing a fine rug so as to provide an egress for her soul from the splendid warp and woof. One may also think of certain related activities, whose clinical equivalent I have termed "99 percentism," and, above all, of wanton acts of destruction in potlatches.

Culture determines what is "correct" behavior (though its correctness does not necessarily make it normal). Hence, "incorrect" (though at times normal) behavior must also be evaluated in cultural terms. For us it is *normal* to sharpen a stick with an outward motion of the knife. It is *normal* for the Sedang Moi to do the opposite: he pulls the knife toward himself. There is no "natural" way of doing the majority of our daily actions. In this narrow sense we can view the schizophrenic's behavior as an alternative to our behavior. But the fact that some schizophrenic activities are duplicated at more primitive stages of culture does not justify viewing the primitive as a lunatic at large. Porteus (1937) sagaciously remarked that the Australian shows so exceptional a capacity to cope with his inhospitable environment that, were he able to cope with the materials of modern culture as well, he would soon inherit the earth.

To sum up: contrary to what some authorities seem to assert, the schizophrenic does not live simply on stimuli emanating from the visceral level and does not respond exclusively to this type of stimuli. He is aware of reality and is interested—at least, in everything that is going on in his fictitious little back yard. In that sense, Bleuler's criticism (1912), that Kraepelin overemphasized the isolation of the schizophrenic, is justified. The schizophrenic's reaction is characterized by so long a hesitancy that it may be considered an absurdly delayed reaction that in the end defeats its own aims, since it never comes to fruition.

The schizophrenic's delusional system is incoherent chiefly because it is built on extrapolation. In keeping with that method, he organizes the world horizontally, although man's nervous system abstracts as a rule from one level to a higher one—that is, vertically. The (delusional) structure of the schizophrenic's image of the world does not conform to the structure of the operations his nervous system performs.

The key word in this context is "operation" and *that* word is not included in the oft-repeated dictum of Korzybski (1933) and his disciples. In fact, the structure of the nervous system could not possibly be structurally analogous to a delusional or even to a realistic representation of the world.

In short, the schizophrenic extrapolates from reality but no longer troubles to check the results of his extrapolations *against reality*. Partly because of this, and partly also because of the fact that the schizophrenic becomes almost one with the physical environment, the partition between object and observer (Devereux 1967c) loses all importance, so that feelings of unreality occur.

The theory of disorientation is compatible with Bleuler's statement (1912) that the schizophrenic misunderstands the external world. This, he feels, is closely connected with schizophrenic negativism.

The heart of the matter, however, is that in order to misjudge the external world one must be conscious of it. I therefore trust that I will not be accused of failing to tackle an important problem, to wit, "Does the patient perceive stimuli and fail to respond to them, or does he fail to perceive stimuli to begin with?" Figuratively speaking, this is tantamount to asking, "Is the break between the furnace and the boiler, or is it between the boiler and the piston?" The problem, so worded, is both meaningless and not susceptible to objective study. The observable data from which this meaningless problem was derived led me to an altogether different problem: that of the progressive dedifferentiation of responses and stimuli, which can be given an operational meaning in the experimental sense of the word.

The preceding conclusions are not necessarily equally applicable to paranoid schizophrenics or to the "paraphrenias,"[15] whose illnesses seem to me to be of an essentially different type. The problems raised by these psychological disorders is beyond the scope of this study.

The reader is reminded that the sociological theory of schizophrenia here proposed is one of several possible ones. I have selected it because it offers certain conveniences of manipulation (Poincaré's criterion of *commodité* [1913]) and contains no concepts that cannot be given an operational meaning.

The following chapter (chap. 10) proposes *another* sociological theory of schizophrenia that also satisfies Poincaré's criterion of *commodité* and is also based on concepts that can be given an operational meaning.

IO

Schizophrenia: An Ethnic Psychosis

or

Schizophrenia without Tears

(1965)

A psychic disorder—whether a neurosis or a psychosis—can be cured only by a psychiatrist or a psychoanalyst who is not himself suffering from the same illness, and then only if the treatment takes place in a social setting that, while professing to wish to cure this illness, does not indirectly encourage and foster its principal manifestations. Now, of all mental diseases, the one most refractory to treatment, schizophrenia, is the most widespread psychosis in modern society. The near impossibility of curing it completely is even held by some to prove that it has an organic basis. This evasive explanation—this subterfuge—is not surprising. Physiology, biochemistry, and histology have a broad back, and it is always easy to blame the unseen and the unknown for all our sins of omission and commission. Unfortunately for this pseudo-explanation, genuine "nuclear" schizophrenia appears to be absent among authentic primitives (Devereux 1961a), though it appears as soon as such societies are subjected to a process of violent acculturation and oppression (chap. 9).

I believe schizophrenia to be almost incurable not because it has an organic basis but because its principal symptoms are systematically encouraged by some of the most characteristic and most powerful—but also most senseless and useless (dysfunctional)—"values" of our civilization. Moreover, since these cultural values and models are sometimes also those of the psychiatrist, he is, of necessity, often quite unable to tackle the problem of schizophrenia and its treatment in a truly objective and scientific spirit. His therapeutic efforts can be hampered quite as much by his ethnocentric and cultural biases and blind spots as by his unconscious idiosyncratic countertransference reactions. It is self-evident that the training of the psychiatrist is incomplete and the didactic psychoanalysis of the psychoanalytic candidate is unfinished until the future therapist ceases to scotomatize *not only* his subjective conflicts *but also* the objective ones of the society into which he was born and in which he functions as a psychotherapist. Consider the circumscribed but concrete oedipal conflict. The therapist must not only become aware of his subjective oedipal problems but must also be able to discern, among the multiple aspects of social reality, the ones that, being elaborations of oedipal structures, systematically favor the genesis and development of oedipal difficulties in the individual and permit him to use cultural materials as symptoms. Indeed, for symptomatic purposes, the neurotic or the psychotic can appropriate any cultural trait—value, dogma, custom, current practice—without having to modify its external manifestations (chap. 2), and this to such an extent that any attempt at diagnosis becomes very hazardous. It is a fact that, when a cultural trait has undergone no obvious modification, it is often quite difficult to determine whether it is being utilized in a normal or a pathological-symptomatic manner. Sometimes the manner in which the patient utilizes a cultural item must be almost grotesquely inappropriate before one realizes that what one is observing is not simply (good, bad, or indifferent) *standard* cultural behavior but the symptomatic exploitation of a cultural item.

I have already cited (chap. 1) the case of the Indian halfbreed who, to avoid any awareness of his oedipal conflict, skillfully, though unconsciously, transposed his hatred of his (Indian) father and his love for his (white) mother into a violent prejudice, both against the Indian race and against racial interbreeding. The grotesque aspect of racial prejudice harbored by an Indian halfbreed made diagnosis easy in this instance. However, had the patient been a white American, the idiosyncratic neurotic element inherent in racial prejudice would have been much more difficult to discern, simply because race prejudice rates as a cultural "value," not just in America but, today, also in countries prejudiced against whites.

The correct diagnosis is infinitely more difficult to make when the neurotic and symptomatic exploitation of the cultural trait is more insidious and less grotesque than it is in this case. Often it takes many months of treatment before one realizes that a patient's manifest generosity masks severe guilt feelings, which must be alleviated by *fines—self-imposed fines*—masquerading as gifts. In one of my patients—an electrical engineer—an extreme helpfulness toward his friends and associates was not true philanthropy but a clever maneuver whose purpose was to control others by making himself indispensable to them. Similarly, an analysis of his considerate, *seemingly* tender, and technically perfect sexual behavior disguised the fact that he viewed women simply as complicated machines; he took pride in his ability to discover what buttons must be pushed, what knobs turned, what levers pulled, to make these complicated machines "work," to make them become excited and have an orgasm, which—and this is significant—was always a clitoral and never a vaginal one.

The congruence between neurotic symptoms and social dogmas can easily be used as a resistance. Thus, in a puritanical society it would be very hard to make a woman patient admit that she is not truly chaste but simply phobic with respect to the realities of sex,[1] just as one would find it difficult to make a Mohave woman patient admit that she is not simply sensual but nymphomaniac. I cite elsewhere (chap. 8) the case of a sex-ridden fourteen-year-old girl whose resistance to therapy was based on an exploitation of puritanical principles. She pretended that her "immorality" made her unworthy of help, and for some months she used this unworthiness as a pretext for refusing to cooperate with her psychotherapist.

There is in every neurosis and psychosis a far-reaching exploitation of cultural items for psychopathological (symptomatic) ends. Hence, many of our most modern diagnostic techniques are useless when handled by psychologists and psychiatrists unable to realize the extent to which severe psychiatric illness can hide behind a culturally acceptable façade by using cultural items quite correctly as to outward *form* but highly symptomatically as regards *substance* and *function*. Treatment becomes exceptionally difficult when the psychotherapist and his patient share inherently dysfunctional social values, beliefs, and practices and when the social setting in which the treatment takes place encourages inherently dereistic modes of behavior. Hence, it is harder to diagnose an idiosyncratically neurotic race prejudice in a southerner than in a New Englander. Moreover, even if diagnosed, the neurotic (subjective) race prejudice of a patient cannot be successfully treated by a psychiatrist who is himself prejudiced. Last but not least, it is easier to treat a neurotic race prejudice in Vermont than in Alabama, simply because the social climate of Vermont does not systematically foster race prejudice, whereas that of Alabama does.

In the diagnosis and therapy of schizophrenia we are confronted with precisely this kind of difficulty, because schizophrenia is the most widespread psychosis—and, indeed, the "type psychosis"—of complex civilized society.

I define as an ethnic psychosis or neurosis any derangement in which:

1. The underlying conflict of the psychosis or neurosis is also present in the majority of the normal people. The conflict in the neu-

rotic or the psychotic is simply *more intense* than it is in other people. In short, the patient is *like* everyone—but more intensely so than anyone else.

2. The symptoms characteristic of an ethnic neurosis or psychosis are not improvised, not invented, by the patient but are furnished ready-made by his cultural milieu. One is actually dealing with what Ralph Linton (1936) called "patterns of misconduct." Indeed, society actually seems to say to the potential neurotic or psychotic: "Don't be insane! But, if you have to be insane, you must manifest your insanity by behaving thus and so—and in no other way. If you deviate from this pattern, you will not be considered insane but something else: a criminal, a witch, a heretic, etc." (chap. 13).

A fairly reliable indication of whether a given psychological derangement is an ethnic (and *not* an *idiosyncratic*) neurosis or psychosis is the frequency with which such cases are diagnosed as "borderline," "ambulatory," or "mixed" or as "hyphenated" conditions (e.g., as paranoid schizophrenia, hebephenic schizophrenia, catatonic schizophrenia, etc.). Moreover, such "hyphenated" diagnoses tend to "pad" the statistical frequency of the ethnic neurosis or psychosis. In the age of Charcot a great many people were diagnosed as "hysterics" because that was the ethnic type neurosis of *that* period—the fashionable neurosis: the "proper way" of being abnormal.

Now, since disturbed people do tend to express their inner conflicts in the form expected by their culture, most neurotics in Charcot's time did *behave* as though they were hysterics. Today, by contrast, even simple neurotics behave intermittently like schizophrenics, or at least like schizoid personalities.

The psychologically ill comply rigorously with social expectations regarding "behavior suitable for the madman." This can best be shown by the fact that a Malay will run *amok* for a great variety of cultural reasons (Wulfften-Pahlte 1933), whereas an American or a European hardly ever runs *amok* for any reason whatsoever. I specify that the term *amok* is taken here in the strict sense of the term— i.e., in its sociocultural and psychological sense and not in the sense in which journalists asserted that a psychotic veteran had "run *amok*" in the streets of Camden, New Jersey. It is essential in this context to underline the distinction between the idiosyncratic character of the crisis of this American and the socially structured character of the seemingly—but only seemingly—similar behavior observed in Malays.

This distinction implies a fundamental psychological difference between this American case and the cases of Malay *amok* runners.

A Malay will run *amok* for many reasons: because he feels hopelessly oppressed and insulted; because—for military or political (assassination) reasons (Anonymous 1930)—he is *ordered* to run *amok* by his superior; because he simply wishes to die in a *Götterdämmerung*-type "blaze of glory"; or because he happens to be ill, feverish, delirious, etc. The Malay is, so to speak, preconditioned—perhaps unwittingly but certainly quite automatically—by Malay culture to react to almost any violent inner or outer stress by running *amok* (chap. 1). In the same sense, Occidental man of today is conditioned by his own culture to react to any state of stress (chap. 9) by schizophrenia-like behavior (symptoms) even when his *real* idiosyncratic conflicts are not of the schizophrenogenic type. He behaves in this manner because the ethnic segment of his personality contains culturally structured schizophrenogenic conflicts—and defenses against these conflicts. I shall discuss, further on, the role these conflicts play in the formation of the general schizophrenic syndrome.

Being "insane"—which is a social status like any other social status (chap. 13)—in a predictable and almost socially prescribed manner has at least two tangible, practical advantages:

1. It insures that one will be *treated* as an insane person instead of as a criminal, a witch, a heretic, or a rebel (chap. 13).

2. It saves one the trouble of *having to invent* one's own symptoms (chap. 1).

The latter is not a negligible advantage, since most people do not like to think; they prefer to remember what they already know. This is particularly true of the neurotic or psychotic, whose illness automatically implies a certain impoverishment, dedifferentiation, and lack of originality of the personality.[2]

Many of Freud's early cases, which he diagnosed as hysterias, are today rediagnosed by some psychoanalysts as schizophrenias. I have little doubt that many of the cases that we diagnose today as schizophrenia will, by the next generation, be rediagnosed as something else. Many of our patients who *seem* to *behave* like schizophrenics are not *basically* schizophrenics at all. They are simply neurotics or psychotics who compliantly, though unconsciously, *masquerade* as schizophrenics because this disorder best fits their ethnic conflicts and because it is what we expect from them, socially as well as psychiatrically.

This hypothesis also explains the failure of attempts to discover *the* organic basis of schizophrenia. Such inquiries *could* not produce positive results even if schizophrenia were genuinely an organic illness, because so many of the patients diagnosed as schizophrenics are not schizophrenics to begin with: they only *behave* like schizophrenics. Thus the claim of certain researchers who profess to have discovered a "schizophrenic serum" is one that I cannot take seriously, for the simple reason that at least some of the patients from whom this serum was "extracted" were not genuine (nuclear) schizophrenics to begin with but only psychiatric patients exhibiting the culturally taught and expected symptoms of schizophrenia.

Were I suddenly "bitten by the organicistic bug" and decided to discover the organic causes of schizophrenia, I would quite certainly operate in an entirely different way. I would *not* take a group of patients *diagnosed* as schizophrenics and try to discover whether all or most of them had a certain type of organic defect or "serum." I would instead take all patients who had *organic defect* A, B, or C and then try to find out how many of *them* were *also* schizophrenic. I would not try to determine how many patients diagnosed as schizophrenic underreacted to thyroid extract; I would instead try to find out how many subjects who did underreact to thyroid extract were schizophrenic.

I might also say that I would be much more impressed with the value of diagnostic psychological tests if, in supposedly basic areas of psychological behavior, these tests did *not* give more or less the same type of result for *all* kinds of "schizophrenias." I am especially skeptical of David Rapaport's famous "thought-disturbance" criterion, which, to my mind, is simply an erudite but nonspecific way of saying that a patient is "crazy." If, as seems certain, every neurosis and psychosis represents a more or less pronounced degree of deindividualization and dedifferentiation, then it is inevitable that *all* neurotics and psychotics will exhibit a certain amount of "thought disturbance."

In addition, thought disorders and dereistic thinking are part and parcel of the culturally prestructured symptoms that our society foists not only on people who are perturbed or under stress but on *all* of its members.

It may be objected, of course, that, since a patient's symptoms must fit his underlying conflict, a hysteric would find no relief if he resorted *only* to the schizophrenic symptoms forced on him, or at least offered to him, from the outside. However, I have already answered this objection, for I stressed, above, that *in our society* the schizophrenic's inner conflicts differ from those of normal people, not in their nature, but in their intensity. The ethnic personality of modern man is basically schizoid and remains schizoid even if—as the result of an idiosyncratic trauma (chap. 1)—he happens to become a hysteric or a manic-depressive. Precisely because the symptoms must fit the conflict, the patient must evolve *not only* symptoms that fit his *idiosyncratic* hysteria but *also* schizoid or schizophrenic symptoms that fit his *ethnic* conflicts.

But there is more to it than this. Rooted in the very nucleus of the personality and reinforced by sociocultural pressures, ethnic symptoms are not only superimposed on a hysterical or other symptomatology but can even *structure* an ensemble of discrete symptoms of a fundamentally hysterical character into a schizophrenic model (*syndrome*). In fact, this theory fits hysteria particularly well. It even explains, at least in part, why—as noted above—certain modern psychoanalysts stubbornly assert that the first hysterics treated by Freud were in reality schizophrenics. As a matter of fact, it is well known that a monosymptomatic hysteria can mask a latent schizophrenia and that it is sometimes difficult to distinguish accurately between the hysteric's *"belle indifférence"* and *"as-if"* behavior, on the one hand, and the indifference (hypotonia) and play-acting of the schizophrenic, on the other.

I even believe that one reason why it is so difficult to treat some patients diagnosed as schizophrenic is that the psychotherapist stubbornly tries to treat the schizophrenic façade and fails to come to grips with the underlying illness—for example, with a hysteria. The following observation seems to substantiate this hypothesis. During the prodromal stage of schizophrenia and sometimes also during the period of recovery, the patient occasionally behaves like a psychopath (as that syndrome is defined in chapter 2) or, more rarely, like a hysteric. That is, the *idiosyncratic* aspects of the conflict seem to manifest themselves precisely during these transitional stages but become hard to discern as soon as the patient begins to "stabilize" his illness (as well as his social status as a "madman") in conformity with the schizophrenia model—that is, in conformity with the most common and the most characteristic ethnic psychosis of our society.

I am inclined to see in this structuring of hysterical or manic-depressive symptoms in conformity with the model of the dominant ethnic psychosis, i.e., schizophrenia, a restitutional symptom, or at least an attempt to adapt to a socially prescribed "pattern of misconduct"—and this in the same sense in which, among certain peoples, shamanism represents an analogous restitutional process (chap. 1). In short, the patient who dons the mask of schizophrenia, instead of consenting to be a culturally "eccentric" hysteric or manic-depressive, displays conformism, because, in our society, being schizophrenic is the "proper" way of being "mad." It goes without saying that this adaptation to the schizophrenic pattern is, as I have shown, greatly facilitated by the fundamentally schizoid structure of modern man's ethnic personality.

I hold that the quasi-restitutional function of the modern patient's adoption of the schizophrenic model and his tendency to "stabilize" his illness—to make it chronic and malignant—are due to the fact that this pattern is rooted in the ethnic character and is reinforced by social pressures. This interpretation is confirmed by certain peculiarities of the *bouffée délirante*, so common in primitive societies. This syndrome, which is somewhat analogous to schizophrenic agitation and may even be an idiosyncratic schizophrenic manifestation, has the peculiarity of being very rapidly reabsorbed—quite often without recourse to an efficacious therapeutic intervention. This is due to the fact that in primitive society the schizophrenic model is not recognized as a "pattern of misconduct" (= how to be mad). Hence, it can neither stabilize idiosyncratic explosions of this kind (see below) nor make them chronic, except through confinement in a psychiatric hospital (Devereux 1978b). These findings also explain why the *bouffées délirantes* so closely resemble hysterical manifestations (which are *the* ethnic disorder of many primitive societies) and also why, just like hysterical seizures, the *bouffées délirantes* so often occur in public, and in a highly exhibitionistic form, instead of occurring outside the group, by means of an asocial turning-inward. I therefore believe that in cases of this kind the idiosyncratic schizophrenic conflict and its schizophrenic symptomatology are structured by and patterned upon the ethnic disorder characteristic of primitives, which happens to be hysteria. This permits a rapid and massive abreaction at the outset, i.e., during the prodromal stage of the disease, and this helps to prevent a malignant stabilization of the disorder in the form of a chronic schizophrenia.

My views are indirectly confirmed by what is usually called "three-day battlefield schizophrenia," a disorder characteristic of the modern soldier and often hard to differentiate from a *bouffée délirante*. As the great psychiatrist and anthropologist W. H. R. Rivers (1920, 1923) noted long ago, modern man receives no *warrior* training (which is different from *military* training) and is therefore provided with no adequate (culturally inculcated) defenses against fear during combat.[3]

This is why the modern combat trauma is idiosyncratic in nature. It manifests itself and is then promptly dissipated by an abreaction experienced in the "primitive" form of a *bouffée délirante* (three-day battlefield schizophrenia); except in rare cases, it does not become stabilized by an adaptation to the schizophrenic model. I conclude from these findings that, *as a rule*, a psychiatric disorder will become chronic and malignant only if it manages to model itself—or is forced to model itself (Devereux 1978b)—on the dominant ethnic neurosis or psychosis—whether this is schizophrenia, hysteria, or some other syndrome.

This conception is not incompatible with classical psychoanalytic theory and is no more revolutionary than Osler's famous observation that "syphilis is the great masquerader," able to imitate a broad range of other illnesses. *In our own society,* schizophrenia is both the great masquerader and the great masquerade. It sometimes disguises itself as a monosymptomatic hysteria or even as psychopathic behavior, especially just before and just after a period of manifest schizophrenic illness. It also provides symptoms (masks) for a variety of other psychological illnesses that in our society simply borrow the symptoms of the "fashionable" illness of our day: schizophrenia.[4]

INCULCATION OF THE SCHIZOID MODEL

I will now show how and in what manner Occidental man is *taught* to be schizoid outside the psychiatric hospital and therefore to be schizophrenic within it.

I will take the most common and most characteristic schizophrenic trends of our society one by one and demonstrate the extent to which they are valued in, and taught by, Occidental society.

1. *Withdrawal, aloofness, hyporeactivity.*—These attitudes are highly valued models in our society and, at the same time, are so characteristic of all schizophrenic symptoms that Angyal (1938) could speak of schizophrenic "bionegativity." Impersonality, cold objectivity, *"le moi est haïssable,"* "never use the first-person singular," do not become emotional, *nil admirari,* the inscrutable "poker face" of the successful diplomat or gambler, "the great stone face" of the "ideal" administrator—these are nowadays the means by which one wins the admiration of one's fellow man and gets ahead in society. The prestige of icy unemotionality is such that even the most sensitive and emotional people profess to despise the emotionality of *others.*[5] One can profitably compare this attitude with the diametrically opposite one obtaining among the Mohave: they despise the whites precisely because of their reserve, for only whites did not weep during the funeral ceremonies for Matavilye, the Mohave god (Devereux 1961a).

The guiding star of our society—the one La Barre (1946) calls the "social cynosure"—is the North Star: the internally frozen man who gives no warmth and can tolerate none in others. Most of our psychoanalytic patients are unable to love. Fewer still are able to tolerate *being* loved. One of my woman patients said: "If a man falls in love with me, I know he is an idiot because he loves a slut—a good-for-nothing." A male patient told me that a girl agreed to become his mistress only on condition that (*a*) he would not fall in love with her and (*b*) that he would also have *other* mistresses, so as to protect *her* from his becoming *emotionally involved with her.* Actually, of course, a great deal of insecurity and self-contempt is hidden behind this mask of total aloofness. One of the nicest men I have known once wistfully said to me: "I envy your capacity to love— even your capacity to suffer. I am a cold fish." The opening sentence of a French prose poem written by a young *non*-French poet is "J'ai toujours souffert de ne pas pouvoir souffrir" ("I have always suffered because of my inability to suffer").

Such people are, of course, capable of *occasional* violent eruptions of emotionality. What they lack is the constant, positive, but moderate, never excessive, emotionality of normal people. For the inhibited there is nothing between catatonic stupor on the one hand and quasi-decerebrate, wooden, catatonic excitement on the other hand. Both are common in our day and age.

Taken as a pattern, this highly schizoid hyporeactivity, absence of affectivity, and lack of emotional involvement are perhaps the surest way of commanding attention, gaining respect, and inviting imitation in Occidental society, even if the pattern manifests itself in the guise of a catatonic agitation that is *also devoid* of true affectivity. In both cases there is a disconcerting smell of the back wards of a mental hospital harboring "burnt-out" schizophrenics.

2. *Absence of affectivity in sexuality.*—This characteristic of modern society is equally characteristic of those who are in revolt against it. The gap between those who claim to be puritans and the exhibitionists who display an alleged lack of inhibition is steadily decreasing. The puritanism of the former is a socially prestigious label ("*appellation contrôlée*") stuck on an empty bottle. Though they engage in intercourse quite as often as some authentically uninhibited groups, puritans totally reject the affective implications of sexuality; as for the people belonging to (allegedly) uninhibited groups, they behave more or less the same way when, as a matter of principle, they engage in chaotic sexuality. Both groups can only *fornicate;* they are unable to make *love.* I have discussed elsewhere (1966b) the case of a woman in analysis who did not so much feel ashamed of having intercourse with her husband as of the fact that she enjoyed it, that it meant something to her. Equally interesting is the case of a fairly promiscuous girl who broke with the first man able to give her a vaginal and heterosexual orgasm. She had been able to have many affairs simply because what was sinful for her was *not* cold-blooded, frigid fornication but full sexual *enjoyment,* involving the emotions.[6] An extreme case is that of a schizoid woman who literally

did not *feel* the existence of her genitals—in fact, who did not even feel that she existed—except during intercourse. In order not to feel dead, she deliberately acquired three lovers, who worked different shifts. She visited each of them every day, passing from one bed to another and fornicating close to twenty hours a day—*so as not to feel dead*. Such sexuality has no affective component. As regards the so-called "juvenile sex-delinquent girl," her fundamental asexuality, even antisexuality, were discussed in enough detail in chapter 8 to require no further comment here. As for schizophrenics, their lack of sexual interest and utter inability to love are notorious. Statistics show that the percentage of virgins among schizophrenics is a great deal higher than in the normal population of comparable age, education, and social background.

It is therefore legitimate to say that, under the pretense of inculcating puritanism, or antipuritanism, Occidental societies and the revolutionary groups developing within them both simply teach people to disguise, under a moral-sounding and socially approved label, their incapacity to love and *to make love* (as distinct from fornicating). This symptom is furnished as obviously to the schizophrenic as to the hysteric, the manic-depressive, and the psychopath. It is most effectively taught to the nymphomaniac and to the sexual athlete (in Kinsey's sense), whose illness consists precisely in being unable to love and to enjoy lovemaking deeply and fully.

3. *Segmentalism and partial involvement* are also major schizoid traits systematically fostered by our society. Most transactions in daily life are extremely segmental, implying little or no *total* personal involvement. Business is business and revolt is revolt and must not be combined with friendship or with love, even if it must sometimes borrow their mask.

Yet, in America, neighborhood stores often advertise their friendliness toward the customer: "Your friendly grocer" or "Service with a smile." It would seem that things in France are now moving in the same direction, for there, too, workaday transactions involving human relationships are beginning to lose their affective tonality. Advertising slogans, like the American ones I have just cited, reflect deeply rooted psychological attitudes. One of my patients appraised the attitudes of his friends and colleagues toward him exclusively in terms of their facial expressions. The presence or absence of a smile was for him the only reliable manifestation of friendliness (chapter 4). One is close here, in a sense, to what Mauss called "the obligatory expression of emotions." In short, the "social smile" of the American is the strict equivalent of the Australian native's *Tränengruss* ("tear-greeting").

Some years ago a sensational American TV show reported on the peculiar business practice of providing expensive call girls free to visiting customers. One hopes that the customers suitably appreciated this "delicate attention," at once deeply impersonal and yet superficially personal. I imagine, however, that these customers would have been greatly surprised had the vice-president of so generous a firm offered them, as a personal token of affection, his wife or daughter, which is what a well-brought-up Eskimo would have done. I have no doubt whatever that so personal a token of friendship would have embarrassed the customer.[7] Modern man, when entering a tobacco shop, is interested only in buying a pack of cigarettes as quickly as possible. He might even resent the tobacconist's attempt to engage in friendly small talk, for this would waste time and raise the specter of an involvement. As it is, two minutes later he may not even remember whether the tobacconist was male or female, young or old, sad or gay. Society operates most efficiently *for business*—or for mass activities—and most destructively for the unfolding of Man by narrowly circumscribing the scope of his affective transactions. Though I am an opponent of Plato's views, I think it would be amusing to watch a professor of Greek lecture to a small-town Parent-Teacher Association on Plato's (implicit) view that the teacher should be in love with his (boy) students! The fact is that, for better or for worse, the Greeks were unable to comprehend, and even less to approve of, purely segmental and impersonal human relations. The very wording of the Hippocratic Oath (26 f.) shows that there was a *need* to prevent the physician from becoming sexually involved with his patients. Despite certain specious comments on a scene in Aristophanes' *Clouds*, I also believe that the most brilliant Greek of the classical age would have been unable to invent the psychoanalytic situation, in which the analyst must remain wholly impersonal; for the impersonal analytic situation is in many ways radically contrary to pre-Platonic Greek culture's conception of interpersonal and social relations. Also—and this fact deserves to be noted—as long as human relations in our society were affective and direct, people found it hard to believe that analysts did not cohabit with their female patients;[8] jokes about affairs between analysts and woman patients were therefore common. If this aspect of analysis has ceased to be a source of jokes today, it is not because people have come to realize that such stories are untrue; it is due to the fact that their own affective aloofness in daily life makes the analyst's professional aloofness more credible to them.

To avoid any misunderstanding, I will state once more that the analytic situation is therapeutically effective *only because the ana-*

lyst remains objective but also benevolent and respectful of his patient's individuality. I simply believe that this brilliant discovery could never have been made by either Socrates or Avicenna. Only members of a society in which segmental and impersonal relations are the *main* fabric of society could have devised the psychoanalytic method. This is not very different from saying that, as long as there were slaves and no one—except, perhaps, Euripides—questioned the legitimacy of slavery, no scientist had any real reason for inventing the steam engine to supply mechanical energy. The steam engine devised by Hero, an Alexandrian Greek, remained a scientific toy or curio (Sachs 1933), and, in keeping with the prejudices of the Platonists, Archimedes had to be persuaded to "degrade" his science by putting it to practical uses for his country's defense (Plutarch, *Life of Marcellus* 14 ff.). Those who condemned Edward Teller acted the same way. But I note that no one seems to blame the Russian physicists for having rendered the same service to the Soviet Union.

With so preponderant a role assigned to impersonal, segmental, purely goal-oriented and efficiency-prizing relationships, it is easy to see where and how the schizophrenic learns the art of remaining uninvolved.

4. *Dereism* involves a radical distortion of reality in order to make it fit an illusory model, evolved in accordance with purely subjective or else cultural needs and demands—or even in accordance with the hallucinations of drug addicts. Julius Caesar's dictum, *Homines id quod volunt credunt* (Men believe what they want to believe), applies to mankind in general, not just to the schizophrenic or to any particular society or historical period. Intelligence is a poor defense against taking one's wishes and even one's delusions for reality; usually it only helps one invent good excuses for behaving unintelligently. The brilliant Athenians, who refused to believe that Philip's Macedonians would ever invade Greece—"Bah! They wouldn't dare!"—were no more and no less dereistic than those American congressmen who, *one week before Pearl Harbor,* renewed and extended the Draft Act by a majority of exactly *one* vote—the Greeks despite the constant warnings of Demosthenes and the Americans despite those of Roosevelt. Dereism is thus not specifically schizophrenic; it is almost a basic component of human nature. Its only specifically schizophrenic element—the latent cleavage that it implies—can be understood only in terms of the next topic to be discussed.

5. *The blurring of the frontier between reality and the imaginary.* Culture-historically, the existence of this dividing line is a relatively recent discovery. In most primitive societies the dream is essentially

consubstantial with reality. Father André Dupeyrat (personal communication), a sound practical psychologist and a good anthropologist, once told me that recently converted Papuans and Melanesians insist on confessing that they have committed adultery even when they have done so only *in dreams*. It suffices to open almost any one of Lucien Lévy-Bruhl's books, or, for that matter, many standard anthropological monographs, to realize that such a conception of the dream is extremely common among primitives. It is no less common, of course, among philosophers, many of whom incarnate the attitude ridiculed by the famous German quip: "Denn nicht sein kann, was nicht sein darf" (What should not be, cannot be). One need only recall Hegel's haughty remark, when someone pointed out to him that, despite his theories, certain things stubbornly kept on being at variance with them: "So much the worse, then, for reality!" The *fact* is that the primitive acts realistically most of the time; the *trouble* is that he does not *know* that he is acting realistically when he bandages a wound but unrealistically when he tries to cure an illness by offering a sacrifice. The Greeks were among the first to differentiate between reality and the imaginary *as categories,* yet in practice they—and Plato in particular—often treated certain of their cherished fantasies as real and treated as fantasies certain things they chose not to believe—just as we do! What is even more significant is that, having made this momentous discovery, the Greeks *could not stand its consequences.* They reacted to the painful discovery of the *difference* between dream and reality first with Platonic idealism and then with what Gilbert Murray (1951) called a "failure of nerve." They *withdrew* from their insight into this basic difference and lapsed into unbridled mystical obscurantism.

The crucial point is that a primitive, who does not distinguish between the real and the imaginary—who does not fully grasp that they are two different categories—is not really schizophrenic when, having *dreamed* of adultery, he confesses to the missionary that he has actually committed adultery, because for him, *and for his society,* dream and reality are consubstantial. He can, like Grubb's (1911) Lengua Indian, believe, *without a sense of contradiction and of an inner split,* that Grubb stole his pumpkin because he *dreamed* that Grubb stole it, and yet admit that, at the time of the supposed theft, Grubb was many miles away and that the pumpkin was, obviously, still in his garden. By contrast, Occidental man, if faced with a contradiction of this kind, would do all he could to rationalize it. Thus, compared with primitive societies, our society is less schizophrenic and our citizenry is more so, because a split of this kind impairs the *ethnic* personality of Occidental man but not the primitive's

227

—and I was able to prove (chap. 1) that there can be no authentic psychosis without damage to the ethnic personality. There *must* be such a split in the members of a society that *professes* to differentiate between the real and the imaginary but admires Carrell for being a mystic and Newton and Millikan for writing childish theological pamphlets. One also saw magazines like *Time* and *Life* champion Edward Teller and yet chide him for being an agnostic. Some forty years ago a psychologist showed that, among scientists, the physicists were the most mystical and the psychologists and psychiatrists were the least so. "Mais nous avons changé tout cela!" (But we have changed all that). Before Freud invented the death instinct, most psychoanalysts were hostile to the occult. Following the invention of that (hypothetical) instinct, both Freud's own papers on telepathy and those of certain of his disciples became predominantly favorable to the extra-sensory-perception hypothesis (Devereux 1953a). It makes one wonder whether the greatest scientists might be the least able to bear the feeling that they—even they!—do not understand perfectly all the riddles of the universe and so refuse most consistently to accept Moses Maimonides' advice: "Teach thy tongue today to say: 'I do not know.' " Yet, there are few tokens of true maturity more convincing than the capacity to suspend judgment and to tolerate one's own lack of omniscience. Many scientists, including some of the greatest, seem to lack this gift and therefore feel compelled to fill in the gaps in their realistic knowledge by sucking Aristophanic bird's-milk "wisdom" out of their elbows. It is a sad spectacle when a scientist begins to engage in "wisdom"-mongering, and Freud was assuredly the last person from whom one would have expected it. His work, more than that of any of his predecessors, clarified the difference between the real and the imaginary and warned against any blurring of the tenuous boundary line.

Our pseudo-rational society insists that we accept a schizophrenic split: that we keep our equilibrium with one foot firmly planted among the transistors of an electronic brain and the other in the revivalistic church around the corner—or even among ectoplasms produced in a spiritualistic séance. The primitive notion that it is actually magic that sanctions and confirms reality is psychologically much less harmful than the view that the telepathy hypothesis is supported by statistics—or, more correctly, by statisticians.

6. *Infantilism,* too, is deeply rooted in our social and cultural matrix. It is well known that schizophrenics—and even some schizoid neurotics—often look much younger than their age. Only when (and if) cured do they begin to look their real age. Our own society makes a fetish of youthful appearance. Some time ago, world-famous

American scientists strenuously tried to look like Princeton under-graduates, with crew cuts, loud sports jackets, and porkpie hats, just as, today, some French scientists have a hippie look. Portly matrons, spreading like Longfellow's proverbial chestnut tree, dress and act like girlish high-school sophomores. Sedate businessmen assembled at sales conferences or American Legion conventions act like not too bright ten-year-olds who have raided their father's liquor cabinet. I have called this self-destructive behavior pattern "honorary adoles-cence" (1956a). The infantilism of our society is also shown by its having made idols out of muscle-bound slobs, who are good at hit-ting a small ball with a big stick or at running a larger one down the field for a touchdown.

A supposedly radical or left-wing novel, *No Pockets in a Shroud* (1937), written by the rebellious novelist Horace McCoy, is, in a sense, a truly frightening document. The hero, a crusading intellec-tual journalist, seeks to clean up a politically corruption-ridden and racially prejudiced town and in the end achieves his goal. He does *not* achieve it, however, by denouncing the complicity between the police and the gangsters or the Ku Klux Klan meetings at which men belonging to a discriminated-against minority are castrated. He does nothing of the kind! He finally awakens the "social conscience" of the city by proving that the local (professional) baseball team—whose members are the *moral idols* of the young!—is thoroughly crooked and has been bribed by gamblers to "throw" games it could have won. The most tragic thing is that McCoy himself seems quite as convinced as the town he describes that the "moral turpitude" of a baseball player is a more serious matter than political corruption or the castration of members of the oppressed minority.

From this kind of systematic encouragement to think, feel, and act as though one were ten years old to genuinely schizophrenic fetal regression is but a short step—*et ce n'est que le premier pas qui coûte!* (and it is only the first step that is hard to take). In this re-spect there is very little difference, either morally or psychiatrically, between the totalitarian system, which seeks to make men into stupid adults, and the *incomplete* democratic system, which tries to turn men into precocious children.

The one thing no "civilized" country tries to do is to turn its citi-zens into intelligent and mature adults, because intelligent adults are supposedly hard to govern. But if they are, that should be an addi-tional reason for doing everything possible to foster an adult citi-zenry, in the best sense of the word; for the ultimate goal of the state is *not* to produce, as Sparta did (Plutarch, *Lycurgus and Numa Com-pared* 4. 3–5), citizens made on the assembly line but to teach citizens to govern themselves. Only a group made up of mature and intelligent adults is able to govern itself.

7. *Fixation and regression* are the means by which the prestige-laden state of infantilism may be achieved. One can remain a baby or one can regress to infancy. Both solutions are highly valued in civilized society and are bolstered by a massive pseudo-sentimentality and by countless variations on the theme of maternal wisdom. In modern society Mother's Day is the root of a private "cult of personality" and institutionalizes a carefully gift-packaged and commercialized pseudo-sentiment. It makes little difference whether all reason stops at the threshold of the semidetached family dwelling or at that of some sacred navel of the world.

Modern man systematically assumes an infantile stance and stubbornly takes his wishes for reality, having been conditioned to do so by his environment. Duly persuaded of the need to give a justification to his existence—as though life were not, in itself, its own justification—he is taught to rely on those who claim to have a hot line to (the currently fashionable) Eternal Truth. Worse still: even the brilliant Athenians, when they had the good fortune to have Pericles as their first magistrate, could tolerate him only by ascribing to him the traits of a charismatic leader capable of saving them from the claws of Hades and the Erinyes, while those hostile to him delighted in the fantasy of being a minority oppressed by a tyrant. Under these circumstances it is truly miraculous that a Pericles now and then manages to get elected—even if for the wrong reasons—and it is more miraculous still that such a man is willing to play the role of first magistrate in a political nursery.

While I am on this subject, I might as well specify that, contrary to current interpretations, I hold that the charismatic leader is not an omniscient and omnipotent paternal imago. He is a mother imago, simply because, once past the oral stage of babyhood, the normal child quickly gives up fantasies of omniscience by proxy. Once he reaches the oedipal stage, he is haunted by Father, the castrating tyrant. Hence, he demands that the politician who solicits his vote reassure him by playing the buffoon, incarnating the good-natured, incompetent dolt—shuffling about in his slippers, as in the comic strips—whose very incapacity guarantees that he will never turn into a castrating oedipal father. Thus, Pericles was repeatedly obliged to play this degrading role before the Athenian assembly. For example, he had to degrade himself to the point of tears and supplications to get the Athenians to spare his mistress, Aspasia. In societies, like Athens or the United States,[9] that are haunted by dread of the tyrannical Father, the more intelligent the candidate, the more he has to waste time on smiling and joking or on playing the buffoon or daddy in slippers, kissing babies and donning Indian warbonnets. He must, above all, limit his speeches to the reassuring affirmation that he is in favor of baseball, motherhood, and apple pie—and against sin. Otherwise he risks being defeated by a veritable land-slide of adverse votes.

But there is more still! One of my European colleagues was won-dering one day why, in more and more matriarchal America, no woman is ever elected president. But this fact is easy to explain. In a matriarchal society, which, dreading tyranny more than anything, manages to neutralize the paternal imago and make it inoffensive, it is the phallic mother who is the genuine phantasmatic castrator: the "Mom," whose destructiveness has been repeatedly stressed by the most informed American psychiatrists. Hence, no woman will ever be elected president as long as America, while dreading tyranny, in-creases the power of women to the point of making of them despots, leeches, and castrators par excellence. A deeply patriarchal society can, from time to time, tolerate a female as head of state, even as tyrannical a woman as Queen Semiramis, the inventor of castration (according to Ammianus Marcellinus 14. 6. 17). No matriarchal so-ciety will ever run the risk of placing the executive power directly in the hands of women. In pre-Hellenic Greece (Devereux 1963), as well as among the Iroquois, the Hopi, and the Khasi,[10] women can be the sole depository of power and its sole legitimate source, but this power is exerted by men in her name. All this has nothing to do with any real or fictitious inferiority of women. My remarks pertain simply to a psychologically verifiable fact: the castrating mother is a more important source of neurotic terror than the castrating fa-ther. This is no doubt due to the fact that the image of the castrating mother is rooted in the deepest layers of what L. S. Kubie calls "gut memory"—the preverbal memory of the anxieties of the baby who is still absolutely dependent on the mother.

The fact that the true statesman, seeking election, is obliged to play the role of the all-knowing mother in order to reassure persons still fixated at the infantile stage of omnipotence by proxy, or must impersonate the inoffensive and inefficient daddy in slippers to ap-pease the fears of those still fixated at the oedipal stage—this is not what really matters. What matters is that, in both cases, the states-man is obliged to highlight and to market an aspect of his "person-ality" that is purely conventional and, from the functional point of view, completely irrelevant. Sometimes he must even play both roles at the same time: Roosevelt managed to play to perfection, now the role of the all-knowing mother, in order to satisfy those who clamored for a charismatic leader, and then that of the easygoing, inoffensive father, for example in the course of his "fireside talks," in order to reassure those haunted by the oedipal fear of a tyrant. He had to play these comedies in order to be elected *despite* his (initially) genuine greatness. There are some exceptions to this rule, but they are extremely rare.[11]

8. *Depersonalization* is inseparable from segmentalism and infantilism. The small child is unable to apprehend *total* personalities; the *hazy*, phantasmatic mother is only an appendage of her breast, which alone is experienced as real (Devereux 1961a, 1966a, 1967a). Needless to say, those who cannot see others as *total* personalities, having an identity in time (Devereux 1966d), cannot see themselves as total personalities either. Little wonder, then, that whereas Freud once saw chiefly symptom neurotics and the psychoanalysts of the '30s and '40s saw chiefly character neurotics, most analysts today see patients who have terrible identity problems and also doubts about external reality (Devereux 1966a, 1967b). Now, such uncertainties are systematically fostered by society. A clear definition of anything whatsoever—even, and chiefly, *of oneself*—presupposes the presence of certain characteristic and clearly accentuated traits and, at the same time, a stable frame of reference. Such definitions require that horses be horses, tables tables, and not that *and also* something else.

To take one point almost at random, one observes in our day a feminization of men and a masculinization of women. During walks along the boulevard Saint-Michel or the boulevard Saint-Germain or the streets of Greenwich Village in New York, it has happened to me more than once to notice a couple so undifferentiated that I was unable to say which of the two was the man and which the woman until they were but a few steps away. One is manifestly dealing here with the phenomenon of *dedifferentiation*. This dedifferentiation, involving a fundamental component, is analogous to the one which, as I have said time and again, is a fundamental characteristic of psychological illness. Now, differentiation is a basic criterion (chap. 9), one that any system of energy must satisfy if it is to produce work. This rule is as valid in sociology as in thermodynamics (Devereux 1967c). When loss of differentiation concerns as fundamental a trait as sexual identity, the illness is ipso facto very severe. Nonetheless, it is this kind of dedifferentiation that some "scientists"—and dressmakers—advocate today (Devereux 1967c).[12]

To come back to the increasing dedifferentiation of men and women (who are equally important and deserve the same social respect): this tendency deprives the "subject" to be defined of certain of his key characteristics and undermines the very foundations of his identity. At the same time, it deprives the observer—who formulates these definitions—of an important part of the constituent elements of his own frame of reference, thereby making him unsure of his own identity.

For one of my patients, raised by a violent and domineering mother and by a passive weakling of a father, the terms "masculine" and "feminine" had lost their normal connotations. For him, his mother was "masculine" and his father "feminine." In the course of the analysis there came a point where, whenever the patient used the term "masculine," I had to ask: "Do you mean masculine like your mother? Or do you mean masculine in the ordinary sense?" *Mutatis mutandis*, I had to ask the same thing when he used the word "feminine." Worse still, this patient literally no longer knew whether he himself was a man or a woman. When he had intercourse with his mistress, there were so many crisscrossing and reciprocally interfering fantasy identifications that, in fantasy, he interpreted what was, objectively speaking, a heterosexual act as a *lesbian* relationship, in which his mistress was the "masculine" tribade and he was the "feminine" lesbian. The confusion of identities cannot go much further (Devereux 1966a, 1967a).

This depersonalization is further reinforced by the social demand that one should be impersonal, unemotional, reticent, inconspicuous, average, neutral, and the like. All these demands amount in the last resort to saying: "Never mind who and what you *really are!* Just *behave as expected* and avoid making yourself *conspicuous* by *being yourself,* by being *different.*"[13] A witty American journalist who had lived for many years in France wrote an amusing little article when, in the 1930s, the newly elected head of the Ku Klux Klan—a dentist, I think—boasted that he was the most average man in America. The American journalist commented: "A Frenchman would never call himself average—not even if he were. Least of all would he dream of *boasting* of it."

Side by side with this loss of a real identity and with the taboo on displaying *real* originality goes the brute commercialization of perfectly nonfunctional and purely external "trademarks": of distinctive "packaging." This is represented by Jayne Mansfield's ample bosom, by Veronica Lake's lock of falling hair, and even by the senior John D. Rockefeller's proverbial gifts of dimes or by the famous Eisenhower smile. Similarly, a patient may refuse to discard a preposterously old and battered sweater, cap, or necktie, which he cherishes as his "trademark," precisely because *only* this (purely external) trademark differentiates him from the other members of the "lonely crowd." He needs a trademark because he has no shreds of a distinctive personality left and no longer has a sense of his own identity. Sometimes he is not even sure that he is real, even to himself. This is not surprising when society systematically depreciates and inhibits the functionally meaningful creative uniqueness of men, when it values only what is nonfunctional: the "trademark," the "packaging," the "image."

In modern society, true individuality—that most precious and socially most valuable of all aspects of the human being—is a source of trouble rather than gratification; far from being rewarded, it is penalized. I note in passing that many "rebels," who erroneously believe that in behaving in an aberrant manner they are manifesting their personality, are simply out-of-context conformists; they do not *affirm themselves* but *reject their milieu.* San Francisco's beatniks rebel by acting out their notion of what a (Japanese) Zen Buddhist is like; New York's Greenwich Village rebels play at being Russian Communists as seriously as Moscow's rebels play at being young American capitalists. This is still simply conformism masquerading as anticonformism (chaps. 3 and 13). True individuality is nowhere in sight and, in most societies, represents no value and brings no rewards. Therefore, hardly anyone dares to be himself.

Yet, only by being maximally himself can man be maximally useful to society. Moreover, he cannot be maximally himself without the help of society. Mozart cannot manufacture his own piano, nor Pasteur his own laboratory equipment; but it is the piano that permits Mozart to be himself—a musician, and it is the laboratory that permits Pasteur to be himself—a scientist.

If society penalizes, depreciates, or, at best, commercializes this aspect of man, a sense of selfhood, a sense of the continuity of oneself in time (Devereux 1966d), and even a real sense of one's existence and reality are made impossible. Depersonalization is thus only a step beyond Mr. Anyone's sacrosanct idea of averageness and is the ultimate—and catastrophic—consequence of this goal. In a healthy society the sense of the self—of selfhood—and a certainty of one's identity and reality—and of the identity and reality of others—are encouraged. This simple finding suffices to explain the unmiraculous "miracle" of Periclean Athens, of Medicean Florence, of mid-seventeenth-century and mid-nineteenth-century France, and of Elizabethan England (Devereux 1956a). The frustration of man's attempts to become individualized and the penalization of his uniqueness lend a nightmarish quality to the sterile drabness of Kokomo, Minsk, or Stendhal's Verrières.[14] All this leads in the end to the twin

234

horrors of concentration camps and Soviet psychiatric "hospitals" for dissenters, who stubbornly persist in being individuals and not cogs in a machine, and to chronic wards in Occidental mental hospitals for those whom society has successfully discouraged from attempting to be real human beings.

CONCLUSIONS

Since I myself have stressed (chap. 1) that each ethnic group has its own typical and privileged "ethnic neurosis (or psychosis)," it will perhaps be objected that too much should not be made of the fact that Occidental society, too, has a characteristic and privileged "ethnic" type disorder. But what is disturbing and disquieting is not, of course, that Occidental society, too, has an ethnic illness but the fact that this illness happens to be *schizophrenia* rather than some relatively benign psychic disorder, such as hysteria, so prevalent in the nineteenth century and still prevalent among many primitive groups; for hysteria, though it is undoubtedly a genuine neurosis, does not involve a radical and extensive disorganization of the ego and so does not vitiate, to the same extent as schizophrenia, the very basis of human relations with others and with reality. A society whose characteristic ethnic neurosis is hysteria can often flourish and function quite "normally," though of course not *quite* as effectively as if it were relatively free of neurotic tendencies. By contrast, a society whose ethnic psychosis is schizophrenia necessarily functions far below its optimum potential. In some cases it can even completely lose its capacity to survive and can collapse more rapidly than would a society in which the percentage of persons suffering from relatively benign neuroses had reached the threshold of "saturation" (Devereux 1956d), even though it is probable that it is precisely at that point that malignant psychoses begin to proliferate.

I am convinced that when the *scientific* history of mental illness is written, it will be possible to prove that societies such as pre-Platonic Athens, which functioned at an almost optimal level, had only ethnic disorders of a relatively benign type, such as hysteria, and that societies in their decline, like Sparta at the beginning of the fourth century B.C. and Rome during its worst period of decadence, had severe ethnic psychoses, such as schizophrenia.

One thing at least is certain: one of the least-recognized historical facts (Devereux 1965a) is the *increase* in the percentage of persons suffering from severe latent neuroses, and especially psychoses, in doomed social systems. Only a fundamental reconsideration of Occidental culture and a radical restructuring of our society in accordance with human principles inspired by reason and common sense can avoid a catastrophe.

Our society must either stop fostering mass schizophrenia or it will simply cease to be. We must either recover our humanity within the framework of reality or perish.

I I

Ethnopsychoanalytic Reflections on Neurotic Fatigue (1966)

I propose to discuss here the psychological and sociological functions of fatigue and the way in which this condition is exploited, especially in ancient and primitive societies.

Practical considerations impose this method of treating the subject. A diagnosis of neurotic fatigue requires the elimination of organic causes at the outset. The ethnologist, however, is rarely a physician, and even the ethnologist-physician has no laboratory in the bush. Moreover, the fact that an individual is neurotic does not necessarily mean that his fatigue, too, is neurotic. In addition, it is sometimes difficult to distinguish between neurotic fatigue and depressive tendencies, especially when one does not speak the patient's language perfectly. Finally, the primitive rarely considers his fatigue to be a symptom of illness and therefore consults neither shaman nor Occidental physician. These considerations explain the paucity of concrete data in both ethnological textbooks and textbooks of tropical —or even exotic—medicine. One must therefore approach the problem of fatigue states first of all within the framework of psycho-socio-cultural relations.

THE PRESTIGE OF ENERGY

Restless and overexcited as we are, we assume that energy is everywhere viewed as a virtue accessible to everyone. Still, in Homer, only Athena is called "the unwearied one"; Zeus himself occasionally dozes off. An Arabic adage asserts that it is better to sit than to stand, to lie than to sit, to sleep than to lie, and to be dead rather than asleep. Hyperactivity is sometimes regarded as not altogether desirable and even dangerous. The Mohave Indians, who are hard workers, claim that hyperactivity—intense and sustained work— exhausts, in the end, not only men but the gods themselves. Their culture hero, Mastamho, exhausted from his labors, undergoes a metamorphosis into a crazy and catatonic fish-eagle. Stuporous and covered with lice, he eats the leavings of other birds (Kroeber 1925;

Devereux 1961a). I do not know the official explanation of the salutation "May you never be tired!", used by the Pathans of Afghanistan; it may perhaps convey the wish that the person so greeted will never have to overexert himself. According to the Afghan psychiatrist Kamal (1978), the notion of "fatigue" plays a crucial role in Afghan nomad beliefs about (probably psychosomatic) illness: the nomad Couchi say that nomads afflicted with fatigue became settled and urbanized. The Melanesians of Dobu called Fortune's (1932) attention to a compulsive worker, for they considered him to be abnormal.

Inactivity may also, by contrast, enjoy enormous prestige. One thinks here of the immobility of Indian yogis; of the indescribable laziness and indifference of Damsan, the mythical hero of the Rhadé tribe in Vietnam (Sabatier 1928), who could nonetheless perform incomparable feats of valor; of the prestige of the mandarin's physical inactivity, made obvious by the fact that his fingernails were never cut; and so forth.

Even normal activity sometimes seems to require special preparation. Stimulants such as coffee, tea, kava, maté, cola, and cocoa were discovered by primitives. A young Sedang Moi woman of South Vietnam explained why she wore on her right forearm (her working arm!) a brass spiral weighing more than a kilogram: the bracelet "strengthened" her arm. In short, the body's normal resources do not seem sufficient. And yet, like many other primitive agriculturalists, the Sadang must engage in work of several days' duration only four or five times a year, and their ten-day corvée, consisting in keeping the roads in repair, used to occur only once a year. What is more, each of these periods of effort was followed by feasting and drinking, "to reward the soul for the effort it had made."

SCHEDULES OF WORK

The practice of intense, sustained, daily work for all is historically new, and I doubt that man, despite his long period of "domestication," is well adjusted to it, for such a schedule does not exist among primitives. Some hunters engage in violent activity, but only for a short time, and primitive agriculturalists also work hard only periodically. The first people to perform monotonous, intense, and continuous work were, I think, the slaves of antiquity: those who labored in the silver mines of Laurium, the copper mines of Egypt, and in the large agricultural, mining, and industrial operations of Rome —and they died of it! There are even racial variations in this respect. By forcing their Indian slaves to work literally "like niggers"—a much more robust race and better adjusted to the tropics—the Spaniards managed to depopulate the Antilles. Thermodynamically, the Chinese is a very efficient "machine." He can convert a bowl of rice into more energy than a white man can. Similar facts are observable even among animals. A tame zebra cannot furnish the same amount of *sustained* work as a horse—a species long bred for this purpose. The elk, though bigger and stronger than the reindeer, is practically useless as a draft animal, for its metabolism predisposes it to overheating, which can be fatal (Hančar 1955). The cheetah, though it is the fastest of the quadrupeds, suffers a heart attack if it is forced to run at top speed for more than ten minutes.

We must therefore consider the possibility that intense work, sustained throughout the year, is incompatible with the realities of human physiology. *Neurotic* fatigue may well be—*at least partially* —an (occasionally *anticipatory*) defense against this kind of requirement. It may not be the result of the amount of work actually done but a *defensive anticipation of the foreseeable consequences* of the quantity of work required by this schedule. Though this is certainly a partial explanation, I think it is nevertheless valid and not to be lost from view.

Society seems to have only three ways of regarding inactivity: it sees it as the result of real fatigue, caused by intense activity; as the result of an obvious illness; and, finally, as the result of "inborn" laziness. The only alternative to work is the prestigious inactivity of the ascetic and the privileged idleness of those who are wealthy enough not to have to work. My best Sedang informant, Mbrieng, a thin, asthenic man, was considered lazy; he shared this view and was ashamed of his laziness, just as he was ashamed of his poverty, which was due to his limited activity. Yet he was an indefatigable informant, capable of doing *intellectual* work eight hours a day, seven days a week (Devereux 1976b).

I now propose to discuss the exploitation of genuine fatigue and the intentional production of a state of fatigue for sociocultural purposes or for psychological ones—or for both.

Fatigue due to real effort can sometimes serve as an alibi. Among the Sedang and among some tribes of the Philippines (Barton 1938), the woman's work is fairly arduous; as a result, her sleep is so deep that she sometimes does not bother to become fully awake when her husband penetrates her. If, during her husband's absence, a man takes advantage of this feminine practice in order to penetrate a woman surreptitiously, she can claim that she was so numbed by sleep that she failed to realize that the man was not her husband— a perfect alibi for forbidden pleasure.

Deliberately induced fatigue is frequent, even in so-called civilized societies. "Chaste" athletes exhaust themselves in order to control their sexual impulses; they claim, quite mistakenly, to "sublimate" them in this way. Neurotic housewives allay their anxiety by frantically sweeping their houses. A woman suffering from serious mitral stenosis brutally overworked her heart: she cleaned her large house from top to bottom every time she had an anxiety attack. Voluntary exhaustion is also manifested in religion. The great Greek athletic games had a religious character; the participants spent their strength in the service of a god. At the time of puberty, young Mohave girls have to do *useless* work (Kroeber 1925)—collecting leaves—in order to *become* hard workers. In many societies, the "possessed" ritual dancers dance until they collapse, utterly exhausted.

Such states of deliberate exhaustion must be viewed as states of quasi-drunkenness—particularly because fatigue is, in fact, a biochemical self-intoxication and because these fatigue states fall into the category of so-called *pleasant languor*. If this way of viewing them is valid, it might be useful to consider this kind of fatigue as a kind of "drug addiction." A kind of parallel exists: some Eskimos try to give pleasure to their children by hanging them by the neck; the anoxemia thus produced is supposedly pleasant (Freuchen 1957).[1] I would therefore compare this "toxicomania of fatigue" to the satiated infant's sleep, which, according to Ferenczi (1922), represents an alimentary "drunkenness." One might even assume the existence of a general category of pleasures elicited simply by a radical change in physiological functioning: from hunger to satiation, from waking to falling asleep, and, more clearly still, from sexual excitement to postcoital relaxation.

EXPLICABLE FATIGUE VS. UNEXPLAINED FATIGUE

Some primitives, when they feel tired even after they have slept well, attribute their fatigue to the adventures of their soul, which had wandered about during their sleep; it is thus their soul that is tired. Shamans, too, wake up very tired if they overwork their souls or send them on travels during sleep or shamanistic seizures (Devereux 1961a [see 2d rev. ed., 1969]).

These observations bring me back to the psychological meaning of *sought-after* fatigue, already alluded to in the preceding paragraphs. Its paradigm is postcoital fatigue, whose principal purpose seems to be to obtain the pleasure that the appeasement of an excitation provides. In fact, there seem to be neurotics for whom orgasm is only a hypnotic, their principal goal being the pleasant tiredness of the postcoital state; that is, the pleasure of orgasm is simply a supplementary "bonus" collected, or expense incurred, en route. Moreover, since Dement (1967) and his team have discovered that *restful* sleep requires dreaming, I am inclined to view dreaming as a "bonus" perfectly comparable with orgasm. One would thus dream *in order to be able subsequently to relax* during sleep. This explanation appears to draw the ultimate consequences from the Freudian hypothesis that the dream is the guardian of sleep. By linking this theory with the phenomenon of hypnagogic fantasies, which open the pathway to sleep, and also with the definition of the dream as the gratification of a wish, one could regard dreams as so many hypnagogic mechanisms, or rather hypnostabilizers, which intervene at the very moment when, without this stabilizing dream, one would wake up.[2]

I mention in passing that there are, in my opinion, two broad categories of hypnotics: those that elicit dreams, so as to enable one to sleep, and those that induce sleep, in order to permit one to dream. The hypnotic to be prescribed for a patient should be selected in accordance with his psychic needs, i.e., in terms of the psychological causes of his insomnia.

Induced fatigue as an act of asceticism has already been mentioned briefly in connection with "chaste" athletes. A young black American, powerfully built and in perfect health, felt worn out and had become impotent. He *systematically* exhausted himself by daily taking three or four strong doses of a laxative, which he did not need in the least. It was a neurotic and ascetic maneuver: he *unconsciously* sought exhaustion and impotence. Once I even analyzed a patient who used sexual *excesses* in order to exhaust himself and thus to become temporarily "chaste." This ascetic practice in reverse was inspired by two symbolic equations: body = penis, and fatigue = impotence ("chastity"). Real fatigue, due to normal and legitimate efforts, diminishes sexual potency very little; it is chiefly in neurotic fatigue that potency is diminished. This may well be one of the sources of the "need" for neurotic fatigue. In fact, the fatigued neurotic often seems to want to experience a "pleasant" fatigue of the postcoital type even as he makes a detour to avoid the "intermediate" bonus (or expense) of orgasm. In cases like this, one can also speak of *anticipatory* fatigue, which takes two forms: a neurotic fatigue that anticipates the tiredness a person would feel *if* he had made the effort required by our society's patterns of work, and a fatigue that anticipates postcoital fatigue and even the exhaustion of sexual excesses. This latter category of fatigue is clearly linked with asceticism, aphanisis, anhedonia, and also with *la belle indifférence* of the hysteric, so admirably described in the Rhadé myth of the hero Damsan (Sabatier 1928), who would not even take the

241

trouble to make love to his two ravishing wives and sought a purely autarkic and narcissistic paradise by means of total "immobilism."

THE SECONDARY GAINS OF NEUROTIC FATIGUE

1. Flight from reality is observable in Bali, where, according to Margaret Mead, people charged with serious crimes sometimes fall asleep on the defendants' bench. Barchillon (1963) gives an excellent account of such flights into sleep in some types of neuroses.

2. Fatigue used as an *opportunity* to manifest "justifiable" neurotic behavior is comparable to drunkenness considered as an extenuating circumstance (alibi). Indeed, the superego, the ego-ideal, and to some extent even the ego are proverbially "soluble in alcohol"; the same is true also of extreme and neurotic fatigue, whose unconscious purpose may well be the ("justifiable") ventilation of certain prohibited neurotic tendencies. Since its effects are related to chronic invalidism, neurotic fatigue may also "justify" the manifestations of a pathological passivity and dependence, for it is at once an alibi and a form of blackmail: "If I am not working, it is not because I am lazy; I am merely exhausted," goes hand in hand with, "Do my work, please—I am too tired to do it myself." A German witticism is to the point: "I do love work! I would gladly spend my days watching other people work." Finally, neurotic fatigue—like asceticism—frequently involves also a disguised manifestation of great hostility toward those who have the right to count on the help of the one who is "tired." By their permanent tiredness, or by becoming hermits preoccupied solely with their own salvation, "immobilist" neurotics wrong their families and even society, which also has a right to their work.

NEUROTIC FATIGUE AND SUBLIMATION

Freud specifies that, for those who are capable of sublimating their aggressive drives, work is a creative pleasure. This implies that neurotic fatigue explicitly reflects a failure to sublimate aggressivity. When an activity does not represent *true* sublimation, when it is only an "acting-out," the fatigue that inhibits it is a simple reaction formation. It is comparable to the fainting of the latent sadist (unaware of his condition) at the sight of blood; his fainting obviously inhibits his ability to leap on the wounded man in order to kill him—but it also prevents him from coming to his aid.[3]

Neurotic fatigue thus seems to permit the neurotic to avoid the guilt feelings that would be triggered in him by a kind of work that did not represent a true sublimation of his aggressivity but was only an acting-out in disguised form. Moreover, as a reaction formation, neurotic fatigue allows the manifestation of unconscious aggressivity (in the form of passive aggressivity) toward those whom the fatigue deprives of the benefits to which they are entitled. This may well have been one of the causes of the purely physical (i.e., not intellectual) fatigue of my Sedang informant Mbrieng. When his wife was about to give birth to their fifth or sixth child and her life was in danger, he refused for quite some time to offer a sacrifice to the spirits, claiming that the crisis was not yet serious enough to warrant mortgaging the family's meager resources in this way. This explanation failed to convince his twelve-year-old daughter, who acted as her mother's midwife; the following day she had a fairly destructive hysterical attack and broke so many pots and other objects that the cost of their replacement—and the compensations paid to the other inhabitants of the long house for the damages her frenzy caused them—considerably strained the family's budget (Devereux 1976b).

I am aware that I have proposed a new theory of neurotic fatigue. I find it plausible *without believing it to be complete*. It seems to fit not only the scanty ethnographical data that we have but also our meager knowledge of this syndrome at the clinical level. I hope that at least a part of this theory will make a valid contribution to our understanding of this neurosis, which is as yet so poorly understood.

Finally, I note that I speak here only of neurotic fatigue. Psychotic fatigue, which may sometimes culminate in psychogenic death—in so-called "voodoo death"—does not come within the scope of this discussion.

12

Masochistic Blackmail: An Ethnopsychiatric Note on Property Destruction in Cargo Cults (1964)

The basic position I take in this note is that, though societies and cultures cannot be "diagnosed" in psychiatric terms, certain social processes can be interpreted psychodynamically—especially those mass eruptions that, because they fly in the face of cultural traditions, cannot readily be channeled into traditional types of activity.

My primary purpose here is to shed light on the well-known fact —too well known to require special documentation—that in many Cargo Cults, and in certain movements related to them, the expected period of happiness and plenty is anticipated by a wholesale destruction of existing resources. Similar phenomena have also been observed in historical societies. Thus, when the false messiah Sabbatai Zevi (called Shabbethai Zebi by Sir Paul Rycaut) stirred up the Jewish communities in the Turkish Empire, "All business was laid aside; none worked or opened shop, unless to clear his warehouse of merchandise at any price. Whoever had a superfluity of household stuff sold it for what he could" (Rycaut 1687).

I suggest that this maneuver—hastening the coming of plenty by self-inflicted impoverishment—is psychologically quite comparable to, e.g., the Crow Indian practice of pretending impoverishment and loneliness in the vision quest so as to *extort compassion* from a potential supernatural protector by an ostentatious display of helplessness. I have discussed this technique of masochistic extortion elsewhere, in some detail (Devereux 1951a [2d rev. ed., 1969]).

I now propose to cite a clinical example, obtained in the course of a psychoanalytic treatment, whose psychodynamics are essentially comparable to the technique of masochistic extortion.

A young man in psychoanalysis for a totally incapacitating agoraphobia (as well as for a number of other related phobias and compulsions), which prevented him from earning a living and forced him to remain as dependent as a child upon his aging parents, had in his childhood often been frightened by his parents, who enforced their commands by saying: "Just wait until we're dead! You'll break your nails and scar your hands trying to dig us out of our graves." They also did many other things to keep him in a position of infantile, passive dependence in both childhood and adolescence but were of course disappointed when, in adulthood, despite considerable intellectual potentialities, he remained essentially a child.

In the course of his analysis the patient spontaneously gained insight into his inexplicable infantilism: "If I remain a child forever, if my very existence continues to depend on the presence of my parents, I can arrest the progress of time. By staying a child, I prevent my parents from becoming old and dying. If I am a dependent child, they simply don't have the right, or even the possibility, of deserting me by dying." (It will be noted that the parents themselves inculcated this patient with the notion of equating their death with a punitive desertion.)

An almost identical story is recorded in Chinese sources in the form of a moralizing account of perfect filial conduct, exemplifying the extreme reverence that Chinese children owe their parents: "Lao Lai-tsu was a man of the country of Ch'u. When he was seventy years old, his parents were still alive. His filial piety was very strong. Constantly clothed in a medley of garments [as children are dressed], when he carried drink to his parents, he pretended to stumble on arriving at the hall,[1] then remained lying on the ground, uttering cries after the manner of little children." Or else, "*with the object of rejuvenating his old parents* (my italics), he remained before them, playing with his long sleeves, or amusing himself with chickens" (Granet 1930).

Needless to say, the real problem is not to determine whether Lao Lai-tsu really existed or behaved in an infantile manner for the purpose of "rejuvenating" his parents. The point is solely that this anecdote was recorded (or invented) in China and was circulated there, eliciting belief, admiration, and therefore (inevitably) an echo in the minds of those who heard or read this story. In other words, the *popularity* of this "edifying" tale is conclusive evidence that the fantasy that one can postpone one's parents' death by pretending to remain a child is a product of the unconscious mind and also appeals to it as a "proof" that its fantasies are defensible and, possibly, correspond to the operations of reality. Many neurotic symptoms have a distinctly "magical" aspect, just as much magic has distinctly neurotic aspects (Devereux 1954c). The practical problem is to determine whether a particular fantasy appears on the *individual* level or belongs to the realm of *culture* and, within the realm of culture, whether it belongs to the cultural mainstream or to its backwaters (Devereux 1954c). I have shown elsewhere (chap. 16 and Devereux 1954a) that a concrete fantasy—corresponding to the "koro" syndrome of the Chinese of Southeast Asia—occurs, despite its outlandishness, in a great variety of contexts.

Cultural anthropology has much to gain by the study of the various contexts, both cultural and individual, in which a given cultural trait, reflecting a fantasy, may manifest itself.

13

Primitive Psychiatric Diagnosis:
A General Theory of the
Diagnostic Process
(1963)

I propose to outline a general theory of the diagnostic process by tackling the problem *historically,* through an analysis of the "total" diagnosis encountered in primitive psychiatry. I believe that modern psychiatric practice can derive useful stimuli from this contribution to the history of medicine.

The chief difficulty in this undertaking is the extreme paucity of information about the diagnostic methods of primitive healers. In the few anthropological studies that do mention the psychiatric disorders of primitive peoples, the patient appears on scene—on the printed page—as an already recognized and more or less completely diagnosed neurotic or psychotic, with no mention of the manner in which this status—for a status it is!—had been assigned to him. Even the few psychiatrists who have studied primitive psychiatric practices describe mainly symptoms and primitive healing techniques and tend to ignore the primitives' diagnostic procedures. Thus, the index of Laubscher's work on Tembu psychopathology (1937) does not list the term "diagnosis," and Yap's excellent paper on *latah* (1952) discusses only the finished and properly labeled "product," not the manner in which the label came to be assigned *by the Malays* to the person suffering from *latah* seizures. To the best of my knowledge, the only work grappling systematically with the problem of diagnostic science in a primitive system of psychiatry is my study of Mohave ethnopsychiatry (Devereux 1961a [2d rev. ed., 1969]).

One can, of course, simply resign oneself to this state of affairs and try to squeeze whatever meaning one can from the meager data available. On the other hand, one can attempt to derive new insights precisely from the paucity of data on diagnosis—for example, by postulating that this lack is due neither to chance nor to incompetence but to certain unanalyzed difficulties inherent in the entire diagnostic process, both primitive and modern. These difficulties, once analyzed, are likely to increase one's understanding of the diagnostic process, substantially, not only at *every* level of cultural development but also qua properly scientific method of investigation. I thus adopt the position that the correct approach is to exploit the paucity of data as a significant and productive fact instead of deploring it and viewing it as an obstacle to insight.

The present study is divided into two major parts.

Part 1 reconstructs the cultural process by which a given individual acquires the status of an abnormal person, or, in psychiatric terms, the process by which he is assigned a diagnostic label. The emotional difficulties inherent in the recognition and labeling of a neurosis or psychosis are also discussed.

In part 2 I attempt to clarify a hitherto almost completely neglected yet crucial question: Is diagnosis made in terms of the logical process of *exclusion,* through which, as in statistics, one creates two populations, one defined as "$X = A$" and the other ("all the rest") defined specifically as "$Y = \bar{A}$" (i.e., Y is non-A), or is diagnosis made in terms of the process of *enumeration:* "$X_1 = A_a$," "$X_2 = A_b$," "$Y_1 = B_a$" or "$Y_2 = B_b$," etc? In ordinary language, I will seek to determine whether, when a person is diagnosed as a psychotic—and perhaps also, specifically, as a schizophrenic or a paranoiac—this diagnosis is achieved by saying "Mr. X is non-normal" or by saying—if something of a barbarism may be permitted—"Mr. X is 'yes-insane.'" Anticipating my findings somewhat, I will demonstrate that—contrary to what is generally assumed and is automatically implied, by linguistic usage, in the term *ab*-normal—the real diagnostic process does not consist in the *negative* determination that Mr. X is non-normal (deviant) but in the *positive* determination that Mr. X is "yes-insane."

For reasons of expository convenience—and also to avoid giving the impression that, in the course of discussions contained in part 1, I am smuggling in, as a latent premise, the point to be proved in part 2—I will, in part 1, seek to treat psychiatric illness neither as "non-normal" nor as "yes-insane" but simply as the logical equivalent of what the student of analytic geometry calls a "singularity" of a curve, such as a maximum, a minimum, or a break of continuity. This approach implicitly fits the now generally accepted thesis that —within the same behavioral continuum—the neurotic or psychotic is simply a distorted specimen of normal man, one in whom certain intrapsychic processes, present in everyone, have become preponderant, to the point of disrupting the balanced functioning of his personality. This finding in turn fits my basic thesis that, from the viewpoint of classical anthropology, "neurotic" or "psychotic" are statuses and, specifically, "achieved statuses," in Linton's sense of that term (1936). Indeed, the process through which someone comes to be labeled "neurotic" or "psychotic" is, from the viewpoint of classical anthropology, highly similar to the attribution of other statuses, while, from the viewpoint of psychiatry, both primitive and modern, it is diagnosis.

This finding implies, in turn, that one must further refine Linton's analysis of status by recognizing that no individual really achieves a given "achieved" status until society actually attributes or grants it to him by acknowledging that he has indeed executed certain *sine qua non* performances that entitle him to it. In fact, the distinction between "ascribed" and "achieved" status is not quite as absolute in practice as it is in theory, as is shown by the well-known quip that the nobleman, too, "achieves" his high status simply by taking the trouble to be born (*se donner la peine de naître*) (Beaumarchais, *The Marriage of Figaro*).

Be that as it may, the position of "madman" is, anthropologically, a genuine status. It is achieved by an individual through his exhibiting certain types of clearly defined behavior, and it is then granted (attributed) to that individual by society, which, in doing so, concedes that the individual in question did actually behave in a manner entitling him to the status (diagnosis) of madman and perhaps also the status of "psychotic" or, even more specifically, that of "paranoiac," etc. At the same time, one must recognize that some individuals whose behavior constitutes a singularity on the behavioral curve fail to achieve the status (diagnosis) "madman"; that others who behave in the same way *do* achieve that status (diagnosis); and that still others, whose behavior does not *quite* correspond to a well-defined point of singularity on the curve, achieve ("undeservedly"?) the status (diagnosis) of "psychotic" or "neurotic." Two examples will illustrate these points.

Case 1.—Some years ago, in the course of a discussion with an eminent psychoanalytic colleague, I insisted that, in view of some aspects of his behavior, a certain influential person should be considered a psychopath. This colleague insisted, however, that the person in question was not a psychopath because, owing to his eminent position, he was able to "get away with it" and to force reality—at least most of the time—into the procrustean bed of his irrational demands and needs.

A well-known historical example of such a personality was Bayan, the ruler (*Kha-khan*) of the Avars, who, driven by his psychotically self-destructive megalomania, frittered away his tribe's manpower in constant—usually only pyrrhically victorious—wars of conquest and did not recover his sanity until the final disastrous battle, in which the Byzantines crushed what was left of Avar military might (Brion 1931).

Case 2.—The Mohave take it for granted that all members of a certain family are—at least potentially—crazy. Hence, the least approximation to certain points of singularity on the Mohave behavioral distribution curve on the part of any member of that family is enough to cause him or her to be considered (diagnosed) as "crazy," although a strictly analogous behavior on the part of someone not belonging to that family would be very differently appraised (Devereux 1961a [2d rev. ed., 1969]).

Two comparable examples will clarify this point:

a) A person who has the reputation of being a great wit can say quite unwitty things and still elicit laughter, for he is *supposed* to be witty at all times.

b) Beethoven is rightly rated as one of the world's greatest composers. As a result, recording companies not only record, but actually manage to sell, even those of Beethoven's compositions (e.g., the *Jena Symphony*) that were written during a neurotically sterile period of his life and are therefore inferior to the works of many second-rate composers.

PART 1: THE DIAGNOSTIC PROCESS

Throughout part 1 I seek to avoid any reference to the problem of whether diagnoses are made in terms of "non-normal" or in terms of "yes-insane." This avoidance will of necessity create stylistic difficulties, since it is contrary to the logical habits and terminologies of anthropologists and psychiatrists to leave such questions undecided. In fact, the need to consider this problem as settled is so deeply ingrained in our thought and language habits that I may at times inadvertently fail to use the necessary circumlocutions to avoid a premature commitment. For this reason I wish to specify in advance that all passages in which, through oversight, I have failed to designate psychiatrically relevant behavior simply as a *"singularity" on the behavioral distribution curve* should be interpreted strictly as references to such "singularities," in the analytical-geometry sense of that term, and not in the sense in which, in ordinary speech, "singularity" means, valuatively, "peculiar," "queer," or the like.

Another specification to be made concerns the differential meaning that will be assigned to such words as "crazy," "insane," or "mad" as distinct from "neurotic," "psychotic," and the like. The terms "crazy," "insane," and "mad" are used exclusively in connection with the recognized status of those whose behavior represents a singularity, and they are to be considered as strictly anthropological terms. By contrast, 'neurotic," or other specifically psychiatric technical terms, will be used in contexts where—regardless of whether society has granted or denied an individual the status of "insane" or "crazy" person—*objective* psychiatric criteria indicate the presence of a genuine psychopathology. (I will leave temporarily undecided the question whether *my* decision, that psychopathology is present, was reached by means of the "non-normal" or the "yes-insane" process of definition.)

Data concerning primitive diagnostic criteria and techniques are especially scanty and inadequate with regard to the most crucial step in diagnosis: the determination that a singularity is present, i.e., that "something" is unusual. By contrast, data concerning *differential* diagnosis, i.e., the specific labeling of a condition *already* defined or diagnosed as a singularity ("something is wrong"), are somewhat more plentiful. Yet, as will be shown, the crucial step in psychiatric diagnosis, both primitive and modern, is not the differentiation of one psychiatric disease category from another but the differentiation between psychological "health" and "illness," and it is on this latter point that the data are scanty in the extreme. For that reason, in part 1 I shall be chiefly concerned with scrutinizing the process by which the presence of a singularity is determined.

Before going any further, I must also specify that a "singularity" can be of two types. It can be a singularity on the *temporal* curve, which plots the lifelong behavioral modalities of the individual (change of personality); or it can be a singularity on the *spatial* curve, which plots the theoretically prescribed (customary) and/or actually observed behavioral modalities of the patient's society or of mankind as a whole. For the sake of brevity, the former will be called "temporal singularities" and the latter "spatial singularities."[1]

"A singularity exists in me (you)"

The first step in diagnosis—whether it is the subjective recognition "Something is wrong with me" or the objective recognition "Something is wrong with you"—is the postulation that "something" is a phenomenon of the "singularity" type. This step actually involves a double insight: "Something is wrong" and "The something that is wrong involves or concerns me (you)." Sometimes such an insight calls for considerable perceptiveness, because mankind is so reluctant to admit that something is not foreseen, understood, and controlled that much effort is wasted in trying to treat new and unusual events (singularities) as though they were but variations on a familiar theme. The situation is further complicated by the fact that the

251

first sign that something unusual is happening may first appear in an ambiguous or highly disguised form. This was already known to Hippocrates (*On Dreams* 87) and Aristotle (*On Divination in Sleep* 426b21 ff.), who, with perfect psychoanalytic acumen, correctly explained why the first intimations of an (organic) illness *may* appear, not in the form of felt organic symptoms, but in the form of dreams. This fact, and the Greeks' explanations of it, were subsequently rediscovered independently by modern analysts, among them Ferenczi (1927a) and Bartemeier (1950).

Logically and technically, one must differentiate between the statements "Something is wrong with me" and "Something is wrong with you." This important difference has been almost entirely neglected by field workers, though diagnostically it is very important whether the patient knows that something is wrong with him or whether others must point it out to him. The importance of this distinction is highlighted by the—now allegedly obsolete—classical technique of differentiating between the neurotic and the psychotic in terms of the presence or absence of insight. Yet, while admittedly somewhat sweeping, this distinction possesses more than a grain of validity, in that, unlike the psychotic, the neurotic is capable of at least a modicum of self-diagnosis, especially in connection with the most crucial diagnostic step: the recognition that "something is wrong *with me.*"

The (logically double) statement "Something is wrong *with me (you)*" can be further expanded by means of three additional steps:

a) Something (unspecified) is wrong with me (you).
b) Something of concern to the *healer* is wrong with me (you).
c) Something *psychological,* of concern to the healer, is wrong with me (you).

I must now discuss these three steps in detail.

a) "Something (unspecified) is wrong with me (you)" does not call for an extended discussion. It simply asserts the presence of a singularity and the attribution of this singularity to the Self or to the other.

b) "Something of concern to the *healer* is wrong with me (you)" is a somewhat more complex statement. It differentiates, for example, between the statements "I am unsuccessful" and "I am neurotically self-destructive." This distinction is sometimes less clear in primitive societies than in classical psychiatry and—though obvious on the logical level—is somewhat less than absolute even within the framework of psychoanalysis.

In primitive society the awareness that one is suddenly unsuccessful may actually suggest that this singularity is due to a (perhaps magically or supernaturally caused) loss of *mana* or something of that sort, whereas in psychoanalysis a previously consistently successful businessman's sudden failure is most of the time rightly viewed as being caused by the eruption of a masochistic need to fail (Laforgue 1944) or, specifically, by an incapacity to tolerate success (Freud 1916). Moreover, in primitive society, which, as Róheim (1930) has pointed out time and again, is often a "therapeutically oriented society," a phenomenon such as a sudden decline in a man's fortunes (allegedly due to witchcraft or to loss of *mana*) and actual organic or psychological illness belong to the same universe of discourse and are of equal concern to the healer. Among the Kikuyu the healer is qualified not only to treat the illness but also to avert ill fate (*thahu*), which can be due to a curse or to a ritual pollution. This being said, and due recognition being granted to the anxiety-arousing potential of a sudden awareness of a decline in one's fortunes, even when (objectively speaking) it is due to a natural calamity, such as an epizootic in the herds is for pastoralists, it is still a fact that, in every primitive society known to me, some behavioral singularities are assigned solely to the healer, while others are assigned to the tribe's chief or to whatever other equivalent of a law court there may be. Thus, the fact that a given stressful situation is routinely assigned to—or claimed by—the healer is already a major diagnostic step.

c) "Something psychological, of concern to the healer, is wrong with me (you)," is a further crucial diagnostic step. For example, the patient who feels a malaise or a pain of some kind may declare, "This is not a symptom of heart disease, but precordial anxiety," or, with less sophistication, "My illness is not an ordinary physical ailment. I am bewitched, or am haunted by ghosts, or have lost all or part of my soul." In most primitive societies the distinction between organic and psychological illness is of course somewhat vague. On the whole, there seem to be many more examples of primitives imputing "psychological" dimensions to organic illness than there are examples of psychological illnesses to which organic concomitants are ascribed. Thus, the organicistically overloaded etiological theory of psychiatric illness formulated by the Mohave shaman Hikyēt reflected his own idiosyncratic biases rather than standard tribal belief (Devereux 1961a [2d rev. ed., 1969]).[2]

The magnitude of this step—and the anxiety it arouses—can hardly be overemphasized. Its significance can be discussed in terms of two completely different frames of reference, both of which highlight its momentousness.

Resistance to the Recognition of Psychological Illness

The recognition that something is wrong with the nucleus of the Self is singularly hard to achieve and even harder to accept. As La Rochefoucauld rightly observed, "Everyone complains of his memory, and no one complains of his judgment." A well-known "get-well" card expresses the same insight: "Your condition is not psychosomatic! You are sick, sick, sick!"

In brief, both socially and subjectively, psychic malfunctioning is experienced as the ultimate insult, and society does little to alleviate this discomfort and feeling of degradation. Hence, an eminent psychoanalyst, who also happens to be a sophisticated physician, once said to me, "To my mind 'psychosomatic' is often simply a bad word —one that conceals the fact that someone made a poor organic diagnosis." In a lighter vein, I feel that the greatest compliment I ever received was the remark of a psychologist who said to me, "In this psychiatric community you are the only analyst who, when you don't like someone, do not say, 'He needs more analysis,' or 'He is paranoid,' but are content to call him an s.o.b., in plain English."

From the viewpoint of both diagnostician and patient, the recognition that a nuclear impairment of the Self is present is—consciously, preconsciously, or unconsciously—viewed not simply as a scientific and diagnostic statement but also as a pseudo-objectively and reconditely worded variant of the contemptuous remark "This guy is nuts!"

This misconception is quite understandable, since one experiences the psyche as the nucleus—or center—of one's Self, while specific acts and even the body as a whole are perceived as more or less peripheral, at least in comparison with the psyche. This significant fact is sometimes consciously recognized even in daily life:

Case 3.—A patient complained that his wife nagged him a great deal and criticized many of his specific actions. When he asked her not to be a nag, she angrily—and irrationally—retorted, "I only criticize your *actions;* your criticism, however, represents a condemnation of my entire *personality.*"

In brief, even if one recognizes that primitive man does not always consider his body to be quite as peripheral to his Self as the dualistically oriented Westerner does, it is a fact that even in primitive society both the subject and the healer experience genuine organic illness as more peripheral—and therefore less upsetting—than psychic illness. This permits the conclusion that psychic illness is the most anxiety-arousing of all disturbances of the Self.

The Threat Posed to the Self by Psychic Illness

A. The psychologically ill patient's behavior represents an extremely painful and anxiety-arousing temptation for the observer to imitate the patient's example by "letting go" of his own unconscious and repressed impulses.

Case 4.—I once asked a friend of mine—a brilliant man who had had so severe an episode of paranoid schizophrenia that he had actually been screened for a lobotomy—whether, during his illness, he had understood the real meaning of the confused utterances of other schizophrenic patients. When he told me that he had understood them, I asked him whether now, i.e., after his full recovery, he could still understand them. He replied, "I am sure that I could—but I would not *allow* myself to understand them, for fear of a relapse."

Case 5.—In a certain medical school, second-year medical students were instructed by the professor of psychiatry to "go down into the unconscious with the interviewed psychotic." One medical student absolutely refused to comply with this directive, saying, "I am sure I can go down there, but I am not sure that I could surface again afterwards."

The contagiousness of mental illness is an axiom in some primitive cultures:

Case 6.—The Sedang Moi believe that people go insane when the ghost of insanity (*kiya ràjok*)—which can be either a genuine (insane) supernatural being or else the ghost of a deceased insane human being—approaches a person, puts his arm around that person's shoulder, and seeks to "make relatives" (*prå hmoy må*) with him (Devereux 1933–35).[3]

Case 7.—In many primitive societies, the shaman who sends out his soul to bring back the soul of a person who has lost his runs the risk that his own soul may not return to him. Among the Mohave, the shaman who sends his soul to the land of the dead to bring back his patient's soul, which had been lured there by the ghost of one of his deceased relatives, runs the risk that his own deceased relatives may persuade *his* soul to stay with them (Devereux 1961a [1969]; Fathauer 1951).

These observations, and certain related phenomena, explain why some potential shamans refuse to become practicing shamans:

Case 8.—Now and then a Sedang Moi on whom the thunder gods seek to bestow shamanistic powers drinks his own urine in order to disgust his would-be benefactors and cause them to take back their gift of power, because he is afraid that he may end up as a soul-eating witch, subject to the death penalty; that is, his angry and terror-stricken fellows may seek to kill him or at least to sell him abroad as a slave (Devereux 1933–35).

Case 9.—When certain young Mohave feel the budding of shamanistic powers within themselves, they panic and, though unable to reject these powers, refuse to acknowledge themselves as shamans or to practice their skill (Devereux 1961a [1969]).

In many primitive groups the brief psychotic episode that usually precedes the acquisition of shamanistic powers is often even more excruciating than the subsequent shamanistic seizures. Such initial psychotic episodes appear to be manifestations of an acute and desperate struggle against the fragmentation of the ego and the return of the repressed and are often accompanied by terrifying hallucinations and severe anxiety attacks. These well-known and properly documented facts are discussed in chapter 1, as is the strange phenomenon of their general scotomization by authors like Ackerknecht (1943), Honigmann (1960), and M. K. Opler (1959).

B. It is of the essence of psychiatric symptoms that they are more or less conspicuously at variance with the mores and, indeed, *must* be *provocatively* at variance with them if they are to gratify the idiosyncratic and socially negativistic needs of the patient (chap. 3). In other words, the psychiatric patient is a "social trouble unit" (Devereux 1937a) and, precisely for that reason, possesses a great deal of what I have called "social mass" (1940 [1978a, chap. 1]); it is, moreover, a social mass that he did *not* possess in his sane state, and he often genuinely enjoys it. As a wit once remarked, a melancholiac would not enjoy his melancholia half as much if it did not greatly inconvenience others. One may also mention in this context an old Melanesian woman, described by Rivers (1926), who, being considered dead, was to be buried alive. She participated in her own funeral rites—in which she starred—in a state of joyful and almost hypomanic exaltation. The element of rebellion in psychopathological symptomatology has also been pointed out by Jenkins and Glickman (1946, 1947).

To return to the problem of self-diagnosis, and specifically to the crucial step the individual takes when he recognizes that something nuclear is radically wrong with him: one must take explicit cognizance of the painfulness of this step—a painfulness constantly mentioned by analytic patients, who feel that even their own analysts despise them for being irrational, weak, or neurotic.

How does the primitive, who recognizes that he is not functioning adequately, cope with this traumatic insight? Let me scrutinize in detail the case of a Sedang Moi who recognized that he was functioning inadequately and, on a very superficial level at least, seemed to accept this fact without further ado, except perhaps for a sense of humiliation.

Case 10.—My father by adoption, Mbrão, formerly village chief (*kan pley*), and in 1933–35, when I knew him, still house chief (*kan hngīi*) of the biggest longhouse of the village of Tea Ha, was an outstandingly able informant who had a spectacular memory despite his great age, which I inferred to be about seventy. Yet, a few years earlier, he had resigned his village chieftainship on the ground that he no longer felt qualified to fill that position. When questioned on this point, he stated: "Formerly I had much 'ear' [reason, judgment]. Now I have little ear. For example, I now occasionally strike my wife, though she is good woman and does not deserve it" (Devereux 1967c).

Superficially, nothing could be clearer than this account of an aged man's awareness of the decline of his mental powers and of the emotional lability which it brought in its train. Actually, however, the situation is far more complex, the key issue being the Sedang conception of "ear" (and of other psychic functions as well). The choice of the *ear* to denote reason is, obviously, related to the Sedang conceptual series "hearing, understanding, reasoning," which seems to reflect their rather passive-aggressive approach to life (Devereux 1964). By contrast, the more actively oriented Mohave, while fully recognizing the existence of impaired understanding, view *muteness* (and *speech impairment* in general)—i.e., impairment of an organ of output rather than one of intake—as the prototype of mental impairment (Devereux 1961a [1969], 1964), an outlook similar to our own tendency to equate stupidity with "dumbness."[4]

Now, though old Mbrão was actually getting just a trifle hard of hearing, his reference to his "loss of ear" pertained, in this context, to a loss of *judgment* rather than hearing. This interpretation of the data perfectly fits the Sedang view that the ear is the seat of reason; they therefore assert that very young children, as well as stupid or senile people, "have no ear," regardless of how sharp their hearing may be.

C. The crucial question is: To what extent is the "ear" (reason) an *integral part* of the Self? The Sedang, like countless other primitives, believe in a detachable soul and in soul loss. In fact, one of the main Sedang souls, the property-and-*mana* soul, constantly fluctuates in size, since it is largely made up of the souls of the persons and things that one owns at a given time. Thus, when one sells a valuable possession, such as a slave, a buffalo, or a gong, the climax of the selling ritual is the transfer of the sold object's soul from the seller to the buyer. Similarly, if one captures a slave, one's *mana*-soul increases; if one's slave or buffalo dies, one's *mana*-soul decreases in size. These beliefs are, obviously, nothing more than variations on the theme of the partially or totally detachable soul (Devereux 1967c).

What should be stressed next is the tendency—seldom noted but easily documented—of primitives and the peoples of antiquity to consider even individual parts of the body to be endowed with a large degree of autonomy. The biblical injunction "If thine eye offend thee, pluck it out" clearly reflects an ascription of autonomy to the offending organ. Seen superficially, the castration of adulterers, the chopping-off of thieves' hands, the crippling of the legs of runaway Kikuyu wives, the punitive raping of promiscuous wives or even of lewd phallic women (Devereux 1961a [1969]), all seem to be simply practical forms of retribution, since they render impossible a repetition of the offense.[5]

On a deeper level, however, such punishments seem directed at the sinning organ itself, because in many cultures it is implicitly held to have a large degree of autonomy and hence to be responsible for its acts. Thus even we speak of "having itchy feet," and we say, "My eyes were bigger than my stomach." Examples of this type can be easily multiplied. Strong confirmatory evidence is also provided by the analysis of psychotic self-mutilations, the most typical varieties of which have been discussed by K. A. Menninger (1938); for acts of self-mutilation definitely suggest that the organ's sinning is perceived as an Ego-alien activity, and that the organ itself is thus to be ejected, so to speak, from the Self-image (the body-ego) and punished, as one punishes a rebellious servitor. This expulsion of the sinning organ from the body-image is especially conspicuous in the case of the sex organs. Even the nonpsychiatrist who keeps his eyes and ears open knows to what extent the penis in particular is viewed almost as a person, endowed with a true autonomy and given pet names. This evidence suggests that at puberty the new and highly localized spontaneous sensations of the penis and the clitoris, which are perceived as wholly autonomous, cause adolescents to ascribe to them a considerable individuality and autonomy, because these spontaneous sensations tend to make the integration of the sex organs with the rest of the body-ego quite difficult (Devereux 1967b).

To return to Mbrāo: it is suggested that, in complaining of a loss of *ear,* he was implicitly complaining—both in cultural and in depth-psychological terms—not of an impairment of his *entire* psychic apparatus but specifically of the desertion of a quasi-autonomous servitor. This strengthens my conviction that the capacity to view all of one's organs and functions as nonautonomous components of the Self is a major achievement in genuine self-integration and a token of true emotional maturity as well. In this context one must distinguish the domain of interpersonal relations from the domain of the intrapsychic images that provide a model for these relations.

D. It is actually possible to identify the two ontogenetic sources of the tendency to ascribe autonomy to various organs and psychic functions.

1. As regards the interpersonal frame of reference, it is a basic psychoanalytic finding that, until about the onset of the Oedipus complex, the child does not evolve true personal relations.[6] The baby is incapable of perceiving the person of the mother as a structural whole, at a given moment in time, or of realizing that the gratifying mother of 2:00 P.M. is truly the same person as the frustrating mother of 3:00 P.M. In the spatial context, the mother is seen as a partial object only: the mother is the breast and the breast is the mother. In the temporal context, changes in the mother's attitude— e.g., from "good" to "bad" or vice versa—determine the child's tendency to effect a split between the "good" mother and the "bad" mother (Devereux 1961a, 1966d). These facts are—or should be— relatively well known, though the spatial problem of the "partial object" has been given more attention in psychoanalytic literature than the temporal problem of the seemingly mutually incompatible or discontinuous successive images of the mother.

2. By contrast, the intrapsychic self-model which serves as a precedent for the ill-articulated or partial interpersonal model of the mother has been neglected, though the two are in fact closely interrelated and seem to form a whole. Indeed, I believe that I am the only one to have pointed out the nearly perfect chronological overlap between the period of partial (or ill-articulated) objects and the initial period of poor coordination of the infant's organs and senses and its deficient sense of its own continuity in time (Devereux 1961a, 1966a, 1967a). This incapacity to perceive a total image operates in both space and time. In the spatial dimension it is the infant's lack of muscular and sensory integration and coordination, as well as its subjective sense of the autonomy of its organs and senses, that prevents it—at least in part—from evolving a *complete* image of the mother. In the time dimension it is the infant's short attention span and its inability to correlate two events or perceptions separated by a certain lapse of time that prevent it from apprehending the self-

identity of its mother as having a continuity in time, persisting through her changes of humor and behavior.

Peripheralization, Etiology, and Diagnosis

On the emotional and primary-process level of thinking (so similar to Lévy-Bruhl's unjustly discarded "prelogical thinking"), the primitive who recognizes that his "singularity" is a psychological malfunctioning of his Self does not reach this insight without *implicitly* hedging it about with important reservations. I am even inclined to suggest that—given the painful and anxiety-arousing nature of the insight "I am crazy"—he can reach this insight *only* because his own culture provides him with means *simultaneously* to recognize the (*not* "his") malfunctioning and to extroject it in a quasi-paranoid manner.

The type of mentality just described continues to haunt even the most sophisticated modern psychiatrists (Devereux 1958a [1978a, chap. 10]). In two insightful papers, Scheflen (1958, 1961), a truly scientific analyst, drew some fascinating parallels between the "germ theory" and the "deficiency theory" of organic illness, on the one hand, and numerous psychodynamic explanations of psychological "illness," on the other, showing the extent to which such conceptual tokens as "mother love" are grossly reified in our supposedly scientific etiological thinking. Scheflen particularly stressed that this type of psychiatric reasoning is rooted in the medical (organic) training of psychiatrists. Going one step further, I suggest that this transposition of organicistic thinking to psychodynamics, by means of the fallacy of misplaced concreteness, is greatly facilitated by the need to deny the possibility of a truly *basic* impairment of the Self —a need that springs from the self-threatening implications of the recognition that the possibility of such impairment does, in fact, exist and can afflict anyone—even the psychiatrist himself.[7]

It might be added that the primitive patient—and often the modern one, as well—usually presents the healer not only with a description of his complaints but with a more or less fully developed, ready-made, home-grown self-diagnosis, complete with clear-cut etiological implications: "I am bewitched," or "It is something I ate, Doctor." The primitive healer may then confirm or modify this self-diagnosis, though—especially in the case of psychiatric patients —he seldom challenges the patient's basic assertion that he is ill, and, if he does challenge it (Devereux 1961a), usually questions the specific self-diagnosis rather than the far more crucial implicit affirmation that "A singularity, of concern to the healer, is present." Similarly, in our society, a general practitioner consulted by a patient who is found to be free of disease is nonetheless likely to accept the patient's implicit assertion that he is *ill*. Having done so, he will then proceed to make the diagnosis "hypochondria" and refer the (would-be organic) patient to a psychiatrist.

The healer's temptation to accept the patient's assertion that his singularity concerns the healer is so great that the Mohave shaman Ahma Humāre, who was not a boastful person, did boast of the following diagnostic feat, which he considered one of the high points of his career as a healer:

Case 11.—Ahma Humāre was consulted by a middle-aged woman who, on the basis of the cessation of her menses and of certain dreams, was convinced that she had contracted the dreaded ghost-pregnancy disease (pseudocyesis). After listening to her, Ahma Humāre sent her home after telling her, correctly, that she was not ill but pregnant (Devereux 1961a).

Thus, there is a basic willingness on the part of the healer to accept the patient's belief that his singularity concerns the healer rather than some other agency of society. On the whole, the healer's readiness to accept the patient's statement that he is ill is greater than his readiness to accept the patient's more specific (nosologically and etiologically worded) self-diagnosis. This finding calls for a brief discussion of the true meaning of the term "diagnosis," which will prepare the ground for the discussion in part 2 of the problem of attribution of status ("ill") and the problem of diagnostic labeling.

This is the point in the diagnostic process at which a label—implying a definite etiology—is about to be applied both to the singularity and to the person to whom that singularity pertains. It is necessary, therefore, to recall that the term "diagnosis" has a very significant meaning. As its etymology indicates, it does not mean simply "to label" or "to identify." Rather, it means specifically "to tell *apart*," "to differentiate *from*."[8] Indeed, when one declares that a given singularity belongs to the realm of psychopathology, one implicitly declares also that it does *not* belong to the realm of criminal law or to some other matrix or social universe of discourse to which various *other* singularities of behavior may be assigned. Likewise, when one diagnoses a patient as a hysteric, one implicitly states also that he is different from a schizophrenic or from a psychopath.

PART 2: THE DIAGNOSTIC LABELING OF THE SINGULARITY

In the preceding pages I have emphasized that one of the most crucial steps in the diagnostic process is the affirmation that the observed singularity is of interest to the healer rather than to some other social agency. This finding is not an academic one, nor was it intended simply as a display of critical ingenuity, i.e., hair-splitting. Indeed, a given singularity can be, and usually is, of concern to various agencies of society and is susceptible of being scrutinized and evaluated in terms of various cultural matrices (chap. 2). This fact is of concern not only to the healer but to the patient himself:

Case 12.—A female patient, intensely though ambivalently attached to her mother, whom she had practically incorporated into her psyche as a sort of internal parasite, strenuously resisted all attempts to make her aware of her (ethically justifiable) hatred of her mother, who had been extremely cruel, self-righteous, and narcissistic. The patient opposed any attempt to make her see that her mother had indeed been cruel and selfish; as she put it: "I cannot condemn my mother without also condemning myself, who am *also* a bad mother. If I am to consider myself neurotic rather than evil, then I must also consider my mother to have been neurotic rather than evil."

The problem created by the great social mass and by the culturally multivalent singularity (chap. 2) of the psychiatric patient is clearly reflected in the history of civilization. In the late Middle Ages, for example, many psychiatrically ill persons were held to be the Church's (and, specifically, the Inquisition's) concern rather than the healer's. This explains why certain books written by and for Inquisitors—such as the celebrated *Malleus Maleficarum* (see Zilboorg and Henry 1941)—which list in detail the signs by which witches may be recognized, are today important source material for the study of the psychiatric disorders that occurred during the Middle Ages; they are in fact more important and illuminating than the many medical treatises of that period.

Somewhat later, the most important and insightful medical works dealing with psychiatric illness—such as those of Weyer, discussed by Zilboorg and Henry (1941)—were precisely the ones that sought to demonstrate that these singularities of behavior should be dealt with by the healer, not the Inquisitor. Many of these important early psychiatric works therefore devoted a great deal of space to jurisdictional polemics.

Many singularities of behavior—which of necessity include elements of social negativism—were, and often still are, defined as "bad" or "criminal" instead of being recognized as psychiatric illnesses (chap. 3). Such behavior as compulsive stealing, homosexuality, and the like is so obnoxious to society that, despite conclusive proof of its psychopathological nature, the law continues to claim jurisdiction over persons displaying it. The law has thus far successfully resisted incorporating into its repertory of thought models of "legal insanity" a large variety of singularities that are demonstrably psychopathological. Certain feeble attempts of early law to exempt the psychotic from punishment—for example, by the declaration *Furiosus satis ipso furore punitur* (The madman is sufficiently punished by his madness)—are more than counterbalanced by legal principles like *Malitia supplet aetatem,* which postulates that a young child, even in a legal system that nominally asserts that he is incapable of committing a legally punishable crime, is no longer immune from criminal prosecution if the crime he commits is of a particularly vicious nature. This explains why, even in twentieth-century America, a fifteen-year-old murderer was tried by a jury and treated like an adult criminal. Indeed, the courts are usually disinclined to accept the plea of insanity whenever it seems possible to *impute* to the criminal a seemingly rational motive for his crime. In other words, when a psychotic shoots a total stranger for no obvious reason, a plea of insanity is usually accepted; if, however, a psychotic kills *and robs* a stranger, the courts tend to reject the plea of "Not guilty by reason of insanity," on the ground that robbery is—for the judge—an "understandable" and "reasonable" motive for murder (Devereux 1957).

Even primitive society is preoccupied with the legal aspects of psychic illness:

Case 13.—An Ashanti king sought to determine "experimentally" whether the legal responsibility of the drunk was greater or smaller than that of the psychotic. He therefore caused a psychotic and an intoxicated person to be brought together in a house, which was then set afire. The psychotic escaped by running away, while the dead-drunk experimental subject, because he was unable to leave, sustained burns. This was held to prove that the legal responsibility of the drunk is smaller than that of the psychotic (Rattray 1927).

In other societies it is the extreme troublesomeness of certain psychotics that removes them from the "jurisdiction" of the healer and subjects them to the jurisdiction of the law.

Case 14.—A Sedang Moi psychotic who is not extremely troublesome and destructive is treated by shamans and sheltered by his relatives, who are responsible for any damage he may cause. If, however, he becomes uncontrollable and/or actually represents a threat to his relatives, they deal with him as they deal with a habitual witch. Since it is not permissible to kill one's relatives outright, the "criminally insane" patient is tied hand and foot and cast into some deserted cave, where—"regrettably" and without any positive act of aggression against him on the part of his relatives—he "just happens" to die of hunger and/or exposure (Devereux 1933–35 [1978a]).

263

Case 15.—The Mohave declare that all shamans are "crazy." Hence, within limits, they can explain—and implicitly justify—the shaman's singularities of behavior by the traditional maxim "It is his nature, he can't help it." If, however, the shaman becomes overtly destructive—that is, if he bewitches people and actually boasts of it —he is killed, like a foe (= criminal) (Kroeber 1925; Devereux 1961a [1969 ed.]).

Case 16.—The Mohave recognize two major types of female promiscuousness, both types being explicitly labeled as *yamomk* (crazy). One of these types is represented by women who suffer from nymphomania (of which several diagnostic subtypes are believed to exist) but whose conduct is otherwise impeccable, in that they are known to be kindly, helpful, good-natured, and industrious. Such women are pitied and are often liked and accepted for their good qualities. They are felt to resemble the type of woman whom the English call "a bad lot, but a good sort" (Devereux 1961a). By contrast, the *kamalōy*, though at times also held to be *yamomk*, is felt to behave objectionably in all areas of conduct; she is aggressive, boastful, and ostentatious about her promiscuousness and is prone to make sarcastic comments about her lovers' sexual organs and performances. Such women, though also recognized to be *yamomk* (crazy), are intensely disliked and, in aboriginal times, were subjected to punitive mass rape and clitoridectomy and, in some extreme cases, even to deliberate attempts to contaminate them with syphilis (Devereux 1948c).

These and many other examples show that culturally determined preconceptions—"thought models" (Devereux 1958a [1978a, chap. 10)—determine whether a given psychiatric patient is assigned to the jurisdiction of the healer, the Church, or the courts.

These findings are of decisive importance for understanding the basic diagnostic process. Everything depends on whether a diagnosis is made in terms of the criterion "*deviation* from the norm" (statistical, nomothetic, etc.)—that is, in terms of "*non*-normal"—or whether it is made in terms of the criterion "fitting certain marginal norms" (statistical, nomothetic, etc.)—that is, in terms of "*yes*-insane."

The data cited regarding jurisdictional disputes over whether a given type of behavioral singularity—and/or the person displaying that singularity—concerns the healer ("sick"), the courts ("bad"), or the Church ("witch") clearly prove that even one of the most basic of all diagnoses, "This singularity is of concern (for example) to the healer," is made *not* in terms of "deviation from the norm" but in terms of "yes-insane" (or of "yes-bad," or of "yes-witch").

The still-raging dispute over the problem of "lay analysis" has, despite some sordidly materalistic overtones, many of the basic characteristics of other jurisdictional disputes over the psychiatric patient (Freud 1926). This polemic, too, operates in terms of positive "yes-insane" models, usually implying clear-cut (organic vs. functional) etiologies. Moreover, just as some psychoanalytic physicians, in claiming exclusive jurisdiction over the psychiatric patient, increasingly seek to rationalize their claim by emphasizing extra-analytic (genetic, hormonal, neural, etc.) factors, so psychoanalytic psychologists seek to rationalize their claim by diluting the essence of Freud's psychoanalytic psychology with large doses of essentially nonanalytic learning theories and the like. So far, the only visible result of this particular jurisdictional dispute has been a distressing distortion and dilution of classical psychoanalytic theory by both contending groups.

The crucial diagnosis "This singularity concerns the healer" is—I repeat—not based on a *deviation* from the norm but on *conformity* with some marginal but clearly specified norm. A given individual is not considered "insane" because he *does not* behave normally, as the majority of his peers allegedly do, but because he *does* behave the way the "insane" are *known, expected,* or *supposed* to behave. This implies, in turn, that if an (objectively psychotic) person does *not* conform to the kind of Lintonian "pattern of misconduct" (Linton 1936) that a given culture "proposes" to the neurotic or the psychotic, he is simply not recognized as "insane" and, *a fortiori,* is not diagnosed as having a particular kind of psychiatric illness.

Case 17.—The late H. M. Adler, M.D., professor of psychiatry at the University of California School of Medicine at San Francisco, told me in 1935 that he had seen, in consultation, a paranoiac whom he did not even attempt to have committed because he was certain that no court would admit that this man was, in fact, acutely and dangerously psychotic.[9]

Case 18.—In nineteenth-century England a certain psychotic was repeatedly declared sane by the courts until, in the course of a new hearing, a person present in the courtroom whispered something into the judge's ear. The judge then stood up and, bowing to the psychotic, said, in substance, that he had not realized that the gentleman was Jesus Christ. The psychotic, who until then had repeatedly managed to convince judges of his sanity, responded by saying that he had wondered for some time when he would finally be recognized for what he was (Krafft-Ebing 1875)!

I believe that many anthropologists refuse to admit that the shaman is psychiatrically ill, chiefly because the "shamanistic model of psychiatric illness" is not part of our official repertoire of "psycho-pathological models."

Misdiagnosis also reveals the importance of these diagnostic thought models. Members of alien cultures are sometimes diagnosed as neurotic or psychotic because their ethnic character causes them to behave in a manner that *accidentally* happens to fit one of our accepted "thought models" of psychiatric illness (Devereux 1951a [1969 ed.]).

It is demonstrable that the thought models of psychiatric illness are known not only to experts (healers and diagnosticians) but also to the laity, including especially those who are about to become psychotic. It is one of my key theses that the incipient psychotic's knowledge of these thought models actively influences the formation of his symptoms. Before discussing this particular point in detail, it is necessary to show the extent to which society at large is aware of these thought models.

The first, and most obvious, proof that they are well known is that the patient consulting the healer often approaches him with a ready-made, home-grown diagnosis. Thus, as reported in Case 11, a middle-aged Mohave woman consulted the shaman Ahma Humāre because she thought she was suffering from a ghost pregnancy. Her reason for thinking so was that she had had certain supposedly pathognomonic dreams and had also ceased to menstruate. Further discussion is superfluous, for I have cited many examples of Mohave self-diagnosis in another work (1961a [2d rev. ed., 1969]).

The second proof of the layman's awareness of psychiatric thought models, briefly referred to in chapter 1, relates to the phenomenon of malingering. In subjects who pretend to be insane, two types of malingering must be distinguished: the ritual and the idiosyncratic.

A. Ritual simulation of insanity always presupposes on the part of the subject a conscious attempt to display singularities of behavior that are explicitly recognized by the group as fitting one of its diagnostic thought models. Such ritual malingerings can be divided into two subtypes.

1. Ritual simulation of insanity as a prophylactic measure to prevent actual psychosis has been reported for the Iroquois (Wallace 1958) and for the Nyakyusa (Wilson 1954). I am reasonably certain that further instances of prophylactic malingering will eventually be found in other groups. I suspect that such malingering is, psychodynamically, a relatively effective prophylactic measure, closely related to the American technique of reducing tensions by getting "roaring drunk." Such a simulation seems to represent a kind of self-induced massive "ventilation," comparable to the hysterically

overdramatic ritual ventilation of grief at primitive—and not so primitive—funerals, after which the dead are supposed to be forgotten. This hypothesis is materially strengthened by the fact that, among the Nyakyusa, the ritual simulation of madness is a part of funeral rites and that, among the Mohave, highly dramatic but actually quite ineffectual female attempts at suicide occur in connection with funerals (Devereux 1961a [2d rev. ed., 1969]). Periods of ostentatious ritual license (Saturnalia) are probably related phenomena.

2. Ritual buffoonery (clowning) has not as yet, to my knowledge, been explicitly recognized as a type of malingering, though relevant data have found their way into even nonpsychologically oriented textbooks of anthropology. Thus, Lowie (1940) reports that members of the Arapaho Crazy Lodge military society acted "as foolishly as possible" during public appearances and—significantly—"spoke by contraries." This choice of words suggests that Lowie understood the connection between this type of buffoonery and the "speaking by contraries" of the typical Plains Indian Crazy-Dog-Wishes-to-Die (chap. 1).[10]

B. The behavior of the Crazy-Dog-Wishes-to-Die is located exactly on the boundary line that separates ritualistic from idiosyncratic malingering, for the Crow Crazy Dog himself determined the time of onset of his quasi-malingering and could, if he managed to survive until the leaves turned yellow, also determine the date of its termination (Lowie 1935).

True purposive malingering is mentioned in the Bible and also by Homer and other Greek authors. A Hebrew king, fleeing his enemies, simulated madness in order to make good his escape. Odysseus feigned insanity at least three times: first, when the "draft board" insisted that he join the army that was to sail against Troy, on which occasion an ingenious improvised draft-board psychiatrist, Palamedes, confronted him with a dilemma that forced him to behave rationally, thus revealing that he was sane (Hyginus *Fabulae* 95). Second, Odysseus feigned psychic and also physical distress when he entered Troy as a spy disguised as a partly unbalanced slave (Odyssey 4. 244 ff.). His third malingering, when, with Athena's help, he feigned senile psychosis, occurred when he was spying on the suitors, who in his absence had besieged Penelope with their attentions (*Od.* 13. 429 ff.).

It is hardly necessary to demonstrate that a *willingness* to feign insanity or feeblemindedness is, psychiatrically, an indication of neurosis. However, another factor should also be stressed: neither a ritual nor an idiosyncratic malingering would achieve its purpose if it failed to fit the thought model of some neurosis or psychosis familiar to the group one was seeking to deceive. In primitive society, where the lay thought model of "insanity" is often almost identical with the professional healer's thought model, malingering is harder to recognize than in Western society, where malingerers often reveal the spuriousness of their symptoms by behaving not in the way that psychiatric textbooks tell us that psychotics behave but in the way that lay opinion imagines that insane persons behave. The lay thought models of psychotic behavior obtaining at a given time appear to be derived from types of psychotic patterns of behavior known to have been prevalent in earlier periods (chap. 1).

It is because both lay and professional thought models of insane behavior exist that certain culturally conventionalized signals, which I have called "signal symptoms" (1961a [1969 ed.]), can be used by the incipient neurotic or psychotic to inform his environment that his status has changed from "normal" to "insane." This signaling represents an authentic form of cooperation between patient and diagnostician and can actually become a conventionalized and nearly contractual routine. Thus, it is a matter of common knowledge that when mental hospitals are visited by groups of psychology or social-work students, many inmates obediently trot out their fanciest symptoms for their visitors' edification.

In many instances the incipient psychotic signals his impending change of status in highly conventionalized ways. Thus Lowie reported for the Crow that the Crazy-Dog-Wishes-to-Die "talks by contraries" or talks "backward" (1935). The Moro about to run *amok* (*juramentado*) often first asks his parents' permission to do so (Ewing 1955). This is especially interesting since, among the Malays, nobles wishing to embark on some illegal venture, such as an attack on another nobleman, often asked the king's permission before breaking the peace. Many other examples of requests for permission to break the law are mentioned in the Malayan stories of Sir Hugh Clifford (1927) and by other authors as well. In some cases the incipient psychotic will actually acquire certain objects or regalia needed for the proper enactment of his psychotic role. The elaborate dress and armoring and other technical preparations resorted to before becoming *juramentado* (for example, one must cause one's penis to point upward, by tying it to a string passed around one's neck) well illustrate this process (Ewing 1955).

How well known these signal symptoms are is shown by the fact that misdiagnoses result when a person happens to produce accidentally—that is, idiosyncratically—certain supposedly pathognomonic signal symptoms:

Case 19.—Tcatc, a vigorous old woman, outspoken even by Mohave standards, once declared, "People sometimes say that I am a shaman—but I only have a temper." In this case, her characterologically determined "temper" was socially misdiagnosed as the signal symptom of a shamanistic neurosis, for, according to the Mohave, "all shamans are crazy" (Devereux 1961a [1969 ed.]).

Case 20.—I told Apen Ismalyk, a Mohave psychotic in partial remission, that, because of his behavior, people believed him to be a budding shaman, but one who refused to practice. He replied, very calmly and matter-of-factly, "They were bound to think that" (Devereux 1961a [1969 ed.]).

Mohave children and adolescents who are violent in their behavior and display uncontrollable impulsiveness in the instinctual sphere are practically maneuvered into becoming shamans by constant comments that their behavior is indicative of shamanistic proclivities. This occurs even when the neurotic child as yet has no such ambitions (Devereux 1961a [1969 ed.]). Thus, the transformation of an idiosyncratic singularity of behavior into a signal symptom is clearly due to a process of *reinforcement,* in the strictest learning-theory sense of that term.

These findings concerning signal symptoms call for a more general inquiry into the articulation of such symptoms with the social process. Signal symptoms having the greatest pathognomonic significance in diagnosis are largely conventional and cultural in origin and therefore vary from group to group. This implies, in turn, that signal symptoms *must* involve, not only socially disapproved behavior, but, specifically, the disapproved behavior that is related to *major* areas of stress in a given society. For example, one reason why Mohave neurotics and psychotics are so consistently and pathognomonically preoccupied with the dead is that Mohave culture emphasizes the obligation to forget the dead and to taboo their names. Now, certain signal symptoms that induce the Mohave to say that shamans (always suspected of being witches) are crazy also characterize the behavior of ghosts: both evil shamans and ghosts are avaricious, rapacious, incestuous, and prone to use their magical powers for the purpose of killing their relatives (Devereux 1961a [1969 ed.]). This strengthens my conviction that ghosts and certain supernatural beings are derived from conceptual models that in a given society subtend the "psychiatric" diagnoses characteristic of that society.

An even more striking example of the *necessarily* antisocial character of all signal symptoms is the prevalence of sexual delinquency as a signal symptom in American adolescent girls. The "sex-delinquent" girl is usually unable to enjoy sex. Sexuality is not, for her,

269

a source of pleasure. It is exclusively a signal symptom, because adults, through their frantic preoccupation with the chastity of adolescent girls, practically outline for these girls how they ought to behave in order to upset adults (chap. 8). This fits the finding that every signal symptom known to me involves an attack on major social values, an offending of important social sensibilities (chap. 3). It is a principle recognized—at least implicitly—by both the misbehaving person and the person observing him that his misbehavior is an act by which "insane" status is claimed.

The sum total of these considerations explains why, as stated elsewhere, practically every case of primitive neurosis or psychosis is a so-called perfect textbook case (chap. 1). The great accuracy with which the "insane" individual conforms to the cultural thought model, or diagnostic category, is due partly to the relatively great internal consistency of every primitive culture and its areas of stress and partly to the fact that primitives *differentiate* less rigorously and systematically than we do between "scientific" and "intuitive" thought. This is not the same as saying that they are more often irrational than we are. I mean only that they do not *know* as clearly as we do—or like to think we do—the difference between irrational and rational thinking (chap. 10).

Thus, the fundamental diagnostic step is taken in terms of the deranged person's positive conformity with a cultural thought model ("*yes*-insane") and not in terms of his nonconformity with society at large ("*non*-normal"). One hopes—perhaps in vain—that this finding will finally lay to rest the unrealistic, and hence grotesquely inadequate, "statistical" and "cultural-relativism" conceptions of psychiatric illness; these serve only to disguise the painful insight that compulsive conformity can itself be a major psychiatric problem (Reider 1950).

What remains to be clarified is the psychiatrically ill patient's willingness and pressing inner need to conform to a marginal cultural pattern—that is, to a strictly Lintonian "pattern of misconduct" (1936)—in a way that actually represents a collaboration between patient, diagnostician, and society at large. In colloquial terms, one may ask: What is in it for the psychotic?

The answer is provided by analysis of deliberately, even monstrously, antisocial or anticonventional actions, which indicate that the acquisition of the status of "insane" involves some tangible satisfactions. These actions lead to a tremendous increase in the rulebreaker's *social mass* (capacity to get attention). He is placed on a kind of pedestal and provided with a more or less supernatural status. The respect given to "those afflicted by Allah" and the oracular powers attributed to the mentally deranged hint at what really takes place when an individual violates some of the most cherished values of his society, especially if the violation assumes a more or less socially prescribed form (Devereux 1954c).

Case 21.—Certain highly specific, attempted or real, cannibalistic acts occurring among the Northern Algonquians serve to signal that the cannibal is a supernatural being: a *windigo*. He has become the human equivalent of the *windigo* ghost, whose victim he himself is believed to have been. Through being devoured inside by a *windigo* ghost, he himself becomes a *windigo*. And, since identification with the enemy is a mean of defense against anxiety (A. Freud 1946), Algonquian children play at *windigo* (Teicher 1960).

The entire problem is presented in a nutshell by Harrison's (1922) demonstration that, for all practical purposes, the Greek heroes' supernatural status was based on their having committed crimes and on the belief that some of them continued to cause harm even after death, often within the precincts of their shrines. This finding clarifies the following data.

Case 22.—An Eskimo woman who had cannibalized her family declared that she could no longer live among humankind (Rasmussen 1927; cf. Boas 1907).

Case 23.—Before hunting the hippopotamus, the Ba-Thonga first cohabits with his daughter so that his terribleness will match that of the beast he wishes to hunt (Junod 1927).

Case 24.—Atreus, wanting revenge for his wife's adultery with his brother Thyestes, tricked Thyestes into eating the flesh of his own children. An oracle then revealed to Thyestes that he could avenge himself on Atreus by committing incest with his own daughter, Pelopia; for the child born of this union, "blameless" Aegisthus, would eventually seduce Atreus' daughter-in-law, Clytemnestra, and would help her kill Atreus' son, Agamemnon (Apollodorus, *Epitome* 10. 5).

Case 25.—In order to recruit killers for its elite units, Sparta (Jeanmaire 1939), as well as the Thirty Tyrants of Athens, Genghis Khan, and Hitler (Alexander 1948), incited the volunteers—and forced the reluctant—to commit monstrously ego-dystonic acts, which put them, once and for all, beyond the pale of society.

Case 26.—It was the privilege and indeed the duty of certain divine kings—the pharaohs, the Incas, the kings of the Azande and those of Hawaii, etc.—to marry their sisters (or daughters), presumably for the purpose of setting themselves clearly apart from the rest of mankind.

Case 27.—The ritual—and dangerous—act of deflowering virgins is in numerous societies assigned either to a group or to persons so highly placed that they are not affected by the dangers resulting from this act (Westermarck 1906–8; Freud 1918; Yates 1930).

Case 28.—Some societies deny that certain crimes—and especially certain horrible crimes—*can* be committed. The Persians believed real parricide to be impossible (Herodotus 1. 137). The Spartans supposedly had no law against adultery (Plutarch, *Life of Lycurgus* 15. 10); they falsely claimed that there was no adultery in Sparta. Yet, wife-lending was lawful (Plutarch, ibid. 15. 6 ff.), King Ariston doubted that he had fathered Demaratus (Herodotus 6. 63), and the real father of Leotychidas, son of King Agis' wife, Timaea, was Alcibiades (Plutarch, *Life of Alcibiades* 23. 7). As to kin-slayers, their situation is often a complicated one. In Greek the same word (*autophonos*) means "murdering one's kin," "suicidal," and "slaying with one's own hand." In societies in which the murderer had to be slain by the victim's kindred, the slaying of a kin-murderer also involved kin murder. Orestes had to face this quandary when commanded by Apollo to kill his mother, who had slain his father, Agamemnon. It is, moreover, conceivable that the horribleness of kin murder put the killer beyond human jurisdiction (see Case 22, above). Some such ideas may explain why the ritual slayer of a divine king could become his successor.

Case 29.—In many tribes, incest and the acquisition of shamanistic powers are closely interconnected.

Case 30.—In Central Australia, the person who dares to commit incest, the *ilturka* man, is "condemned with admiration" (Róheim 1932). He is, however, sometimes punished in an indirect manner: when a strong band—seeking to avenge a "magical" murder—undertakes a punitive expedition against a weaker group, the latter may placate the attackers by handing over to them, for slaying, their *ilturka* (incestuous) men and/or by lending the tribe's women to the attackers.

Case 31.—The most curious example of the social *extraterritoriality* of the insane is the traditional freedom of speech granted to them and to those who simulate insanity. Thus Solon pretended to be insane so that he could violate with impunity the law that forbade all citizens to exhort the Athenians to reconquer Salamis (Plutarch, *Life of Solon* 8). Brutus and Lorenzaccio de' Medici resorted to similar expedients. It was this privilege that made the court jester or "fool" an important source of information for kings, since he alone could presume to tell unpleasant truths. However, the court fool had to signal his status at all times by wearing the traditional garb of fools and by speaking in a properly "foolish" manner (cf. the saying *Ridendo castigat mores*).

In all of these cases the acquisition of a quasi-supernormal or extraterritorial status is explicitly achieved by means of acts that closely approximate the proper (though marginal) thought model of "insane behavior"; the fact that these acts also deviate from the norm is here of only secondary interest. Indeed, where royal power is acquired or demonstrated by means of incest, which is taboo for commoners, one could not acquire a divine king's status by performing some *other* tabooed act, *not* specifically correlated by society itself with divine royal status.

SUMMARY

In primitive psychiatry explicitly, and in modern psychiatry implicitly, diagnosis is made in terms of the patient's conforming to a marginal model of "singularities of behavior" and not in terms of his deviation from the norm. Where behavior deviates from the norm but does not fit any clearly defined psychiatric thought model, the deviant is likely to be treated as a criminal rather than a "lunatic." These findings deprive of scientific significance all statistical and culturally relativistic approaches to the problem of normality and abnormality.

14

Pathogenic Dreams in Non-Western Societies (1966)

Causality and the Pathogenic Dream

The history of anthropology reveals that a great many concepts that seemed singularly clear and precise when first introduced into anthropological discourse tend to become vaguer and more evanescent when increased factual knowledge makes it possible to subject them to a more careful scrutiny. The history of the concept of totemism is an example of this process (Lévi-Strauss 1962).

In the first part of this essay I shall seek to demonstrate that the seemingly very precise concept of pathogenic dreams is actually far from precise. It appears precise only because it has not been carefully scrutinized and also because most data pertaining to dreams commonly thought to be pathogenic are incomplete.

The central difficulty in the anthropological, psychoanalytic, and phenomenological study of so-called pathogenic dreams stems from the fact that the term "pathogenic" clearly implies causality. Now, it is well known that the definition of causality, in practice as well as theory, has been one of the most vexing problems of both science and the philosophy of science. To take a famous example, many scientists and logicians hold that the Heisenberg indeterminacy principle at least partially undermines the concept of causality, whereas Einstein, Bertrand Russell (1927), and some other authorities feel that it is not incompatible with the laws of causality for the simple reason that it has no bearing whatever upon the problem of causality. If difficulties and controversies of this kind can arise in the exact sciences, then the student of cultural and behavioral phenomena may be excused for experiencing difficulties in connection with concepts that imply causality.

Superficially, the definition of the pathogenic dream is quite simple: Any dream that causes an illness is a pathogenic dream. Unfortunately, as soon as this simple definition, and the data from which it is derived, are subjected to closer scrutiny, one realizes that—in Henri Poincaré's words—one has been guilty of labeling the problem instead of solving it. In the first section of this essay I shall seek to remedy this scientifically untenable and intolerable situation.

The starting points in any situation in which a pathogenic dream is said to have occurred are two empirical data: (1) a dream and (2) an illness.

It cannot be sufficiently stressed that at this juncture the two data must be treated as discrete phenomena—as two isolated items on a trait list including all known behavioral phenomena.

Next, one may, or may not, observe a third phenomenon, which is of an entirely different order. It belongs, in Bertrand Russell's terminology (1903, 1919), to a different "mathematical type," in that it is a statement about two statements concerning empirical phenomena: "a dream" and "an illness." This statement—which can be either an individual, idiosyncratic assertion or a cultural tenet or both—asserts that the two phenomena under consideration are *somehow* connected. In other words, the existence of *a* nexus is predicated, but the *nature* of the nexus remains *unspecified*. In particular, at this point it is not even asserted that the (unspecified) nexus between "dream" and "illness" is a *causal* one. What is more, at this stage of the reasoning not even the concept of a temporal *sequence* is introduced into the informants' discourses. This means, in practice, that at this point the two phenomena that the informants have—legitimately or illegitimately—conjoined, by the imputation of some unspecified nexus, can also occur either simultaneously, perhaps in the form of having a dream and falling ill simultaneously, or the illness may precede the dream, in which case the dream may be viewed, not as pathogenic, but as symptomatic or pathognomonic. In brief, in such cases one surreptitiously introduces a special type of causality, which Petzoldt, who calls it "simultaneous causality," utilizes to explain the coherence of spatial (simultaneous) structures as opposed to the coherence of temporal (sequential) structures. Since it has been surreptitiously introduced, this inference must be discarded at once, at least at this stage of one's reasoning.

In principle, one's own position, and that of one's informants, with regard to the predication of an *unspecified* nexus between a dream and an illness is comparable to that of a statistician who finds a high degree of correlation between two phenomena but is unable to explain the actual connection between them in a causal way. This type of "correlation" is so common that statisticians sometimes amuse themselves by thinking up pairs of phenomena that, despite the existence of a statistically highly significant correlation between them, are not causally connected. One well-known "correlation" of this type is the one between the birth of babies and the coincident appearance of the doctor's black bags at the time and place of birth. I have pointed out elsewhere (1953a) that nearly all experimental studies in parapsychology are of this type. Indeed, in strictly logical terms, even if a given experimental subject in a clairvoyance study guesses right every time, one simply imputes an *unspecified* nexus to two discrete phenomena as long as one is unable to suggest any *clearly specified mechanism* connecting the appearance of a certain card and the ("correct") utterance of the subject. And one imputes a nexus not because logic obliges one to do so but because of a subjective need to impute some kind of order to nature and its phenomena. It may be objected that, according to Mach, there are no laws *in* nature other than those which one puts *into* nature. I feel, however, that *at this point* one has not even operated in accordance with Mach's principle. Even less has one operated in terms of the type of reasoning propounded by Saint Thomas Aquinas in his *Summa contra gentes* ("By the conformity between intellect and things truth is defined"), by Spinoza ("The order and connection of ideas is the same as the order and connection of things"), or by James Clark Maxwell (mathematical physics is possible because the laws of numbers happen to parallel the laws of bodies). Rather, one —or one's informant—has satisfied a purely emotionally determined Sumnerian "strain toward consistency," which, as psychoanalysis has shown, is the mother not of rationality but of rationalizations.

In brief, at this stage of the inquiry, one has simply discovered that the native informant chooses to assert that a nexus, as yet unspecified, exists between a dream and an illness. It cannot be stressed sufficiently that, strictly speaking, the informant is not (yet?) speaking of *pathogenic* dreams, since he has not (yet?) specified that the imputed nexus is a causal one. Even less has he specified the *mechanism by which* a causal connection comes into being and becomes operative. To take, for a moment, only the special case of the actual sequence "antecedent dream, subsequent illness": when one predicates a nexus between the two and possibly asserts also that the nexus is a causal one, the logical status of one's statement is strictly that of the well-known fallacy *Post hoc ergo propter hoc.*

If one turns for a moment to empirical field data, one finds, if one is careful, that available data seldom go beyond this point and that, quite illegitimately, the concept "pathogenic dream" is introduced at precisely this point. At the risk of seeming critical of field workers, I must confess that in many cases the actual published data cause me to wonder:

1. Whether, at this point, it is the field worker or the native in-

formant who introduces the concept of a (causally) pathogenic dream

2. Whether the field worker stopped his inquiry too soon and therefore failed to obtain precise and specific information about native beliefs concerning the *nature* of the causal nexus between the antecedent dream and the subsequent illness.

The first of these questions I cannot answer with any degree of certainty. Indeed, one mostly goes into the field so eager to discover the exotic, and therefore seduces one's informants so consistently to elaborate the unfamiliar and the strange, that sometimes a kind of *folie à deux* comes into being between informant and field worker —a tacit and unconscious contract to ignore all practicality and logic. This collusion is amusingly epitomized by Róheim's quip that, quite often, the only savage in the field is the visiting anthropologist.

With respect to the second question, I feel that I can speak with somewhat more assurance. I am almost certain that no truly exhaustive investigation of native dream theory exists, not even for the dream-oriented and dream-obsessed River Yumans—and this despite the fact that both conventional anthropologists (Kroeber 1925; Gifford 1926; Wallace 1947) and psychoanalytic anthropologists (Róheim 1932; Devereux 1957b [1978a, chap. 9], 1961a [1969 ed.], etc.) have specifically studied their dream life. The simple fact is that each new investigation reveals River Yuman dream theory to be far more complex than it previously appeared to be.

On a worldwide scale, it is evident that our information concerning the range and variety of primitive dream theories is fragmentary and that in this respect little progress has been made since Lincoln (1935) wrote his book on dreams in primitive cultures. This is due partly to the general tendency to expect very little from primitive informants in the way of theoretical complexity or multiple or variegated types of explanations and partly to the fact that, when the anthropologist hears of one dream theory that is officially emphasized and functionally important, he is quasi-hypnotized by it and calls off any search for dream theories of a different type, less prominent but equally traditional. Thus, though it is quite certain that among the Iroquois the theory of the "soul-wish-manifesting" dream is the most striking and socially most important dream theory (Wallace 1958), I cannot help harboring the conviction that a number of additional Iroquois tenets pertaining to dreams also exist but have not hitherto been recorded and/or adequately exploited.

This point is, methodologically, of some importance and should be substantiated, at least by means of a parallel example. Without exception, all earlier published data concerning the River Yumans had described only the official—and both functionally and behaviorally important—theory that twins are heavenly visitors, who are welcomed with joy and are readily granted special privileges. Only much later did I discover (Devereux 1941) the existence of a second theory concerning twins, completely different, and emotionally rather than behaviorally important. This second theory views twins as contemptibly acquisitive ghosts, whose sole purpose in returning to earth is to obtain a second set of funeral gifts from the living. The official emphasis on the first theory and its extreme elaboration simply diverted anthropologists from the task of exploring further the range of Mohave and other River Yuman beliefs concerning twins.

I suspect that something of this order occurred also in connection with the Iroquois. In their case the functionally important "wish-of-the-soul" dream theory short-circuited interest in supplementary, or possibly even contradictory, dream theories. A hint of a different dream theory is furnished by an incident, cited without any indication of its source, by Linton (1956). An Iroquois extorted a certain gift from a white officer on the ground that he had dreamed of having received it as a gift. When, subsequently, the white officer turned the tables on the Iroquois and, also on the basis of an (alleged) dream, extracted a (much-desired) return gift from him, the Iroquois informed the officer that, from that day forward, neither he nor the officer would have any further (wish-of-the soul) dreams.

As regards the Mohave in particular, the more data I accumulated regarding Mohave dreams, and the more I analyzed them, the more I was impressed by the range, scope, and variety of Mohave dream theories. On the basis of the preceding considerations, I am therefore inclined to believe that the logical incompleteness or arbitrariness of the connections that primitives (allegedly) believe to exist between an antecedent dream and a subsequent illness may be due more to an incomplete inquiry in the field than to a distressing fragmentariness of native dream theory.

To return now to the problem of the logical aspects of so-called pathogenic dreams: the postulation (or imputation) of an unspecified nexus between dream and illness demands at once that the *nature* of this nexus be specified and be shown to be of a causal nature. At this point one meets with utter chaos. In many cases one simply has no information. In other cases, the field worker applies to all dreams the portion of native dream theory that is known to him. This latter finding may partly explain why, in discussing the general problem of such sequences as "antecedent dream, subsequent event," Lévy-Bruhl (1922) (an unjustly neglected genius) found that in many cases he could not determine whether the antecedent dream was the efficient cause or was simply the prophetic intimation (omen) of some subsequent event. He therefore concluded that, in a genuine though complex sense, the omen dream actually also "causes" the event it foretells. One might perhaps amend this formulation somewhat and suggest that the haziness of the boundary between omen dream and causal dream is often due more to the fact that both occurrences are part of a rigidly deterministic (kismet-type) conception of the order of events in time than to a direct causation of the event (or illness) by the dream.

There is a broad range of phenomena in which an antecedent dream is linked to a subsequent illness in a manner only remotely connected with causality, even if one conceives of causality in the most elastic sense possible. A good example of this is one aspect of the Iroquois-type soul-wish dream. If Kamchadal *A* dreams that *B* is doing something for him and *B* fails, in reality, to comply with *A*'s demand, then not only the frustrated dreamer but also the frustrating and uncooperative person dreamed about will fall ill (Steller 1774). It requires further study to determine whether *A*'s wish dream should be viewed as a *pathogenic* dream with regard to *B*'s illness *even though* the Kamchadal themselves see a clear-cut—though not explicitly specified (pathogenic)—nexus between them.

A similar difficulty arises when *A* dreams that *B* will fall ill and *B* does, in fact, fall ill, with or without *B*'s having learned that *A* had dreamed that he (*B*) would become ill. One can, of course, seek to dispose of the matter by asserting that in such instances *A*'s dream is not pathogenic within the primitive meaning of that term and should therefore be considered as an omen dream rather than a causal one. I am inclined to question this simple-seeming explanation, quite apart from Lévy-Bruhl's cogent argument that the omen dream is, in a sense, also a causal dream, at least within the purview of native logic. Indeed, Lévy-Bruhl (1922) himself cites the following case: A Lengua man dreamed that he ate a tabooed bird and, on arising, confidently declared that his (absent) child had had a fretful (sick?) night as a result of this dream (Grubb 1911). In this case a true (primitive) causal nexus is predicated between the father's dream and the child's (a priori inferred) illness. The argument runs as follows: If fathers eat this tabooed bird, their children will become ill. The father dreamed of having violated this taboo. Dreams being real experiences of the soul, the taboo had actually been violated, and this necessarily caused the child's illness. *Ergo:* Individual *A* can have a "genuinely" pathogenic dream causing the illness of *B*.

Instead of rambling all over the ethnological map of the world, I limit myself, in the second part of this study, to an exploration of the various types of connections believed to exist between dream and illness in Mohave culture. I do so chiefly because, as stated above, the whole problem of pathogenic dreams is so complex and so poorly documented that the exploration of the problem in depth in a single culture whose dream theories are relatively well understood is more likely to clarify matters than would a poorly documented comparative approach to a few cultures only. This, however, is not all. I have postulated elsewhere (1955b) that something resembling the mathematician's ergodic hypothesis also exists in the social and behavioral sciences, so that at least the range and meaning of phenomena, typology, and patterns of connections between phenomena can be ascertained with equal precision by four means:

1. The study of a single individual in depth (e.g., through psychoanalysis)
2. The cross-sectional study of many individuals (e.g., through Rorschach tests)
3. The study of a single culture in depth (intensive field work)
4. The cross-sectional study of a large number of cultures (comparative method)

In the second part of this study, I shall use the third of these four approaches. I present it without further justification, since I have already provided empirical proof of the validity of this cultural ergodic hypothesis in the work just cited (Devereux 1955b).

DREAM AND ILLNESS IN MOHAVE CULTURE

The first point to be made in a discussion of dream and illness in Mohave culture is that the very existence of illnesses of *various* types —for example, the existence of *a* gastrointestinal disorder, as distinct from the concrete gastrointestinal illness of a given Mohave individual here and now—is in a sense derived from a pathogenic dream in the broadest sense of the term. The Mohave believe that all illnesses were foreordained, established, and experienced at the time of Creation. The event of Creation included (in principle) at least one concrete case of every illness (e.g., it included *a* gastroenteritis) and at least one actual cure of that illness. The illness "gastroenteritis" exists because at the time of Creation a case of this illness occurred, and it thus became not only a precedent but a "prophecy" that such illnesses would occur subsequently. Each case of this illness—a hundred years ago, today, and a hundred years hence—is thus a duplication of the mythical precedent and an implementation of the "prophecy" that the prototypal illness represented.

The Creation *myth* is, moreover, not a finished product. The Creation myth as recorded, let us say, in 1900 reports simply those portions of the myth that had been revealed in dream up to that time. Thus, when firearms were introduced and caused bullet wounds, a shaman promptly dreamed of having witnessed the portion of the Creation that pertained to the primordial, prototypal, and precedent-setting bullet wound and its cure. In principle, a Mohave shaman may dream tomorrow or the next day of the creation of radiation burns or space sickness and of its primordial healing. These new dreams automatically call for the completion of previously known versions of the Creation myth, just as the discovery of a new fossil demands that last year's handbook of paleontology be brought up to date.

Of course, the Mohave do not explicitly affirm that the original act of creation was a dream, in the sense in which some Australians speak of the time of Creation as "dream time." But the Mohave do hold certain beliefs concerning Creation, in which Creation as an act and the Creation myth as a dream differ no more than Tweedledum from Tweedledee. Indeed, the future Mohave shaman witnesses in his mother's womb the portions of the Creation that pertain to his future therapeutic specialty. He even specifies that he has witnessed the actual act of Creation, saying: "I know it, I was there." At the same time, he insists that the creators repeated or reenacted Creation for his benefit while he was still in the womb. Now, there is a basic paradox in this latter statement; for the Mohave hold that all their gods are dead and have been dead since Creation and that the culture hero or quasi-god Mastamho, exhausted by his labors, became a (catatonic?) osprey, or fish-eagle, and so no longer intervenes in human affairs (Kroeber 1925, 1948; Devereux 1961a). Now, if the gods are dead, one cannot quite see how they could reenact Creation for the unborn shaman. Hence, his statement, "I know it, I was there," necessarily predicates that the shamanistic dream can move backward in time. This implies that in his "intrauterine" dream he witnessed the *true, original* illness event and recreated it. This event serves as the prototype of the illness that he will later cure, and it is the nucleus of his "intrauterine" experience. In this very definite sense his intrauterine dream is an act of creation; his dream is pathogenic with regard to the occurrence of a *type* or *category* of illness (e.g., the clinical entity gastroenteritis), though it is not pathogenic, *at the time of the dream,* with regard to the gastroenteritis a concrete Mohave individual *A* will have on 1 June 1962 and which the shaman will have caused through witchcraft, by inducing a pathogenic dream in the victim.

Later on, in adolescence, the shaman will once more—and this time explicitly—dream of this part of Creation and will have a déjà vu experience in two senses: he will remember having witnessed the same scene in the womb and will feel that what he witnessed in the womb was the act of Creation itself.

Sometimes, later in life, under the impetus of some strong and significant stimulus, he may have further dreams, also accompanied by a sense of déjà vu—for example, of having already witnessed *in utero* some other illness and its cure. Ahma Humāre, a shaman who was not an obstetrician, saw his unborn child die in the womb of his dead parturient wife. Shortly thereafter he had the proper obstetrical dreams and became *also* an obstetrical shaman (Devereux 1948b). The same thing must have taken place when the first Mohave shaman had the necessary dreams that enabled him to heal bullet wounds.

In brief, all knowledge about Creation is acquired in dream, and the Creation myth is held to be a dream-revealed guide to reality. Moreover, the nature of shamanistic "intrauterine" experiences seems to imply that reality is a product of dream—a reality that necessarily includes the various illness categories represented by precedent-setting illnesses. Needless to say, the Mohave are not alone in feeling that reality, or portions of reality, are the products of dreaming. Some other groups explicitly state that the gods and even the ancestors create portions of reality by dreaming them. In Hindu theology a certain tenet clearly suggests that the world is a dream of Brahma. Even the Gospel according to Saint John, by expressing the conception that the world was created through or from the Word (Logos), indicates that man tends, in one way or another, to see reality as a projection of psychic forces and materials. This principle is applied by the Mohave to cultural reality as well. The dream alone puts the stamp of cultural validity on learning. Anyone can learn to sing a medicine song, but its singing is therapeutically ineffective and remains a purely extracultural, individual act unless it is backed and validated by the proper shamanistic learning dreams. Likewise, in theory, a newly introduced item or fact becomes a Mohave *cultural* item only if someone dreams that that item or fact was already present at the time of Creation. In short, the dream is both the funnel that admits and the sieve that rejects facts and events in regard to Mohave culture. It is the sole legitimate means by which new elements can be culturally "naturalized."

I add, in passing, a theoretical point of some importance. Anthropologists have carefully explored the value-meaning-affect matrix of cultures, as well as the trait-item content of cultures. It seems necessary to add to these two levels of culture a third one: the standard mechanism by which a new item—an invention, a borrowed trait or attitude, an individual's subjective experience, and so on—acquires the status of a cultural item and becomes, so to speak, culturally "naturalized." I suggest that in Mohave culture this role is assigned to the dream and that *the Mohave interpret their culture in terms of dreams rather than dreams in terms of their culture*—at least in theory.

To sum up these findings, with special reference to pathogenic dreams creating illness *categories* in Mohave culture: it seems fairly clear that nosological *entities* (as distinct from individual cases of illness) are "caused" by certain dreams and that these "pathogenic" dreams form that portion of the Creation myth that pertains to the coming-into-being of illnesses through precedent-setting primordial events, which play both a causal and a prophetic role with regard to individual cases of illness occurring in the future and "caused" by real dreams.

All this should surprise no one, since, as psychoanalytic findings show, all theories of genesis, creation, and the like are the intellectual consequences of the child's curiosity about birth in general and its own coming-into-being in particular. To cite only a simple case, Abraham (1927) has shown that a certain competent chemist's decision to specialize in the study of the state called "status nascendi" was ultimately rooted in his infantile interest in the origin of babies and, one suspects, interest in his own origin as well.

Now that it has been demonstrated that a stylized "pathogenic" dream (the Creation myth) accounts in Mohave culture for the existence of illness in general and of all clinical entities in particular, the next objective is to scrutinize the relationship between pathogenic dreams and the concrete illness of a given person at a given time. At this point, one is struggling not with a paucity of data but with a veritable embarrassment of riches. All of Mohave life and culture unfolds itself in an atmosphere of dreams. Kroeber (1925) called Mohave culture a dream culture, for dreams literally cluster around every salient event of life and every important cultural item. Just as nothing good can happen, and no capacity or power to be successful can be acquired, without an appropriate dream (Kroeber 1925; W. J. Wallace 1947; Devereux 1937a, 1957b [1978a, chap. 9]; 1961a; etc.), so no calamity, no illness, can occur without appropriate dreams (ibid.) Bad dreams are called either *sumatc itcem* (Wallace's spelling is *achemk*) or *sumatc alayk*. Wallace states that the first of these terms is applied specifically to dreams related to failures in undertakings and the second to dreams of illness and death. My own informants definitely did not follow this terminological distinction in practice, but this does not necessarily imply that Wallace is wrong or was misinformed. The difference between his informants' views and my informants' practice may reflect nothing more than the extreme elasticity of Mohave culture. Wallace also specifies that *sumatc alayk* dreams are omens of illness. As will be shown, this latter specification is somewhat narrow and quite debatable.

Every dream related in any way to illness is held to be pathognomonic and to possess diagnostic value. In brief, from the Mohave diagnostician's point of view, any dream related to illness can, functionally, be treated as a symptom. Indeed, in every illness the diagnostician promptly investigates the patient's dreams, so as to make the proper diagnosis and prognosis. Admittedly, no data exist concerning the diagnostic and prognostic use of dreams in the treatment of such obvious accidents as injuries resulting from horse kicks and the like. On the basis of the general pattern of Mohave healing sciences, however, I am inclined to suspect that even in such cases an inquiry may be made into dreams, though probably only for prognostic purposes and/or in order to ascertain whether or not the injury (a "straight" or natural illness, like a "straight" gastroenteritis) is complicated (made "not straight") by an admixture of witchcraft, viewed as a "secondary invader," which makes the illness "not straight" (Devereux 1961a). This, however, is admittedly a speculation and need concern me no further in the present context.

The fact that any recent or "relevant" dream—whatever its ultimate relationship to the illness may be—is used for diagnostic and prognostic purposes necessarily implies that both pathogenic dreams, in the strict sense of the term, and omen dreams are also viewed, apart from their causative or prophetic function, as symptoms of the illness and as (prognostically important) indicators of its gravity. Now, it is obvious that dreams can be exploited diagnostically and/or prognostically only if there is a body of theory concerning the meaning of various kinds of manifest dream content—that is, only if there exists an oneirocritic science.

Dream interpretation can be of three types: paralleling the manifest content (e.g., coitus with a woman means good luck); running counter to the manifest content (e.g., luck in a love intrigue is foretold among the Malays by dreams of being bitten by a snake); and symbolic. The last is so rare that, according to Hundt (1935), the only symbolically interpreted dream in Homer is that of Penelope, which, as I have shown elsewhere (1957a), happens to be the key to the latent content of much of the *Odyssey*.

Broadly speaking, much of Mohave dreaming in connection with illness—and also much general dreaming—is interpreted parallel to the dream content. Unpleasant dreams, experienced as such *regardless of their manifest content,* dreams whose manifest content is unpleasant, and dreams that contain some element that by definition pertains to illness (e.g., dreams about ghosts) would all be interpreted as bad dreams. Since illness-and-death is practically the prototype of "badness," unpleasant dreams are sometimes interpreted as heralding sickness even if they contain no specific element *traditionally* associated with a particular illness. Moreover, some dreams are held to foretell illness or trouble even when they contain nothing specifically unpleasant. Thus, on narrating a dream of mine to the Mohave, I received from one informant a favorable interpretation, but a second informant declared that the first informant must have been too tactful to tell me its real meaning and asserted that it foretold some bad luck or illness (Devereux 1961a).

In view of the well-known influence that culture and culturally and subjectively determined expectations have on dreamwork (Devereux 1951a), it is fairly certain that a person who more or less consciously suspects that he has a certain illness will sooner or later produce the type of dream that his culture habitually correlates with that type of illness. This process is further facilitated by the fact that many "classical" diagnostic dreams do, in fact, pertain to quite basic fears, repressed wishes, and anxieties. Among the Mohave, they are exemplified by dreams of incestuous coitus with the dead. In such instances the cultural tenet that illness X presupposes a certain type of dream is, for all practical purposes, a "self-fulfilling prophecy," in Merton's sense (1949).

Such pathognomonic dreams can also be scrutinized from the opposite point of view, that is, as the products of unconscious autoscopy, or self-diagnosis, in dream. The dynamics of such dreams were already clearly understood in classical Greece. Hippocrates (*On Dreams* 86 ff.) and Aristotle (*On Divination in Sleep* 462b21 ff.) held that they reveal a latent illness. Both taught that this is due to the fact that in dreams one's attention is focused entirely on oneself and is withdrawn from distracting external reality. This point of view fully dovetails with the findings of Ferenczi (1927a) and Bartemeier (1950). It implies in turn that, both in psychoanalytic theory and in Mohave belief, such dreams are neither pathogenic nor omen dreams: they are self-diagnostic dreams and the products of autoscopy in dream.

A related group of dreams can be viewed, without unduly stretching the meaning of Mohave dream theory and medicine, as manifestations of an internal struggle involving the drives, or such entities as health and illness, which have taken the organism as a whole as their battleground and which manifest themselves also in dream. Again one is dealing largely with pathognomonic and symptomatic dreams rather than strictly pathogenic or omen dreams. It is hardly necessary to add that whenever such autoscopic or symptomatic dreams precede the obvious onset of illness, a certain laxity in speech and thought habits permits them to be defined as pathogenic or omen dreams; yet even a brief supplementary inquiry usually reveals that no such meaning is implied by the Mohave themselves.

In the strictest sense of the term there are, then, only two types of pathogenic dreams in Mohave culture:

1. Dreams in the course of which the organism falls ill because the soul experiences certain harmful adventures in dream. These experiences may also include the invasion of the psyche by an alien power, such as the power of a witch, an enemy, or a ghost.
2. Dreams that are so upsetting that the patient reacts to them with illness.

Actually, the distinction between these two categories is far from sharp. A dream that seriously upsets the dreamer is almost always one that involves a pathogenically dangerous adventure of the soul. Thus, a Mohave woman became upset, anorexic, and severely depressed after dreaming that a dead relative cooked and served her a fish and that, after beginning to eat the fish, she realized that the head of the fish was the head of her dead mother. Since dreams about ghosts, and especially about the ghosts of relatives, are known to cause illness and are particularly dangerous if they involve being fed by, or engaging in coitus with, these ghosts, the dream in question—though said to have "caused" the woman's illness because it was upsetting—was actually a pathogenic dream of the type "illness bringing adventures of the soul." In fact, it proved very upsetting precisely because it was quite obviously a pathogenic dream of this type.

Strictly speaking, the only truly pathogenic Mohave dreams are those in which the soul undergoes some illness-causing adventure (a visit to the land of the dead, for example) and those in which the soul (and the dream) is invaded by the power of a malignant adversary, such as a witch.

286

A subspecies of this type of pathogenic dream is the dream that both causes and reveals the nature of the impending illness but fails to lead to the proper type of activity on awakening. In some instances of this type it is the dream itself that prevents the patient from taking the proper action on awakening. The fact that one is being bewitched is revealed to one in dreams. Sometimes the evil witch disguises his identity by borrowing the shadow-soul of another shaman; at other times he assumes an entirely different kind of disguise, one that cannot be recognized at all. By these means he simultaneously achieves his twofold aim of bewitching his victim and preventing him from knowing his magical assailant's name and revealing it on awakening, so as to save his life. In other instances the witch simply "closes the lips" of the prospective victim, making him (or her) actually desirous of succumbing to witchcraft and thus inducing him not to reveal the identity of the witch, though only this revelation could save him.

Such dreams are doubly pathogenic, albeit on two distinct levels. The dream itself is, and portrays, the invasion of the victim by the power of the witch. Simultaneously, the victim is prevented from saving himself on awakening, either by being unable to recognize his assailant, or by being unable to utter his name if he does recognize him, or by remaining silent because he is unwilling to be saved.

This, then, is the sum total of what exists in the way of *genuine* pathogenic dreams in Mohave society. Of course, grouped around this nucleus are such pathogenic dreams as those of people who become insane because they have dreamed of Mastamho in his final insane avatar. These, however, still represent only bona fide pathogenic adventures of the soul, though of a somewhat special kind.

As regards omen dreams, I have already indicated that, on closer scrutiny, the dream is linked to the illness, even in Mohave thought, by altogether nonprophetic mechanisms. I suspect that the same will prove true of many other omen dreams pertaining to illness if one takes the trouble to reinvestigate illness-omen dreams in the field with some measure of psychological sophistication. I even venture to suggest that, if only one knew enough about dream theory in the ancient Near East, the many illness-omen dreams listed by Oppenheim (1956) would be recognized, at least initially, as either pathogenic or symptomatic-autoscopic dreams. For there can be no doubt that, as oneirocritic science snowballed, *omina* of illness were ground out by oneirocritic craftsmen as fugues once emerged by the yard from the contrapuntal sausage machines of the baroque masters, including Bach himself.

CHAPTER FOURTEEN

Conclusions

In the study of primitive medicine one often meets with reports that a dream is believed to be connected in some way with an illness. The dream and the illness between which informants postulate a nexus may occur either in sequence or simultaneously. Unless the scholar is able to demonstrate that native dream theory itself specifies the *nature* of the nexus between dream and illness and further specifies that this nexus is a *causal* one, he is not entitled to speak of genuinely pathogenic dreams. He can speak only of omen dreams, generalized fate-foretelling dreams, symptomatic, pathognomonic, or autoscopic dreams. Only where the *nature* of the nexus is specified and also explicitly stated to be *causal* is it legitimate to speak of pathogenic dreams. Owing to defective data, many nonpathogenic dreams have been misidentified as pathogenic. Conversely, owing to lack of adequate information about native dream theory, some definitely pathogenic dreams have been mistaken for omen dreams and the like. A more thorough exploration not only of native dreaming and dreams but of native dream *theory* and its influence on both dreaming and waking thought is one of the most urgent tasks of psychologically oriented anthropology.

15

Cultural Factors in Psychoanalytic Therapy

(1953)

A technical discussion of the influence of cultural factors upon the course and technique of psychoanalytic therapy should, in principle, begin with a preliminary analysis of the nature of culture and of its vicissitudes in psychological health and illness and in psychoanalytic therapy. But since some of this material has already been touched upon in chapter 2, I shall present here my conclusions only, in a more or less axiomatic form.

CULTURE AS A CHARACTERISTIC HUMAN TRAIT
Definition of Terms

In the following discussion I differentiate between *Homo sapiens,* or genus *Homo,* as a biological organism and *man* as a human being.

1. *Homo sapiens* is the current end product of an evolutionary process toward a very high degree of differentiation and individualization. The principal and uniquely characteristic trait of *Homo sapiens*—the "constant of human nature"—is the extreme plasticity and variability of his behavior.

2. These four characteristics of genus *Homo*—differentiation, individualization, plasticity, and variability of behavior—represent a unitary and consistent biological potentiality that is actualized in the acquisition of a distinctively human psyche and culture.

3. The possession of a human psyche and culture is uniquely characteristic of man and further stimulates and expands *Homo sapiens'* biologically determined tendency toward differentiation, individualization, plasticity, and variability of behavior.

4. Although the human psyche and culture are the resultants of a biological potentiality, whose actualization they represent, neither the human psyche nor culture may be thought of as *biological* characteristics of genus *Homo.* They must be thought of as distinctively *human* characteristics of *man.*

5. The human psyche and culture are, both methodologically and functionally, inseparable complementary concepts.

6. Since culture represents an actualization of a basic biological potentiality of genus *Homo*, whenever man functions as a "creator, creature, manipulator, and carrier" (Simmons 1942) of culture, he satisfies one of his most fundamental needs, which cannot be frustrated without dire consequences for the human psyche and for man's status as a human being. This is cogently demonstrated by Davis's study (1940) of a young girl who had been almost completely deprived of cultural experiences.[1]

7. The "culturalization" of man is contingent upon, and is a resultant of, the replacing of the rigid, direct, and massive *manifestations* of biological impulses—and especially of aggressive rather than genital impulses—by plastic, economical, and accurately context- and goal-adapted behavior. Such behavior has a high survival value and is in conformity with *Homo sapiens*' biological potentialities for differentiation and individualization. In other words, *Homo sapiens*, in actualizing and implementing his biological potentialities (his capacities for differentiated, individualized, plastic, and variable behavior), acquires the status of *man* and functions as a human being.

8. It is an illusion that culture constricts behavior. If culture constricted behavior, then culture would not actualize but would destroy *Homo sapiens*' biological potentialities for differentiation, individualization, plasticity, and variability of behavior, so that the being possessed of culture would be more *Homo sapiens* than *man*, which is obviously a fallacy. In reality, culture expands the scope, range, variability, efficiency, and appropriateness of behavior (chap. 2) by substituting for massive and impulse-determined motility and affect-governed discharge a partial, specific, and narrowly goal- and context-determined motility and affect discharge. Several misconceptions are responsible for the illusion that culture constricts behavior. The first of these is the inappropriate use of a far too narrow biological frame of reference: one that fits genus *Homo* but not mankind and ignores the biologically determined trend toward differentiation and individualization in the evolution of *Homo sapiens*. The second misconception is derived from observation of the effects of "sick" cultures, which force their members into patterns of pathological, or at least passive and nonspontaneous, adaptation. The source of the third misconception is clinical experience itself, for the patients one treats are in analysis precisely because they themselves constrict and distort their aggressive impulses instead of sublimating, individualizing, and adapting them to reality.

9. A healthy society encourages, for its own sake, the fullest actualization of *Homo sapiens*' potentialities for individualization and differentiation. As Mill (*On Liberty,* 1859) and MacIver (1936)

pointed out long ago, maximum individualization and maximum socialization go hand in hand; indeed, just as man cannot unfold all of his inherent potentialities without the help of society, society cannot derive the utmost benefit from any of its members unless each one is permitted and helped to unfold all of his potentialities to the fullest possible extent. In fact, the more man is differentiated, the more he needs society's support for his self-actualization. I stress that a successful sublimation disguises and distorts the underlying antisocial impulse far less than a suppression or a repression does. For example, if the underlying impulse happens to be a body-destruction fantasy, it will be sublimated more productively, more creatively, and more individualistically by the surgeon than by the butcher or the rabid antivivisectionist (Devereux 1961c [1975, chap. 1]).

10. By contrast, a "sick society" cannot tolerate individualization and individualized sublimations and therefore favors dedifferentiation, loss of individuality, suppression, repression, reaction formation, and other regressive manifestations of this type.

11. The illusion that culture is necessarily constrictive and anti-instinctual is contradicted by the clinical fact that the analysis of the infantile and unconscious sources of a sublimation not only fails to destroy that sublimation but, on the contrary, actually strengthens it. This point was made with exceptional clarity by Jokl (1950).

12. The cultural frame of reference enables the observer to "structure"—that is, to understand, control, and predict—the behavior of normal persons. The psychoanalytic frame of reference enables the observer to "structure," in this sense, the behavior of abnormal persons.[2]

13. Personality disorders of various kinds, including those that arise in the course of the transference neuroses, represent a partial dedifferentiation and deindividualization—in other words, a partial regression of *man* to *Homo sapiens*. For this reason, children (and abnormal persons) belonging to our society resemble their counterparts in other cultures far more than the normal members of our society resemble the normal members of other ethnic groups, simply because normals are more highly differentiated and more fully individualized than the child (= *Homo sapiens*) and the abnormal person. These observed differences can best be understood in terms of the concept *man*, while the observed similarities can best be understood in terms of the concept *Homo sapiens*.

14. All of these considerations, taken together, again explain why the behavior of abnormal persons seems incomprehensible when one insists on analyzing it in exclusively sociocultural terms. If, however,

one views this abnormal behavior *also* in biological terms—that is, at least partly in terms of the concept *Homo sapiens*—it becomes understandable, predictable, and controllable—*more* understandable, predictable, and controllable, in fact, than the far more complex, overdetermined, differentiated, and individualized behavior of normal man (Devereux 1951g, 1952).

15. These considerations explain why the manner in which abnormal persons manipulate and experience cultural material has great diagnostic value (chap. 2). They also suggest that in really deep psychoanalytic therapy it is less essential for the analyst to be fully informed about the patient's specific cultural background ahead of time than in more superficial forms of psychotherapy (Devereux 1951a). This point will be elaborated in detail further on.

16. The psychoanalyst must, however, possess a very sound understanding of the nature and function of "culture per se"—as distinct from familiarity with any particular culture—because culture is a universal phenomenon and a trait uniquely characteristic of man and because the broad *categories* of culture—as distinct from their concrete *content* in any particular culture—are also universal phenomena.[3] A simple illustrative example may help to clarify this seemingly complex statement. I once sought to diagnose an Indian of whose culture I knew next to nothing. This Indian reported that he had left his mother at the foot of a hill; he had then *ridden* to the top of the hill and there had met his father *and his mother*. Although this sounded like a clear-cut case of delusion or hallucination, my awareness of the cultural category "classificatory kinship systems" caused me to inquire whether the mother the patient had left at the bottom of the hill was the *same* mother he had met at the top. The patient immediately explained that the "mother" he had met on top of the hill was actually his mother's sister, whom, in accordance with the kinship system of his tribe, he also called "mother." In brief, in this particular instance it was not my (nonexistent) familiarity with the patient's tribal culture that enabled me to differentiate between a cultural practice and a delusion. What enabled me to do so was my familiarity with the categories of culture per se—of culture as a universal human phenomenon.

17. Whenever the psychotherapist utilizes his concrete familiarity with the patient's tribal culture, he engages in the practice of intercultural psychotherapy. Whenever he utilizes his knowledge of the nature of culture per se, and of universal cultural categories, he engages in the practice of metacultural psychotherapy (Devereux 1951g).[4]

THE RELATIONSHIP BETWEEN PSYCHOANALYSIS AND ETHNOLOGY

Both psychoanalysis and ethnology study what is distinctively human in man, that is, what differentiates man, seen as a person-in-culture, from *Homo sapiens,* viewed in a biological frame of reference. Psychoanalysis is particularly concerned with what is distinctively human in the human psyche, while ethnology is primarily interested in what is uniquely and characteristically human in culture and society. In this sense both psychoanalysis and ethnology are branches of "Anthropology" as defined by Kant, that is, the science of that which is distinctively human in man. However, as I have pointed out elsewhere (Devereux 1945 [1978a, chap. 4]), psychoanalysis and ethnology yield complementary, not additive, insights.[5] On the theoretical level there is actually a Heisenberg-Bohr type of indeterminacy relationship (Devereux 1945 [1978a, chap. 4], 1961b [1978a, chap. 5], 1967c) between the psychoanalytic and the ethnological understanding of human behavior. In practice, convenience and economy of effort alone determine when and at what point it is desirable to discontinue further inquiry in psychoanalytic terms and to start analyzing the phenomenon under consideration in ethnological terms—and of course, vice versa. Though this is a purely heuristic solution of the problem, it is sufficiently accurate for present purposes.

I stress in this context that both psychoanalysis and ethnology study what is distinctively and uniquely human in man and that both sciences are concerned with individuality and differentiation but use different modalities of exploring these phenomena.

This does not mean that psychoanalysis and ethnology systematically neglect similarities and uniformities. In fact, when psychoanalysts and ethnologists formulate general laws about the human psyche and about culture and cultural behavior, these laws usually pertain to various consistent processes of differentiation and individualization rather than to their end products, which are extremely diversified. They are, in fact, so diversified that an attempt to strip them of their quality of variability frequently also deprives them of their very essence, meaning, and reality. Thus, psychoanalytic and ethnological laws pertain to processes of differentiation and individualization but leave relatively unexplained the phenomenological diversity of the *end products* of these processes. This is not a defect of psychoanalytic and ethnological theorizing. It is, on the contrary, the natural consequence of a theoretical approach eminently suited to the nature of the phenomena these sciences study. In another context (1951a) I have examined in detail the differential significance of concrete cultures in the etiology, symptomatology, and therapy of neuroses and psychoses, while in chapter 2 I have analyzed the vicissitudes of cultural material in various forms of mental illness. Here I only state once again that every observation relative to "psychological health," "maturity," and "immaturity" is in the present frame of reference only an indirect allusion to degrees of differentiation and individualization—that is, to degrees of sublimation. The more serious the patient's "illness," and the deeper his "regression" (which may be permanent or only temporary, that is, limited to a certain stage of his psychoanalysis), the more restricted will be the cultural role of cultural items in his behavior and the more frequent will be the process of "deculturation."[6]

Having highlighted, in these remarks, the decisive role of cultural factors in psychoanalytic therapy, I now turn to an examination of some modalities of their manifestations in the therapeutic context.

CULTURAL FACTORS IN PSYCHOANALYTIC THERAPY

I wish to call especial attention to the fact that in this section I shall draw on data from the psychoanalysis of patients belonging to non-Occidental cultures, chiefly because one tends to be more objective about this kind of information, which is seen, as it were, *in vitro*. Actually, all the problems encountered in the course of these analyses arise also, for example, in didactic psychoanalysis, that is, in situations where both patient and analyst have the same social and cultural background, are of the same age group, and are perhaps even of the same sex (Nathan 1977). In fact, all the problems to be mentioned occur in even more pressing and critical form in an analytic relationship in which there is no cultural distance than in the psychoanalysis of a patient belonging to a foreign culture. The reason why this is so—and *must* be so—is easy to understand. When the patient is, for instance, an Indian, the "exotic" character of his culture frees the analyst from those of his own scotomata that have a cultural origin, and this favors—at least to some extent—his "cultural neutrality," which is something altogether different from "cultural relativism." Functionally, the real equivalent of cultural neutrality is "emotional neutrality" (the absence of countertransference taken in its usual sense), which the analyst is supposed to have acquired in the course of his own didactic analysis.

"Emotional neutrality" must not be confused, however, with "cultural neutrality," for the one does not necessarily imply the other. A good ethnologist may well achieve a certain degree of cultural neutrality without acquiring the slightest trace of emotional neutrality.

Similarly, a didactic analysis may enable the psychoanalyst to achieve emotional neutrality, but this does not necessarily make him neutral on the cultural level as well.

In other words, the analyst can achieve a complete neutrality only if he resolves not only his emotional but his cultural conflicts. For example, with regard to the oedipal conflict, he must analyze both his subjective oedipal conflict and the form taken by the oedipal conflict in the culture to which he belongs; that is, he must be aware of the means his culture uses to inhibit oedipal manifestations in some ways while encouraging them in others, and he must know the *manner* in which the oedipal conflict is integrated with the totality of his culture. No one can consider himself analyzed until he has undergone this twofold analysis.

Any individual engaged in analyzing others will find that his analytic work is considerably hampered by his culturally determined scotomata and countertransference reactions. This is particularly true if he works with patients of the same sociocultural background as his own. Instead of elaborating the matter here, I refer the reader to chapters 9 and 10, where I examine in detail the problems of the diagnosis and therapy of schizophrenic patients in a society that *systematically* encourages an absurdly schizoid life-style.

Although the remarks to follow are based on a fairly broad clinical experience with non-Occidental or only marginally Occidental patients, the majority of my examples will be drawn from my analysis of a Plains Indian woman whose case admirably illustrates the influences a patient's culture exerts on both psychological disorder and its therapy.

The most important cultural influence exerted by cultural factors on psychoanalytic therapy is, in a sense, the analyst's own interest in the cultural materials furnished by the patient. This interest is a special aspect of the problem of countertransference as a whole; that is, it is not basically different from the countertransference problems that are bound to arise in any research-oriented psychotherapeutic situation. The analytic patient is usually quite sensitive to the analyst's cultural interests and is able to exploit them in the elaboration of his own resistances. Depending on the course of the analysis, he will either gratify these interests indirectly, by endlessly discussing the practices of his tribe, supposedly to gratify the analyst's curiosity, or else he will use his analyst's cultural interests in a way that permits him to manifest more overt kinds of resistance, which I shall discuss later.

The patient sometimes even turns the tables on the analyst and, always as a resistance, develops a special interest in his analyst's native culture or degree of Americanization. Two of my native-born but culturally marginal white American analytic patients were rather curious about my cultural background and—since both of them were rather proud of their verbal skills—confessed that they used stilted modes of expression in order to "teach" me new English words and better English.[7] They also speculated on whether I *truly* understood the American cultural meaning of some of their actions, and they sometimes resisted certain correct but ego-dystonic interpretations of their inhibitions by making disparaging remarks about the manners and morals of foreigners (= the analyst).

Occasionally, of course, my interest as an ethnologist in a patient's description of some hitherto unrecorded custom may momentarily have kept me from focusing my full attention on the unconscious and characterological material revealed by such productions. Still, it is occasionally legitimate to deliberately stimulate the production of cultural material. I am thinking, for example, of the case of a highly acculturated (Americanized) Indian woman patient with whom I used this technique in order to encourage a temporary regression likely to facilitate the recall of infantile experiences that had taken place in an aboriginal cultural setting. Usually this technique works fairly well, though sometimes it leads only to dry, factual recitations, which have to be viewed as resistances.

I must admit that on certain—fortunately, very rare—occasions my attempts to view a given event in the patient's life from the native point of view were ingenious rather than cogent. This happened mostly when I was "taken in" by a special kind of resistance that is, in fact, simply the patient's negative response to his analyst's cultural interests. Indeed, the native patient soon becomes aware of his analyst's cultural interests and evolves an "overcompliant resistance," which consists in the copious production of cultural material, more or less irrelevant from an analytic point of view. Such data are just so many "red herrings," intended to divert him from his analytic duties by arousing his interests in cultural material. This is not an unusual occurrence; my study of articles reporting alleged feats of telepathy shows that spectacular "acting-out," "telepathic" feats, and other unusual performances in the course of an analysis, also seek to divert the analyst's attention from the latent to the manifest content of the patient's productions (Devereux 1953a).

One distinctive type of resistance evolved in response to the analyst's extra-analytic cultural interests is the patient's resentment over what he (mistakenly) construes to be interest in him as an Indian informant rather than as a patient and a person. A querulous Indian woman patient mentioned with great anger that, during her military service, an illustrated magazine wanted to publish her photograph in order to show that Indian women as well as men served in the American armed forces. She vigorously emphasized that she wanted neither favorable nor unfavorable notice for her ethnic personality; she wished to be viewed simply as a person. This demand —apparently reasonable—pertained in part to the transference relationship and was primarily motivated by her need to deny her Indian origins and, through them, her (castrated) femininity and her sexuality as well. Another Indian patient, in psychotherapy, reported the following dream: "I resented the persons I had just met, for, even before asking my name, they asked me whether I was an Indian" (Devereux 1951a). The analyst must therefore at all costs avoid giving free rein to his cultural interests—or to any other non-analytic interest—during the analytic hour.

Yet, until a truly satisfactory technique of metacultural psychotherapy is evolved, both the psychotherapist and the analyst must be interested in the specific cultural background of the patient and must seek to understand the patient's productions in terms of the patient's culture, not their own (Devereux 1951a). In psychoanalysis, as distinct from psychotherapy, the analyst can sometimes—simply by remaining silent long enough—obtain the data needed to situate the patient in the correct cultural perspective. This procedure is, unfortunately, far from ideal, not only because it is wasteful of the patient's time and money, but especially because it does not conform to the principles governing the proper timing of confrontations and interpretations (Devereux 1951b).

For the time being, the only way out of this difficulty is for the analyst to learn about the patient's culture beforehand. Then, when he comes up against data with which he is already familiar, the raw ethnographic facts produced by the patient will fascinate him less and will therefore fail to divert him from his strictly analytic tasks. Hence, I have never undertaken a psychotherapy or a psychoanalysis with a patient belonging to a culture other than my own without first reading up on the patient's culture. Unfortunately, probably no culture has ever been fully described by ethnographers. Hence, even though I had prepared myself for the analysis of my Plains Indian woman patient by reading everything that had been published about her tribe, I was on one occasion so startled by her reference to a hitherto unrecorded tribal custom that for a few minutes I was more interested in further exploring this cultural material than in asking myself what unconscious impulses motivated her narrative and lay concealed beneath it.

These observations show that the analyst's own culturally oriented interests sometimes play into the hands of the patient—a fact that the patient promptly exploits to the hilt. The remedy for this is careful preparation for the analysis of "primitives" and, above all, a constant awareness that one's real task is to analyze the patient, not to collect ethnographic data. Needless to say, the temptation involved is not restricted to the analysis of persons belonging to other cultures. The analyst who is an apprentice stamp collector and happens to analyze an expert stamp dealer may allow himself to be so "seduced" by his patient's lecture on the Antigua penny puce that he fails to ask himself what this monologue seeks to accomplish or what it conceals. Soon after these lines were written, several colleagues reminded me that Freud himself had to transfer to another analyst a patient who was an Egyptologist, because Freud's own interest in Egyptology threatened to interfere with the analysis.

Traditional practices and attitudes can also be used as resistances. An Indian woman analysand often chose to play the role of the stolid Indian when she did not wish to face some ego-dystonic insight. When confronted with the spuriousness of her stolidity, she laughingly admitted that she had deliberately used this typically Indian defense—the "ugh resistance," as we came to call it—against "the nosy paleface." The same patient also exploited to the limit her legitimate grievance over the fact that she had been discriminated against because of her race. Since she knew that, in this connection, the analyst's sympathies were entirely on her side, she blamed all her misfortunes on discrimination. I finally had to break down this resistance by showing her a cartoon clipped from *Time* magazine, in which an analyst tells his Indian patient: "I think we are getting somewhere, Mr. Great Cloud Shadow. Your neurosis apparently stems from a submerged resentment against your ancestors for disposing of Manhattan Island for only twenty-four dollars." This "interpretation" proved so effective that, ever after, even the most cursory reference to "Mr. Great Cloud Shadow" or to "Manhattan Island" sufficed to stop her previously interminable "Lo! the poor Indian!" monologues. In fact, whenever the patient subsequently spoke of being discriminated against, this simply indicated that she was resorting to a last-ditch defense, using an already interpreted and obviously ineffective resistance, before giving in and accepting some new and ego-dystonic insight.

The next point I wish to take up concerns the latent meaning of the patient's manifest behavior and verbal productions. My Indian woman analysand had just had her fourth psychotic episode—her first since the analysis began. Passive and mute, she stubbornly hid under her blanket, although her general attitude was obviously

friendly—even seductive. When I realized that the time-tested analytic interpretations "You are playing dead," "You have something
to hide," "You are playing the baby," produced no results, I remembered that I was not only a psychoanalyst but also an ethnologist
and said, "You are playing the role of the Indian maiden who si-
lently hides under her buffalo robe while her suitor is courting her."
The next instant the patient literally popped out from under her
blanket and behaved in an almost completely normal and rational
manner for several days in a row. This incident stands in need of
detailed analysis.

The "culturalist" will view it as an almost perfect demonstration
of the culture-bound nature of symptoms and symbols. From his
point of view, had this patient belonged to our own society, her behavior would have meant that she was playing dead or that she was
in a state of infantile regression; but in terms of her own culture, as
a Plains Indian woman, it meant that she was the courted maiden.
Unfortunately, this interpretation of the facts is so exceedingly right
in one sense that it is absolutely wrong in another sense. Actually,
the situation is far more complex.

The fact that the patient did not react to the remark "You are
playing dead" but did react to the interpretation "You are playing
the Indian bride" simply shows that I had made a technical mistake.
I had ignored the basic rule that one should interpret whatever fits
the patient's current preoccupations—those that are uppermost in
the patient's mind and just on the threshold of the Conscious. The
interpretation "You are playing dead" was ineffective because it was
an untimely *interpretation,* whereas the remark "You are playing
the bride" was effective because it was a completely timely *confrontation*[8] and close enough to the Conscious to be really accepted.

Indeed, the patient, hospitalized as a borderline psychotic, had
her fourth psychotic break precisely because she was unable to tolerate and to manage her "incestuous" positive transference. Hence
she was thrown into a panic by the accusations of an envious fellow
patient, who, having noticed our daily analytic sessions, claimed
that I saw my patient so often only because she let me have intercourse with her—an accusation that fitted only too well the transference wishes of my patient. When I stubbornly kept on interpreting her behavior and failed to act like a proper *Indian* suitor by
courting her, the patient openly asked me at about that time to court
her in the *European* manner, that is, by kissing her hand. When this
request, too, was merely interpreted, the patient took up the "bride
motif" in a third way—this time specifically in terms of *American*
culture. One day this patient, who had a slight motor disability,

stumbled so often while walking at my side down the hospital corridor, shod in clumsy hospital slippers ("scuffies"), that she "had"
to lean on my arm. After letting her do so for a few steps, I noticed
that she walked with half-closed eyes and that her face bore the *conventional* ecstatic expression of the new bride walking down the
aisle of the church on her husband's arm. When I quietly remarked,
"All we need now is Mendelssohn!" the patient immediately let go
of my arm and, without a trace of resentment, began to march down
the corridor with the step of a Grenadier Guard.

These data indicate that the remark "You are playing the role of
a courted girl" was effective because it was timely and pertained to
the positive transference that at that stage of the analysis was so
close to the threshold of the patient's Conscious that a very simple
confrontation, couched—like the majority of confrontations—in
cultural terms, sufficed to make her understand it.

My next task is to show that the "deep" interpretations, "You are
playing dead," "You are playing the role of a baby, "You have something to hide," were not erroneous but simply inopportune because
poorly timed, that is, premature. Everything that is known of the
stylized and traditional passivity of Plains Indian women in courtship and in sex, of their strikingly masochistic and infantile approach
to genital behavior, and of their attempts to pretend that they are
chaste even when they are not gives a clinical psychoanalytic *meaning* to their (culturally determined) *practice* of passively submitting
to courtship while hiding under a buffalo robe. It seems unnecessary to document here in detail this kind of information, which is
supported by copious ethnographical data (Devereux 1951a).

My patient's attitude toward sexuality was manifestly that of the
Plains Indian woman. She assured me that she had been a virginal
bride and told me a long and entirely untrue story about the details
of her defloration on her wedding night. She (falsely) claimed that
she had been a faithful wife. She had so often exposed herself to
rape that it is hard to understand how she managed to escape with
only one. She placed all responsibility for her sexual acts on the men
who had allegedly "seduced" her. She connected the notion of sexuality with that of castration and fantasied that all prostitutes are
greatly oversexed women, whose internal genital organs, the ova-
ries and the womb, have been excised. She reported that as a child
she had injured her vulva (that is, had "castrated" herself) when,
while raiding the cookie jar, located on a high shelf, she had slipped
and fallen astride the open door of the lower kitchen cabinet. In
adult life she menstruated, or rather, hemorrhaged, for months at

a time, and, in her fantasies, she connected the idea of death with sexual activity.

This being the case, the confrontation, "You are playing the role of the bride," was simply the *timely* formulation of such deeper, but untimely, interpretations as "You are playing dead," etc. The latter interpretations were also true—"truer," perhaps, than the confrontation that had proved effective—but they were premature. This woman's unconscious did not differ from other people's and her fantasies had nothing unique about them. Like any other patient, she used symbols and symbolic acts to express her conflicts and wishes, and the symbols she used were of a *type* that a similarly motivated patient belonging to our own culture would have used. The only distinctive thing about her symbolic acts was the culturally determined *manner* in which she played the role of the passive (and symbolically dead) bride. Being a Plains Indian, she hid under a blanket, where a white American woman patient might perhaps have played the romantic role of a young bride in her coffin.

It is therefore incumbent upon the analyst not to ignore the supplementary cultural meaning of the patient's symbolic acts. Needless to say, the symbolic actions of members of our own society also have cultural connotations that constitute additions to their properly symbolic connotations, but these are so familiar that one sometimes tends to overlook them and to behave as though they did not exist or were parts of the basic symbol. As regards psychoanalytic technique, the point to be stressed here is that these supplementary cultural meanings lend themselves better to confrontations than to interpretations, and it is in general desirable to make these confrontations before one proceeds to interpret the unconscious fantasy material that these symbols seek to express.

Another difficulty in the analysis of culturally "distant" patients is due to the neurotic's tendency to distort the underlying culturally and psychologically standardized meaning of his cultural experiences, with which the analyst, for his part, is unfamiliar. An example will illustrate this point. One night in July my Indian woman patient dreamed that she was sitting on her bed, noticed that it was snowing outside, and felt surprised that it should snow in summer. Her associations referred to a variety of oral topics, including milk, breasts, the fact that she was given coffee as early as the sixth month of her life, and her loathing for milk and her liking for a certain blood-red soft drink, whose "bland taste" she praised extravagantly. The unconscious content of these associations was her resentment over the fact that, by the standards of her tribe, she had been weaned rather early and had therefore developed a spiteful and almost consciously compensatory need to reject milk and to deny her obvious dependency cravings. She then proceeded by a series of further associations to describe the principal rite of her tribe, in the course of which the *bare-breasted* wife of the ritual leader has intercourse with a number of men. Since I knew that the patient was—verbally at least—quite prudish, I expected her to denounce the *sexual* "immorality" of this rite. I was therefore greatly surprised to learn that what the patient actually objected to in this rite was the fact that the ritual leader's wife wore the aboriginal costume, *which left her breasts bare.* Although the patient's account of this previously unrecorded detail of the rite so fascinated me that I was tempted to explore the matter further from the ethnological point of view, the startling nature of this ordinarily (verbally) prudish patient's objections to the rite served to remind me in time of my analytic obligations. I concluded from her diatribe that, impelled by her strong neurotic oral demands, she had assigned an oral meaning to a ritual whose true cultural meaning was a phallic and genital one. In other words, whereas the real center of the ceremony was a series of ritual sexual acts, for this neurotic and orally demanding patient the rite centered on the fact that the ritual leader's wife was bare-breasted. What she begrudged these men was not the sexual pleasure women gave them but the fact that, being men, they could, under the guise of *sexual activity*, gain access to a woman's breasts, which she, being a woman, could not do. Remembering her dream of falling snow, I was able to interpret the important associative material she had given me at that time—only some of which could be mentioned here—as reflections of the patient's desire to obtain (seminal) milk from her analyst while denying him oral access to her own breasts, which she carefully and even aggressively kept covered[9] in order to underscore her superiority to "wild Injuns," as she called them.

Special difficulties arise in connection with the interpretation of material produced by more or less fully acculturated—that is "Americanized"—"Indians." This material sometimes threatens to enmesh the excessively "culturalistic" analyst in a logically fallacious and therapeutically deleterious network of "culturalistic" pseudo-insights. Thus, when a well-acculturated Indian patient reports that in a certain stressful situation he behaved in the "aboriginal" manner, the extreme culturalist may become so preoccupied with sociological problems of cultural duality, culture conflict, etc., that he will fail to give due consideration to the clearly regressive implications of the patient's behavior under stress. When my Indian analysand, who had a college diploma in medical biology, contracted a minor chronic ailment that American physicians seemed unable to cure, she finally went to a native therapeutic peyote meeting, in the hope that this could cure her. From the analytic and therapeutic point of view her behavior has to be interpreted primarily as a regressive act rather than simply as a bit of cultural traditionalism. In other words, this action of a highly acculturated Indian medical biology major has to be interpreted exactly as one would interpret the behavior of an American physician born of immigrant peasant parents who, deeply disturbed by the discovery that he had in inoperable cancer, suddenly decided to consult the urban equivalent of the village witch his parents would have consulted in the "old country." Indeed, in normal circumstances this Indian patient sneered at those of her people who were naive enough to seek peyote cures. What is analytically relevant in this incident is thus not the fact that the patient had been *raised* by parents who believed in peyote cures—for this makes her behavior only culturally, not psychoanalytically, understandable[10]—but the fact that she had *regressed* sufficiently to resort to a subjectively anachronistic anxiety-allaying device that she ordinarily ridiculed as a "wild Injun superstition."

Nothing said in the preceding paragraph constitutes a denial of the empirically tested and theoretically defensible thesis that basic cultural attitudes and the tribal ethos continue to play a major role in the acculturated Indian's personality makeup long after he has forgotten the ancient traditions and practices of his tribe (Devereux 1951a). Every human being has many magical attitudes, partly repressed and partly sublimated (Devereux 1954c, 1956c), and one cannot expect the acculturated Indian to be an exception to this rule. What was regressive in the behavior of this Indian patient was not the fact that she had certain unconscious magical attitudes but the sudden return of these repressed attitudes, which she then *acted out,* in accord with cultural tradition, by seeking a peyote cure.

The last technical problem I propose to discuss is, superficially at least, a fairly complex one, although in practice it can be handled strictly in accordance with the classical rule that one should interpret whatever is nearest to the threshold of the Conscious. In the analysis of culturally "distant" patients, adherence to this rule sometimes requires the analyst to interpret at a fairly early stage certain matters that are usually not interpreted to Occidental patients until they have been in analysis for several months. When such situations arise, the psychoanalyst may be tempted to deviate from the classical rule and to justify this deviation by assuming that the early (pseudo-premature) production of seemingly very "deep" and "traumatic" material may possibly be indicative of a latent psychosis (Devereux 1960b). While such a possibility should never be ruled out a priori, one must bear in mind that a wish or conflict that in one culture must be very deeply repressed may, in another, be only slightly repressed. For example, a tendency to indulge in magical thinking or in fantasies of primary or delegated omnipotence may be interpreted fairly early to an Indian, whose culture does not cathect cold rationality and objectivity to the extent that ours claims —but only claims—to do (chap. 10). On the other hand, a Plains Indian male's cowardice, homosexual dependency cravings, and the like should be interpreted to him fairly cautiously and, whenever possible, only after a fairly stable transference has been established. In a similar sense, castration anxiety may be interpreted fairly early to an Indian cowboy accustomed to castrating livestock, while his incestuous impulses will have to be handled rather carefully, since in many primitive tribes the incest taboo is very severe and applies not only to one's biological family but also to most members of one's extended kin (Devereux 1951a). An important corollary of these considerations is that, contrary to traditional rule-of-thumb practice, dreams may be interpreted even in the first analytic hour to a patient in whose culture dreaming—and the interpretation of dreams —plays an important role. One reason why it is fairly safe to do so is that, at least at the beginning of the analysis, most of the dreams reported to the analyst by patients whose tribes assign an important place to dream life are likely to be precisely those stylized dreams whose manifest content will already have been more or less consciously "corrected" or elaborated to make them fit more nearly the tribal model of the exemplary or "important" dream.

Psychoanalysis and ethnology are, of all the sciences, the ones that deal most systematically with man's distinctively and uniquely human characteristics. Though the human psyche and culture are functionally inseparable, the insights provided by psychoanalysis and those provided by ethnology are not additive but complementary (Devereux 1945 [1978a, chap. 4], 1961b [1978a, chap. 5]). Culture is experienced in different ways by normals and by various types of psychiatric patients. The characteristic transformations and vicissitudes of cultural material in normals, immature persons, neurotics, psychotics, and psychopaths can, moreover, be described operationally (chap. 2).

On the basis of these findings, I have outlined certain technical rules for the analysis of culturally "distant" patients and have illustrated, by means of clinical examples, some of the problems arising in the course of such analyses.

16

Psychoanalysis as Anthropological Field Work: Data and Theoretical Implications (1957)

In this study I propose to examine the usefulness of psychoanalysis as a specialized anthropological field technique. It seems unnecessary in this context to describe the technique of research psychoanalysis since, at least in principle, there exists only one generalized system of classical psychoanalytic technique, directly deducible from the basic conceptual scheme of the science of psychoanalytic psychology. My study is limited to an examination of the type, quality, and anthropological import of data obtained by psychoanalyzing persons who belong to non-Occidental cultures, followed by a presentation of the theoretical consequences of these data.

As with every other specialized anthropological field technique, psychoanalysis has areas of maximum and minimum productiveness. Thus, psychoanalysis cannot provide the necessary data for a well-rounded ethnography of a given tribe. Therefore, even though an analysand who belongs to some thoroughly studied Indian tribe occasionally mentions a previously unreported culture trait, this fact deserves only passing mention in the present discussion.

By contrast, research psychoanalysis is an extremely efficient means of eliciting information concerning the matrix of values and meanings to which a given item is assigned. Such data are of great interest to the anthropologist, since no action, attitude, or material object is a cultural item unless it is embedded in a matrix of values and meanings. Thus, Lowie (1935) has shown that neither the occurrence nor the nonoccurrence of coitus between the ape and his daughter can shed light on the anthropological problem of incest, since the fact that a certain female is his daughter means nothing to the ape. Hence, it cannot motivate the ape to refrain from incest, nor can it induce him to copulate with his daughter either for cultural or for neurotic reasons (Devereux 1965c [1978a, chap. 7]).[1]

In brief, coitus between biologically related individuals can be

305

incest and its nonoccurrence can represent an *avoidance of incest* only in a human—that is, cultural—setting. The same thing is true of all other inherently possible actions, attitudes, or ideas; they do not become cultural items unless they are embedded in a matrix of values, meanings, and other such factors. It is this that establishes between the trait and the rest of the culture a horizontal-functional and vertical-hierarchical "compendence" (here meaning "hanging together"). Moreover, these "compendences" are reciprocally convertible or, better still, complementary (Devereux 1945 [1978a, chap. 4], 1961b [1978a, chap. 5], 1967c).

Any item has at least four matrices: a *biological,* an *experiential,* a *cultural,* and a *neurotic* matrix (chap. 2). Psychoanalysis is exceptionally suitable for obtaining information about the matrices to which the analysand assigns a given item, since his statements never appear "out of context," in the sense in which an anthropologist, filling out a trait-list questionnaire, obtains data more or less out of context.

A dim awareness of the fact that any cultural item has several cultural matrices prompted Edward Sapir to affirm that every member of a society has his own culture. While this statement, so expressed, is certainly unacceptable, it has the merit of directing attention to the multiplicity of matrices in which a given item may be embedded.

At present, anthropologists have no effective schema for analyzing and classifying the various cultural matrices in which a given trait may be embedded. However, Linton (1936) did develop a scheme for classifying *all* traits composing a culture. He differentiated between *universals,* such as language; *specialities,* as exemplified by the techniques of various crafts; *alternatives* between which each person belonging to a particular culture is free to choose without gain or loss of prestige; and—as an afterthought—*patterns of misconduct,* which say, in effect: "Don't do it, but, if you do, you must proceed thus and so." Once one recognizes that a given cultural item may belong to two or more of these categories and not solely to one of them, Linton's scheme becomes applicable also to the analysis and classification of the various matrices in which a given item may be embedded.

A simple example will illustrate this point. In American society, the universal matrix of rolling pins is cookery. Their secondary matrix is a certain "pattern of misconduct," since the folklore of American humor specifies that women may use rolling pins to chastise their erring husbands. However, such an act represents not simple misconduct but socially patterned misconduct because the use of rolling pins in domestic strife, though it is not approved behavior, is nevertheless behavior recognized as "typical"—as behavior toward which society reacts by means of a standardized attitude, namely, humorous tolerance. By contrast, the use of rolling pins in battles between women or for beating children or dogs is misconduct pure and simple; it is not recognized as typical, and it elicits unqualified condemnation.

It is important that what is today the secondary matrix of a trait may formerly have been its primary matrix. The original primary matrix of playing cards—derived from the tarot—was not "entertainment" but "divination." Yet today, fortune-telling is certainly a secondary matrix—and one that in the framework of law, at least, is a pattern of misconduct, just as, in a psychiatric context, playing solitaire for oracular purposes is neurotic behavior (Devereux 1954c, 1968b). Certain societies may even define a particular act, known to occur in other societies, as extracultural and hence as—in a way—"impossible." They will therefore refuse to assign it to any matrix whatever. Thus Sparta had no laws against adultery, for the Spartans believed themselves incapable of committing that particular crime (Plutarch, *Moralia* 228c). Similarly, Mohave society has neither the concept of theft nor social mechanisms capable of coping with it. If a child "swipes" a melon from someone's melon patch, the owner of the field not only will not call this a theft but—like Hivsū Tupōma—will take pride in the fact that the child preferred his melons to those of his neighbor. When a white stole a Mohave's fine horse, the Mohave simply did not know how to react to so "inconceivable" a deed (Devereux 1961a).

One further, and more or less heuristic, distinction to be made at this point is the one between items and matrices belonging to the live *mainstream* of culture and those that belong to its *marginal segments*—its (almost) dry tributaries. Thus science and religion belong to the mainstream of our culture, while superstition belongs to one of its marginal and, in a sense, even "pattern-of-misconduct" segments (Devereux 1956c). It is a matter of some importance whether, in a given culture and at a given time, the principal matrix of an item belongs to the mainstream of culture or to one of its marginal segments. Thus, even after two world wars, the primary matrix of the rifle in the United States is still a relatively marginal segment of culture (hunting), though, in an age of cold wars, its secondary matrix (warfare) is a major aspect of the cultural mainstream.

Personal factors in the broadest sense of the term—including even the ethnic character—will determine into which context or matrix (cultural, neurotic, or other) an analysand will decide to place a given item. I shall neglect for a moment all matrices other than the cultural ones and shall examine only the manner in which such multiple matrices appear in psychoanalytic work and the anthropological significance of the data so obtained. However, before one can study the variety of matrices to which a given item may be assigned, one must first discuss a very basic type of duality that can be observed in every known culture.

Although classical scholars have systematically stressed the rationality of the Greeks and their pursuit of the ideal of the golden mean, Dodds (1951) was able to show that irrationality and orgiastic ecstasy played an equally decisive role in Greek cultural dynamics and in the formation of the Greek character. It is known today that the ostentatiously Apollonian façade of Pueblo culture (Benedict 1934a) screens a witches' cauldron of meanness, envy, hate, and fear (Ellis 1951). The social implementation of the Kwakiutl chief's notoriously "paranoid" grandiose competitiveness (Benedict 1934b) is made possible only by the extreme cooperativeness of the Kwakiutl commoner (Linton 1956). Fortune (1932) has been accused of wantonly distorting our traditional conception of Omaha culture (Fletcher and La Flesche 1906), whereas in reality he simply illuminated the reverse side of the coin (Devereux 1967c).[2] I have ventured to suggest that, far from being primarily reality-oriented, American efficiency chiefly seeks to keep unpleasant reality at arm's length (Devereux 1946a).

In fact, a great deal of evidence suggests that the extreme elaboration of some cultural item does not in all cases necessarily prove that the item occupies a nuclear position in the culture (Devereux 1951a). Thus, most Mohave engaged in warfare, while only a few were transvestites; yet just as many Mohave culture traits are associated with institutionalized homosexuality (Devereux 1937b) as with warfare (Fathauer 1951; Stewart 1947). It is even probable that some inherently secondary practices can survive only if they are socially implemented and culturally elaborated out of all proportion to their real importance (Devereux 1951a). Hence, the proper way to determine the nuclearity or marginality of a given cultural cluster is not to count the number of traits associated with it but to determine how many items are *forcibly* brought within its scope. Thus, the most objective measure of the importance and pervasiveness of the idea of temptation and salvation in medieval society is not the number of cathedrals but the fact that the *Gesta Romanorum* (Grässe 1905) interpreted chess as a symbol of the quest for salvation and so forced it into the procrustean bed of theology and established an artificial "compendence" between the two.

Every culture appears to contain important and culturally sanctioned systems of thought and institutions that actually negate its very basis and sometimes even all of reality (chap. 1). For Saint Augustine, as well as for a great pope, all worldly government was basically evil and quite incompatible with the City of God. Brahmanism, a nuclear feature of Hindu civilization, went so far as to assert that reality is nothing but *maya,* or illusion. More generally, culture itself produces all the value systems in terms of which culture as a whole is criticized and sometimes arbitrarily condemned (chap. 1).

On a less abstract level, one and the same item may have two mutually contradictory matrices. All students of the Mohave, and of the River Yumans in general, have recorded the belief that twins are visitors from heaven, to be welcomed with open arms and showered with honors, gifts, and privileges (Kroeber 1925; Devereux 1941). However, the simple question, "What is better, a twin or an ordinary person?" enabled me to obtain a highly developed secondary set of Mohave beliefs in which twins are viewed as the unwelcome, graspingly acquisitive ghosts of dead persons who become reincarnated solely to die for a second time and so obtain a second set of funeral gifts to take back to the land of the dead (Devereux 1961a).[3] I shall discuss below the methodological import of the fact that anthropologists did not so much as suspect the existence of this second set of beliefs concerning twins.

An even simpler example is the dual matrix of the cultural item "dog." In terms of one cultural matrix the dog is man's best friend. The nature of the second matrix to which the dog is assigned is revealed by such expressions as "dirty dog," "bitch," and the like.

The anthropologically sophisticated psychoanalyst often discovers that the analysand's subjective ambivalences are closely related to the characteristic basic ambivalences of his culture. A Plains Indian, whose tribe hunted for many centuries, had a dream that clearly expressed feelings of guilt over the killing of animals: the fox he shot turned into a baby (Devereux 1951a). While partly subjective and neurotic, this guilt was, at the same time, deeply embedded in the culture of his tribe: the buffalo, the staple food of that tribe, was not simply "meat on the hoof" but also a sacred animal that played a great role in power-giving visions, rituals, and other tribal institutions. In fact, many tribes go to great lengths to conciliate and to honor the game the hunter kills (Devereux 1946b).

In some instances the analysand, instead of assigning a given item to the *manifest* content of its primary matrix, tends to emphasize the latent or implicit meaning of both the trait and the matrix to which it is traditionally assigned.

All Plains Indian societies are characterized by an unusually high degree of sibling rivalry. Sioux Indians boast that their parents loved them so much that they refrained from marital relations for years in order to delay the birth of younger siblings (Devereux 1951a [2d rev. ed., 1969]). The Blackfoot expect the man who was a "favorite" or "honored" child to be an especially generous giver (Goldfrank 1945). Masculine competitiveness in general is also highly institutionalized (Lowie 1935). This characteristically intense sibling rivalry is the cultural matrix of the pathologically callous reactions of a Plains Indian woman analysand to a rather gruesome tribal tale about a baby who left its cradle every night to cannibalize other babies and then stealthily returned to its cradle with bits of human flesh stuck between its teeth. This woman told me that she never wearied of this tale and that she felt sorry for the little cannibal, who must have experienced a great deal of discomfort, due to the bits of human flesh caught between its teeth. "I wanted to pick his teeth to make him comfortable again."

It stands to reason that this pathological reaction was determined largely by this woman's own life history. Because of her mother's illness, she had, by tribal standards, been weaned quite prematurely and, to make things worse, had watched her younger siblings being nursed for two years or more. As a result, she developed an intense reaction formation against her longing for the maternal breast. Further details were given in chapter 15. Here I concern myself solely with the nexus between her early weaning and her jealousy toward her siblings, which in her case had important cultural components. In brief, because of her neurosis, she responded not to the manifest but to the latent content of the story; the manifest cultural matrix in which she placed the *narrative* was not "folklore" but rather "sibling rivalry," and it was thus from the latter that the tale's *content* drew its inspiration. However, she was able to disguise the real nature of her response, even from herself, and professed to enjoy the story as folk literature. This made her sadistic fantasy seem vicarious and culturally sanctioned and, therefore, at least moderately ego-syntonic (Devereux 1961c).

The reverse maneuver may also be observed, especially in the development of sublimations. Thus, the gifted inventor of an ego-dystonic sadistic fantasy may turn it into a short story (Devereux 1961c); by depersonalizing and culturalizing his fantasy, he assigns it to the cultural realm of literature rather than the subjective realm of anxiety-arousing daydreams. Moreover, just as one feels less responsible for one's dreams than for one's waking thoughts (Freud 1925), so the socially accepted redefinition of an ego-dystonic fantasy as "simply" the *raw material* of a literary narrative permits the "author" to feel less responsible for his fantasy than he did at first (Devereux 1961c and chap. 15). In fact, the limited responsibility one feels for the content of one's dreams was systematically exploited in the treatment of a Plains Indian, who was encouraged to "dream out" his conflicts before coming to grips with them in the therapeutic hour (Devereux 1951a). Society itself readily sanctions such maneuvers and agrees to see "inspiration" of extrapsychic origin where, as Kris rightly pointed out (1952), there is nothing more than a *supposed* "regression in the service of the ego."[4]

The fact that a subjective production is extrojected and assigned to the realm of culture seems to give it all the attributes of "mature" and "well-socialized" cultural behavior. Abraham's patient must have felt extremely mature and socially responsible when he transmuted his curiosity about the origin of babies into a scientific interest in the chemical state called "status nascendi" (Abraham 1927). Moreover, had the child who defined flatus as an adult prerogative (Ferenczi 1927b) grown up to be a composer, he would have felt very mature when, instead of expelling flatus, he scored the fortissimo climax of his symphony for the brass ensemble.[5]

Both analysands and ordinary informants may, on occasion, voice not the manifest but the latent content of an item or matrix. Ahma Humāre, an especially cooperative Mohave informant, explained the *hikwīr* disease as follows. Certain bodies of water are inhabited by supernatural aquatic snakes, whose chief has two heads, one at each end of his body;[6] if these snakes attack a person either in real life or in dream, the victim contracts the *hikwīr* illness. It is quite certain that this account embodies the official Mohave belief about the *hikwīr* illness. Yet the equally reliable and well-informed shaman Hivsū Tupōma gave a wholly different explanation of this illness: Should a woman, in the course of a swimming party, have intercourse with a man underwater, she will contract the *hikwīr* illness (Devereux 1961a).

Now, even though these two accounts of the *hikwīr* illness diverge widely on the manifest level, Hivsū Tupōma's "unorthodox" theory is neither a lie nor a strictly personal opinion. It is simply an explicit, nonsymbolic, and nonmythological statement of the latent content of the official theory,[7] made possible by the informant's uninhibited love of ribaldry. It translates the snake symbol into its real referent, the male organ, and equates underwater intercourse with an underwater attack. Hence Hivsū Tupōma's account of the *hikwīr* illness is as genuine a part of Mohave culture as the officially sanctioned theories of the other informant. This finding supports the statement,

311

made elsewhere (Devereux 1953b, 1955b), that the latent content of even the most divergent versions of a given myth is always the same, just as the latent content of a tendentious lie is identical with the truth that the liar seeks to distort or deny (Devereux 1970) or as, according to Lévi-Strauss (1958), the structure of a myth remains invariant in all its transformations and variants.

In short, the discovery of the latent matrix of a given item is as legitimate an anthropological goal as the discovery of the official and manifest matrix of that trait.

I cannot and do not wish to deny that an awareness of the multiplicity of manifest and latent matrices to which an item may be assigned appreciably complicates the task of the anthropologist who seeks to clarify the basic pattern of a given culture. However, as a great mathematician once pointed out, nature is completely unconcerned with (mathematical) analytic difficulties. Hence, like the psychoanalyst, the anthropologist would be well advised to remember the wise counsel of the same mathematician: "Seek simplicity, but distrust it." A failure to distrust simplicity has led to many grossly oversimplified formulations of cultural patterns and of the character structure of ethnic groups and even individuals (Devereux 1961b [1978a, chap. 5], 1967c).

The analysand's tendency to emphasize the secondary matrix of a trait instead of its primary matrix (chap. 2) or to specify the latent rather than the manifest content of the matrix to which a trait belongs is, of course, subjectively determined. But this does not mean that the information he gives is not quite as much a part of his culture as is the official matrix of a given item or the manifest content of a given belief. This thesis can be proved by showing that idiosyncratic and even neurotic motives may induce an analysand to place a given item in its *primary* matrix. A Plains Indian cowboy always referred to the cultural item "horse" in its proper and primary cultural context. Nevertheless, his repeated references to geldings and to "proud cut"[8] horses were simply veiled attempts to inform me that he had a severe potency disturbance (1951a [see rev. ed. 1969]).

A neurotic compulsion to emphasize the subsidiary rather than the primary matrix to which some item may be assigned can also yield valuable anthropological information. A halfbreed Indian refused to place his father in the most natural cultural matrix, "head of the family"; instead, he assigned him to the culturally less nuclear matrix "inferior races." This halfbreed's intense race prejudice enabled him to deny the violence of his oedipal conflicts and to define sexual relations between his father and his mother solely as the "defiling of a pure white woman by a lousy Indian" (chap. 1). Nevertheless, this strikingly neurotic maneuver sheds a great deal of light on the latent content of the cultural matrix "race prejudice," as well as on the manner in which the marginal segments of a culture may be exploited—with only a minimum of conscious guilt feelings—for the expression and implementation of socially unacceptable and highly ego-dystonic wishes and fantasies. In the same way, the aforementioned Plains Indian woman could wallow in cannibalistic fantasies simply by defining her enjoyment of these fantasies as an appreciation of tribal lore.[9]

The assigning of newly acquired cultural items to some traditional matrix is a common occurrence in acculturated analysands. A Plains Indian analysand reported that, when he first left for boarding school, his mother accompanied him to the interurban bus station singing "strongheart songs," as though he were setting out on the warpath for the first time. Such maneuvers shed a great deal of light on the dynamics of acculturation in general, and especially on those of "antagonistic acculturation," where alien cultural *means* are borrowed precisely in order to preserve certain indigenous *ends* more effectively (Devereux 1943 [1978a, chap. 8]).

The reverse of antagonistic acculturation is represented by the attempt to fit obsolete indigenous items into the matrix of a newly adopted pattern. This process is exemplified by the transformation of indigenous deities into Christian demons or by the destruction of native ritual objects and property in semi-Christian messianic cults, as exemplified by "cargo cults" (Berndt 1952–53; chap. 12, above). Several examples of such a reinterpretation of native cultural items by a Plains Indian analysand have been published elsewhere (Devereux 1951a [rev. ed., 1969]). An anthropological analysis of the way in which the Manus detached some items of their aboriginal culture from their original matrices and placed them in the matrices of their postwar culture will be found in Mead's *New Lives for Old* (1956).

I described in chapter 2 the distinctive ways in which various types of neurotics and psychotics distort, reinterpret, and totally or partially deculturalize the culture items that they use (or abuse) in conformity with their personal conflicts and delusions. Here I mention only in passing that the deculturalization of a cultural item in psychosis (chap. 2) is the *reverse* of the process by which a cultural matrix is assigned to an initially noncultural item.

In short, no item is a part of culture unless it is assigned to a cultural matrix of meanings, values, and implications. What matters most to the ethnopsychiatrist is the multiplicity and the occasional mutual incompatibility of the several matrices to which an item may be assigned, either by a culture itself or by an individual belonging to it.

These findings permit one to define culture as both an inner experience and a way of experiencing. Indeed, the person participating in a culture does not experience it simply as something external—as something that buffets him about the way a more or less patterned set of crosscurrents might. Unless he is completely psychotic (chap. 2), he experiences culture as something deeply internalized, something that is an integral component of his psychic structure and psychic economy (Henry 1951). Hence, it suffices to stress that culture is chiefly a manner of experiencing the components as well as the pattern of man's world or life space (*Lebensraum*). To return to the pseudo-problem of "incest" among apes, culture alone determines whether a nubile female is experienced as a sexual object or as a sexually tabooed daughter. If the nubile female whom culture defines as a tabooed daughter is, nevertheless, experienced chiefly as a sexually attractive female, neurosis and/or socially prohibited behavior is certainly imminent. Likewise, culture alone determines whether the flesh of the pig is, or is not, defined as food. On a broader level, culture alone determines whether one defines mankind as a whole as fundamentally evil or whether, like the Arunta to whom a missionary tried to explain the doctrine of original sin, one replies indignantly: "All Arunta are good!" Social models determine even the manner in which one views psychiatric problems. Nonscientific cultural thought models are responsible for some psychiatrists' obsession with the diagnostic value of mere adjustment and for a great deal of "neurologizing psychiatry," or naive organicism, as well (Devereux 1958a [1978a, chap. 10]; Scheflen 1958, 1961). In fact, all great advances in science seem to presuppose either major sociocultural changes or a borrowing of alien scientific knowledge *without* the cultural matrices to which such knowledge is assigned by the lending culture. This kind of borrowing is exceptionally obvious in the process by which early Ionian, Arab, and Renaissance science came into being (Devereux 1958a [1978a, chap. 10]).[10]

The cycle of matrix-free discovery or borrowing—comparable, perhaps, to Hartmann's concept of the conflict-free sphere of the ego (1950)—followed by stultification through the establishment of forced "compendences" between the findings of science and the irrational substratum of culture, repeats itself constantly in the history of the sciences. Science progresses only so long as it is not forcibly fitted into the procrustean bed of culture's irrational substratum; it declines whenever the conception of, or demand for, Mohammedan, Christian, German, Marxist, or even democratic science arises. I imagine it is this aspect of culturally neutral science that Weston La Barre (1954) had in mind when he spoke of the glorious tradition of "scientific rowdyism."[11] Society has a right to demand that the scientist be a responsible citizen. However, once a society demands that science itself cease to be an unkempt urchin and become culturally and ideologically housebroken, it automatically forfeits its scientific leadership to a society more tolerant of the basic cultural —that is, ideological—neutrality of science. The bureaucratization of a science and the transformation of professional organizations into "guardians of orthodoxy" or "defenders of the (revolutionary) anti-faith faith" are also alarming symptoms of scientific decline. As a truly classical psychoanalyst, I can afford to say: "A bon entendeur, salut!" or, "If the cap fits, wear it!"

Now, since culture is a patterned way of experiencing oneself as well as the rest of the world, the manner in which members of a given culture experience a certain item is often at variance with objective reality, as well as with the manner in which that item is experienced in another culture.

I therefore advance the thesis that the full understanding of any given cultural item presupposes not only an understanding in depth of the many discrete matrices in which it may be embedded but also an understanding of the complex (overt and covert) relationships obtaining between the various matrices of a single trait. Thus, it is not sufficient to realize that the item "twins" has two, mutually contradictory, matrices in Mohave society. One must also realize that these two matrices are conjugate—that they complete each other in that they implement the two poles of a fundamentally ambivalent attitude toward twins, whose birth creates problems for even modern families that do not lead economically marginal existences. In fact, the birth of twins, precisely because it is an exceptional event, serves to crystallize a great many of the normally inhibited resentments of both the parents and the older siblings—not to mention the fact that, since infant mortality is higher in twin than in single births, in primitive groups the birth of twins is almost invariably a harbinger of grief and mourning.

Unfortunately for the field worker, it is extremely difficult to determine every single matrix to which a given item is assigned. The position of the theoretician who, on the basis of published field reports, seeks to obtain a well-rounded understanding of the meaning of a given cultural item, either in one culture or in a large number of cultures, is even more difficult, since the average ethnography usually mentions only one of the matrices of a given item.

It is my belief that the careful field worker studying a given tribe will find it quite easy to locate the various matrices to which an item belongs if he bears in mind the variety of matrices to which that item is assigned in *other* cultures. The second set of Mohave beliefs concerning twins would certainly not have remained undetected for nearly half a century had field workers remembered that in certain other culture areas twins are openly rejected and sometimes even killed. Nor can the most caninophile field worker long remain ignorant of the secondary and hostile matrix of the item "dog" in Western culture if he remembers that the Arab considers the dog to be unclean. Conversely, not even the most caninophobic student of Arab culture will remain unaware of the tremendous prestige the greyhound has in Arab society if he remembers that the starving Australian native sometimes ate his child rather than his dingo dog (chap. 5).

I now propose to select an extraordinarily weird item, which certainly did not diffuse from China to the South American Tupari or from Zoroastrian Balkh to a Greenland Eskimo village. This item is the "reversible or retractable penis." Among the Tupari (Caspar 1953) and the Tapirape (Wagley and Galvão 1948), every boy routinely learns to luxate his penis, so that, except when he is urinating or copulating, it is completely tucked inside his body. In South China (Kobler 1948) and in Indonesia (Wulfften-Pahlte 1935) it is believed that the penis may retract into the abdomen, with lethal results; this imaginary illness, as well as the extreme panic that it elicits, is called *koro* in Indonesia. The Mohave Indians jokingly claim that the transvestite "pounds his penis to make it go inside and look like a vagina" (Devereux 1937b). An Eskimo woman who had been told to give birth to a boy managed to persuade everyone that she had done so by maintaining that, due to the premature arrival on the scene on the part of the boy's (nude) older sister, the neonate's penis retracted, turning him into a woman (Freuchen 1957). Legend reports that Zarathustra cured the king's favorite horse, whose legs had retracted into its body (Stoll 1904). Roman (Petronius's *Satyricon*) as well as fifteenth-century ([Philippe le Bon] 1486) and eighteenth-century literature contains a number of spicy anecdotes concerning retraction of the penis. Reuss (1937) described the case of a German psychotic who, three times in succession, stuffed his penis down his own urethra, the way one turns a sleeve inside out. I have published elsewhere a neurotic American woman's dream that specifically *denied* that the penis can retract into the body (1954a). An experienced psychoanalyst told me about a patient who wished to cover his entire body with a rubber sheathing; when this sheath was removed, the portion covering the penis could be inverted to resemble a vagina and permit "autocohabitation."[12] Another competent analyst reports that a neurotic adolescent was afraid that his penis might retract into his abodmen, turning his urethra into a uterus. At times one of my patients felt that, during the analytic session, his penis was about to withdraw into his abdomen. [*Addendum 1979:* A curious oversight on the part of Freud (1911) was first discerned by Nathan (1978). Freud either did not realize—or attached no importance to the fact—that what Schreber described in detail and called "unmanning" was actually the retraction of the penis into the abdomen and its transformation into a vagina.] According to Aelian (*On the Nature of Animals*), certain beavers, knowing that they are hunted for their testicles but not prepared to castrate themselves preventively, as some of them are believed to do, retract their testicles, making them enter their bellies, so as to make the hunters believe that they have no testicles.

No real understanding of the idea of the reversible penis is possible unless one takes into account all of the matrices to which it is assigned in various cultures, including traditional costume, dangerous illness, tribal humor, socially accepted lie, magical cure, erotic anecdote, psychotic behavior, neurotic fantasy, neurotic denial, and even mythozoology.

Equally weird and equally culturally implemented are fantasies concerning beings without anuses. These fantasies assume such diversified forms and occur in such a variety of cultural areas that their occurrence can hardly be explained in terms of diffusion. Since I have discussed this fantasy elsewhere (1954b), and since Lévi-Strauss has analyzed this tale systematically (1966), I simply note that this series of data leads to the same conclusions as does the fantasy of penis-retraction.

I realize that my position represents an at least partial endorsement of the currently despised "comparative method." The fact remains that this method was productive of important anthropological insights. Its sole drawback was that the method itself was never properly justified. I now propose to offer a systematic justification of that method.

I take as my point of departure the mathematician's ergodic hypothesis. It postulates that the results of a million consecutive tosses of a coin are the same as the results of the simultaneous tossing of a million identical coins. This hypothesis is generally accepted as valid even though mathematicians differ as to whether it has ever been actually proved. I have discussed its application to the sciences of man elsewhere (1955b [rev. ed., 1976]).

A complete exploration of the meanings, values, and connotations of a given item can be obtained by psychoanalyzing a single individual, by the cross-sectional study of a large number of subjects, by the complete anthropological exploration of all matrices to which that item belongs in a given culture, or by a reasonably complete survey of the *primary* matrices to which this item is assigned in a large number of cultures. Each approach will yield exactly the same insights into the real meaning of that item. I believe that, had I been able to analyze every single ramification of the dream in which my woman analysand ostentatiously denied that the penis could retract into the abdomen, I would have obtained subjective equivalents of every known cultural context of this belief. I am equally convinced that an exhaustive study of all ramifications of the *koro* pattern in Java would yield the complete range of data, beliefs, etc., pertaining to the retractable penis in *other* cultures. Conversely, a list of the forms in which this idea is expressed in a large number of different cultures is also, at the same time, a catalogue of the matrices in which this idea may appear in a given culture and an inventory of the individual connotations that an analysand may, on various conscious or unconscious levels, assign to this idea.

Needless to say, this thesis is hard to prove, though extremely telling factual evidence can be mustered in its support.

1. An exhaustive survey of data on abortion in 300 primitive cultures did not disclose a single custom, idea, or attitude that analysts have not found also in Occidental women who had aborted, or wished to abort, or had abortion dreams or fantasies.

2. On the basis of the Mohave belief that if a woman violates a certain pregnancy taboo she will miscarry, I inferred (1955b [rev. ed., 1976]) that there must exist at least one tribe in which women deliberately violate certain pregnancy taboos in order to abort. One year later, after surveying a hundred additional groups, I discovered precisely this predicted practice among the Maori (Goldie 1904).

3. On the basis of predominantly African data I concluded that an unmarried girl's illegitimate child is often fantasied to be the offspring of the girl's own father. My book was already in galley proof when, in connection with another investigation, I encountered this very belief among the African Fan (Trilles 1912). I have, moreover, just discovered, in J. P. Vernant's (1963) analysis of Athenian *epiklēros* girls, certain elements suggesting the presence of analogous fantasies.

4. A Sedang girl who was impregnated and then aborted by her own father pretended that she bled because she had been bitten by leeches—which are used as a means of procuring abortions in Persia (Devereux 1955b [rev. ed., 1976]).

5. An Aleut abortionist refused to discuss her practices and instead chose to discuss—of all things—*baskets,* which, like other containers, are well-known symbols of the female genitalia, especially the uterus (Shade 1949).

I am therefore led to conclude that the uniformity of the human psyche implies also the uniformity of human Culture with a capital C. Just like individuals, cultures differ from each other chiefly in the manner in which the constituent items are juxtaposed and arranged into patterns and structures. They also differ in terms of the fact that the *primary* matrix of a certain item in one culture may be its *secondary* matrix or *latent content* in another culture; the reverse, of course, also holds true. In fact, the systematic affirmation of one belief necessarily implies the denial of the opposite belief, and this denial is quite as much a constituent element of a culture as the affirmation is. Thus, the unqualified affirmation of absolute monotheism in Islam indicates the presence of (latent or rejected) polytheistic ideas. As Moses Hadas has recently noted, it is in *one* God that the atheist does *not* believe. A psychoanalytic analogy may clarify this statement.

A certain person dreamed that three fish, named Matthew, Mark, and Luke, were swimming in a fishbowl. A short analysis of this dream disclosed that the real subject of the dream was *John,* whose name was *ostentatiously* omitted from the dream (Devereux 1956a).

On the basis of the preceding considerations, the precise nature of the logical nexus between culture and the human mind can be formulated as follows:

1. Historically, culture and the human mind are coemergents and presuppose each other (chap. 15).

2. Attempts to derive culture *genetically* from the nature of the human psyche are quite as meaningless as attempts to derive the human psyche *genetically* from culture.

3. The infant's acquisition of Culture per se (as distinct from Eskimo or Hottentot culture) and his transformation from an immature specimen of the (zoological) genus *Homo* into a human being occur simultaneously. This functionally indivisible dual process may be designated by the term *humanization* and must be differentiated from the acquisition of a *specific* culture, which may be called "ethnicization." For example, in learning to *speak,* the child becomes human; in learning to speak *Sioux,* he becomes a certain kind of

Plains Indian. Humanization through the acquisition of Culture actualizes the human being's potentialities; ethnicization simply provides one set of specific means for their actualization (Devereux 1956a).

4. The only psychological system the anthropologist can use is the one whose focus is not genus *Homo* (defined zoologically) but *zōon politikon*—the creature who lives in a socioculturally organized community, not in a biologically organized gregarious herd or beehive. Only psychoanalysis satisfies this criterion; no sound anthropology is possible without it.

5. The only science of man the psychoanalyst can use is one that studies man's distinctively and uniquely human behavior. Only anthropology satisfies this criterion; no sound psychoanalysis is possible without it.

6. Psychoanalysis and anthropology alike must take account of man's characteristics that are not species-bound, i.e., the characteristics he shares with beings that are cultureless and have no human psyche—in other words, man's biological nature. However, that nature must be viewed, not as a true *causa causans* of culture and the human psyche, but solely as the terrain on which culture and the human mind may develop, as the raw material with which culture and the human mind operate, and as an internal limitation on the theoretically almost unlimited variability of culture and of the mind. The traits that man shares with other primates can no more explain his psyche and culture than the nature of iron can explain the structure and function of a chronometer. Any science of man that refuses to recognize this fact is not science but science fiction.

7. Psychoanalysis and anthropology must hang together lest they hang separately in an age of automation and electronic brains, an age that has returned to the philosophy of Roman slave-keepers and has extended to mankind as a whole the concept of the slave as a kind of machine. The *total* disorganization that some advocate as the very essence of freedom is also a technique of enslavement, for the technique that deprives man of all organization is the first condition of his slavehood. A new science that would combine psychoanalysis and anthropology in accordance with the principles of complementarity (Devereux 1978a)—that is, without fusing them—is the last bulwark of the concept of man as an end in himself.

Notes

PREFACE

1. Chapter 11 was written in French; chapters 8 and 10, though written in English, were first published in French translation.

2. Another volume of my selected papers has a similar history. *Ethnopsychoanalysis* (Devereux 1978a) originally appeared in book form as a French translation of a collection of papers most of which had originally been written and published in English. This French version was translated into Spanish (1975), Italian (1975), German (1978), and then back into English (1978).

CHAPTER ONE

1. For the concept of transcultural psychotherapy, see pp. 70 and 334, n. 4.

2. See Devereux 1961c [1975, chap. 1] for a brief discussion of sublimation.

3. This is the classical view. In my opinion it needs some revisions, preferably in terms of the Hartmann-Kris-Loewenstein (1947, 1950) theory of the undifferentiated infantile ego or even in terms of Fairbairn's (1954) view that it is the id that splits off from the infantile ego, not the ego that splits off from the infantile id. The classical view has to be refined in terms of a more sophisticated conception of the ego (Devereux 1966d), and particularly of the primitive ego of the infant. I mention this problem in order to indicate that I am aware of its existence, though I cannot discuss it in this context.

4. These are not pleonastic expressions (Devereux 1967c).

5. In a previously published article (Devereux and Hoffman 1961d) it was proposed that the diagnostician's principal task is to evaluate the patient's strengths rather than his weaknesses, his "credit" rather than his "debit" side.

6. This finding led me to propose (Devereux 1956a) that the superego contains the residual precipitate of those experiences a child cannot master with its own means at the time they occur.

7. This finding leads one to ask whether the early diffusion of emotional ties over a whole segment of society (kin group, village), which is so characteristic of primitive societies, may not be an (unconsciously evolved) prophylactic cultural defense, which, by decreasing the child's exclusive emotional dependence on its parents—whose predictable life-span in primitive societies is often fairly short—reduces the intensity of the trauma resulting from the parents' death. This diffusion of emotional ties is socially fostered by establishing, e.g., a functional equivalence between the mother and the mother's sister by means of a classificatory kinship system (chap. 9). If correct, this hypothesis would account for some of the characterological differences between primitives, whose parents have a short life-span, and advanced groups, characterized by a greater longevity of the parent age group. Of course, in the latter types of societies, where the

321

child's emotional ties are less diffuse (Devereux 1942c), becoming an orphan early in life is more likely to be an atypical experience and therefore more likely to be traumatic than among primitives, since in advanced societies children have few extrafamilial emotional ties and, in addition, remain socially immature for a long time.

8. I have discussed elsewhere (Devereux 1955c, 1965a) the breakdown of cultural defenses in situations of sudden historicocultural discontinuity.

9. Henri Ey, cited in Bastide 1965.

10. I refer here simply to Stewart's data and do not mean to endorse his highly heterodox interpretation of this phenomenon.

11. The distinction between "a" and "any" is to be taken in Bertrand Russell's sense (1903, 1919).

12. When I was still a relatively "green" psychoanalytic candidate, I once remarked to my analytic supervisor that my patient "had quite an Oedipus complex." The supervisor very aptly replied, "Who hasn't?"

13. By contrast, sublimations resulting from insight create no new problems and are therefore permanently effective (Jokl 1950).

14. The same kind of provocative and self-destructive behavior has been observed in witches of other culture areas as well.

15. The argument proposed by M. K. Opler (1959) is a case in point. He claims that Kroeber and I rely on material drawn exclusively from California Indians. This is simply not true; moreover, even if it were true, it would not be relevant, because similar data have been recorded in many other regions. Even Ackerknecht, the originator of the sophism that an individual can be simultaneously autonormal and heterogeneous, cites data from northern Eurasia, central Asia, India, Indonesia, Melanesia, Polynesia, South Africa, and other regions. Opler adds that some of the California tribes referred to by Kroeber were subjected to brutal oppression, and this is indeed true. By contrast, the Mohave were never persecuted. As for Genghis Khan's Mongols, Tamerlane's Turks, and the Bantu of Dingaan or Chaka, they were more aggressive than submissive. Further comment on this topic seems superfluous.

16. I am indebted to Harold Rosen, of the department of psychiatry at Johns Hopkins University, for detailed information about just such a case, which I have briefly summarized elsewhere (Devereux 1956a).

17. The brilliant punning intellectual described by Freud (1905b) did not manifest a comparable exaltation.

18. *Witzelsucht* (a "toxicomania" of punning) may also be observed in some neurological illnesses, perhaps as a consequence of the "dissolving" of higher functions, which entails the "liberation" of inferior functions, in Jackson's (1931–32) sense of the terms.

19. I hope to discuss on another occasion the way the *Cratylus* also reflects an abnormal aspect of Plato himself.

20. For a systematic presentation of Greek materials relative to this distinction, see Dodds (1951), especially chapter 3, "The Blessings of Madness."

21. In the sense in which one may concurrently have both pneumonia and a broken leg.

22. It goes without saying that one need not be a shaman in order to dream in a hallucinatory manner that one is being attacked by ghosts, though the severely perturbed shaman will *no doubt* have hallucinations of this type more often and more systematically than other people do. The

intrusion of irrational cultural beliefs into the delusional pattern of individuals who are not shamans will be discussed further on.

23. It is unnecessary to enumerate once more the great personages of the world of intelligence or of social history who confirm this rule.

24. Likewise, the patient and self-denying wife of a chronic alcoholic may turn into an alcoholic shrew as soon as her husband stops drinking.

25. Metaphorically speaking, the shaman still has at his disposal his grandfather's bow and arrows, whereas the nonshaman is obliged to try to shoot rifle bullets with a child-size bow bought at the corner five-and-dime.

26. A bow cannot compete with a submachinegun, nor a horse with an airplane, nor the shamanistic curing ritual with penicillin, although the latter's supernaturalistic aspects may continue to coexist with penicillin treatments. Cf. my account of why I had to pretend to be a shaman when taking care of Sedang patients.

27. This explains the ease with which syncretistic cults—crisis cults—are born and spread and also the answer that Geza, the last of the pagan rulers of ancient Hungary, made to a bishop who blamed him for serving Jehovah and his pagan gods at the same time: "I am rich enough to serve them both."

28. Pirenne (1939) correctly stressed the important role played by the Roman sociopolitical structure, on the one hand, and the tribal organization of the barbarian invaders on the other, in the formation of the functional and active ethos underlying medieval "Christian" society. He neglects to mention, however, how small a contribution was made to medieval society by the ethos and aspirations of the first oppressed Christians (slaves, poor people, publicans, and others). In my opinion, medieval society had only a thin veneer of true Christian spirit. Christianity, distorted in order to satisfy the demands of a system of brutal oppression, served only to rationalize fundamentally non-Christian sociopolitical models. The nostalgic dream of modern man, who sees medieval society as deeply imbued with the religion of Christ, is one thing; sociocultural reality is another.

29. See chapter 2 for the various forms of neurotic manipulation of cultural materials.

30. After all, no ophthalmologist claims that, because "in the kingdom of the blind the one-eyed man is king," being one-eyed is normal. Boyer is far too sophisticated a scholar to use this reasoning, but it is just the kind of thing, I am sure, that cultural relativists would not hesitate to advance.

31. I say "usually" advisedly, for whereas the Mohave have a whole series of psychiatric labels ("categories") (Devereux 1961a), the Sedang Moi, who show little interest in psychology, identify only the insane (*ràjok*), the neurotic or eccentric or queer individual (*kok*), and the good-for-nothing (*plam ploy*).

32. These advantages outweigh the disadvantage—if indeed it is one—of being accused by the champions of cultural relativism (such as M. K. Opler) of proposing theories that apply only to those specific disorders and the cultures in which they occur. I have made only one concession in this respect: I cite only a very few examples drawn from my own field data.

33. This disdain is a far from recent development. Boardman (1964) notes that in ancient Egypt the Greek colonist was as thoroughly hated as he was needed.

34. A partial analysis of the causes of a society's disavowal of itself,

and, specifically, the formulation of this in terms of *irrational ideologies,* is given below.

35. The situation is actually even more complex. Ganser's syndrome, observed chiefly among imprisoned persons (who have a good "obvious" reason for malingering), is often misdiagnosed as malingering because in many respects its symptoms fit the behavior patterns that modern culture ascribes apriori to the insane. Since a detailed analysis of the psychodynamics of this similarity would take me too far afield, I will simply suggest that Ganser's syndrome may well be the "ethnic psychosis" of imprisoned persons.

36. Some years after I developed this concept, Jenkins independently emphasized the *variable* importance of pure rebelliousness in different mental disorders (Jenkins and Glickman 1946, 1947).

37. A documentary film by Dr. L. Chertok proves, however, that *la grande hystérie* still exists, even in Paris.

38. This example is of interest in that anality plays a decisive role in all obsessional neuroses and that money often symbolizes feces.

39. For these distinctions, see chapter 7.

40. This perhaps explains why the psychoanalytic theory of hysteria has been on dead center for several decades. The course on the theory of hysteria that I took around 1950 was based almost exclusively on Freud's early writings about this syndrome.

41. It is claimed that fewer than sixty families of the Hungarian nobility can now trace their origins to the time prior to the battle of Mohács, at the beginning of the sixteenth century.

42. The tribe he belonged to lived formerly not in wigwams but in tipis.

43. Franz Alexander has reported a similar observation to me: the exploitation of a double cultural allegiance in a patient of Japanese descent, born in Hawaii.

44. Cultural items intended for quite other purposes can also be used as symptoms and defenses. This process will be examined later (chap. 2).

45. Adelman (1955) also notes the uniformity of reports concerning the course of the *latah* attack.

46. Worse still, these flagrant violations of military discipline more often than not went unpunished, whereas anyone violating the discipline during a buffalo hunt was severely whipped by the tribe's police society.

47. The same is true of a number of traits characteristic of the psychopath (chap. 2).

48. The only Mohave man who attempted to commit suicide during a funeral was a father who tried to throw himself on the funeral pyre of his son, whom his own hardheartedness had pushed to suicide (Devereux 1961a [2d rev. ed., 1969]).

49. Compare: hashish–*hashshashin* (hashish addict)–assassin.

50. If this hypothesis proves correct, it would explain why the tripod was a particularly precious object as early as Homer. It was often dedicated to Apollo, god of prophecy.

51. Compare Aeschylus *Agamemnon* 410 ff.: the mourning of Menelaus for his runaway wife (Devereux 1968c, 1976a).

52. This terminology differs intentionally from that of Durkheim.

53. This happens, for example, in the case of the marriage relationship. Only when a marriage is about to break up does one hear about the "duties" of the spouses toward each other: the husband's "duty" to provide

for his wife and the wife's to behave in such-and-such ways toward her husband. This, incidentally, may be one of the reasons why divorce is less frequent in countries that permit divorce by mutual consent than in those that require proof of a "violation of contract." Similarly, the pope ceased to exercise in fact an effective universal sovereignty as soon as the theologians felt impelled to specify that he is (1) a spiritual head and (2) a temporal leader and brought in, to support their propositions, a flagrant forgery—the *Donation* of the Emperor Constantine.

54. This is not to suggest that I am in agreement with those who claim to diagnose schizophrenia where Freud diagnosed hysteria. Vienna in 1890 is not New York or London in 1970.

55. The real natures and functions of the *ipā tahānā* status in Mohave society are rather poorly understood. One can be certain only of the fact that "commemorative services" were celebrated solely in honor of the *ipā tahānā*, both those nobly born and those who had acquired noble status by their warlike feats. It is highly probable that a coward of noble origin incurred greater scorn than did one of common birth. Similarly, a French aristocrat of the sixteenth century who exhibited cowardice was more despised than an equally cowardly bourgeois, though he did not lose his title of nobility because of his cowardice.

56. For a description of the luxurious life of Alexander the Great's generals, see Plutarch, *Life of Alexander* 40.

57. Linton (1956) rightly complained that he could nowhere find a truly satisfactory definition of hysteria. This was no doubt due to the fact that our textbook definitions were based on Occidental clinical data. He would probably not have had this kind of difficulty while looking for a definition of so-called "nuclear" schizophrenia, which is made especially explicit by Occidental clinical data.

58. In B. Russell's sense (1903, 1919).

59. I am indebted for this example to Richard L. Jenkins, M.D., who discussed this paper when it was presented before the Anthropological Society of Washington, D.C. I add that such cases confirm my view that the crux of mental health is the capacity to readjust.

60. I was duly recognized as a shaman because I twice found Neolithic stone axes, which only shamans are supposed to be able to locate (Devereux 1967c).

61. Similar considerations justify Burnet's opinion (1930) that Empedocles, too, was a shaman.

62. I can acknowledge in only a general way the influence of certain psychiatric and psychological writings of W. H. R. Rivers (1920, 1923, 1926) on the development of my ethnopsychiatric theories.

CHAPTER TWO

1. *Ausgegliedert:* detached by "disarticulation" from a coherent configuration (*Gestalt*).

2. For the symbolic equation hearth (oven) = vagina, see Herodotus 5. 92.

3. For an analysis of neurotic displacements from one area of biological organization to another in the interpretation of cultural materials, see chapter 15. An analysis of sexual "sliding" among the ancient Greeks has been published elsewhere (Devereux 1967b).

4. For a systematic discussion of the logical differences between (social) law and the (individual) superego, see Devereux 1940 (1978a, chap. 1).

5. For marriage as a compromise solution see Devereux 1965c (1978a, chap. 7).

6. The conceptual bases of this statement have been discussed elsewhere (Devereux 1945), in connection with an analysis of the pseudo-dichotomy between "nature" and "nurture."

7. In the same sense, a painter interested in balancing tone values may legitimately wish to place a large mass in the center of his painting without being overly concerned about whether it will represent a black horse or a red automobile.

8. *Eingebettet:* "immersed in" or "integrated into" a coherent configuration (*Gestalt*).

9. These examples are not as far-fetched as they may seem. Trick arrangements of this type also occur in art. One may think in this context of several musical compositions whose theme is B-A-C-H (B-flat, A, C, B) or of certain themes of Villa-Lobos, whose written contour follows the contour of the Brazilian mountains or the New York skyline.

10. I remind the reader that I originally called this type of psychiatry "transcultural" (1951a) but have had to give up using this term—which I created in order to refer specifically to this type of psychotherapy—because it has been usurped by others, who use it to denote the whole of ethnopsychiatry. I have therefore replaced it with the term "metacultural."

11. The term "normal development" is used here to denote the maturation process, in the course of which only the usual "developmental neuroses" (that is, the so-called infantile neuroses) occur. The unique characteristic of such developmental neuroses is that they can disappear without any psychiatric help, simply by being "outgrown" by means of the impetus inherent in the very processes of development and psychosexual maturation. Moreover, unlike the true neuroses of children, developmental neuroses cause no residual pathological distortions of the personality.

12. A relatively nonpathological feeling of being "tested" can, in certain cases, be culturally determined, as witness the psychotherapy of the Plains Indian woman in whose culture the "test theme" played an important role (chap. 15).

13. The reverse of this procedure would be the attempt to translate Freud's *Three Essays on the Theory of Sexuality* (Freud 1905a) into a baby's babblings.

14. A fictitious tribal name.

CHAPTER THREE

1. I am intentionally restricting my discussion here to behavior *only*. Neurosis and psychosis, as illnesses, cannot be defined simply as "deviations" from the social norm (chap. 13).

2. As the Hellenist Moses Hadas has wittily observed, in our society the atheist *disbelieves* in *one* God.

3. Part of this theory was presented in outline form before the French Society of Psychosomatic Medicine in 1965.

4. Róheim (1932) had already recognized the problematic character of these stages for the study of primitive childhood.

5. Needless to say, I cite this definition without attributing a mystical —Jungian—meaning to the "universal problem." I define this "universal

problem" in a perfectly concrete way, as the totality of real problems, material as well as psychological, that man must face both as a biological organism and as a member of society. Thus my definition of the problem is rigorously scientific and makes no concession to mysticism, metaphysics, or "philosophy," in the ordinary sense of the word.

6. Diodorus of Sicily made the same observation in his *Historical Library* 1. 89.

7. Almost the same metaphor is found in a recent book by Lorenz (1965).

CHAPTER FOUR

1. This quip is, however, wrongly ascribed to Talleyrand, who was only quoting Edward Young (1682–1765) (Young 1770).

2. A slat of wood tied to the end of a thong, so called because, when whirled, the slat produces an intermittent roaring sound. It is used in religious rites.

3. According to Lorenz (1954), the monkey is terrified by any unexpected type of aggression—for example, when his handler bites him.

CHAPTER FIVE

1. We can judge of the lack of interest in the subject by referring to Grinstein's thematic *Index of Psychoanalytic Writings* (1960).

2. Compare the conspiracy to kill the infant Cypselus, of whom it was prophesied that he would displace the Bacchiadae and become tyrant of Corinth (Herodotus 5. 92).

3. A cursory glance at the abortion techniques tabulated in my book provides the following information: twelve tribes use unspecified "overexertion," and twenty more use a specified form of overexertion, such as "jumping off high places." The latter is still in common use in Europe, and Hippocrates himself, taking pity on a pregnant girl musician, advised her to dance and leap strenuously (Ploss, Bartels, and Bartels 1927).

4. In the film *The Gold Rush*, Charlie Chaplin and his fellow sufferer Big Jim, a big, hairy brute, are starving in an Alaskan cabin. While experiencing a hallucination triggered by hunger, Big Jim *sees* his victim—Chaplin—as a rooster skipping about the cabin. Only *after* having thus metamorphosed Chaplin does Jim try to kill and eat him.

5. In scientific French, *l'analyse* means differential and integral calculus.

6. In a discussion of the "reality" of telepathy (Freud 1916–17).

7. This phenomenon, as well as the phenomenon of the noninhibition of this reflex, should doubtless be understood in terms of Hughling Jackson's theories (1931–32) concerning the mechanisms of dissolution and liberation.

8. I cannot here take into account the fact that several species of fish eat their young, since fish neither raise nor recognize their offspring. Moreover, when, to explain the bitch's eating both its young and the placenta, Lorenz (1966) appeals to a kind of instinct to eat anything small and weak, he is gratuitously multiplying hypotheses.

9. Lorenz (1966) appears to believe that I overlooked this mechanism. Had he read this study closely, he would have found in it a number of references to this mechanism.

10. For examples of a young snake biting the breast, see Stesichorus frag. 42 (Page) and Aeschylus *Choephoroi* 532 f.

11. This fantasy is a striking parallel of the zoological fact that the crocodile keeps its maw open so that a small bird can pick its teeth and mouth clean of food debris and worms.

12. In this patient's tribe the normal weaning age was between the ages of two and three and a half. Owing to her mother's illness, she had been weaned suddenly and prematurely.

13. This may illustrate the equivalence of cat and vagina. In French argot, *la chatte* denotes the vagina, as does English "pussy."

14. Adult cannibalism and cannibalistic fantasies have been systematically ignored in the literature; one need only look at Grinstein's *Index* (1960), which, under the two headings "Anthropophagy" and "Cannibalism" lists a total of four papers—two under each of these headings. Cross-references to "Oral Sadism" and the like concern works that either pertain chiefly to infantile cannibalistic fantasies or consist of analyses of the infantile sources of such impulses.

15. Greek mythology is replete with such data: the infant Dionysus, devoured by the Titans, is himself a cannibal in his adult "omophagous" role (a reactive fantasy). Pelops was cooked by his father, and Demeter consumed his shoulder blade (she was, at the time, in a state of severe depression because of the loss of her daughter, Persephone, and so had cannibalistic impulses). Thyestes "unwittingly" ate his children, who had been cooked and served to him. Itys was murdered and cooked by his vindictive mother, Procne, who then fed his flesh to his father, Tereus. Cannibalistic sacrifice of a child was made to Zeus Lycaeus (Burkert 1972). And so forth.

16. Similarly, as Lowie (1935) rightly stressed, an animal, for whom the term "parent" has no meaning, cannot commit incest. Yet, human beings —including even Aristotle, who was not only a great thinker but also an excellent naturalist and an especially fine observer of animal behavior— do impute even to animals a "horror of incest." The same objection applies to Melanie Klein's conception of "oedipal" impulses during the first year of life. In order for a child to have "oedipal" (as distinct from simply "sexual" or "aggressive") impulses, it must first understand the meaning of kinship (Devereux 1965c [1978a, chap. 7]), which is one reason why, with an unerring sureness of touch and acuity of observation, Freud situated the genesis of the "oedipal" impulse in the third or fourth year of life, when the child begins to be able to assign a real meaning to the terms "father" and "mother."

CHAPTER SIX

1. See below for the equation ankle = penis.

2. I think that the following observation sheds some light on one aspect of the process of sublimation. In the course of only a few months of therapy, a major change occurred in the patient's drawings of the human body. In his pretherapy sketches the figures were represented as more than relaxed. They almost seemed to sag and collapse, as though they were snowmen or wax figures melting in the sun. In his later sketches there was a marked sense of muscle tonicity, even in those showing figures in repose, and his posttherapy drawings were characterized by particularly vigorous contours.

3. I note that the cannibalistic sacrifice of children to Zeus Lycaeus included specifically the consumption of the child's *intestines* (Cook 1914, vol. 1).

4. Some disturbed individuals correlate the size of stools with the size of the abdomen, anus, or buttocks and correlate the quantity of urine with the volume of the bladder or the size of the penis (Devereux 1966b).

5. I am deliberately using this formulation ("traumatizing" rather than "wounding") because John of Antioch (fragment 8, C. Müller, *Fragmenta Historicorum Graecorum*, vol. 4, p. 545) states that Oedipus's feet were simply compressed by a hollowed-out piece of wood.

6. The Greek word *toxon*, "bow," gives us our word "toxic."

CHAPTER SEVEN

1. The quotation is from De Quincey's "On Murder, Considered as One of the Fine Arts."

CHAPTER EIGHT

1. An inability to concern oneself with the unconscious determinants of manifest acts is shown by the fact that the self-blinding of Oedipus is invariably interpreted *only* as an upward-displaced and symbolic self-castration, though it was also—and perhaps even primarily—self-punishment for the visual parapraxis, or scotoma, that had prevented Oedipus from recognizing his parents, even though he was an "expert" in recognizing the real identity of people whose appearance had changed with age. This expertness was revealed by his ability to solve the riddle of the Sphinx, which required the recognition that the child crawling on all fours, the adult walking on two legs, and the aged person hobbling along with the help of a third leg (a cane) are the same individual. Moreover, the very nature of this riddle, which concerns *legs,* shows that it has a particular relevance for Oedipus, who had *swollen* feet (Devereux 1959b [1975]).

2. Cutting off the unfaithful wife's nose is a traditional form of punishment in many primitive societies.

3. This maneuver is far from unique. I have elsewhere (1951c) stated that traditional curses reveal the dominant stresses and strains of a culture, while individually invented curses lay bare the fears of the one who uses them. Thus the extremely common Sedang Moi curse "May the tiger eat you!" would fall flat in New York. Likewise, Róheim (1932) pointed out that the insult "Fuck your father!" enrages the Somali but not the Arab, since the latter frequently indulges in homosexual acts.

4. One of the deans of modern anthropology—a man of impeccable morals and respectability—once remarked to me, in the course of a conversation, that in all his field work and readings about primitives he had never came across a tribe whose sexual mores were as insensate as those of Western society.

5. The fact that the (never completely cited) Latin maxim makes a specific exception for man reinforces the thesis that our society is so consistently puritanical that it will even distort into its opposite a maxim about the joys of mature human sexuality.

6. By contrast, when a Roman was awarded a triumphant entrance to Rome, he was accompanied by a slave whose sole duty was to keep reminding him that, despite the triumph, he too was mortal.

7. This seemingly extreme statement is an almost literal quotation from the *Mémoires* (1928) of Elisabeth de Gramont, daughter of the duc de Gramont and, subsequently, wife of the duc de Clermont-Tonnerre. In the same work she also reports overhearing, at a society ball, the remark of a

young aristocrat, who suggested to his friends that they leave the ball and go to Maxim's—a famous nightclub frequented by high-class prostitutes —because the smell of the debutantes' armpits disgusted him. Even more explicit is the statement of a highly intelligent young American woman who in her late teens had led a rather dissolute life: "When I was about nineteen, I had a lover who used to take me on visits to Negro prostitutes. These women were kind to me, and I learned from them all I know about feminine cleanliness." At the beginning of this century, an aristocratic Central European bride asked her sophisticated husband to teach her the grooming techniques of expensive prostitutes, whose cleanliness and attractiveness she envied.

8. A similarly untenable procedure would be the attempt to evolve an image of "natural man" solely on the basis of a study of the wretched inmates of Nazi concentration camps at the moment of their liberation.

CHAPTER NINE

1. Among the Sedang Moi, 5 percent of the population are either seriously neurotic or psychotic.

2. Thus patrilineal and matrilineal descent are mutually exclusive in a given tribe. Conversely, a tribe that makes pottery usually knows also how to cook its food in baked-clay vessels.

3. I disregard for the moment the (obvious) fact that some of these formulations are manifestly false and sometimes even deliberately specious.

4. It is hardly necessary to add that this state of affairs in no way implies the absence of the Oedipus complex.

5. For a discussion of several of the traumatic effects of initiation rites, see Devereux 1956a.

6. A good analogy is offered by the various meanings a word can have, depending on the context in which it occurs.

7. Some years after the original publication of this article, Sinclair Lewis expressed the same opinion in public.

8. For some legitimate examples of this type of reconstruction and extrapolation, see Devereux 1967c.

9. This useful device of dating—but nothing else—has been borrowed from Korzybski (1933).

10. Several years after this article was first published, Adlai Stevenson used exactly the same phrase to describe the state of the world when he was running for president of the United States. His casual remark had great impact, whereas my logical argument went unnoticed. Not being Cyrano de Bergerac, I refuse to say,

C'est justice, et j'approuve au seuil de mon tombeau
Molière a du génie et Christian était beau,

because it happens to me a little too often.

11. Work is produced by the flow of heat (kinetic energy) from a warm body to a cold body.

12. This interpretation, suggested to a schizoid agoraphobic, produced an improvement as sudden as it was lasting.

13. I had already reached this conclusion when I wrote this study in 1938, but external constraints prevented me from including it in the original text. [Cf. Devereux 1978a, chap. 2.]

14. [*Addendum 1969:* When I had analyzed a number of "word salads," which had been recorded verbatim, I discovered that, by carefully sorting

out the words, it was sometimes possible to reconstruct, without changing their *temporal* order, two or even several relatively coherent statements whose constituent elements had apparently become scrambled. This finding tends to weaken Ehrenwald's theory (1948) of the "heteropsychic" origin of at least a part of the psychotic's verbal productions and delusions.]

15. The term is in quotation marks because I am far from sure that the "paraphrenias" are autonomous clinical entities.

Chapter Ten

1. Very few Hellenists realize that Hippolytus, as depicted by Euripides, is neither chaste nor even excessively chaste but has a neurotic phobia of sexuality in general—and that it is so that Euripides meant to represent him. A Mohave or Tahitian Hellenist would not have been deceived.

2. Manifestly, there is more real originality in one of La Rochefoucauld's maxims or in an epigram of Simonides than in the most extravagant divagation of the schizophrenic; let the poets and artists who search for the weird at any price bear this in mind (Devereux 1961c [1975, chap. 1]). Villon was not a great poet *because* of his neurosis but *despite* it. Paraphrasing the advice Baudelaire (*Les Paradis artificiels*) gave to a young poet, who asked him whether the use of opium would make a better poet of him, I would say: Neither opium nor madness can bring out in a man something he does not already own.

3. During some forty-five years of ethnopsychiatric research I have never encountered, in the ethnological literature or elsewhere, a single well-attested case of "war neurosis" (three-day battlefield schizophrenia) in a warlike primitive tribe under conditions of native warfare—and this apart from the fact that a cowardly Plains Indian could always find safety in the marginal status of the transvestite (chap. 1).

4. We find much the same phenomenon in art. In the days of Berlioz, Chopin, Schumann, and Liszt, even the affectively coldest and most aloof composer had to pretend that he was romantic and emotional. Today, even the most emotional and exalted composer feels compelled to compose coldly mechanical music, which might just as well have been ground out by the yard by an IBM computer (Devereux 1961c).

5. The American who when drunk is violent and sentimental, even to the point of tearfulness, virtuously despises emotional people when he is sober. I well remember the 1920s, when the almost hysterically emotional *Action Française* used to heap ridicule on "le violoncelle de Briand." Alain Besançon (1967) admirably analyzed the strange figure of the New Man— the indifferent, disembodied, emotionally frozen ideal of the Russian intelligentsia, which was itself so deeply emotional and passionate in reality. Few people show themselves in real life more violently emotional than the theoreticians of contemporary "acedia" (a word to the wise!).

6. This girl quickly got rid of her parrot when she realized that she was becoming attached to it.

7. In a highly revealing passage, Plutarch (*Erotikon* 760B) noted, apropos of events that occurred in Rome and Argos, that, though some Greeks consented to yield their wives to tyrants, none of them ever yielded his young male lover. Nothing sheds a more brutal light on the nature of marital relations in societies that fostered male homosexuality. It seems to me, however, that in Athens the relation between the spouses was less degraded than some believe. In Aristophanes' *Lysistrata*, the men, deprived

of sexual relations, ardently wish to make love to their own wives and not to prostitutes, young boys, or catamites. Similarly, at the end of Xenophon's *Symposium*, the married men, who have just seen a dance mimicking passionate sexual relations, rush home to satisfy their aroused passion in the arms of their wives, while the single men swear to get married as soon as possible. For a more detailed discussion of this point, see Devereux 1967b.

8. I have been credibly informed that the servants of a psychoanalytic clinic located in an economically backward and highly emotional country gave the analysts a great deal of trouble, for they used to peek through the keyholes of the consulting rooms and even through the transoms, convinced that, sooner or later, they would witness a sexual act.

9. Even the most conventional and conservative historians admit that a considerable part of the American Constitution is intended to reassure those who dread a federal "tyranny." The Athenians' panic dread of tyranny has been analyzed in depth by Andrewes (1956) and by Forrest (1966).

10. Among the matrilineal Khasi, milk was considered an excrement (Gurdon 1904).

11. The American voters knew a day of greatness and glory when they elected Truman because of his courage and frankness. The Athenians and the English had their hour of greatness when the former chose to follow Themistocles and the latter elected Churchill, though both could promise nothing but "blood and sweat and tears."

12. See, for example, the learned but very specious analysis of courtly love by Nelli (1966) and the astounding conclusions he draws from it regarding our own culture. See also the recent (1969) fashion of handbags for "men."

13. *Mutatis mutandis*, the rebel is also subjected to the same imperative (chap. 3).

14. There is no contradiction here. Stendhal's critique of the nineteenth century is at once the product and the glory of the nineteenth century. The twentieth century is unable to produce a critique that is both constructive and affirmative.

CHAPTER ELEVEN

1. A sexual pervert had the habit of hanging himself periodically because this caused him to ejaculate. In the end he accidentally killed himself.

2. The perfect example of this is the transformation of some external stimulus, likely to awaken the sleeper, into "dreamable" material (Devereux 1976a, chap. 8).

3. See also an Arizona Indian's blood phobia (Hrdlička 1908) and the proneness to faint at the sight of blood exhibited by a servant of the sheik Ousama, a Syrian lord of the period of the Crusades (Hitti 1929).

CHAPTER TWELVE

1. I assume that, in doing so, he upset the beverage he had brought for his parents, frustrating them "accidentally on purpose."

CHAPTER THIRTEEN

1. The term "spatial" is quite appropriate in this context, since society and the behavior of its members can be viewed as a multidimensional en-

semble, i.e., as a "space" in the sense in which that term is used in mathematics (Devereux 1940 [1978a, chap. 1]).

2. I hardly need add that, within the context of this paragraph, the term "psychological" must be interpreted in a broad and almost figurative sense, which includes also witchcraft, haunting by ghosts, and other unusual phenomena of that sort. In other words, what is meant here by "psychological" is simply the primitive's subjective or objective assertion that the "singularity" affects primarily the *"Self"*—the very nucleus of the total personality.

3. This means that he is attempting to create a contractual kinship relationship of the type Kemlin (1917) calls a (nonmatrimonial) alliance.

4. The connection dumb = mute, stupid is more convincing in English than in French. *Barbaroi*, the name the Greeks gave to non-Greeks, to whom they felt superior, was thought to mimic the "confused" speech of strangers.

5. The mass raping of adulterous wives among the Cheyenne (Llewellyn and Hoebel 1941) is apparently meant to condition such women against sex. The mass raping and clitoridectomization of the phallic-aggressive Mohave *kamalōy* (Devereux 1948c) and the raping of the masculine lesbian (Devereux 1937b, 1961a [2d rev. ed., 1969]) are supposed to refeminize them. I note in passing that only the lesbian who plays the masculine role is raped in this manner; her partner is not.

6. I have explained elsewhere (1966a) why, precisely because I accept without any reservations Freud's theory of "object" relations, I prefer to speak of "personal" relations. Indeed, both etymologically and semantically the term "object" brings to mind exactly the opposite of what Freud calls "object relations." Hence I reserve the term "(partial) object relations" for relations with the "(partial) objects" of the pregenital stages, for *these* relations do involve genuine "(partial) objects," i.e., nonpersons.

7. On the basis of my own clinical experience, I am inclined to question the increasing tendency to diagnose (in order to avoid anxiety and pessimism) as "borderline" certain conditions that in my estimation are genuine psychoses, although of moderate intensity and/or affecting only limited areas of the personality in a truly incapacitating way. The general problem of hyphenated or "mixed" diagnoses is discussed in chapter 9.

8. This implies that the expression "differential diagnosis" is a pleonasm (see Liddell-Scott-Jones, *A Greek-English Lexicon*, 9th ed. s.v. διάγνωσις).

9. The reader is reminded that paranoiacs are notoriously hard to identify, for they manage to justify their delusions in a most "logical" manner and display great skill in concealing them.

10. Thus, though Lowie always disclaimed knowledge of psychology, he was by temperament a good practical psychologist, with a feeling for the psychological.

CHAPTER FIFTEEN

1. Insofar as reliance may be placed on reports of so-called "wolf-children" in India (Gesell 1941; Mandelbaum 1943; Singh 1942), their data also support the views just expressed.

2. This formulation is in accordance with Mach's dictum that there are no laws in nature apart from those we *put into*, or *ascribe to*, nature in the course of our attempts to generalize from our observations of discrete phenomena.

3. This is implicit in Durkheim's conception of *les catégories de l'esprit humain*. Indeed, every culture "has" a kinship system, an economic system, a system of laws, of knowledge, of religion, and so forth, though the actual kinship system, for example, may differ from tribe to tribe. In the present context—that is, as regards the *use* one makes of these categories in scientific discourse—it is totally irrelevant whether these "structuring" categories *exist in* culture or are *put into* or *ascribed to* culture by the observer, who may even himself be a member of the culture under consideration (chap. 16).

4. It is desirable to remind the reader of the reasons that led me to modify my terminology. Originally, I invented the term "transcultural psychotherapy" to stress the difference between this approach and "cross-cultural psychotherapy." Unfortunately, the term was borrowed (without reference to its authorship, of course) and, what is more serious, was stripped of the special meaning I had given it. Thus "transcultural psychiatry" acquired the meaning of "cross-cultural psychiatry" and, even more broadly, of ethnopsychiatry. As it is impossible for me to reverse this shift of meaning, I am forced to dissociate myself from it by offering "metacultural psychotherapy" as a replacement for "transcultural psychotherapy" [1969].

5. Indeed, the more fully one understands the deeper psychological factors that impelled John Doe to give his wife a pair of earrings on their first wedding anniversary, the less fully one understands this act in social and cultural terms, that is, in terms of the customs, mores, and folkways regulating the relationship between spouses, the celebration of anniversaries, the choice of appropriate gifts, and so forth, in our own society.

6. The "deculturation" of a cultural item refers to the process by which it is stripped of the meaning it has in the culture. If, for example, I use a violin for firewood, I am "deculturating" it (chap. 2).

7. The desire of these patients to "teach" me English may have been partly motivated by the fact that, in my analytic work, I always use the simplest and most homely modes of expression at my disposal. In addition, I usually avoid all abstractions, using, instead, figurative expressions consisting, whenever possible, of visual types of imagery, because my ethnological field experience has led me to believe that visual figures of speech are especially easily understood and may even be particularly suitable for communication with at least the upper layers of the unconscious.

8. I have discussed elsewhere (1951b) the distinction between confrontations and interpretations, especially as regards timing.

9. At the beginning of the analysis, she once angrily accused me of staring at her breasts, which I could have stared at all day long without seeing anything worth the trouble, since she was perfectly flat-chested—a fact she could apparently not acknowledge, particularly because breasts also represented phallic organs for her.

10. This incident well illustrates the relationship of complementarity between the cultural and the psychoanalytic understanding of human behavior.

CHAPTER SIXTEEN

1. An ape cannot commit incest because, like Thyestes, he is advised to do so by an oracle (Apollodorus 2. 13–14; Hyginus, *Fabulae* 87–88; Servius on Virgil's *Aeneid* 11. 262); or because, like a Ba Thonga big-game hunter

(Junod 1927), he wishes to become as terrible as the beast he hunts; or because, like an Azande king (Ford 1951), it is his royal privilege; or because, as in Swedish peasant families (Riemer 1940), a sick woman's adolescent daughter first becomes her father's housekeeper and then his mistress.

2. This is indirectly confirmed by the studies of Mead (1932).

3. This finding proves that the frenzied destruction of property at funerals represents "spiteful giving" (Devereux 1961a).

4. I say "supposed" because, even though such cases assuredly involve regression, a "regression in the service of the ego" seems impossible to me (though I concede that everything depends on the manner in which "the ego" is defined).

5. Pseudo-sublimations such as shamanism will be ignored in this context since their neurotic basis is discussed in chapter 1.

6. One thinks here at once of the Greek *amphisbaina*.

7. Compare how El-Kronos "first" decapitated his daughter and "then" circumcised himself (Philo of Byblos).

8. An incompletely castrated horse, capable of having erections and at times even able to engage in coitus but incapable of procreation.

9. For a discussion of the neurotic exploitation of marginal cultural phenomena, such as magical thinking and superstition, see Devereux 1954c.

10. This might explain why Hungary, one of the last European countries to be modernized, has produced so many first-rate scientists and why Russia, whose modernization is even more recent, was the first to devise spaceships. The speed with which China evolved atomic and nuclear power seems to have surprised some. It did not surprise me, for, taking into account the still more recent modernization of China, I predicted it in a lecture given at Columbia University in 1960.

11. But not of the rowdyism of the scientist!

12. A striking detail remains to be noted. Neither this colleague nor I (until quite recently) realized that a simple "cohabitation" with the (condom-like) rubber sheathing of one's own penis would have been possible (from the inside) *without* first stepping out of this rubber "skin" and then pushing inside the portion that had formerly covered the penis, so as to provide the shed (and inflated?) rubber "skin" with a "vagina." This complicated fantasy-maneuver must have been inspired by an unconscious wish to create a female double of oneself with whom one could copulate as though it were a female twin.

Bibliography

WORKS BY GEORGE DEVEREUX

Where republication data are given in parentheses at the end of an item, the later, revised, edition should be consulted.

1933–35 Sedang Field Notes. Ms.

1937a Functioning Units in Hà(rhn)de:a(ng) Society. *Primitive Man* 10:1–7.

1937b Institutionalized Homosexuality of the Mohave Indians. *Human Biology* 9:498–527.

1937c L'Envoûtement chez les Indiens mohave. *Journal de la Société des Américanistes de Paris* n.s. 29:405–12.

1938 Principles of Hà(rhn)de:a(ng) Divination. *Man* 38:125–27.

1939a Maladjustment and Social Neurosis. *American Sociological Review* 4:844–51.

1939b Mohave Culture and Personality. *Character and Personality* 8:91–109.

1939c The Social and Cultural Implications of Incest among the Mohave Indians. *Psychoanalytic Quarterly* 8:510–33.

1940 A Conceptual Scheme of Society. *American Journal of Sociology* 54:687–706. (Now chap. 1 of Devereux 1978a.)

1941 Mohave Beliefs concerning Twins. *American Anthropologist* n.s. 43:573–92.

1942a Social Structure and the Economy of Affective Bonds. *Psychoanalytic Review* 29:303–14.

1942b The Mental Hygiene of the American Indian. *Mental Hygiene* 26:71–84.

1942c Primitive Psychiatry (Part 2). *Bulletin of the History of Medicine* 11:522–42.

1943 Antagonistic Acculturation. With E. M. Loeb. *American Sociological Review* 7:133–47. (Now chap. 8 of Devereux 1978a.)

1944a A Note on Classical Chinese Penological Thought. *Journal of Criminal Psychopathology* 5:735–44.

1944b The Social Structure of a Schizophrenia Ward and Its Therapeutic Fitness. *Journal of Clinical Psychopathology* 6:231–65.

1945 The Logical Foundations of Culture and Personality Studies. *Transactions of the New York Academy of Sciences* 2d ser. 7:110–30. (Now chap. 4 of Devereux 1978a.)

1946a Quelques aspects de la psychanalyse aux Etats-Unis. *Les Temps modernes* 1:229–315.

1946b La Chasse collective au lapin chez les Hopi, Oraibi, Arizona.

Journal de la Société des Américanistes de Paris n.s. 33:63–90.

1947   Mohave Orality: An Analysis of Nursing and Weaning Customs. *Psychoanalytic Quarterly* 16:519–46.

1948a   Mohave Pregnancy. *Acta Americana* 6:89–116.

1948b   Mohave Indian Obstetrics. *American Imago* 5:95–139.

1948c   The Mohave Indian Kamalo:y. *Journal of Clinical Psychopathology* 9:433–57.

1949a   The Psychological "Date" of Dreams. *Psychiatric Quarterly Supplement* 23:127–30.

1949b   Post-Partum Parental Observances of the Mohave Indians. *Transactions of the Kansas Academy of Science* 52:458–65.

1950a   Heterosexual Behavior of the Mohave Indians. In *Psychoanalysis and the Social Sciences,* edited by Géza Róheim, vol. 2. New York: International Universities Press.

1950b   Education and Discipline in Mohave Society. *Primitive Man* 23:85–102.

1951a   *Reality and Dream: The Psychotherapy of a Plains Indian.* New York. (2d rev. ed., New York: New York University Press and Anchor Books, 1969.)

1951b   Some Criteria for the Timing of Confrontation and Interpretations. *International Journal of Psycho-Analysis* 32:19–24.

1951c   Mohave Indian Verbal and Motor Profanity. In *Psychoanalysis and the Social Sciences,* vol. 3, edited by Warner Muensterberger and Sidney Axelrad. New York.

1951d   The Primal Scene and Juvenile Heterosexuality in Mohave Society. In *Psychoanalysis and Culture,* edited by G. B. Wilbur and Warner Muensterberger. New York.

1951e   Cultural and Characterological Traits of the Mohave Related to the Anal Stage of Psychosexual Development. *Psychoanalytic Quarterly* 20:398–422.

1951f   Three Technical Problems in the Psychotherapy of Plains Indian Patients. *American Journal of Psychotherapy* 5:411–23.

1951g   Logical Status and Methodological Problems of Research in Clinical Psychiatry. *Psychiatry* 14:327–30.

1952   Practical Problems of Conceptual Psychiatric Research. *Psychiatry* 15:189–92.

1953a   *Psychoanalysis and the Occult.* George Devereux, ed. New York: International Universities Press. (Reprinted, 1970.)

1953b   Why Oedipus Killed Laius: A Note on the Complementary Oedipus Complex. *International Journal of Psycho-Analysis* 34:132–41.

1954a   Primitive Genital Mutilations in a Neurotic's Dream. *Journal of the American Psychoanalytic Association* 2:483–92.

1954b   The Denial of the Anus in Neurosis and Culture. *Bulletin of the Philadelphia Association for Psychoanalysis* 4:24–47.

1954c   Belief, Superstition, and Symptom. *Samiksa* 8:210–15.

1955a   Anthropological Data Suggesting Unexplored Unconscious

Attitudes toward and in Unwed Mothers. *Archives of Criminal Psychodynamics* 1:564–76.

1955b   *A Study of Abortion in Primitive Societies.* New York: Julian. (Now see Devereux 1976c.)

1955c   Charismatic Leadership and Crisis. In *Psychoanalysis and the Social Sciences,* vol. 4, edited by Warner Muensterberger and Sidney Axelrad. New York.

1955d   A Counteroedipal Episode in Homer's *Iliad. Bulletin of the Philadelphia Association for Psychoanalysis* 4:90–97.

1956a   *Therapeutic Education.* New York: Harper & Bros.

1956b   Mohave Dreams of Omen and Power. *Tomorrow* 4:17–24.

1956c   The Origins of Shamanistic Power as Reflected in a Neurosis. *Revue internationale d'ethnopsychologie normale et pathologique* 1:19–28.

1956d   Review of Eaton and Weil 1955. *American Anthropologist* 58:211–12.

1957a   Penelope's Character. *Psychoanalytic Quarterly* 26:378–86.

1957b   Dream Learning and Individual Ritual Differences in Mohave Shamanism. *American Anthropologist* 59:1036–45. (Now chap. 9 of Devereux 1978a.)

1957c   The Criminal Responsibility of the Insane. Ms. Address given at the inauguration of the W. A. Bryant Center of Worcester State Hospital, Worcester, Mass.

1958a   Cultural Thought Models in Primitive and Modern Psychiatric Theories. *Psychiatry* 21:359–74. (Now chap. 10 of Devereux 1978a.)

1958b   The Anthropological Roots of Psychoanalysis. In *Psychoanalytic Education,* vol. 5 of *Science and Psychoanalysis,* edited by Jules Masserman. New York: Grune & Stratton.

1959a   The Nature of the Bizarre. *Journal of the Hillside Hospital* 8:266–78.

1959b   Why Oedipus Blinded Himself. Ms. Lecture, Harvard Medical School, Department of Psychiatry. (Now published as "The Self-Blinding of Oidipous in Sophokles' *Oidipous Tyrannos,*" *Journal of Hellenic Studies* 93 [1973]:36–49.)

1960a   The Female Castration Complex and Its Repercussions in Modesty, Appearance, and Courtship Etiquette. *American Imago* 17:1–19.

1960b   Schizophrenia vs. Neurosis and the Use of "Premature" Deep Interpretations as Confrontations in Classical and in Direct Analysis. *Psychiatric Quarterly* 34:710–21.

1961a   Mohave Ethnopsychiatry and Suicide. *Bureau of American Ethnology Bulletin* no. 175. (2d rev. ed. Washington, D.C.: Smithsonian Institution, 1969.)

1961b   Two Types of Modal Personality Models. In *Studying Personality Cross-Culturally,* edited by Bert Kaplan. Evanston, Ill.: Row, Peterson. (Now chap. 5 of Devereux 1978a.)

1961c   Art and Mythology: A General Theory. In *Studying Personality Cross-Culturally,* edited by Bert Kaplan. Evanston, Ill.: Row, Peterson. (A French translation appears in *Tragédie et poésie grecques,* chap. 1. Paris: Flammarion, 1975.)

1961d   The Non-Recognition of the Patient by the Therapist. With F. H. Hoffman. *Psychoanalysis and Psychoanalytic Review* 48:41–61.

1963   Sociopolitical Function of the Oedipus Myth in Early Greece. *Psychoanalytic Quarterly* 32:205–14.

1964   Ethnopsychological Aspects of the Terms "Deaf" and "Dumb." *Anthropological Quarterly* 37:68–71.

1965a   La Psychanalyse et l'histoire: Une application à l'histoire de Sparte. *Annales* 20:18–44.

1965b   A Psychoanalytic Study of Contraception. *Journal of Sex Research* 1:105–34.

1965c   Considérations ethnopsychanalytiques sur la notion de parenté. *L'Homme* 5:224–47. (Appears in English as chap. 7 of Devereux 1978a.)

1966a   Loss of Identity, Impairment of Relationships, Reading Disability. *Psychoanalytic Quarterly* 35:18–39.

1966b   Mumbling. *Journal of the American Psychoanalytic Association* 14:478–84.

1966c   La Nature du stress. *Revue de médecine psychosomatique* 8:103–13. (Appears in English as chap. 2 of Devereux 1978a.)

1966d   Transference, Screen Memory, and the Temporal Ego. *Journal of Nervous and Mental Disease* 143:318–23.

1967a   La Rénonciation à l'identité: défense contre l'anéantissement. *Revue française de psychanalyse* 31:101–42.

1967b   Greek Pseudo-Homosexuality. *Symbolae Osloenses* 42:69–92.

1967c   *From Anxiety to Method in the Behavioral Sciences.* Paris and The Hague: Mouton.

1967d   Observation and Belief in Aischylos' Accounts of Dreams. *Psychotherapy and Psychosomatics* 15:114–34. (Appears in French as "L'Observation et la croyance dans la narration des rêves chez Aischylos" in *Tragédie et poésie grecques,* chap. 3. Paris: Flammarion, 1975.)

1968a   L'Image de l'enfant dans deux tribus, mohave et sedang, et son importance pour la psychiatrie infantile. *Revue de neuropsychiatrie infantile* 16:375–90.

1968b   Considérations psychanalytiques sur la divination, particulièrement en Grèce. In *La Divination,* edited by A. Caquot and M. Leibovici, vol. 2. Paris: Presses Universitaires de France.

1968c   L'Etat dépressif et le rêve de Ménélas. *Revue des études grecques* 81:12–15. (Incorporated into chap. 3 of Devereux 1976a.)

1968d Orthopraxis. *Psychiatric Quarterly* 42:726–37.

1970 La Naissance d'Aphrodite. In *Echanges et communications* (*Mélanges Lévi-Strauss*). Paris and The Hague: Mouton.

1975 *Tragédie et poésie grecques*. Paris: Flammarion.

1976a *Dreams in Greek Tragedy*. Oxford: Blackwell. Berkeley: University of California Press.

1976b Autocaractérisations de quatre Sedang. In *L'Autre et ailleurs,* edited by Jean Poirier and François Raveau. Paris: Berger-Lévrault.

1976c *A Study of Abortion in Primitive Societies*. 2d rev. ed. New York: International Universities Press.

1978a *Ethnopsychoanalysis: Psychoanalysis and Anthropology as Complementary Frames of Reference*. Berkeley: University of California Press.

1978b The Cultural Implementation of Defense Mechanisms. *Ethnopsychiatrica* 1:79–116.

1978c Culture and Symptomatology. *Ethnopsychiatrica* 1:201–12.

WORKS BY OTHER AUTHORS

Aberle, D. F. 1952. Arctic Hysteria and Latah in Mongolia. *Transactions of the New York Academy of Sciences* 2d ser. 14:291–97.

Abraham, Karl. 1927. Restrictions and Transformations of Scoptophilia in Psycho-Neurotics. *Selected Papers of Karl Abraham, M.D.* London: Hogarth Press.

Ackerknecht, Erwin Heinz. 1943. Psychopathology, Primitive Medicine, and Primitive Culture. *Bulletin of the History of Medicine* 14: 30–67.

Adelman, Fred. 1955. Toward a Psycho-Cultural Interpretation of Latah. *Davidson Journal of Anthropology* 1:69–76.

Alexander, Franz. 1931. Buddhistic Training as an Artificial Catatonia. *Psychoanalytic Review* 18:129–45.

Alexander, Leo. 1948. Sociopsychologic Structure of the S.S. *Archives of Neurology and Psychiatry* 59:622–34.

Andrewes, Antony. 1956. *The Greek Tyrants*. London: Hutchinson's University Library.

Angyal, András. 1938. The Concept of Bionegativity. *Psychiatry* 1: 303–7.

Anonymous. n.d. *Gems of Chinese Literature* (The Progress). n.p.

Anonymous. 1930. *Hikayat Hang Toeah*. 3 vols. Java: Balei Poestaka Veltevreden. (German translation, *Hikayat Hang Tuah*. 2 vols. Munich: Georg Müller, 1922.)

Anton, G. 1904. Nerven- und Geisteserkrankungen in der Zeit der Geschlechtsreife. *Wiener klinische Wochenschrift* 17:1161–67.

Arensberg, Conrad M. 1950. *The Irish Countryman: An Anthropological Study*. Rev. ed. New York: Macmillan.

———, and Kimball, Solon T. 1940. *Family and Community in Ireland*. Cambridge, Mass.: Harvard University Press.

Aubin, H. 1939. Introduction à l'étude de la psychiatrie chez les Noirs. *Annales médico-psychologiques* 97:1–29, 181–213.

Barbosa, Duarte (d. 1521; supposed author). 1921. *The Book of Duarte Barbosa*, vol. 1. In 2 vols. Translated from the Portuguese text and edited by Mansel Longworth Dames. London: The Hakluyt Society.

Barchillon, José. 1963. Analysis of a Woman with Incipient Rheumatoid Arthritis. *International Journal of Psycho-Analysis* 44:163–77.

Bartemeier, L. H. 1950. Illness following Dream. *International Journal of Psycho-Analysis* 31:8–11.

Barton, Roy Franklin. 1938. *Philippine Pagans*. London.

Bastide, Roger. 1965. *Sociologie des maladies mentales*. Paris: Flammarion. (English translation by Jean McNeil, *The Sociology of Mental Disorders*. London: Routledge & Kegan Paul, 1972.)

Beatty, Kenneth James. 1915. *Human Leopards: An Account of the Trials of Human Leopards before the Special Commission Court*. With a Preface by Sir William Brandford Griffith. London: H. Rees.

Benedict, Ruth. 1934a. *Patterns of Culture*. Boston and New York: Houghton Mifflin. (Paperback ed., 1961.)

———. 1934b. Anthropology and the Abnormal. *Journal of General Psychology* 10:59–82.

———. 1938. Continuities and Discontinuities in Cultural Conditioning. *Psychiatry* 1:161–67.

Bérard, Victor. 1927–32. *Les Navigations d'Ulysse*. 5 vols. Paris: A. Colin.

Bernatzik, Hugo A. 1958. With the collaboration of Emmy Bernatzik. *The Spirits of the Yellow Leaves*. London: R. Hale. (Published in German as *Die Geister der gelben Blätter*. Gütersloh: C. Bertelsmann, 1951.)

Berndt, R. M. 1952–53. A Cargo Movement in the East Central Highlands of New Guinea. *Oceania* 23:40–65, 137–58, 202–34.

Besançon, Alain. 1967. *Le Tsarévitch immolé: La symbolique de la li dans la culture russe*. Paris: Plon, 1967.

———. 1977. *Les origines intellectuelles du léninisme*. Paris: Callman-Lévy.

Bleuler, Eugen. 1912. *The Theory of Schizophrenic Negativism*. Nervous and Mental Disease Monographs, no. 11.

Boardman, John. 1964. *The Greeks Overseas*. Harmondsworth, Eng.: Pelican.

Boas, Franz. 1907. The Eskimo of Baffin Land and Hudson Bay. *American Museum of Natural History Bulletin*, no. 15.

Boehm, Felix. 1935. Anthropophagy: Its Forms and Motives. *International Journal of Psycho-Analysis* 16:9–21.

Bogoras, Waldemar. 1904–9. The Chukchee. *The Jesup North Pacific Expedition, Memoir of the American Museum of Natural History* 7:1.

Boyer, L. B. 1961. Notes on the Personality Structure of a North American Indian Shaman. *Journal of the Hillside Hospital* 10:14–33.

———. 1962. Remarks on the Personality of Shamans. Pp. 233–54 in

The Psychoanalytic Study of Society, vol. 2, edited by Warner Muenster-berg and Sidney Axelrad. New York: International Universities Press.

―――. 1964. Further Remarks concerning Shamans and Shamanism. *Israel Annals of Psychiatry and Related Disciplines* 2:235–57.

―――; Klopfer, Bruno; and Kawai, Hayao. 1964. Comparisons of the Shamans and Pseudo-Shamans of the Apaches of the Mescalero Indian Reservation: A Rorschach Study. *Journal of Projective Techniques* 28: 173–80.

Bridgman, Percy Williams. 1932. *The Logic of Modern Physics*. New York: Macmillan.

Brion, Marcel. 1931. *La Vie des Huns*. Paris: Gallimard.

Burnet, John. 1930. *Early Greek Philosophy*. London: Black.

Burkert, Walter. 1972. *Homo necans*. Berlin: de Gruyter.

Burrow, Trigant. 1937. *The Biology of Human Conflict*. New York: Macmillan.

Cannon, Walter Bradford. 1939. *The Wisdom of the Body*. New York: Norton.

Caspar, Franz. 1953. Some Sex Beliefs and Practices of the Tupari Indians (Western Brazil). *Revista do Museu Paulista* n.s. 7:203–44.

Chanson de Damsan: Légende radé du XVIe siècle. 1927. Transcribed in French by Leopold Sabatier. Paris: Leblanc & Trautmann.

Chowning, Ann. 1961. Amok and Aggression in the d'Entrecasteaux. Pp. 78–83 in the *Proceedings* of the 1961 Annual Spring Meeting of the American Ethnological Society (Seattle, Wash.).

Cleckley, Hervey Milton. 1950. *The Mask of Sanity: An Attempt to Clarify Some Issues about the Psychopathic Personality*. 2d ed. Saint Louis: Mosby.

Clermont Tonnerre, Elisabeth (de Gramont), duchesse de. 1928. *Mé-moires*. Vol. 1: *Au temps des équipages*. Paris: B. Grasset.

Clifford, Sir Hugh. 1898. *Studies in Brown Humanity: Being Scrawls & Smudges in Sepia, White, and Yellow*. London: G. Richards.

―――. 1922a. The Amok of Dâto' Kâja Bîji Dĕrja. In *The Further Side of Silence*. Garden City, N.Y.: Doubleday, Page.

―――. 1922b. The Experiences of Râja Haji Hamid. Ibid.

―――. 1927. In the Days When the Land Was Free. In *Court and Kampong: Being Tales and Sketches of Native Life in the Malay Penin-sula*. London: G. Richards.

Coodley, Alfred. 1966. Discussion of Devereux, "The Cannibalistic Impulses of Children" (1966; now chap. 5 of this book). *Psychoanalytic Forum* 1:125.

Cook, A. B. 1914, 1940. *Zeus: A Study in Ancient Religion*. Vols. 1, 3. Cambridge, Eng.: At the University Press.

Corbett, James Edward. 1946. *Man-Eaters of Kumaon*. London and New York: Oxford University Press.

Correa, Gaspar (16th century). 1858. *Lendas da India*. 2 vols. London.

Czaplicka, Marie Antoinette. 1914. *Aboriginal Siberia: A Study in So-*

cial Anthropology. With a Preface by R. R. Marett. Oxford: Clarendon Press.

Davis, Kingsley. 1937. The Sociology of Prostitution. *American Sociological Review* 2:744–55.

————. 1939. Illegitimacy and the Social Structure. *American Journal of Sociology* 45:215–33.

————. 1940. A Case of Extreme Social Isolation of a Child. *American Journal of Sociology* 45:554–65.

Dekker, Edward Douwes. *See* Multatuli.

Dembowitz, N. 1945. Psychiatry amongst West African Troops. *Journal of the Royal Army Medical Corps* 84:70–74.

Dement, W. C. 1967. The Psychophysiology of the Dream. In *The Dream and Human Societies*, edited by G. E. von Grunebaum and Roger Caillois. Berkeley and Los Angeles: University of California Press.

Deutsch, Helene. 1944–45. *The Psychology of Women: A Psychoanalytic Interpretation*. With a Foreword by Stanley Cobb. 2 vols. New York: Grune & Stratton.

Dhunjibhoy, J. E. 1930. A Brief Résumé of the Types of Insanity Commonly Met With in India, with a Full Description of "Indian Hemp Insanity," Peculiar to the Country. *Journal of Mental Science* 76:254–64.

Dodds, E. R. 1951. *The Greeks and the Irrational*. Berkeley: University of California Press.

————. 1965. *Pagan and Christian in an Age of Anxiety: Some Aspects of Religious Experience from Marcus Aurelius to Constantine*. Cambridge, Eng.: At the University Press.

Dollard, John. 1937. *Caste and Class in a Southern Town*. New Haven: Yale University Press. London: Oxford University Press.

———— et al. 1939. *Frustration and Aggression*. New Haven: Yale University Press. London: Oxford University Press.

Domarus, Eilhard von. 1948. Anthropology and Psychotherapy. *American Journal of Psychotherapy* 2:603–14.

Dumas, Georges. 1946. *Le Surnaturel et les dieux d'après la maladie mentale*. Paris.

Dumézil, Georges. 1958. *L'Idéologie tripartie des Indo-Européens*. Brussels: Latomus.

Dunham, H. Warren. 1937. The Ecology of Functional Psychoses in Chicago. *American Sociological Review* 2:467–79.

Dupeyrat, André. 1954. *Savage Papua: A Missionary among Cannibals*. Preface by Paul Claudel. Translated by Erik and Denyse Demauny. New York: Dutton.

Durkheim, Emile. 1912. *Les Formes élémentaires de la vie religieuse*. Paris: Alcan. (English translation by Joseph W. Swain, *Elementary Forms of the Religious Life*. Glencoe, Ill.: Free Press, 1954. Reprinted, London: Allen & Unwin, 1976.)

Dyson, W. S., and Fuchs, V. E. 1937. The Elmolo. *Journal of the Royal Anthropological Institute* 67:327–38.

Eaton, Joseph W., and Weil, Robert J. 1955. *Culture and Mental Dis-*

orders: A Comparative Study of the Hutterites and Other Populations.
Glencoe, Ill.: Free Press.

Ehrenwald, Jan. 1948. *Telepathy and Medical Psychology.* New York, Norton.

Ekstein, Rudolf. 1966. Discussion of Devereux, "The Cannibalistic Impulses of Children" (1966; now chap. 5 of this book). *Psychoanalytic Forum* 1:127–28.

Ellis, F. H. 1951. Patterns of Aggression and the War Cult in Southwestern Pueblos. *Southwestern Journal of Anthropology* 7:177–201.

Encyclopaedia Britannica. 1910. 11th ed. Article "Amuck Running."

Ewing, J. F. 1955. Juramentado: Institutionalized Suicide among the Moros of the Philippines. *Anthropological Quarterly* 28:148–55.

Fabing, H. D. 1956. On Going Berserk: A Neurochemical Inquiry. *American Journal of Psychiatry* 113:409–15.

Fairbairn, W. R. D. 1954. *An Object-Relations Theory of the Personality.* New York: Basic Books.

Faris, Robert E. L. 1934. Some Observations on the Incidence of Schizophrenia in Primitive Societies. *Journal of Abnormal and Social Psychology* 29:30–31.

———, and Dunham, H. Warren. 1939. *Mental Disorders in Urban Areas.* Chicago: University of Chicago Press.

Fathauer, George H. 1951. The Mohave "Ghost Doctor." *American Anthropologist* 53:605–7.

———. 1954. The Structure and Causation of Mohave Warfare. *Southwestern Journal of Anthropology* 10:97–118.

Fauconnier, Henri. 1930. *Malaisie.* Paris. (English translation by Eric Sutton, *The Soul of Malaya.* Oxford University Press, 1965.)

Ferenczi, Sándor. 1922. Stages in the Development of the Sense of Reality. In *Sex in Psycho-Analysis: Contributions to Psycho-Analysis.* Translated from the German by Ernest Jones, M.D. Boston: Badger. (Reprinted, New York: Basic Books, 1950.)

———. 1927a. Thinking and Muscle Innervation. In *Further Contributions to the Theory and Technique of Psycho-Analysis,* compiled by John Rickman; translated from the German by Jane Isabel Suttie et al. New York: Boni & Liveright. (Reprinted, New York: Basic Books, 1952.)

———. 1927b. Flatus as an Adult Prerogative. Ibid.

———. 1955. Confusion of Tongues between Adults and Children. In *Final Contributions to the Problems and Methods of Psychoanalysis.* Translated by Eric Mosbacher et al. With an Introduction by Clara Thompson. New York: Basic Books.

Fletcher, A. C., and La Flesche, F. 1906. The Omaha Tribe. *Bureau of American Ethnology Annual Report,* no. 27. Washington, D.C.

Ford, Clellan S., and Beach, Frank A. 1951. *Patterns of Sexual Behavior.* Foreword by Robert L. Dickinson. New York: Harper & Bros.

Forrest, W. G. 1966. *The Emergence of Greek Democracy: The Character of Greek Politics, 800–400 B.C.* London: Weidenfeld & Nicolson.

———. 1968. *A History of Sparta, 950–192 B.C.* London: Hutchinson.

Fortune, Reo F. 1932a. Omaha Secret Societies. *Columbia University Contributions to Anthropology*, vol. 14. (Reprinted, New York: AMS Press, 1976.)

———. 1932b. *Sorcerers of Dobu.* With an Introduction by B. Malinowski. London: Routledge.

François, H. K. B. von. 1929. *Napoleon I.* Berlin.

Freuchen, Peter. 1957. Personal communication.

Freud, Anna. 1946. *The Ego and the Mechanisms of Defense.* Translated from the German by Cecil Baines. New York: International Universities Press.

Freud, Sigmund. 1900. The Interpretation of Dreams. *SE,** vols. 4–5.

———. 1905a. Three Essays on the Theory of Sexuality. *SE*, vol. 7.

———. 1905b. Jokes and Their Relation to the Unconscious. *SE*, vol. 8.

———. 1907. Obsessive Actions and Religious Practices. *SE*, vol. 9.

———. 1911. Psycho-Analytic Notes on an Autobiographical Account of a Case of Paranoia. *SE*, vol. 9.

———. 1912a. On the Universal Tendency to Debasement in the Sphere of Love. *SE*, vol. 9.

———. 1912b. A Note on the Unconscious in Psycho-Analysis. *SE*, vol. 12.

———. 1912–13. Totem and Taboo. *SE*, vol. 13.

———. 1913. The Occurrence in Dreams of Material from Fairy-Tales. *SE*, vol. 12.

———. 1915. Repression. *SE*, vol. 14.

———. 1916. Those Wrecked by Success: Some Character-Types Met with in Psycho-Analytic Work, Part 2. *SE*, vol. 14.

———. 1916–17. New Introductory Lectures on Psycho-Analysis. *SE*, vol. 22.

———. 1918 [1917]. The Taboo of Virginity. *SE*, vol. 11.

———. 1919. The Uncanny. *SE*, vol. 17.

———. 1921. Group Psychology and the Analysis of the Ego. *SE*, vol. 18.

———. 1922. Some Neurotic Mechanisms in Jealousy, Paranoia, and Homosexuality. *SE*, vol. 18.

———. 1925. Moral Responsibility for the Content of Dreams. *SE*, vol. 19.

———. 1926. The Question of Lay Analysis. *SE*, vol. 20.

———. 1941 [1921]. Psycho-Analysis and Telepathy. *SE*, vol. 18.

Fromm, Erich. 1941. *Escape from Freedom.* New York: Farrar & Rinehart. (Avon paperback ed., 1971.)

Fromm-Reichmann, Frieda. 1946. Remarks on the Philosophy of Mental Disorder. *Psychiatry* 9:293–308.

———

* The English *Standard Edition* of Freud's works, translated from the German under the general editorship of James Strachey, in collaboration with Anna Freud. 24 vols. London: Hogarth Press, 1953–74.

Gesell, Arnold L. 1941. *Wolf Child and Human Child: The Life History of Kamala, the Wolf Girl.* New York and London: Harper & Bros.

Gifford, E. W. 1926. Yuma Dreams and Omens. *Journal of American Folklore* 39:39–66.

Gluckman, Max. 1954. *Rituals of Rebellion in South-East Africa.* Manchester, Eng.

Goldfrank, Esther Schiff. 1945. Changing Configurations in the Social Organization of a Blackfoot Tribe during the Reserve Period. *American Ethnological Society Monograph* 8.

Goldie, W. H. 1904. Maori Medical Lore. *Transactions of the New Zealand Institute* 37:1–120.

Granet, Marcel. 1930. *Chinese Civilization.* Translated from the French by Kathleen E. Innes and Mabel K. Brailsford. Reprint ed., New York: AMS Press, 1972.

Grinstein, Alexander. 1960. *The Index of Psychoanalytic Writings,* vol. 5. Preface by Ernest Jones, M.D. New York: International Universities Press.

Grousset, René. 1941. *L'Empire des steppes: Attila, Gengis-Khan, Tamarlan.* Paris: Payot. (English translation by Naomi Walford, *The Empire of the Steppes.* New Brunswick, N.J.: Rutgers University Press, 1970.)

Grubb, Wilfrid B. 1911. *An Unknown People in a Unknown Land.* London: Seeley.

Gurdon, P. R. T. 1904. Note on the Khasis, Syntengs, and Allied Tribes Inhabiting the Khasi and Jaintia Hills District in Assam. *Journal of the Asiatic Society of Bengal* 73, pt. 3, no. 4:57–74. Calcutta.

Hallowell, A. I. 1945. Sociopsychological Aspects of Acculturation. In *The Science of Man in the World Crisis,* edited by Ralph Linton. New York: Columbia University Press.

————. 1946. Some Psychological Characteristics of the Northeastern Indians. In *Man in Northeastern North America: Papers of the Robert S. Peabody Foundation for Archaeology,* vol. 3. Andover, Mass.

Hančar, Franz. 1955. *Das Pferd in prähistorischer und frührer historischer Zeit.* Vienna: Herold.

Handy, E. S. C.; Pukui, M. K.; and Livermore, K. 1934. Outline of Hawaiian Physical Therapeutics. *B. P. Bishop Museum Bulletin,* no. 26.

Harrison, Jane Ellen. 1922. *Prolegomena to the Study of Greek Religion.* 3d ed. Cambridge, Eng.: At the University Press.

Hartmann, Heinz. 1950. Comments on the Psychoanalytic Theory of the Ego. In *The Psychoanalytic Study of the Child,* edited by Ruth S. Eissler et al., vol. 5. New York: International Universities Press.

————; Kris, Ernst; and Loewenstein, Rudolph. 1947. Comments on the Formation of Psychic Structure. Ibid., vol. 2.

Hawke, C. C. 1950. Castration and Sex Crimes. *Journal of the Kansas Medical Society* 51:470–73.

Henry, Jules. 1951. The Inner Experience of Culture. *Psychiatry* 14: 87–103.

Hitschmann, E., and Bergler, E. 1936. Frigidity in Women. *Nervous and Mental Disease Monographs*, no. 60. New York.

Hollingshead, August de B., and Redlich, Frederick C. 1958. *Social Class and Mental Illness: A Community Study*. New York: Wiley.

Honigmann, John. 1954. *Culture and Personality*. New York: Harper & Bros. (Reprinted, Westwood Conn.: Greenwood Press, 1973.)

———. 1960. Review of M. K. Opler, ed., *Culture and Mental Health*. *American Anthropologist* n.s. 62:920–92.

Howitt, Alfred W. 1904. *The Native Tribes of South-East Australia*. London and New York: Macmillan.

Hrdlička, Aleš. 1908. Physiological and Medical Observations among the Indians of Southwestern United States and Northern Mexico. *Bureau of American Ethnology Bulletin*, no. 34. Washington, D.C.

Hundt, Joachim. 1935. *Der Traumglaube bei Homer*. Greifswald: Dallmeyer.

Hurley, Victor. 1936. *The Swish of the Kris: The Story of the Moros*. New York: Dutton.

Hymes, Dell. 1961. Linguistic Aspects of Cross-Cultural Personality Study. In *Studying Personality Cross-Culturally*, edited by Bert Kaplan. Evanston, Ill.: Row, Peterson.

Jackson, Hughlings. 1931–32. *The Selected Writings*, edited by J. Taylor et al. 2 vols. London.

Jeanmaire, H. 1939. Couroi et Courètes. *Travaux et mémoires de l'Université de Lille*, vol. 21.

Jenkins, R. L., and Glickman, Sylvia. 1946. Common Syndromes in Child Psychiatry. *American Journal of Orthopsychiatry* 16:244–61.

———. 1947. Patterns of Personality Organization among Delinquents. *The Nervous Child* 6:329–39.

Jokl, R. H. 1950. Psychic Determinism and Preservation of Sublimation in Classical Psychoanalytic Procedure. *Bulletin of the Menninger Clinic* 14:207–19.

[Jones, G. I.] 1951. *Basutoland Medicine Murder*. London: H. M. Stationery Office.

Jung, C. G. 1928. *Two Essays on Analytical Psychology*. Translated from the German by H. G. and C. F. Baynes. London: Baillière, Tindall & Cox.

Junod, Henri A. 1927. *The Life of a South African Tribe*. 2d rev. ed. 2 vols. London: Macmillan.

Kamal, Said. 1978. Observations ethnopsychiatriques des nomades d'Afghanistan. *Ethnopsychiatrica* 1:163–71.

Kardiner, Abram. 1939. *The Individual and His Society: The Psychodynamics of Primitive Social Organization*. With a foreword and two ethnological reports by Ralph Linton. New York: Columbia University Press.

Kemlin, J. E. 1917. Les Alliances chez les Reungao. *Bulletin de l'Ecole française d'Extrême-Orient* 17:1–119.

Kempf, Edward J. 1917. The Social and Sexual Behavior of Infrahuman

Primates, with Some Comparable Facts in Human Behavior. *Psychoanalytic Review* 4:127–54.

―――. 1920. *Psychopathology*. Saint Louis: Mosby.

Kobler, F. 1948. Description of an Acute Castration Fear, Based on Superstition. *Psychoanalytic Review* 35:285–89.

Korzybski, Alfred. 1933. *Science and Sanity: An Introduction to Non-Aristotelian Systems and General Semantics*. Lancaster, Pa., and New York: International Non-Aristotelian Library. (4th ed., Lakeville, Conn.: Institute of General Semantics, 1958.)

Krafft-Ebing, Richard von. 1875. *Lehrbuch der gerichtlichen Psychopathologie*. Stuttgart: F. Enke.

Kris, Ernst. 1952. *Psychoanalytic Explorations in Art*. New York: International Universities Press.

Kroeber, A. L. 1925. Handbook of the Indians of California. *Bureau of American Ethnology Bulletin*, no. 78. Washington, D.C. (Reprinted, Saint Clair Shores, Mich.: Scholarly Press, 1972.)

―――. 1934. Cultural Anthropology. In *The Problem of Mental Disorder*, edited by Madison Bentley and E. V. Cowdry. New York and London: McGraw-Hill. (Reprinted in Kroeber 1952.)

―――. 1948a. *Anthropology: Race, Language, Culture, Psychology, Prehistory*. Rev. ed. New York: Harcourt Brace.

―――. 1948b. Seven Mohave Myths. *University of California Anthropological Records*, vol. 9, no. 1.

―――. 1952. *The Nature of Culture*. Chicago: University of Chicago Press.

Kubie, Lawrence S. 1952. Problems and Techniques of Psychoanalytic Validation and Progress. In *Psychoanalysis as a Science*, edited by E. Pumpian-Mindlan. Stanford, Cal.: Stanford University Press.

―――. 1958. *Neurotic Distortion of the Creative Process*. Lawrence, Kans.: University of Kansas Press. (Noonday paperback ed., New York: Farrar, Straus & Giroux, 1961.)

La Barre, Weston. 1946. Social Cynosure and Social Structure. *Journal of Personality* 14:169–83.

―――. 1947. The Cultural Basis of Emotions and Gestures. *Journal of Personality* 16:49–64.

―――. 1954. *The Human Animal*. Chicago: University of Chicago Press. (Phoenix paperback ed., Chicago: University of Chicago Press, 1960.)

―――. 1966. The Dream, Charisma, and the Culture Hero. In *The Dream and Human Societies*, edited by G. E. von Grunebaum and Roger Caillois. Berkeley: University of California Press.

―――. 1970. *The Ghost Dance: The Origins of Religion*. New York: Doubleday.

Laforgue, René. 1944. *Psychopathologie de l'échec*. Paris: Payot.

Landes, Ruth. 1938. The Ojibwa Woman. *Columbia University Contributions to Anthropology*, no. 31. New York. (Reprinted, New York: AMS Press, 1969.)

Laubscher, B. J. F. 1937. *Sex, Custom, and Psychopathology.* London: Routledge & Kegan Paul.

Lévi-Strauss, Claude. 1949. *Les Structures élémentaires de la parenté.* Paris: Presses universitaires de France. (English rev. ed., *The Elementary Structures of Kinship.* Translated by James Harle Bell, John Richard von Sturmer, and Rodney Needham. London: Eyre & Spottiswoode, 1969. Paperback ed., Boston: Beacon Press, 1969.)

———. 1958. *Anthropologie structurale.* Paris: Plon. (English translation, *Structural Anthropology.* Vol. 1 translated by Claire Jacobson and Brooke Grundfest Schoepf; vol. 2 translated by M. Layton. New York: Basic Books, 1963, 1976.)

———. 1962. *Le Totémisme aujourd'hui.* Paris: Presses universitaires de France. (English translation by Rodney Needham, *Totemism.* Boston: Beacon Press, 1963.)

———. 1966. *Du miel aux cendres.* Paris: Plon. (English translation by John and Doreen Weightman, *From Honey to Ashes.* Vol. 2 of *An Introduction to a Science of Mythology.* New York: Harper & Row, 1973.)

Lévy-Bruhl, Lucien. 1910. *Les Fonctions mentales dans les sociétés inférieures.* Paris: Alcan.

———. 1922. *La Mentalité primitive.* Paris: Alcan. (English translation by Lilian A. Clare, *Primitive Mentality.* New York: Macmillan, 1923.)

———. 1927. *L'Ame primitive.* Paris: Alcan. (English translation by Lilian A. Clare, *The "Soul" of the Primitive.* New York: Macmillan, 1928.)

———. 1931. *Le Surnaturel et la nature dans la mentalité primitive.* Paris: Alcan.

Liddell, H. G., and Scott, Robert. 1940. *A Greek-English Lexicon.* Revised by H. S. Jones. 9th ed. Oxford: Clarendon Press.

Lincoln, Jackson S. 1935. *The Dream in Primitive Cultures.* London: Cresset Press.

Linton, Ralph. 1924. Totemism and the A.E.F. *American Anthropologist* 25:295–300.

———. 1933. The Tanala, a Hill Tribe of Madagascar. *Field Museum of Natural History, Anthropological Series,* vol. 22.

———. 1936. *The Study of Man.* New York: Appleton-Century.

———. 1938. Culture, Society, and the Individual. *Journal of Abnormal and Social Psychology* 33:425–36.

———. 1939. Foreword and two ethnological reports in Abram Kardiner, *The Individual and His Society.* New York: Columbia University Press. (Reprinted, Westport, Conn.: Greenwood, 1974.)

———. 1945. Contributions to *The Psychological Frontiers of Society,* edited by Abram Kardiner et al. New York: Columbia University Press.

———. 1956. Contribution to *Culture and Mental Disorders,* edited by George Devereux. Springfield, Ill.: Thomas.

Llewellyn, Karl N., and Hoebel, E. Adamson. 1941. *The Cheyenne Way: Conflict and Case Law in Primitive Jurisprudence.* Civilization of the American Indian, no. 21. Norman, Okla.: University of Oklahoma Press.

Lorenz, Konrad. 1954. *Man Meets Dog.* Translated by Marjorie Kerr Wilson. London: Methuen. (Penguin ed., 1965.)

———. 1965. *Das sogenannte Böse.* Vienna. (English translation by Marjorie Kerr Wilson, *On Aggression.* New York: Harcourt, Brace & World, 1966. Bantam paperback, 1967.)

———. 1966. Discussion of Devereux, "The Cannibalistic Impulses of Parents" (1966; now chap. 5 of this book). *Psychoanalytic Forum* 1: 128–29.

Lowenfeld, Henry. 1944. Some Aspects of a Compulsion Neurosis in a Changing Civilization. *Psychoanalytic Quarterly* 13:1–15.

Lowie, Robert H. 1924. *Primitive Religion.* New York: Boni & Liveright. (Paperback ed., Liveright, 1970.)

———. 1925a. Takes-the-Pipe, A Crow Warrior. In *American Indian Life,* edited by Elsie C. Parsons. New York: Viking Press. (Paperback ed., Lincoln: University of Nebraska Press, 1967.)

———. 1925b. A Crow Woman's Tale. Ibid.

———. 1925c. A Trial of Shamans. Ibid.

———. 1929. *Are We Civilized? Human Culture in Perspective.* New York: Harcourt, Brace.

———. 1933. The Family as a Social Unit. *Papers of the Michigan Academy of Science, Arts and Letters* 18:53–69.

———. 1935. *The Crow Indians.* New York: Farrar & Rinehart. (Paperback ed., New York: Holt, Rinehart & Winston, 1956.)

———. 1940. *An Introduction to Cultural Anthropology.* New York: Farrar & Rinehart.

Lundborg, H. 1902. Beitrag zur klinischen Analyse des Negativismus bei Geisteskranken. *Zentralblatt für Nervenheilkunde und Psychiatrie* 13:553–60.

McFarland, R. A. 1932. The Psychological Effects of Oxygen Deprivation (Anoxemia) on Human Behavior. *Archives of Psychology,* vol. 145.

MacIver, Robert M. 1936. *Community: A Sociological Study, Being an Attempt to Set Out the Nature and Fundamental Laws of Social Life.* London: Macmillan.

Maier, N. R. F. 1939. *Studies of Abnormal Behavior in the Rat.* New York and London: Harper & Bros.

Malinowski, Bronislaw. 1926. *Crime and Custom in Savage Society.* London: K. Paul, Trench, Trubner. New York: Harcourt, Brace. (Reprinted in the International Library of Psychological Philosophy and Scientific Mathematics Series, New York: Humanities Press, 1970.)

———. 1927a. *The Father in Primitive Psychology.* London: K. Paul, Trench, Trubner. (Paperback ed., New York: Norton, 1966.)

———. 1927b. *Sex and Repression in Savage Society.* London: K. Paul, Trench, Trubner. (Reprinted in the International Library of Psychological Philosophy and Scientific Mathematics Series, New York: Humanities Press, 1953.)

———. 1932. *The Sexual Life of Savages in North-Western Melanesia.* With a Preface by Havelock Ellis. 3d ed. London: Routledge. (Paperback ed., New York: Harcourt, Brace, Jovanovich, 1962.)

———. 1934. Preface to *Law and Order in Polynesia,* by H. Ian Hogbin. New York: Harcourt, Brace. (Reprint ed., New York: Cooper Square, 1973.)

———. 1944. *A Scientific Theory of Culture and Other Essays.* Chapel Hill: University of North Carolina Press.

Mandelbaum, David G. 1943. Wolf-Child Histories from India. *Journal of Social Psychology* 17:25–44.

Mauss, Marcel. 1950. *Sociologie et anthropologie.* With an Introduction by Claude Lévi-Strauss. Paris: Presses universitaires de France.

Mead, Margaret. 1928. *Coming of Age in Samoa.* New York: Morrow. (Paperback ed., Morrow, 1971.)

———. 1932. *The Changing Culture of an Indian Tribe.* New York, Columbia University Press. (Reprinted, New York: AMS Press.)

———. 1949. *Male and Female.* New York: Morrow. (Reprinted, Westport, Conn.: Greenwood, 1977.)

———. 1956. *New Lives for Old: Cultural Transformation—Manus 1928–53.* New York: Morrow. (Paperback ed., Morrow, 1976.)

———, and Métraux, Rhoda, eds. 1953. *The Study of Culture at a Distance.* Chicago: University of Chicago Press.

Mendelssohn, Peter. 1931. *Paris über mir.* Leipzig.

Menninger, Karl A. 1938. *Man against Himself.* New York: Harcourt, Brace.

Merton, Robert K. 1949. *Social Theory and Social Structure.* Glencoe, Ill.: Free Press.

Meyerson, Emile. *De l'explication dans les sciences.* Paris: Payot.

Montagu, Ashley. 1939. Adolescent Sterility. *Quarterly Review of Biology* 14:13–34, 192–219.

Multatuli (pseud. of Edward Douwes Dekker). 1868. *Max Havelaar.* Edinburgh.

Murdock, G. P. 1949. *Social Structure.* New York: Free Press. (Reprinted, Free Press, 1965.)

Murray, Gilbert. 1951. *Five Stages of Greek Religion.* 3d ed. Boston: Beacon Press. (Reprinted, Westport, Conn.: Greenwood, 1976.)

———. 1960. *The Rise of the Greek Epic.* 4th ed. Oxford: Oxford University Press.

Nathan, Tobie. 1977. *Sexualité idéologique et névrose.* Claix (Isère): La Pensée Sauvage.

———. 1978a. Considérations ethnopsychiatriques sur le traitement analytique des psychoses. *Ethnopsychiatrica* 1:15–42.

———. 1978b. Ethnopsychanalyse des psychoses. *Ethnopsychiatrica* 1: 213–42.

Neher, Andrew. 1961. Auditory Driving Observed with Scalp Electrodes in Normal Subjects. *Electroencephalography and Clinical Neurophysiology* 13:449–51.

————. 1962. A Physiological Explanation of Unusual Behavior in Ceremonies Involving Drums. *Human Biology* 34:151–60.

Neihardt, J. G. 1932. *Black Elk Speaks*. New York: Morrow. (Paperback ed., Simon & Schuster Pocket Books.)

Nelli, R. 1966. L'Amour courtois. In *Sexualité humaine*. Paris: Centre d'études Laënnec.

Opler, M. E. 1936. Some Points of Comparison and Contrast between the Treatment of Functional Disorders by Apache Shamans and Modern Psychiatric Practice. *American Journal of Psychiatry* 92:1371–87.

Opler, M. K. 1959. Dream Analysis in Ute Indian Therapy. In *Culture and Mental Health,* edited by M. K. Opler. New York: Macmillan.

Oppenheim, A. L. 1956. The Interpretation of Dreams in the Ancient Near East. *Transactions of the American Philosophical Society* n.s. 46, pt. 3:177–373.

Orr, Douglass W. 1941. Pregnancy Following the Decision to Adopt. *Psychosomatic Medicine* 3:441–46.

Osborn, R. (pseud. of Reuben Osbert). 1959. *Freud and Marx: A Dialectical Study*. With an Introduction by John Strachey. London: Gollancz.

Parsons, Talcott. 1939. The Professions and Social Structure. *Social Forces* 17:457–67.

Philippe le Bon, duke of Bourgogne (compiler?) 1486. *Les Cent Nouvelles Nouvelles*. Paris.

Pirenne, Henri. 1939. *Mohammed and Charlemagne*. Translated by Bernard Miall from the French of the 10th edition of *Mahomet et Charlemagne*. New York: Norton.

Ploss, Hermann H.; Bartels, Max; and Bartels, Paul. 1927. *Das Weib in der Natur- und Völkerkunde*. 11th ed. Berlin. (English translation, *Woman: An Historical, Gynaecological and Anthropological Compendium*. London: Heinemann, 1935.)

Poincaré, Henri. 1901. *Electricité et optique*. 2d rev. ed. Paris: Carré & Naud.

————. 1913. *The Foundations of Science*. Translated by George B. Halsted. With an Introduction by Josiah Royce. New York and Garrison, N.Y.: Science Press.

Porteus, S. D. 1937. *Primitive Intelligence and Environment*. New York: Macmillan.

Pukui, Mary. 1942. Hawaiian Beliefs and Customs during Birth, Infancy, and Childhood. *B. P. Bishop Museum Occasional Papers*, no. 16.

Rasmussen, Knud. 1927. *Across Arctic America*. New York: Putnam.

Rattray, Robert S. 1927. *Religion and Art in Ashanti*. Oxford: Clarendon Press.

Reich, Wilhelm. 1945. *Character-Analysis*. Translated from the German by Theodore P. Wolfe. 2d ed. New York: Orgone Institute Press.

Reider, N. S. 1950. The Concept of Normality. *Psychoanalytic Quarterly* 19:43–51.

Reik, Theodore. 1925. *Geständniszwang und Strafbedürfnis*. Leipzig: Internationaler Psychoanalytischer Verlag.

————. 1931. *Ritual: Psycho-Analytic Studies.* With a Preface by S. Freud. Translated from the second German edition by Douglas Bryan. London: Hogarth Press and the Institute of Psycho-Analysis. (Paperback ed., Westport, Conn.: Greenwood, 1975.)

————. 1932. *Der unbekannte Mörder.* Vienna. English translation by Dr. Katherine Jones, *The Unknown Murderer.* London: Hogarth Press and the Institute of Psycho-Analysis, 1936.

————. 1948. *Listening with the Third Ear.* New York: Farrar, Straus. (Paperback ed., New York: Harcourt, Brace, Jovanovich, 1977.)

Reuss, H. 1937. Ein Fall von anatomischen Narzismus (Auto-cohabitatio in Urethram). *Deutsche Zeitschrift für die gesamte gerichtliche Medizin* 28:340–46.

Riemer, S. 1940. A Research Note on Incest. *American Journal of Sociology* 45:566–75.

Rivers, W. H. R. 1920. *Instinct and the Unconscious.* Cambridge, Eng.: At the University Press.

————. 1923. *Conflict and Dream.* London: K. Paul, Trench, Trubner. New York: Harcourt, Brace.

————. 1926. *Psychology and Ethnology.* With a Preface and an Introduction by G. Elliot Smith. London: K. Paul, Trench, Trubner. New York: Harcourt, Brace.

Rohan-Csermák, Géza de. 1949. Istensegitségiek Állatorvoslása. *Ethnographia* (Budapest) 60:236–66.

Róheim, Géza. 1930. *Animism, Magic, and the Divine King.* New York: Knopf.

————. 1932. Psychoanalysis of Primitive Cultural Types. *International Journal of Psycho-Analysis* 13:1–224.

————. 1933a. A Primitive Ember. In *Lélekelemzési Tanulmányok* [Ferenczi Festschrift]. Magyarországi Pszichoanalitikai Egyesület Tagjai. Budapest: B. Somlo.

————. 1933b. Women and Their Life in Central Australia. *Journal of the Royal Anthropological Institute* 63:207–65.

————. 1934. *The Riddle of the Sphinx, or Human Origins.* Translated from the German by R. Money Kyrle. With a Preface by Ernest Jones, M.D. London: Hogarth Press and the Institute of Psycho-Analysis.

————. 1937. The Nescience of the Aranda. *British Journal of Medical Psychology* 17:343–60.

————. 1940. The Garden of Eden. *Psychoanalytic Review* 27:1–26, 177–99.

————. 1950. *Psychoanalysis and Anthropology.* New York: International Universities Press.

————. 1951. Hungarian Shamanism. In *Psychoanalysis and the Social Sciences,* edited by Géza Róheim, vol. 3. New York: International Universities Press.

Roscher, W. H. 1896. Das von der "Kynanthropie" handelnde Fragment des Marcellus von Side. *Abhandlungen der philologisch-histo-*

rischen Classe der Königlich Sächsischen Gesellschaft der Wissenschaften, vol. 17, no. 3.

Rose, H. J. 1960. *A Handbook of Greek Literature from Homer to the Age of Lucian.* New York: Dutton.

Rosen, Harold, and Erickson, M. H. 1954. The Hypnotic and Hypnotherapeutic Investigation and Determination of Symptom-Function. *Journal of Clinical and Experimental Hypnosis* 2:201–19.

Rosenberg, S. 1875. *Reistochten naar de Geelvinkbaai op Nieuw Guinea 1869–1870.* The Hague.

Roth, H. L. 1899. *The Aborigines of Tasmania.* 2d ed. Halifax, Eng.

Russell, Bertrand. 1903. *Principles of Mathematics,* vol. 1. Cambridge, Eng.: At the University Press.

———. 1919. *Introduction to Mathematical Philosophy.* London: Allen & Unwin. New York: Macmillan.

———. 1927. *The Analysis of Matter.* New York: Harcourt, Brace.

Rycaut, Sir Paul. 1687. *The History of the Turkish Empire.* London.

Sachs, Hanns. 1933. The Delay of the Machine Age. *Psychoanalytic Quarterly* 2:404–24.

———. 1942. *The Creative Unconscious.* Cambridge, Mass.: Sci-Art Publishers.

Scheflen, A. E. 1958. An Analysis of a Thought Model Which Persists in Psychiatry. *Psychosomatic Medicine* 20:235–41.

———. 1961. A Common Defect in Extrapolation: Explaining Psychic and Social Processes in Terms of Feeding. *Psychiatry* 24:143–52.

Schreber, Daniel P. 1903. *Denkwürdigkeiten eines Nervenkranken.* Leipzig: Oswald Mutze. (English translation by Ida MacAlpine and Richard A. Hunter, *Memoirs of My Nervous Illness.* Cambridge, Mass.: Robert Bentley, 1955.)

Seligman, Charles G. 1932. Anthropological Perspective and Psychological Theory (Huxley Memorial Lecture). *Journal of the Royal Anthropological Institute* 62:193–228.

Shade, C. 1949. "Ethnological Notes on the Aleuts." B.A. Honors Thesis, Department of Anthropology, Harvard University.

Simmons, Leo W., ed. 1942. *Sun Chief: The Autobiography of a Hopi Indian.* Rev. ed. New Haven: Yale University Press. (Paperback ed., 1963.)

Singh, J. A. L., and Zingg, R. M. 1942. *Wolf Children and Feral Man.* New York: Harper. (Reprinted, Hamden, Conn.: Shoe String Press, 1966.)

Skliar, N., and Starikowa, K. 1929. Zur vergleichenden Psychiatrie. *Archiv für Psychiatrie und Nervenkrankheiten* 88:554–85.

Smith, Homer W. 1932. *Kamongo.* New York: Viking.

Sorokin, P. A. 1937–41. *Social and Cultural Dynamics.* 4 vols. New York: American Book.

Sperling, Otto. 1950. The Interpretation of Trauma as a Command. *Psychoanalytic Quarterly* 19:352–70.

Spitz, R. A. 1935. Frühkindliches Erleben und Erwachsenenkultur bei den Primitiven. *Imago* 21:367–87.

———. 1945. Hospitalism. In *The Psychoanalytic Study of the Child*, edited by Ruth S. Eissler et al., vol. 1. New York: International Universities Press.

———. 1946a. Hospitalism: A Follow-up Report. Ibid., vol. 2.

———. 1946b. Anaclitic Depression. Ibid.

———. 1949. The Role of Ecological Factors in Emotional Development in Infancy. *Child Development* 20:145–55.

Steller, G. W. 1774. *Beschreibung von dem Lande Kamtschatka.* Frankfurt and Leipzig.

Stewart, K. M. 1947. Mohave Warfare. *Southwestern Journal of Anthropology* 3:257–78.

Stewart, Kilton. 1954. *Pygmies and Dream Giants.* New York: Norton. (Torchbook paperback ed., New York: Harper & Row, 1975.)

Stoll, Otto. 1904. *Suggestion und Hypnotismus in der Völkerpsychologie.* 2d ed. Leipzig: Veit.

Storch, Alfred. 1924. The Primitive Archaic Forms of Inner Experience and Thought in Schizophrenia. English translation by Clara Willard. *Nervous and Mental Disease Monograph,* no. 36. (Originally published in German as *Das archaisch-primitive Erleben und Denken der Schizophrenen.* Berlin: Springer, 1923.)

Strehlow, C. 1907–21. *Die Aranda- und Loritja-Stämme in Zentral Australia.* Frankfurt-am-Main.

Teicher, M. I. 1960. The Windigo Psychosis. In *Proceedings* of the 1960 Annual Spring Meeting of the American Ethnological Society (Seattle, Wash.).

Teoh, Jin-Inn. 1972. The Changing Psychopathology of Amok. *Psychiatry* 35:345–50.

Thompson, Laura. 1948. Attitudes and Acculturation. *American Anthropologist* n.s. 50:200–215.

Toennies, Ferdinand. 1926. *Gemeinschaft und Gesellschaft.* 7th ed. Berlin. (English translation by Charles P. Loomis, *Community and Society.* East Lansing: Michigan State University Press, 1957.)

Tolman, Edward C. 1951. *Collected Papers in Psychology.* Berkeley and Los Angeles: University of California Press.

Trilles, H. 1912. Le Totémisme chez les Fan. *Collection internationale de monographies ethnographiques, Bibliothèque Anthropos,* vol. 1, no. 4. Münster.

Usamah ibn Murshid ibn Munqidh. 1929. *An Arab-Syrian Gentleman and Warrior in the Period of the Crusades: Memoirs of Usamah ibn-Munqidh.* Translated by Philip K. Hitti. New York: Columbia University Press.

Van Loon, F. H. G. 1920. Amok and Lattah. *Journal of Abnormal and Social Psychology* 21:434–44.

Velten, C. 1903. *Sitten und Gebräuche der Suaheli, nebst einem Anhang über Rechtsgewohnheiten der Suaheli.* Göttingen.

Veniaminov, I. 1840. *Zapiski ob Ostrovakh Unalashkinskago Otdela* [Notes on the Islands of the Unalaska District]. 3 vols. Saint Petersburg.

Vernant, J.-P. 1963. Hestia-Hermès. *L'Homme* 3:12–50. (Reprinted in *Mythe et pensée chez les grecs*. 2d ed. Paris: Maspéro, 1965.)

Wagley, C., and Galvão, E. 1948. The Tapirapé. In *Handbook of the South American Indians,* edited by J. H. Steward, vol. 3. Bureau of American Ethnology Bulletin, no. 143. Washington, D.C.

Wallace, Anthony F. C. 1951. Some Psychological Determinants of Culture Change in an Iroquoian Community. In *Symposium on Local Diversity in Iroquois Culture,* edited by W. N. Fenton. Bureau of American Ethnology Bulletin, no. 149. Washington, D.C.

————. 1958. Dreams and Wishes of the Soul. *American Anthropologist* 60:234–48.

————. 1961. *Culture and Personality.* New York: Random House. (2d ed., 1970.)

Wallace, W. J. 1947. The Dream in Mohave Life. *Journal of American Folklore* 60:252–58.

Wardlaw, H. S. Halcro. 1932. Some Aspects of the Adaptation of Living Organisms to Their Environment. *Smithsonian Report for 1931,* pp. 339–411.

Wegrocki, H. J. 1939. A Critique of Cultural and Statistical Concepts of Abnormality. *Journal of Abnormal and Social Psychology* 34:166–78.

Westermarck, E. A. 1906–8. *The Origin and Development of the Moral Ideas.* 2 vols. London and New York: Macmillan.

White, L. A. 1969. *The Science of Culture: A Study of Man and Civilization.* 2d ed. New York: Farrar, Straus & Giroux.

Wilson, Monica. 1954. Nyakyusa Ritual and Symbolism. *American Anthropologist* 56:228–41.

Winiarz, Wiktor, and Wielawski, Joseph. 1936. Imu—A Psychoneurosis Occurring among the Ainus. *Psychoanalytic Review* 23:181–86.

Wissler, Clark. 1923. *Man and Culture.* New York: Crowell.

Wulfften-Pahlte, P. M. Van. 1933. Amok. *Nederlandsch Tijdschrift voor Geneeskunde* 77:983–91.

————. 1935. Koro, eine merkwürdige Angsthysterie. *Internationale Zeitschrift für Psychoanalyse* 21:249–57.

Yap, P. M. 1952. The Latah Reaction: Its Pathodynamics and Nosological Position. *Journal of Mental Science* 98:515–64.

Yates, S. L. 1930. An Investigation of the Psychological Factors in Virginity and Ritual Defloration. *International Journal of Psycho-Analysis* 11:167–84.

Young, Edward. 1770. *The Works of Edward Young.* 4 vols. Edinburgh.

Zilboorg, Gregory, and Henry, G. W. 1941. *A History of Medical Psychology.* New York: Norton.

Zuckerman, Sir Solly. 1932. *The Social Life of Monkeys and Apes.* New York: Harcourt, Brace. London: K. Paul, Trench, Trubner.

Index